THE HISTORIES

GAIUS (or Publius: the evidence is ambiguous) CORNELIUS TACITUS is widely regarded as the greatest of all Latin historians. We know relatively little about his life. He was born around AD 56, and is known to have engaged in the standard political career of a young Roman aristocrat, holding the offices of quaestor (in 81 or 82), praetor (in 88), and consul (in 97), along with a variety of other administrative and military posts, including (by 88) membership of the college of priests known as the *quindecemviri sacris faciundis*. He was governor of Asia (a province of the empire consisting of part of modern Turkey) in 112–13. In a high-profile trial in 100 he and his friend Pliny the Younger successfully prosecuted Marius Priscus for corruption while governor of Africa. Tacitus probably lived beyond 117; but his precise date of death is unknown. He was betrothed in 77 to the daughter of Julius Agricola, later governor of Britain, and married her shortly afterwards: her name, however, is unknown.

Tacitus' writings include the *Agricola* and the *Germania*, both published in 98. The date of a third work, the *Dialogue on Orators*, is disputed; some have thought it his first work, but it may well post-date both the *Agricola* and the *Germania*. All three of these survive complete. His major works were the *Histories* (published around 109) and the *Annals* (published some time after 117); only about a third of the former and just over half the latter survive.

D. S. LEVINE is Professor of Classics, New York University. He was educated at the City of London School and Brasenose College, Oxford; his writings include *Religion in Livy* (Leiden, 1993) and articles on Sallust and Tacitus.

OXFORD WORLD'S CLASSICS

*For over 100 years Oxford World's Classics have brought
readers closer to the world's great literature. Now with over 700
titles—from the 4,000-year-old myths of Mesopotamia to the
twentieth century's greatest novels—the series makes available
lesser-known as well as celebrated writing.*

*The pocket-sized hardbacks of the early years contained
introductions by Virginia Woolf, T. S. Eliot, Graham Greene,
and other literary figures which enriched the experience of reading.
Today the series is recognized for its fine scholarship and
reliability in texts that span world literature, drama and poetry,
religion, philosophy and politics. Each edition includes perceptive
commentary and essential background information to meet the
changing needs of readers.*

OXFORD WORLD'S CLASSICS

TACITUS

The Histories

Translated by

W. H. FYFE

Revised and edited by

D. S. LEVENE

OXFORD
UNIVERSITY PRESS

OXFORD

UNIVERSITY PRESS

Great Clarendon Street, Oxford OX2 6DP

Oxford University Press is a department of the University of Oxford.
It furthers the University's objective of excellence in research, scholarship,
and education by publishing worldwide in

Oxford New York

Athens Auckland Bangkok Bogotá Buenos Aires Cape Town
Chennai Dar es Salaam Delhi Florence Hong Kong Istanbul Karachi
Kolkata Kuala Lumpur Madrid Melbourne Mexico City Mumbai Nairobi
Paris São Paulo Shanghai Singapore Taipei Tokyo Toronto Warsaw

with associated companies in Berlin Ibadan

Oxford is a registered trade mark of Oxford University Press
in the UK and in certain other countries

Published in the United States
by Oxford University Press Inc., New York

First published as an World's Classics paperback 1997
First published as an Oxford World's Classics paperback 1999
Reissued 2008

British Library Cataloguing in Publication Data

Data available

Library of Congress Cataloging in Publication Data

Tacitus, Cornelius
[Historiae. English]
The histories / Tacitus; translated by W. H. Fyfe; revised and
edited by D. S. Levene.
(Oxford world's classics)
Includes bibliographical references and index.
1. Rome—History—Flavians, 69–96. 2. Rome—History—Civil War,
68–69. I. Levene, D. S. II. Title. III. Series.
DG286.T313 1997 937'.07—dc20 96–32812

ISBN 978–0–19–954070–9

17

Printed and bound in Great Britain by Clays Ltd, Elcograf S.p.A.

CONTENTS

CONTENTS

INTRODUCTION

Tacitus the Historian

The historian Cornelius Tacitus is the writer who, more than any other, has defined for later generations our picture of the Roman Empire. He was born around AD 56, shortly after the Emperor Nero came to the throne. Under Nero's successors he engaged in a political career, at which he achieved considerable success, gaining the quaestorship in 81 or 82, the praetorship in 88, and the consulship in 97, and later becoming governor of Asia (a province of the empire consisting of part of modern Turkey). In addition, a fragmentary funerary inscription from Rome has recently been conjectured to be that of Tacitus.[1] If correct, this allows us to fill in further gaps in his career, including the information that he was tribune (presumably around 85), and that his quaestorship had been the most prestigious of all: he was 'quaestor Augusti', who attended the Emperor himself. This post was normally reserved for those of the highest background: even as a young man Tacitus was marked out for outstanding political success.

But Tacitus' significance lies less in his own political experiences than in his application of them to his historical works. Other Roman historians had been politically involved—many ancient theorists, indeed, saw such experience as an essential prerequisite for the writing of political history. Yet none ever focused such subtlety and complexity of analysis onto the inner workings of Roman political and military power.

His earlier works were short: the *Agricola*, a biography of his father-in-law Julius Agricola, a notable governor of Britain, and the *Germania*, an ethnographic study of the tribes of Germany. Both appeared at the end of the century, shortly

[1] The inscription is Corpus Inscriptionum Latinarum vi. 1574: the identification with Tacitus is made by Geza Alföldy, *Mitteilungen des Deutschen Archaeologischen Instituts: Römischen Abteilung*, 102 (1995), 251–68.

after his consulship. The date of a third work, the *Dialogue on Orators*, a debate on the place of rhetoric in contemporary Rome, is disputed; some have thought it his first work, but it may well postdate both the *Agricola* and the *Germania*. But Tacitus' reputation rests above all upon his two final writings: the large-scale historical masterpieces of his maturity, the *Histories* and the *Annals*.

Between them, the *Histories* and the *Annals* covered the whole history of Rome from AD 14 to 96. The *Annals*, though written second, dealt with the earlier part of that period, taking the story down to the death of Nero in 68. The *Histories*, the earlier of the two works, described the civil wars succeeding Nero's death, the eventual emergence of Vespasian as emperor, and the reigns of the three emperors of the Flavian dynasty: Vespasian and his sons Titus and Domitian.

When complete, the *Histories* contained (probably) twelve books, the *Annals* eighteen. However, substantial portions of both works are now lost. The collapse of the Roman Empire in Western Europe was followed by a period when few pagan authors were prized enough to have copies made of their writings; much of Latin literature perished as a result. The earliest surviving manuscript of the *Histories* dates from the eleventh century, and all subsequent copies are usually thought to derive from it. It contains barely a third of the total work: Books 1–4 are intact, but the manuscript breaks off in mid-sentence something like a quarter of the way through Book 5. The same manuscript gives us most of Books 11–16 of the *Annals*; another provides the bulk of Books 1–6. The remainder of that work, too, has vanished.

The third of the *Histories* that is left to us treats just two years: AD 69–70; the missing portion of the work will have dealt with the following twenty-six years up to the death of Domitian. The reason for this unbalanced coverage is the uniquely eventful AD 69. It is known as the 'Year of the Four Emperors': in the vacuum left by the deposition and death of Nero, four men successively claimed the throne, each with his own armies behind him. The four were Galba, Otho, Vitellius, and Vespasian; and a year of virtually continuous civil war and struggles for power concluded with Vespasian, his rivals dead, established as the sole authority. That murderous competition Tacitus recounts in detail in his first three books.

Books 4–6 probably described the rest of Vespasian's reign, to his death in 79; Books 7–12 then dealt with the brief reign of Titus, and the longer one of Domitian—Tacitus seems to have had a penchant for structuring his works in groups of six books. Book 4 and the surviving portion of Book 5 cover only the first months of that period, as two provincial revolts simultaneously were to be recounted, one by the Germans, the other by the Jews; and it is with those revolts that these books are largely concerned.

The Background

Until the middle of the first century BC, Rome was a republic, ruled not by one man, but a succession of annually elected officials (though in practice the election process was strongly dominated by the wealthy classes). The supreme officials were the two consuls; they were, however, advised by a Senate consisting of all ex-office holders; and from the ranks of these came the military commanders and provincial governors who controlled the empire.

However, in the last half-century of the Republic the system broke down. A series of civil wars was fought out between leading political and military figures, not least Julius Caesar, who temporarily vanquished his rivals and established himself as sole ruler. But on his assassination in 44 BC civil war began anew; only in 31 BC did it come to an end, when Octavian, Caesar's great-nephew and heir, defeated Mark Antony, leaving himself alone in control. He ostensibly restored the institutions of the Republic, but reserved for himself a new role in the state: 'princeps' or 'leading man'. He adopted the name 'Augustus', and in effect took supreme power in his own hands—the first emperor of Rome. On his death in AD 14, the throne passed to his stepson Tiberius; thence to Tiberius' great-nephew Gaius (often known as Caligula), to Gaius' uncle Claudius, and finally to Claudius' stepson Nero. These first five emperors all came from two of the ancient aristocratic families of Rome, the Julii and the Claudii, and hence are often referred to as the 'Julio-Claudian' dynasty.

Nero's rule became increasingly capricious and tyrannical; and in 68 he was faced with two rebellions by provincial governors, one in Gaul under Vindex, another in Spain under Galba. His army successfully defeated the first, but then itself threatened to turn against him. Nero fled Rome, as the city troops, followed by the Senate, declared for Galba. He committed suicide, leaving no heir within his family; the Senate voted to make Galba emperor. His rule, however, was hardly secure. At this point Tacitus' *Histories* begin.

Sources and Methods

Tacitus was an adolescent in 69–70, and possibly witnessed one or two of the events that he describes in the *Histories*. From time to time he also made use of personal informants; he is known in later life to have associated with several of the participants in the civil war; he seems also to have consulted some documentary material. But for the bulk of his information he, in common with most surviving ancient historians, was not doing original research, but relied upon earlier published histories and memoirs of the period, now lost to us. Since Tacitus (again like other ancient historians) cites sources by name extremely rarely, it is a matter of controversy which he used at any given point.

Sometimes he followed these sources closely, but often he adapted them, slanting his narrative in order to highlight his favoured themes. In some areas ancient historical practice granted the historian considerable leeway to alter what was handed down to him. It was an accepted convention, for example, that the speeches in a historical work might bear little or no resemblance to anything that the characters had really said. Such speeches largely consisted of free compositions by which the historian might indicate the type of arguments that a character might plausibly have used; but they also became vehicles for the historian, without necessarily endorsing the viewpoint expressed, to explore key issues relevant to the period. Thus, for example, the question of the succession—whether an emperor should select his heir from within his own family, or should adopt an outsider—is examined in the *Histories* from different standpoints by both Galba (1. 15–16) and Mucianus (2. 76–7).

Not only the words, however, but also the deeds of the characters were subject to manipulation. Tacitus shows himself perfectly capable, when it suits him, of adapting chronology, conflating repeated events into a single episode, or elaborating a description with details derived more from literary convention than the available evidence. In this he once again simply follows the practices of his predecessors; such an approach to his material, unacceptable though it would be to a modern historian, is nevertheless typical of ancient historical writing. Both of his most famous historical forerunners at Rome, Sallust and Livy, were capable of being similarly cavalier, and Tacitus' debt to both is clear: the *Histories* contain not simply numerous verbal reminiscences of Sallustian or Livian phrasing but sometimes entire episodes modelled upon his great predecessors (e.g. 4. 68 ff.).

Despite this, Tacitus' account shows on the whole a fair degree of accuracy, certainly in the outlines of his narrative, but even in particular episodes. Relatively little documentary material (such as inscriptions) survives; but where such documents intersect with Tacitus' account, they tend to confirm it. His battle scenes can be compared to the actual topography of the battlegrounds; unlike Livy's battles, they usually fit the known features of the landscape closely. Few modern historians doubt that he provides for us not merely the most comprehensive but also the most reliable sustained account of the period; but if he is the only source for an event, one must keep a wary eye for those areas where adaptation or reworking of his source material may have occurred.

A good general sense of the direction of Tacitus' manipulations may be obtained by comparing his account with those of the other historians of the period: the biographies of all the emperors down to Domitian written by his younger Roman contemporary Suetonius; the biographies of Galba and Otho by his older Greek contemporary Plutarch; the history of the Jewish War written in Greek by Josephus, a Jewish commander turned pro-Flavian historian; and finally the later history of Rome written by the third-century senator Cassius Dio. None of these is Tacitus' equal either as historian or as writer; but the comparison can indicate to the reader those areas where Tacitus may actively be distorting, or at any rate selecting one of several alternative versions of events that were available to him. The notes to this translation, accordingly, frequently refer to those other historians, so as to demonstrate what is distinctive about Tacitus' own account.

Understanding Tacitus

Tacitus' biting wit is famous. Again and again individuals, groups, events are summed up with a pungent, cynical, and often paradoxical epigram. Virtually every page furnishes examples: 'The troops could be punished though not controlled' (4. 27); 'At last, for lack of the truth, Galba yielded to the consensus of error' (1. 35); '[He] excused them from the services which they refused to render' (3. 58); 'Good men owe their power to their virtues; he was one of that worst sort who derive it from their vices' (3. 77); 'More careful of their safety than of their authority' (4. 48); 'He played the slave to gain a throne' (1. 36); 'Petitioning for peace, though war there was none' (1. 63); and, perhaps most famous of all, his obituary on the Emperor Galba (1. 49): 'He had the qualifications to be a ruler—if only he had not ruled.'

By such comments Tacitus, so it seems, makes his interpretations and views clear: one has the consistent sense of a powerful mind seeing beneath specious appearances and fair words, and setting out instead the realities of power and the moral depravity of civil war. So also is he a master of innuendo, his narrative coloured by hints of vicious undercurrents and sinister motives underlying even the most straightforward of events. Once again examples abound. The hints at 1. 39 and 1. 42, for instance, that Galba's colleague Vinius was complicit in his murder ('His whole life and reputation give reason to suppose that he was an accomplice in the crime of which he was the cause'); the 'mercy' of Otho when he pardons Celsus at 1. 71, where the calculating nature of his

ostensibly virtuous action is made explicit ('Otho now wanted
to earn a name for clemency by pardoning a well-known man
who had fought against his party'); the senators who admired
Otho 'and in their hearts unanimously favoured Vitellius'
(2. 53); and much of the narrative of Vitellius' own behaviour,
such as his hypocritical attitude towards Junius Blaesus (2. 58,
3. 38–9).

Today it is usually thought undesirable for a historian consistently and overtly to instil his biases and his interpretations
into his narrative, especially when he does so by imputing to
characters thoughts and motives for which he presents no
evidence. Yet it is an approach to historiography that was
widespread among the ancients; and it does at any rate seem
to provide the reader with an overwhelming sense of a clear,
distinctive, and powerful analysis of the Roman Empire. If
that analysis is thought one-sided, its very conspicuousness
appears to provide the modern historian with straightforward
evidence for the direction of Tacitus' partiality, which can
then be compensated for when one assembles one's own
account of the period.

However, it would be misleading to think that these overt
comments make Tacitus' opinions easy to determine. For the
form and nature of his observations encourage the reader to
attempt to combine them into an overall picture; but reconciling them in practice proves a far from simple task. Vinius' role
in the murder of Galba provides an excellent example. For
while, as quoted above, at Galba's death Tacitus suggests
clearly that he believed in Vinius' complicity, earlier (1. 32–4)
he had shown Vinius strongly advocating that Galba protect
himself by remaining in the palace. Tacitus himself is em-
phatic that this was the policy that Galba *should* have followed: he describes Icelus' alternative as leading to 'the ruin of
his country'. The implication in Tacitus is that Vinius is giving
Galba the best possible chance of success; in the parallel
passage of Plutarch, Vinius is far less forceful in advocating
his proposal, and the author does not explicitly endorse its
good sense. It seems that Tacitus, far from uncomplicatedly
propagating the view that Vinius was a conspirator, is actually
muddying the waters by undermining that view in advance.

The sententious nature of his comments seems to compel one to give them the widest application; yet actually reconciling them with each other leads only to doubt and conflict.

A similar problem is caused by rumour. Tacitus portrays a world governed by rumour, a world where whispered information, whether true or false, is one of the prime agents that can transform history. Vitellius' rebellion originates in and is promoted by rumours of atrocities committed by Galba (1. 51, 1. 54); rumour turns Rome to panic under Otho (1. 85); it leads Otho's army to insubordination (2. 23), and Civilis' Germans to break openly with Rome (4. 54). Rumours first designate Vespasian for the throne (2. 73), and are actively employed by Mucianus and the other Flavians in support of their cause (2. 83, 3. 54). The false rumours of Lucius Piso's rebellion in Africa not only lead to Piso's murder but are strongly indicated by Tacitus to come close to being self-fulfilling: it is precisely those rumours that lead Piso to contemplate the very action of which he is falsely accused (4. 38, 4. 48–50).

Yet rumour is more than a simple actor in the historical events: it is one of Tacitus' chief vehicles for commenting upon those events, as he places sinister interpretations and innuendoes into the mouths of unspecified observers. One example is the rumour he reports at 2. 60 of Caecilius Simplex's attempt to purchase the consulship from Vitellius. No other version is given, and the imputation against Simplex is thus allowed by Tacitus to stand, if not directly endorsed by the author, at least implicitly so, because unchallenged. Or 3. 65, with the reports of a jealous rivalry between Vespasian and his brother Flavius Sabinus, leading to the latter's refusal to lead the City Garrison against Vitellius. Here Tacitus does offer a 'more charitable explanation'—that Sabinus was of gentle character—but the more damaging innuendoes still retain their force, not least because they offer the evidence of specific past actions, which the 'more charitable explanation' fails to refute.

But assessing the precise status of such rumours—how far Tacitus himself is endorsing their contents—is continually problematic; and this is only accentuated when one has to

weight them against Tacitus' more direct statements. His
treatment of Vinius once again provides an example of these
problems. At 1. 13 Tacitus reports a rumour that Otho was
due to marry Vinius' daughter: this provides what he otherwise never gives—a motive for Vinius to have joined Otho in
his rebellion. But how seriously should one take this rumour?
Only a few lines before (1. 12) he has shown that other, false
rumours about Galba's plans to adopt an heir are clearly
prompted by malice against Vinius himself ('Many were influenced by foolish hopes and spread self-interested rumours
pointing to some friend or patron, thereby also gratifying their
hatred for Titus Vinius, whose unpopularity waxed daily with
his power'). Rumour in the latter case is a means for deceiving
oneself and others, and a vehicle for venting hatred against
Vinius. In such a context, can a further rumour about
Vinius—the rumour of Otho's relationship with him—be presenting the authorial standpoint? The question is left entirely
open.

   It is little surprise, in the face of this, that readers have often
despaired of pinning down Tacitus' interpretations of Roman
history: all we have to rely on, it seems, is multiple and
contradictory viewpoints of doubtful validity. One seems at
times to be looking into a bottomless pit where nothing at all
makes sense. One can see why many commentators have
preferred to deny that a consistent interpretation is to be
found at all. Tacitus' ambiguous treatment of the Flavian
commander Antonius Primus, for example, has often been
ascribed to his use of multiple sources: some pro-Antonius,
which present him with the highest motives and the virtues of
the best of generals; others seeking, after his quarrel with
Mucianus and fall from Vespasian's favour, to load onto his
shoulders all the guilt of Flavian atrocities. On this view,
Tacitus has drawn on both of these at different times, and
failed to observe—or care—that they have led him into
contradiction.

   At times the case for such a reading is strong. For example,
the contradiction between the violence against the city of
Rome shown by the Flavian troops (and blamed on their
generals) at 4. 1 and the specific statement at 4. 39 that

Antonius and Arrius Varus 'were popular in Rome, because they had used no violence off the field of battle'. It is possible that Tacitus is seeking to demonstrate the fickleness and brutality of the Roman mob, by hinting at their shifting support; but the clear factual inconsistency is hard to explain in this way alone, and it may well be preferable to conclude that he has simply reproduced contradictory material from his sources.

But at other times, especially when the passages in question are more closely juxtaposed, such an account is much less satisfactory. For example, Antonius' vigorous suppression of the mutinies in his army at 3. 10–11 is undercut by the belief, which Tacitus reports, that he was himself the instigator of them ('It was even supposed by some that [Antonius] had cunningly promoted both outbreaks, to secure for himself the full profit of the war'). But the combination of these two (very typical, as discussed above, of Tacitus) fits perfectly his portrayal of Antonius from his first appearance (2. 86)—a man on the one hand 'by no means contemptible in war', on the other 'invaluable in riots and sedition'. Tacitus consistently shows Antonius as someone of the finest *military* qualities, and the ability to quell insubordination among one's troops was, for a Roman, a central military virtue. But at the same time, Antonius' more dubious morality in wider matters is never far from the story's surface: and the possibility is raised, as here, that this can lead him to actions that are not only wrong in themselves but specifically undermine the very virtues for which he is being praised.

Antonius' actions at the sack of Cremona conform to a similar pattern. Like any good commander, he makes a speech restraining his troops and advising instead practical measures that they must take to ensure victory (3. 20). His speech superficially conforms to the canons of military virtue; but he noticeably does not seek to dissuade the soldiers from sacking the town on principle; and Tacitus leaves it open whether it was his idea to point to the town to encourage his men during the battle (3. 27–8). This in turn matches exactly his reported behaviour directly prior to the town's destruction (3. 32–4): he is not perhaps directly responsible for the atrocities (the town is already burning when he cracks his joke 'It will not be long before it is hot'), but shows no interest in keeping his soldiers from them. To attribute the double-sidedness of this portrait of Antonius to Tacitus' incompetent combination of contradictory sources is to overlook the way in which he does precisely juxtapose contradictory views of Antonius and unite them into a single complex portrait. The very fascination of Tacitus' Antonius lies in his combination of the practical virtues of the military commander with a moral unscrupulousness that leads to the potential annulment even of many of the positive results of his attractive qualities.

Thus it *is* possible to make sense of Tacitus' contradictions and complications, although they lead us to an overall picture that is far from simple, a picture that eschews clear morals and explanations. Indeed, Tacitus' reader is faced with a not dissimilar dilemma to Tacitus' characters: the necessity of finding one's way beneath the surface meaning of the story, and attempting to piece together the author's account from contrasting fragments of information. If assessing the truth in rumours is difficult for us, Tacitus shows it as equally difficult for his characters. But it provides the only way for them—and us—to make sense of the hidden undercurrents governing events in imperial Rome.

Germans and Jews

No section of Tacitus' work is more famous than his account of the Jews at the opening of Book 5. It is the most substantial surviving treatment of Jewish history and religion by a pagan writer of the ancient world; as a result it has often been read by those interested in Jewish history as in effect a self-contained piece, in isolation from the rest of the work.

Its fame, however, has hardly benefited Tacitus' reputation as a historian; for no part of his writing shows him to a worse advantage. His account of Jewish origins is appallingly garbled, and the garbling appears all the more blatant as a result of the remarkable and, for Tacitus, unpredictable sequence of events that turned the Jewish sacred writings into the central text of later European culture. This is the one part of Tacitus' work where numerous non-specialist readers can instantly spot the errors, and indeed can do so more confidently than would have been possible for most of his Roman contemporaries. Moreover, Tacitus' manifest hostility to Jews and Judaism leaves him vulnerable on another score. The modern revulsion against racism in general and anti-Semitism in particular means that this hostility leaps to the reader's attention and draws a strongly adverse response. For while one may view indulgently Tacitus' biases when they concern individuals and institutions long dead, in the case of the Jews his writings are seen in the light of subsequent history. It is only a slight exaggeration to say that, for many readers, a clear line runs from Tacitus via the Inquisition through to Auschwitz.

Yet to read Tacitus instinctively in such a manner can be counterproductive, leading to serious misinterpretation of the work. For the most interesting question is *why* Tacitus should have presented such an account of the Jews. One must appreciate that, for him, Jews are not the central focus of his interest, even though they may be for many modern readers. What is fundamentally informing his picture is a literary background and a wider historical context in which Jews play only a small role; and his distortions and hostility, real though they are, stem above all from those more general considerations.

First, it should be made clear that Tacitus' garblings are not invented by him: virtually everything that he writes he has drawn from earlier, generally Greek, sources. He can be convicted of carelessness, in that, had he cared to, he could certainly have found more authoritative accounts by Jews themselves; but there is no reason to think that he was aware just how unreliable his information was. From what he presumably saw as broadly accurate sources, he selected the information that would enable him to create his desired picture.

The most striking feature of Tacitus' account of Jews is the notion of *inversion*: Jews, for him, are people who turn the familiar Roman world upside down. This is quite explicit at 5. 4: 'Moses introduced a new cult, which was the opposite of all other religions. All that we hold sacred they held profane, and

they allowed practices which we abominate.' He finds the
origin of Jewish sacrificial rites and circumcision precisely in
the desire to reverse current practices; he sees Jews as rejecting
the fundamental Roman ties of family, patriotism, and national religion. Unlike Romans, they bury rather than cremate
the dead; and, of course, the non-anthropomorphic monothe-
ism of Judaism is entirely alien to the cults familiar to the
Romans, a point that Tacitus reinforces by specifically contrasting it with the superficially similar cult of Bacchus.
Tacitus moreover contradicts himself here, since he has previously relayed the (false) information that Jews had an image
of an ass in the Temple. But this likewise is governed by the
inversion of known practices; the ass was seen as a lowly
creature, hardly appropriate for a central cult image. The
same consideration drives his eccentric account of the Exodus:
a need to explain the paradoxes of Judaism. From it he derives
aetiologies for, among other things, the ass, the sacrifices, the
taboo on pork, the Sabbath, and the general Jewish rejection
of the rest of mankind.

Such an approach to foreign cultures did not originate with
Tacitus. There was a long literary tradition of ethnography
which treated other races as the reverse of one's own, a
tradition going back at least to Herodotus' famous (and inac-
curate) account of the Egyptians in very similar terms. Tacitus
provides for his work a digression with exotic overtones along
lines recognizable and attractive to his readers. But ethnographic writing can serve wider ideological purposes. By treating another culture as the reverse of one's own, one helps
construct and reinforce a particular notion of what one's own
culture is. That this is true of Tacitus can be seen if one
examines his Jewish digression against its wider context.

If no part of Tacitus' historical writing is better known than
his description of the Jews, perhaps no part is less known than
his account in Books 4 and 5 of the revolt of Civilis in
Germany, in the middle of which the surviving part of his
discussion of Judaism appears. An apparently inconsequential
episode, almost unknown (apart from the odd passing reference) from other sources, yet an episode to which Tacitus has
devoted virtually an entire book of his work. But the sheer fact

of its prominence in his narrative shows its importance to him; and a dominant theme within it is the question that it raises of what it is to be a Roman.

This issue had earlier been flagged several times in Books 1–3, where the armies of Otho, Vitellius, and Vespasian each were shown at times behaving towards Italy as foreign conquerors, and appearing in various other ways un-Roman. Thus of Otho's troops: 'As though on foreign soil and among an enemy's towns, they burnt, ravaged, plundered' (2. 12). The Vitellian Caecina at first contrasts with this: he 'seemed to have left his cruelty and profligacy on the other side of the Alps' (2. 20); but he paradoxically does so while wearing Gallic costume, and soon the Vitellians too are acting in the manner of alien victors: 'the fields were ravaged like an enemy country' (2. 87); the wild soldiers are unable to cope with city life (2. 88), and Vitellius tries to ride triumphantly into Rome as its captor, before being dissuaded by his friends (2. 89). Then the Flavians follow suit: Antonius' armies 'taste the joys of plundering their compatriots' (3. 15), and he is seen 'harrying Italy like a conquered country' (3. 49). In the moral chaos of the times, the Romans themselves abandon Roman values. But with Civilis the theme plays an ever more central role.

Tacitus refers to the war against Civilis as 'a civil and a foreign war at once' (4. 22; also 2. 69), and this phrase sets the issue starkly. Are the Romans fighting other Romans, or is this a war against foreigners, one that is in consequence less morally problematic for a Roman reader? Civilis and his followers are ambiguous. On the one hand, they exhibit features that are typically Roman. They have served with the Roman army and sometimes display the disciplined and courageous behaviour that is, for a Roman, paradigmatic of Roman military virtue; it is their Roman opponents who act with the indiscipline and cowardice associated with barbarians (4. 20, 33, 37). Their leaders, not least Civilis himself, whose very name is emphatically Roman (presumably the result of his having been granted Roman citizenship), use the language of Roman imperialism; their avowed aim is to set up a German and Gallic empire in parallel to the Roman one (e.g. 4. 59:

'The Empire of All Gaul'; also 4. 63, 69). Civilis, like a good Roman commander, keeps his men under control, while his Roman counterpart hands over authority to his mutinous troops (4. 24–5, 34–5). Sabinus claims descent from Julius Caesar, and actually takes the name 'Caesar' for himself (4. 55, 67); Classicus dresses in a Roman uniform (4. 59).

Yet at the same time as showing the Romanness of the rebels, Tacitus has them appearing in other respects as alien and foreign. Even when employing Roman tactics, they often combine them with barbarian wildness (4. 22–3, 28–9); in battle they engage in wild cries (4. 18). They use traditional German rites and customs (e.g. 4. 15); Civilis ruddles his hair and grows it long, and associates with a god-priestess (4. 61, 65). In short, a consistent feature of this narrative is that the clear boundaries between Roman and non-Roman are broken down. Tacitus thereby exposes a fundamental problem of Roman imperialism: how far are the Romanized subjects truly part of the empire; how far are they truly Roman? And can Romans accept a definition of 'being a Roman' that would permit a Civilis or a Classicus, with all their barbarian elements, to be defined as members of their own culture?

With the advent of Petillius Cerialis, however, the barriers begin to be reasserted. At 4. 73–4 Cerialis appeals to the Gauls precisely by stressing their own closeness to Rome and by treating Civilis and the Germans as hostile foreigners. Tacitus at least in part endorses this, now calling the war 'foreign service' with his own voice (4. 72); and after Cerialis' speech he begins to portray the rebels less as Roman, more as unequivocally alien and barbaric (e.g. 4. 78, 5. 15, 5. 17).

It is at this point that the digression on Judaism appears. It can now be seen that his Jews both parallel and fail to parallel the Germans. Like the Germans, the Jews are in revolt; like the Germans, the Jews' revolt is a consequence of oppression by Roman officials (4. 14, 5. 9); like the Germans, the Jews have imperial ambitions of their own (5. 13). Yet with the Jews, there is no problem. Unlike the Germans, they are a people entirely alien to Rome, and in fighting them one is dealing with an unequivocally foreign enemy. In short, the Jewish War for Tacitus is there as a foil to the German War: a war that is everything that the German War might have been but for a long time was not. His account of Judaism is hostile and simplistic, but that is precisely what heightens the contrast with the problematic complexities of his picture of the Germans, where the very notions of 'Roman' and 'foreign' had for a time appeared to be collapsing. Tacitus' fundamental concern, as in the rest of his work, is in exploring the significance and workings of the Roman Empire itself. Germans and Jews alike are simply an instrument to that end.

TRANSLATOR'S NOTE

Tacitus' Latin style is notoriously idiosyncratic. His writing is extremely compressed and obscure, laconic epigrams abounding; his vocabulary is often poetic and archaic; his sentences irregularly constructed, with standard Latin grammar and syntax contorted to supply an appropriate phrase. An English translation that sought to capture much of this would be virtually unreadable; the best a translator can do in practice is to give some sense of the biting and lapidary quality of the original, without sacrificing intelligibility.

The basis for this translation is the 1912 translation by W. H. Fyfe; however, it has been very substantially altered. Fyfe for the most part managed to avoid the vices of the worst classical translators of his day; there is little of the biblical pastiche or the excessive literalness that mars the work of many of his contemporaries. Nevertheless, he occasionally employed terms that sound inappropriate in modern English; these I have tried to remove. More often his determination to avoid excessive literalness led him into excessive verbosity, turning the epigrammatic wit of Tacitus into something rather ponderous; I have rewritten many such passages so as to introduce a more Tacitean brevity. Finally, Fyfe on numerous occasions seems to have misinterpreted Tacitus' Latin; in these cases I have corrected the translation to bring it into line with the best modern understanding of the text. The introductory material and notes are entirely my own.

In translating geographical names I have adopted the following principles. With towns, mountains, islands, and rivers I have kept ancient names, *except* in cases where the modern English name is so familiar that to retain the ancient name would appear pedantic and alienating: thus I speak of 'Jerusalem' (not 'Hierosolyma'), the 'Rhine' (not the 'Rhenus'), and 'Cologne' (not 'Colonia Agrippinensis'). Inevitably this has involved one or two borderline decisions that may appear arbitrary to some readers. In all cases where the ancient name is used, the modern name appears in the glossary, and is footnoted on the occasion of the site's first appearance in the text.

With Roman provinces and other wide geographical areas, I have used the ancient name *except* when there is *both* a clear etymological link between the ancient name and the modern, *and* when the area denoted by the name has remained constant between then and now. For example, I speak of 'Britain', 'Spain', and 'Italy' (not 'Britannia', 'Hispania', and 'Italia'); but 'Helvetia' (not 'Switzerland'), 'Belgica' (not 'Belgium'), and 'Judaea' (not 'Israel'). Unfamiliar provinces may be found on the map of the Roman Empire. It should be noted that the names 'Africa' and 'Asia' in Roman times denoted not the continents, but relatively small provinces in North Africa and Asia Minor respectively.

All calendar dates have been translated into their modern equivalents. For distances I have retained the Latin calculations in the text: thus 'five miles' refers to 'Roman miles', not English ones. A Roman mile was around 1,618 yards, about 92 per cent of an English mile. In the introduction and notes, all year dates are AD unless otherwise stated.

The paragraph numbers are those standardly employed to refer to Tacitus. As usual with such paragraphing in classical prose authors, they derive not from the ancient world, but from early printed editions. In Tacitus' case it is disputed whether they originate with Gruterus' edition or with Pichena's (both published in Frankfurt in 1607).

Finally, I should like to thank those who have helped me during the preparation of this translation: in particular Helen DeWitt, David Hunt, Eric Levene, Norma Levene, Barbara Levick, John Moles, Jocelyne Nelis-Clément, Leighton Reynolds, Clemence Schultze, and especially Judith Luna of OUP and Tony Woodman.

NOTE ON THE IMPERIAL
ROMAN STATE

At the top of the tree was the EMPEROR: he held supreme power in the state. However, a number of functions were devolved upon others, and there was a standard career structure followed by those members of the upper classes with political ambitions. One would hold in succession various political offices known as MAGISTRACIES: first one became QUAESTOR (normal minimum age 25) then (though this step could be omitted) either TRIBUNE (not to be confused with the military officer with the same title: see below) or AEDILE. All these had minor administrative or judicial duties. Under the Republic tribunes had been elected to serve the interests of the citizen body, and had then had considerable powers, including the right of veto over senatorial enactments; hence the Emperor held tribunician power. Ordinary tribunes still in theory possessed some of these powers, but it was now exceptionally rare for them to be used. After this one might become PRAETOR (normal minimum age 30), with more senior functions; this office also entitled one to hold various important posts in the imperial service.

Finally one might reach the post of CONSUL. Consuls had been the supreme officials of the Republic, and retained considerable prestige under the Empire. Two served at a time; originally they held office for a full year, but the need to provide ex-consuls to serve in various senior administrative capacities led to several pairs holding the office in succession during a year. To be first holder of the office in a calendar year, however, was still highly prestigious, not least because one's name was then enshrined in the official date of that year; the Emperor himself often took one of these slots. The consulship, unlike the other magistracies, might be held more than once by a suitably distinguished candidate.

Those who had held any one of these offices formed together the SENATE (along with a few others who had been specifically honoured with senatorial rank). The Senate's function was essentially advisory, though it still wielded considerable authority, especially at times of crisis. All magistracies except the consulship were elected by the Senate (though the Emperor's support for a particular candidate guaranteed his election). Consuls were appointed by the Emperor himself.

Occasionally two CENSORS were appointed to review the membership of the Senate. These would be senior ex-consuls; one would typically be the Emperor himself. They had the power to expel those considered unfit (see below). More commonly, however, the Emperor, who had censorial power, reviewed the lists alone.

Roman Society

Rome was a strongly hierarchical society, though movement between the classes was often possible. The laws of CITIZENSHIP were complex, but it by now essentially included all descended from the early Romans and Italians, as well as significant numbers of foreigners who had been granted it, and could then transmit it to their descendants; it carried with it various rights and privileges. If a citizen freed a slave, that FREEDMAN also could claim citizenship, though with various disabilities (which did not apply to his descendants).

The upper class was the SENATORS, involved with the politics and administration of the state (see above). Wealthy citizens who would not or (because of their lower family background) could not be politically involved might be enrolled as KNIGHTS (or EQUESTRIANS), who likewise had considerable privileges and prestige (freedmen, however, were not normally eligible for this category). There was a property qualification for both of these classes; periodically the CENSORS (see above) would check the lists, and remove those thought either morally or financially unfit.

Below them was the mass of ordinary citizens. Many of these would have close attachments to particular members of the upper classes, for example through having been slaves in their households. This relationship was formalized; the inferior group were known as CLIENTS, and they owed various

duties to their upper-class PATRONS. SLAVES formed the lowest
group of all; they lived essentially without indepedent legal
rights, and were liable to forms of brutal punishment at their
master's whim.

Provincial Administration

The senator's career would normally be interspersed with
various spells abroad in the army (see below) or as a civilian
administrator. The Roman Empire was divided into a number
of PROVINCES. The supreme official in a province was the
GOVERNOR, normally either an ex-praetor or an ex-consul
(depending on the province), appointed either directly by the
Emperor, or (in certain provinces) by lots drawn in the Senate;
these were called PRO-CONSULS. However, the least important provinces were governed by knights appointed by the
Emperor; these imperial agents were known as PROCURATORS.
In the more senior provinces the procurator would still be a
knight reporting back to the Emperor, but would not be in
supreme control. Egypt was a special case: its economic importance meant that senators were not even permitted to visit
it without the Emperor's permission, lest they use it as a
powerbase against Rome; hence it too was governed by a
knight.

The Roman Army

A LEGION at full strength consisted of around 5,000 heavily
armed infantry; each man signed up for a term of twenty
years. All legions were numbered; there could, however, be
several legions with the same number (there were, for example, three 'Third Legions' in AD 69). They were therefore
also often referred to by nicknames (such as VII Gemina or
XXI Rapax).

The GOVERNOR of a province would usually have supreme
command over the legions in that province (however, if he
was only a PROCURATOR—see above—he would not normally
control legions, but would have a more limited command
over the AUXILIARY troops in his province—see below). Below

the governor were the LEGIONARY COMMANDERS for the separate legions; these were normally ex-praetors. On the commander's staff were several MILITARY TRIBUNES—usually young men serving there as a step on the political ladder.

Each legion was divided into 59 or 60 centuries, most of 80 men apiece, and each under the control of a CENTURION. The centurion of the first century of a legion was the SENIOR CENTURION of that legion. A group of six centuries formed a COHORT, a term also used for regiments of auxiliary infantry and of the Praetorian Guards (see below). Every legion had a STANDARD in the shape of an EAGLE on a pole, carried by the STANDARD-BEARER, a promoted soldier who also had responsibility for the legionaries' pay. The army would also carry other images and symbols with it; while smaller units within the legion likewise had their own standards and bearers.

Legionaries were Roman citizens. In addition, companies were enrolled in the provinces as AUXILIARIES; these provided the army with its cavalry and light infantry. Their commanders were, however, usually young Romans using the post as a stage in their political career.

At Rome itself were stationed the crack troops of the Empire; the PRAETORIAN GUARDS (often referred to in this translation simply as the GUARDS). Their commanders, who were usually knights, were the two PREFECTS OF THE GUARDS; the officers below them were called TRIBUNES (not to be confused with the magistrates holding this title: see above), who normally had been promoted there after having been SENIOR CENTURION in a legion (see above). An élite group of the Guards was attached to the Emperor as BODY GUARDS. Other troops in and around the city were the WATCH and the CITY GARRISON, the latter under the command of a senior ex-consul, the CITY PREFECT.

NOTE ON ROMAN NAMES

In the late Republic a male Roman citizen generally had three names: a *personal name*, a *clan name*, and a *surname*—for example Marcus Tullius Cicero. The *clan name* ('Tullius') would be borne not only by his extended family, but also by various people, such as freed slaves, who gained citizenship through him: thus Cicero's secretary Tiro on being freed took the name Marcus Tullius Tiro. Hence sharing a clan name often did not involve a blood relationship.

The *surname* ('Cicero') was usually inherited within families, though might be a nickname personal to an individual; thus brothers, for example, might sometimes have different surnames.

Few *personal names* were available to choose from: the main ones were Appius, Aulus, Decimus, Gaius, Gnaeus, Lucius, Marcus, Publius, Quintus, Servius, Sextus, Tiberius, and Titus. These might be used alone by close family and intimate friends, but outside those circles a Roman would typically be addressed by surname alone, or by a combination of personal name and *either* clan name *or* surname—'Marcus Tullius' or 'Marcus Cicero'.

Under the Empire, however, the situation became vastly more complex. People often took extra surnames reflecting, for example, adoptions or maternal family background. People sometimes even took multiple clan names for similar reasons. Sometimes surnames were placed first and treated as personal names. And, while the Republican forms of address still sometimes continued, it was far more common to refer to someone formally by a clan name and surname together (e.g. 'Petillius Cerialis', not 'Quintus Petillius'): this is the usual practice in Tacitus. And with the single name by which people were commonly identified, no particular rule was followed: it might be a clan name (as with the Emperors Claudius and Vitellius), a surname (as with the Emperors Nero, Otho, and Vespasian), or even a personal name (as with the Emperors Tiberius, Gaius, and Titus).

Female names under the Republic had normally been simply a feminine version of the father's clan name—thus Cicero's daughter was called 'Tullia'. Once again under the Empire this often became more complex, and women would sometimes have names derived from, for example, their maternal family background, or from surnames; now too women would sometimes have more than one name.

This translation employs the names that Tacitus himself uses; in the index, however, the full names (where these are known) are given, to assist cross-referencing with other works where different versions of the person's name might be used. Except in the cases of the Emperors Tiberius, Gaius, and Titus, however, the alphabetization ignores the personal names listed above: so 'Titus Vinius' should be looked up under 'Vinius', not 'Titus'.

NOTE ON THE TEXT

Our knowledge of Tacitus' *Histories* (and of *Annals* Books
11–16) comes from a single eleventh-century manuscript in
Beneventan script: the so-called 'Second Medicean'. A number
of fifteenth-century manuscripts also survive; but almost certainly these all derive from copies made from the Second
Medicean itself,[1] and so give us no independent knowledge of
the text. Only at 1. 69–75 and 1. 86–2. 2, where pages are
missing from the Second Medicean, does the evidence of these
later manuscripts become vital, for they were copied before
the pages were lost.

The most widely used modern texts of Tacitus are the
Oxford Classical Text of C. D. Fisher, and the Teubner text of
H. Heubner. In cases of significant dispute, I have adopted the
following readings in this translation:

	World's Classics	Fisher	Heubner
1. 2	opimum	†opimum	opimum
1. 3	necessitates fortiter toleratae	necessitates fortiter toleratae	necessitates, ipsa necessitas fortiter tolerata
1. 11	legio [Lipsius]	legiones	legiones
1. 35	resistens	resistens	sistens
1. 41	Vercilionem	Vergilionem	Vercilionem
1. 43	Staius	Statius	Staius
1. 52	aviditate imperandi	aviditate imperandi	[aviditate imperandi]
1. 58	sedatis	stratis	sedatis
1. 70	acciti	exciti	acciti
1. 76	set	set	et
1. 77	Saevino Propinquo [Andresen]	†Saevino P . . .	Scaevino Paquio
2. 4	ardor	†labor	ardor
2. 9	corpus	corpus	caput

---

[1] The most recent critical text of the *Histories*, by K. Wellesley (Stuttgart, 1989),
argues for the independence of a group of the later manuscripts, but his claims have
so far failed to receive scholarly support.

2. 18	quin	quin	[qui]
2. 20	[barbarum tecgmen]	[barbarum tecgmen]	barbarum tegumen
2. 49	obnoxii [Wellesley]	noxa	noxa
2. 55	vita cessisse [Halm]	cessisse	cessisse
2. 100	patuit	Patavii	patuit
3. 5	quam iussorum	†commissior†	quam iussorum
3. 6–7	principia belli secundum Flavianos data. vulgata victoria	principia belli secundum Flavianos data. vulgata victoria	volgata victoria, post principia belli secundum Flavianos data
3. 13	militibus principem auferre	militem auferre	militibus principem auferre
3. 15	cursabant	curabant	cursabant
3. 18	forte ducti [Halm]	[forte victi]	forte iuncti
3. 44	inclinatus	inditus	inclinatus
3. 69	cecidisset	cecidisset	cessisset
3. 72	pretio? stetit, <dum> pro patria bellavimus.	pretio stetit? pro patria bellavimus?	pretio? stetit, <dum> pro patria bellavimus.
3. 80	pulsantur	pulsantur	palantur
3. 84	aggeres	aggeres	aggerem
4. 4	novum	bonum	novum
4. 5	[regione Italiae Carecina] e municipio	[regione Italiae Carecina] e municipio	[regione Italiae] <e> Carecinae municipio
4. 6	inanior [Wellesley]	maior	maior
4. 12	<quo> arma equosque retinens integris turmis Rhenum perrumperet.	arma equosque retinens integris turmis Rhenum perrumpere . . .	<quo> arma equosque retinens integris turmis Rhenum perrumperet.
4. 13	Iulius Paulus et Iulius Civilis	Iulius Paulus et Iulius Civilis	Iulius Civilis et Claudius Paulus
4. 15	proxima [occupata]	proximo †occupata†	proxima [occupata]
4. 22	Romanorum	Romanorum	[Romanorum]
4. 28	[Romanorum nomen]	[Romanorum nomen]	Romanorum <in> nomen
4. 29	concursus	casus	concursus
4. 35	desertos se	desertos se	desertos <se derelictos>que
4. 37	incruentati, quia dispersos	incruenti: in via dispersos	incruentati, quia dispersos
4. 40	iustum iudicium	iustum iudicium	iustam vindictam
4. 65	formido [Wellesley]	condicio	condicio
5. 14	sextae	tertiae decimae	sextae

In accordance with standard classical editorial conventions, [ ] indicates an editorial deletion of words found in the manuscript; < > indicates an editorial supplement to the manuscript; ... signals a lacuna in the text. † indicates that the editor regards the text as intractably corrupt.

SELECT BIBLIOGRAPHY

Note: there are voluminous studies on every aspect of Tacitus. This bibliography is highly selective; in general it also gives preference to works in English, and to books rather than articles.

Latin texts of the Histories

Ed. C. D. Fisher (Oxford, 1910).
Ed. H. Heubner (Leipzig, 1978).
Ed. K. Wellesley (Stuttgart, 1989).

Commentaries

Chilver, G. E. F., *A Historical Commentary on Tacitus'* Histories *I and II* (Oxford, 1979).
——— *A Historical Commentary on Tacitus'* Histories *IV and V* (Oxford, 1985) (completed G. B. Townend).
Heubner; H., *P. Cornelius Tacitus: Die Historien* (5 vols., Heidelberg, 1963–82).
Wellesley, K., *Cornelius Tacitus: The Histories Book III* (Sydney, 1972).

Ancient Historiography

Fornara, C. W., *The Nature of History in Ancient Greece and Rome* (Berkeley and Los Angeles, 1985).
Kraus, C. S., and Woodman, A. J., *Latin Historians* (Oxford, 1997).
Marincola, J., *Authority and Tradition in Ancient Historiography* (Cambridge,1997).
Plass, P., *Wit and the Writing of History* (Madison, 1988).
Wiseman, T. P., *Clio's Cosmetics* (Leicester, 1979).
Woodman, A. J., *Rhetoric in Classical Historiography: Four Studies* (London, 1988).

General Books on Tacitus

Luce, T. J., and Woodman, A. J. (eds.), *Tacitus and the Tacitean Tradition* (Princeton, 1993).
Martin, R., *Tacitus* (London, 1981).
Mellor, R., *Tacitus* (New York, 1993).
Syme, R., *Tacitus* (2 vols., Oxford, 1958).

There are essays on all aspects of Tacitus, many in English, in *Aufstieg und Niedergang der römischen Welt*, vols. 2. 33. 2, 2. 33. 3, 2. 33. 4, 2. 33. 5 (Berlin, 1990–1).

Studies of Individual Sections of the Histories

Ash, R., *Ordering Anarchy: Armies and Leaders in Tacitus' Histories* (London, 1999).

Baxter, R. T. S., 'Virgil's Influence on Tacitus "Histories" 3', *Classical Philology*, 66 (1971), 93–107.

Briessmann, A., *Tacitus und das flavische Geschichtsbild* (Hermes Einzelschriften 10: Wiesbaden, 1955).

Keitel, E., 'Otho's Exhortations in Tacitus' *Histories*', Greece and Rome, 34 (1987), 73–82.

—— '*Foedum spectaculum* and Related Motifs in Tacitus *Histories* II–III', Rheinisches Museum, 135 (1992), 342–51.

Levene, D. S., 'Pity, Fear and the Historical Audience: Tacitus on the Fall of Vitellius', in S. M. Braund and C. Gill (eds.), *The Passions in Roman Thought and Literature* (Cambridge, 1997), 128–49.

Morgan, M. G., 'The Smell of Victory: Vitellius at Bedriacum, Tacitus *Histories* 2. 70', *Classical Philology*, 87 (1992), 14–29.

—— 'The Three Minor Pretenders in Tacitus *Histories* 2', *Latomus*, 52 (1993), 769–96.

—— 'The Unity of Tacitus, *Histories* 1. 12–20', *Athenaeum*, 81 (1993), 567–86.

—— 'Rogues' March: Caecina and Valens in *Histories* 1. 61–70', *Museum Helveticum*, 51 (1994), 103–25.

Shochat, Y., 'Tacitus' Attitude to Otho', *Latomus*, 40 (1981), 365–77.

Wellesley, K., 'Suggestio Falsi in Tacitus', *Rheinisches Museum*, 103 (1960), 272–88.

—— 'A Major Crux in Tacitus: *Histories* 2. 40', *Journal of Roman Studies*, 61 (1971), 28–51.

Woodman, A. J., 'Self-Imitation and the Substance of History', in D. West and A. J. Woodman (eds.), *Creative Imitation and Latin Literature* (Cambridge, 1979), 143–55.

The History of the Period of the Histories

Brunt, P. A., 'Tacitus on the Batavian Revolt', *Latomus*, 19 (1960), 494–517. Reprinted in *Roman Imperial Themes* (Oxford, 1990), which includes other important studies of this period of the Roman Empire.

Goodman, M., *The Ruling Class of Judaea* (Cambridge, 1987).

—— *The Roman World: 44 BC–AD 180* (London, 1997).

Millar, F., *The Emperor in the Roman World* (2nd edn. London, 1992).

Murison, C. L., *Galba, Otho and Vitellius: Careers and Controversies* (Hildesheim, 1993).

Talbert, R. J. A., *The Senate of Imperial Rome* (Princeton, 1984).

Webster, G., *The Roman Imperial Army of the 1st and 2nd centuries AD* (3rd edn. London, 1985).

Wellesley, K., *The Long Year AD 69* (2nd edn. Bristol, 1989).

CHRONOLOGY OF THE LIFE OF TACITUS AND THE PERIOD OF THE *HISTORIES*

Note: a number of the dates given here are probable rather than certainly attested. With the revolt of Civilis, accurate dates are especially hard to come by, as Tacitus himself is our only source, and he is often vague on chronology in this section.

AD 54   Death of the Emperor Claudius; accession of Nero.

*c.*56   Birth of Tacitus.

68   (9 June) Suicide of Nero (1. 4). (16 June) Galba, in Spain, learns of Nero's death and his own elevation to the throne.

Execution of Nymphidius Sabinus, Prefect of the Guard (1. 5); murder of Fonteius Capito, governor of Lower Germany, and Clodius Macer, governor of Africa (1. 7).

(Sept./Oct.) Galba enters Rome. Massacre at the Mulvian Bridge (1. 6).

(end Nov.) Vitellius arrives in Lower Germany as governor (1. 9, 1. 52).

69   (1 Jan.) Mutiny of troops of Upper Germany (1. 12, 1. 55–6). (2–3 Jan.) The armies of Upper Germany and of Lower Germany salute Vitellius as emperor (1. 57). (10 Jan.) Galba adopts Piso Licinianus as his successor (1. 18). (15 Jan.) Otho declared emperor in Rome and recognized by Praetorian Guard (1. 27–38). Murder of Galba, Vinius, and Piso (1. 41–3). Otho recognized by the Senate (1. 47).

(Jan.–Feb.) Vitellian armies under Caecina and Valens march on Italy (1. 62–70).

(late Feb.–early Mar.) Otho dispatches an advance guard under Annius Gallus and Vestricius Spurinna; he sends his fleet to Narbonese Gaul (1. 87, 2. 11).

Caecina crosses the Alps (1. 70).

(15 Mar.) Otho leaves Rome (1. 90). (second half Mar.) Spurinna repulses Caecina from Placentia (2. 21–2). Valens crosses into Italy.

(5 Apr.) Battle at Castores. Caecina defeated (2. 24–6).
(c.8 Apr.) Valens joins Caecina at Cremona (2. 30). (c.10
Apr.) Othonian council of war at Bedriacum (2. 32–3).
(14 Apr.) First Battle of Bedriacum. Othonian defeat
(2. 41–5). (16 Apr.) Otho commits suicide at Brixellum
(2. 49). (19 Apr.) Vitellius recognized as emperor by
the Senate (2. 55).

(late Apr./early May) Vitellius greeted by generals at
Lyons (2. 59).

(c.24 May) Vitellius visits the battlefield at Bedriacum
(2. 70).

(June–July) Vitellius advances to Rome (2. 71, 2. 87–8).

(1 July) Vespasian proclaimed emperor at Alexandria (2.
79). (3 July) Vespasian proclaimed at Caesarea (2. 79).
(16/17 July) Vitellius enters Rome (2. 89).

(late July–Aug.) Mucianus moves west; Vespasian holds
Egypt; Titus takes command in Judaea (2. 82–3).

(late Aug./early Sept.) Antonius Primus and Arrius Varus
invade Italy (3. 6). Civilis receives a letter from Antonius
and begins to plan his rebellion (4. 13). He allies himself
with the Canninefates (4. 15–16).

(c.17 Sept.) Caecina marches to meet the invasion (2. 99–
100). (c.19 Sept.) Antonius surprises a Vitellian detachment at Forum Alieni (3. 6). (c.23 Sept.) The Pannonian
legions arrive at Padua (3. 7). (c.25 Sept.) Valens marches
north from Rome (3. 36).

(late Sept./early Oct.) Civilis defeats the Roman armies
near Vetera (4. 18); he persuades the Batavian auxiliaries
to join his revolt (4. 19).

(c.4 Oct.) Antonius reaches Verona (3. 8). (c.12 Oct.) The
fleet at Ravenna declares for Vespasian (2. 101, 3. 12).
(mid-Oct.) Civilis attacks the camp at Vetera (4. 21–3);
Hordeonius Flaccus sends troops from Mogontiacum to
its relief (4. 24). (c.17 Oct.) The Moesian legions arrive at
Verona (3. 10). (18 Oct.) Caecina attempts treachery, and
is imprisoned by his army; they march towards Cremona
(3. 13–14). (22–3 Oct.) Antonius marches to intercept
them (3. 15). (24–5 Oct.) Second Battle of Bedriacum.
Vitellian forces defeated (3. 16–31). (26–9 Oct.) Sack of
Cremona (3. 32–4). (end Oct.) Civilis besieges Vetera (4.
28–30).

(early Nov.) German troops swear allegiance to Vespasian (4. 31). (*c.*19 Nov.) The Vitellians hold the Apennines at Mevania (3. 55). Vitellius himself leaves Rome a few days later to join them. (*c.*20 Nov.) Antonius advances to Fanum Fortunae (3. 50). (*c.*28 Nov.) Mutiny of the fleet at Misenum (3. 57). (end Nov.) Capture of Valens (3. 43).

(*c.*1 Dec.) Vitellius returns to Rome (3. 56). His remaining troops are moved to Narnia (3. 58). (*c.*7 Dec.) Tarracina seized by Misenum rebels (3. 57). Antonius reaches Carsulae (3. 60). (*c.*10 Dec.) Valens executed at Urbinum (3. 62). (*c.*15 Dec.) Surrender of Vitellians at Narnia (3. 63). (16 Dec.) Antonius marches to Ocriculum; he sends Cerialis ahead to Rome (3. 78). (*c.*17 Dec.) Lucius Vitellius captures Tarracina (3. 77). (18 Dec.) Vitellius tries unsuccessfully to abdicate (3. 67–8). Flavius Sabinus besieged in the Capitol (3. 69). (19 Dec.) Capitol stormed; Temple of Jupiter burned. Sabinus captured and killed (3. 70–4). Cerialis defeated outside Rome (3. 79). (19–20 Dec.) Antonius marches to Rome (3. 79). (20 Dec.) Capture of Rome. Vitellius killed (3. 82–5). (*c.*21 Dec.) Vespasian recognized as emperor by the Senate (4. 3). (end Dec.) Mucianus reaches Rome (4. 11). Mutiny in Novaesium; murder of Hordeonius Flaccus. Vocula relieves Mogontiacum (4. 36–7).

70   (1 Jan.) Meeting of the Senate (4. 39). (9 Jan.) Meeting of the Senate; attack on prosecutors under Nero (4. 40–3). (15 Jan.) Meeting of the Senate: attack on prosecutors dropped (4. 45–5). (first half Jan.) Murder of Piso in Africa (4. 48–50). Classicus, Tutor, and Sabinus join Civilis' rebellion (4. 55–6).

(Spring) Vocula advances to save Vetera, but is driven back to Novaesium and there is murdered (4. 56–9). Rhine army swears allegiance to Gallic Empire (4. 59–60).

(Apr./early May) Titus encamps before Jerusalem (5. 1); John of Gischala captures the Temple from Eleazar (5. 12).

(21 June) Ceremony to begin the restoration of the Capitol (4. 53).

(Summer) Mucianus and Domitian start from Rome with reinforcements (4. 68). Petillius Cerialis reaches Mogontiacum (4. 71); he captures Trier (4. 72–5) and the rebel camp (4. 76–8). Germans massacred in Cologne (4. 79). Civilis defeats Cerialis near Vetera, but is then forced to retreat (5. 14–19).

(Aug.) Fall of Jerusalem.

(Aug./Sept.) Vespasian leaves Alexandria for Rome.

(end Sept.) Surrender of Civilis (5. 24–6).

c.76   Tacitus embarks on his career, appointed by Vespasian to one of the junior posts (the 'Vigintivirate') designed for aspiring young politicians. His position (if Alföldy's identification is accepted—see Introduction p. vii) was that of *decemvir stlitibus iudicandis*, serving as president of certain civil law-courts.

77   Tacitus betrothed to the daughter of the consul Julius Agricola, future governor of Britain; he marries her shortly after. Her name is unknown.

79   Death of Vespasian; accession of Titus.

81   Death of Titus; accession of Domitian.

81 or 82   Tacitus becomes quaestor; he may have been (following Alföldy) *quaestor Augusti*, in attendance on the Emperor.

c.85   Tacitus (probably) becomes tribune.

88   Tacitus becomes praetor. By now he was also a member of the senior college of priests called the 'Board of Fifteen' (the *quindecimviri sacris faciundis*).

89/90–3   Tacitus absent from Rome on military and/or civilian provincial service; the precise posts are unknown, but may well have included a term as a legionary commander.

93   Death of Agricola, Tacitus' father-in-law.

96   Assassination of Domitian; accession of Nerva.

97   (second half) Tacitus becomes consul.

98   Death of Nerva; accession of Trajan. Tacitus publishes the *Agricola* and the *Germania*.

100   Tacitus and his friend Pliny the Younger successfully prosecute Marius Priscus for corruption while governor of Africa.

105–6   Tacitus is by now researching and writing the *Histories*; it is not known when he began.

c.109   Tacitus publishes the *Histories*.

112–13   Tacitus is governor of Asia.

*c.*114   Tacitus begins work on the *Annals*.

117   Death of Trajan; accession of Hadrian.

The date of publication of the *Dialogue on Orators* is unknown; reasonable suggestions have included 102 and 107. It is fairly certain that Tacitus outlived Trajan and was still writing the *Annals* in the first part of Hadrian's reign. Beyond this, the publication date of the *Annals* and the date of Tacitus' death are both unknown.

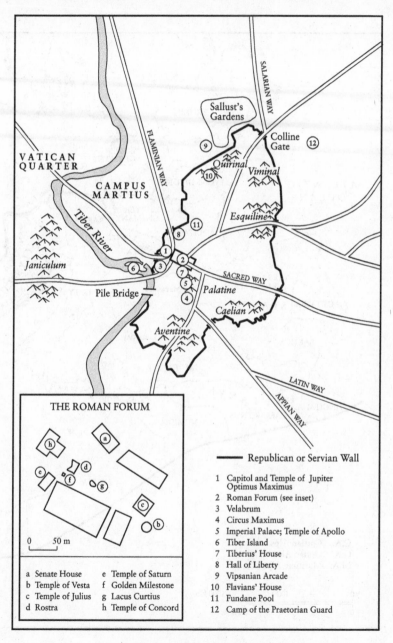

THE ROMAN FORUM

0   50 m

a Senate House   e Temple of Saturn
b Temple of Vesta   f Golden Milestone
c Temple of Julius g Lacus Curtius
d Rostra   h Temple of Concord

——— Republican or Servian Wall

1 Capitol and Temple of Jupiter
   Optimus Maximus
2 Roman Forum (see inset)
3 Velabrum
4 Circus Maximus
5 Imperial Palace; Temple of Apollo
6 Tiber Island
7 Tiberius' House
8 Hall of Liberty
9 Vipsanian Arcade
10 Flavians' House
11 Fundane Pool
12 Camp of the Praetorian Guard

MAP 1   Plan of Rome in AD 69–70

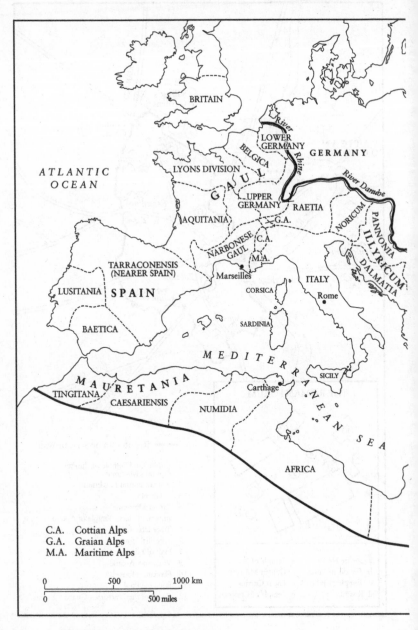

MAP 2   The Roman Empire in AD 69–70

C.A.   Cottian Alps
G.A.   Graian Alps
M.A.   Maritime Alps

0   500   1000 km
0   500 miles

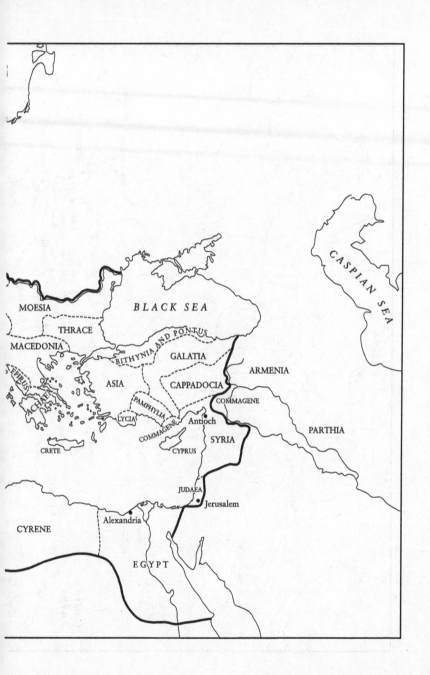

MOESIA

THRACE

MACEDONIA

BLACK SEA

EPIRUS

ACHAEA

CRETE

BITHYNIA AND PONTUS

GALATIA

ASIA

CAPPADOCIA

PAMPHYLIA

LYCIA

COMMAGENE

CYPRUS

Antioch

SYRIA

ARMENIA

COMMAGENE

PARTHIA

CASPIAN SEA

JUDAEA

Jerusalem

CYRENE

Alexandria

E G Y P T

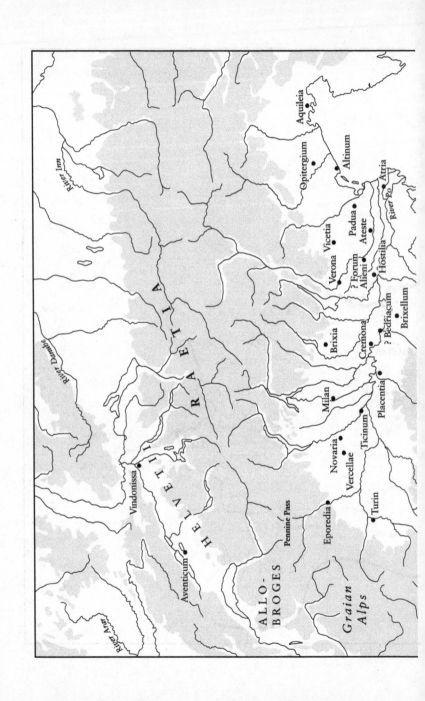

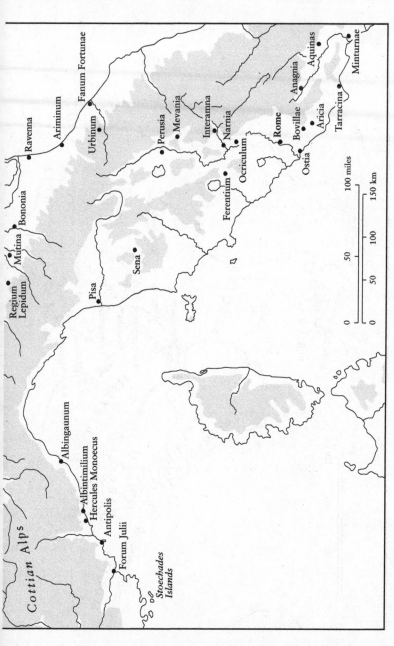

MAP 3   Northern and Central Italy in AD 69–70

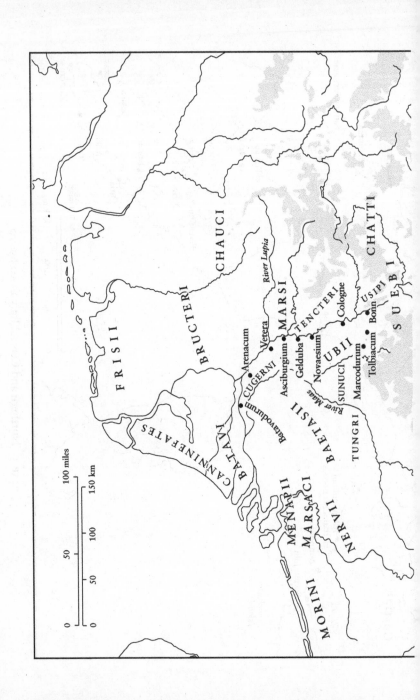

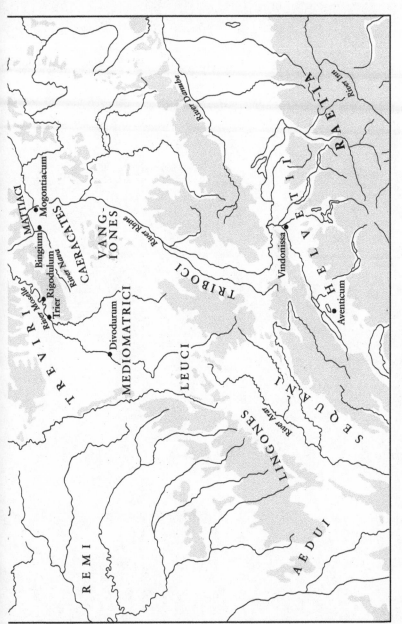

MAP 4 Germany in AD 69–70

THE HISTORIES

BOOK ONE

I propose to begin my work with the year when Servius Galba 1
was consul for the second time* and Titus Vinius was his
colleague.* Many historians have dealt with the 820 years of
the earlier period beginning with the foundation of Rome,*
and the story of the Roman Republic has been told with equal
eloquence and independence. After the Battle of Actium,*
when the interests of peace were served by the centralization
of all authority in the hands of one man, that literary genius
fell idle. At the same time truth was shattered under a variety
of blows. Initially it was ignorance of politics, which were no
longer a citizen's concern; later came the taste for flattery or,
conversely, hatred of the ruling house. So between malice on
one side and servility on the other the interests of posterity
were neglected. But historians find that flattery soon incurs
the stigma of slavishness and earns for them the contempt of
their readers, whereas people readily open their ears to slander
and envy, since malice gives the false impression of independence. From Galba, Otho, and Vitellius, I have experienced
nothing either to my advantage or my hurt. I cannot deny
that I owe the launching of my career to Vespasian, or that
I was advanced by Titus and still further promoted by
Domitian; but those who lay claim to unbiased accuracy must
speak of no man with either hatred or affection. I have reserved for my old age, if life is spared to me, the reigns of
the deified Nerva and of the Emperor Trajan,* which afford
a richer and a safer theme: for it is the rare fortune of these
days that you may think what you like and say what you
think.

The story I now commence is rich in vicissitudes, grim with 2
warfare, torn by civil strife, a tale of horror even during times
of peace. Four emperors slain by the sword. Three civil wars:
often entwined with these, an even larger number of foreign
wars. Successes in the East, disaster in the West, disturbance
in Illyricum, disaffection in Gaul. The conquest of Britain,
immediately given up; the rising of the Sarmatian and Suebic

tribes. Dacia had the privilege of inflicting and receiving defeat at our hands, and a pretender claiming to be Nero almost deluded the Parthians also into declaring war. Now too Italy was smitten with new disasters, or disasters it had not witnessed for a long period of years. Towns along the rich coast of Campania were swallowed by the earth or buried from above. The city was devastated by fires, her most ancient temples were destroyed, and the Capitol itself was fired by Roman hands. Sacred rites were grossly profaned, and there was adultery among the great. The sea swarmed with exiles, and cliffs were red with blood. Worse horrors reigned in the city. To be rich or well born, to hold office or refuse it, was a crime: merit of any kind meant certain ruin. Nor were the informers more hated for their crimes than for their prizes: some carried off a priesthood or the consulship as their spoil, others won administrative office and a place at the heart of power: the hatred and fear they inspired worked universal havoc. Slaves were bribed against their masters, freedmen against their patrons, and, if a man had no enemies, he was ruined by his friends.

3   However, the period was not so utterly barren as to yield no examples of heroism. Mothers accompanied sons in flight, wives followed husbands into exile: one saw here a kinsman's courage and there a son-in-law's devotion: slaves obstinately faithful even on the rack: distinguished men bravely facing the utmost straits and matching in their end the famous deaths of older times. Besides these manifold disasters to mankind, there were portents in the sky and on the earth, thunderbolts and other premonitions of good and of evil, some doubtful, some obvious. Indeed, never has it been proved by such terrible disasters to Rome or by such clear evidence that the gods are concerned not with our peace of mind, but rather with vengeance.

4   Before I begin my task, it seems best to go back and consider the state of affairs in the city, the temper of the armies, the condition of the provinces, and to determine the elements of strength and weakness in the different quarters of the world. By this means we may see not only the actual course of

events, whose outcome is largely governed by chance, but also why and how they occurred.

The death of Nero, after the first outburst of joy with which it had been greeted, soon had aroused conflicting feelings not only among the senators, the people, and the soldiers in the city, but also among all the generals and their troops abroad. It had divulged a secret of state: an emperor could be made elsewhere than at Rome.* Still, the Senate was overjoyed. They had immediately taken advantage of their liberty to act under less constraint before an absent emperor, new to the throne. The delight of the leading knights fell little short of the Senate's. Respectable citizens who were attached to the great families, clients or freedmen who had seen their patrons condemned or exiled, now revived their hopes. The base mob, who had grown familiar with the pleasures of the theatre and the circus, the most degraded of the slaves, and men who had squandered their property and lived on Nero's discreditable bounty, all were miserable and greedy for news.*

The troops in the city had long soaked themselves in alle- 5 giance to the Caesars, and it was more by the pressure of intrigue than of their own inclination that they came to desert Nero. They soon realized that the donation promised in Galba's name was not to be paid to them,* and that peace would not, like war, offer opportunity for great services and rich rewards. Since they also saw that in their bid for the new Emperor's favour they had been forestalled by the army which proclaimed him, they were ripe for revolution; and they were further incited by their villainous Prefect Nymphidius Sabinus,* who was plotting to be emperor himself. As a matter of fact, he was detected in the course of his plan and was dealt with. But, though the ringleader was removed, many of the troops still felt conscious of their treason, and some could be heard berating Galba's senility and avarice. His severity—a quality once admired and set high in soldiers' estimation—only annoyed troops whose contempt for the old methods of discipline had been fostered by fourteen years of service under Nero. They had come to love the emperors' vices as much as they had formerly feared their virtues. Moreover,

Galba had let fall a remark which augured well for Rome, but spelt danger to himself. 'I do not buy my soldiers,' he said, 'I select them'—yet these words were inconsistent with everything else that was going on.

6   Galba was old and ill. Of his two lieutenants, Titus Vinius was the vilest of men and Cornelius Laco the laziest. Between them, they burdened Galba with the odium of Vinius' crimes, and ruined him by the disdain for Laco's inefficiency.

His march from Spain was slow and stained with bloodshed. He executed Cingonius Varro, the consul-elect, and Petronius Turpilianus,* an ex-consul, the former as an accomplice of Nymphidius, the latter as one of Nero's generals. They were both denied any opportunity of a hearing or defence, and died apparently innocent. On his arrival at Rome the butchery of thousands of unarmed soldiers* gave an ill omen to his entry, and alarmed even the men who did the slaughter.

The city was filled with strange troops. A legion had been brought from Spain,* and the regiment of marines enrolled by Nero still remained. Moreover, there were several detachments from Germany, Britain, and Illyricum, which had themselves been selected by Nero, dispatched to the Caspian Pass for the projected war against the Albani, and subsequently recalled to crush the revolt of Vindex.* These were all fine fuel for a revolution; although their favour centred on nobody in particular, they were at the disposal of anyone who had enterprise.

7   It happened by chance that the news of the deaths of Clodius Macer and of Fonteius Capito* arrived in Rome simultaneously. Macer, who was undoubtedly raising a disturbance in Africa, was put to death by the procurator Trebonius Garrutianus, acting under Galba's orders: Capito had made a similar attempt in Germany and was killed by two legionary commanders, Cornelius Aquinus and Fabius Valens,* without waiting for instructions. While Capito had a foul reputation for avarice and loose living, some people yet believed that he had withheld his hand from treason. His officers, they supposed, had urged him to declare war, and, when they could not persuade him, had themselves arranged to accuse and entrap him; Galba, from weakness of character,

or perhaps because he was afraid to inquire too far, approved what had happened for good or for ill, since it was past alteration. At any rate both executions were unpopular.

Now that Galba was detested, everything he did, whether right or wrong, brought upon him equal detestation. His freedmen were all-powerful: money could do anything: his slaves were eager to capitalize on their unexpected fortune, and with so elderly an emperor were losing no time. The evils of the new court were those of the old, and while equally oppressive were not so easily excused. Even Galba's age seemed comic and despicable to a populace that was used to the young Nero and compared emperors, as such people will, in point of looks and personal attraction.*

Such, then, was the variety of feeling at Rome, as was 8 natural in so vast a population. To turn to the provinces: Spain was under the command of Cluvius Rufus,* a man of great eloquence, and more skilled in the arts of peace than of war. The Gallic provinces had not forgotten Vindex: moreover, they were bound to Galba by his recent grant of Roman citizenship and his rebate of their tribute for the future. The tribes, however, which lay nearest to the armies stationed in Germany had not received these honours: some had even lost part of their territory and were equally aggrieved when they sized up their own injuries and their neighbours' benefits.

The troops in Germany, proud of their recent victory, but fearful that they had supported the wrong side, were uneasy and indignant: a very dangerous state for so strong a force to be in. They had been slow to desert Nero, and Verginius* had not immediately declared for Galba. Whether he really did not want the throne is doubtful: without question his soldiers made him the offer. The death of Fonteius Capito aroused the indignation even of those who had no business complaining. However, they still lacked a leader: Galba had sent for Verginius under a pretence of friendship, and, when he was not allowed to return and was even subject to prosecution, the soldiers interpreted the accusation as being against themselves.

The army of Upper Germany felt no respect for their gover- 9 nor, Hordeonius Flaccus.* Weakened by age and an affliction of the feet, he was without resolution or authority, and could not have controlled even the mildest troops. These fiery spirits were only further inflamed when they felt such a weak hand on the reins. The legions of Lower Germany had been for some time without a governor, until Galba's appointee, Aulus Vitellius, appeared. He was the son of the Lucius Vitellius who had been censor and thrice consul;* this, it seemed, was sufficient reason.

The army in Britain showed no bad feeling. All through the disturbance of the civil wars no troops kept cleaner hands. This may have been because they were so far away and severed by the sea, or perhaps frequent engagements had taught them to keep their rancour for the enemy. Quiet ruled in Illyricum also, although the legions, which had been summoned by Nero, while lingering in Italy had made overtures to Verginius. But the armies lay far apart (always a sound assistance to the preservation of military loyalty), and the men could neither share vices nor join forces.

10   The East was still untroubled. Licinius Mucianus held Syria with four legions.* He was a man who was equally talked about in good fortune as in bad. As a youth he was ambitious and cultivated the friendship of the great. Later he found himself in straitened circumstances and a slippery position; moreover, Claudius' displeasure was suspected. He was relegated to the remoteness of Asia, where he came as near to being an exile as afterwards to being an emperor. He was a strange mixture of luxury and industry, courtesy and arrogance, of good and bad. In leisure he was self-indulgent, but he revealed considerable flair when on service. His outward behaviour was praiseworthy, though ill was spoken of his private life. However, with those who were under him or near him, and with his colleagues, he gained great influence by various devices: the sort of man who would more readily make an emperor than be one.

The Jewish War* was being conducted by Flavius Vespasian—appointed by Nero—with three legions. He had no ill-will against Galba, and nothing to hope from his fall. Indeed he had sent his son Titus to carry his compliments and offer allegiance, an incident we must reserve for its proper place. It was only after Vespasian's rise that we came to believe in the mysterious movings of Providence, and supposed that portents and oracles had predestined the throne for him and his family.

Ever since the days of the deified Augustus, knights of Rome 11 have been the uncrowned kings of Egypt and of the garrison that controls it. The province being difficult to reach, a rich source of corn, torn and tossed by fanaticism and licentiousness, ignorant of law, unused to civil government, it seemed wiser to keep it in the control of the Household.* The governor at that date was Tiberius Alexander,* himself a native of Egypt.

Africa and its legion, now that Clodius Macer had been executed, were ready to put up with any ruler after their experience of a petty master. The two Mauretanias, Raetia, Noricum, Thrace, and the other provinces governed by procurators* had their sympathies determined by the neighbourhood of troops, and always caught their likes or dislikes from the strongest army. The ungarrisoned provinces, and chief amongst these Italy, were destined to be the prize of war, and lay at the mercy of any master.

Such was the state of the Roman world when Servius Galba, consul for the second time, and Titus Vinius his colleague,* inaugurated the year which was their last, and almost the last for the commonwealth of Rome.

A few days after 1 January a dispatch arrived from Belgica, 12 in which the procurator Pompeius Propinquus announced that the legions of Upper Germany had broken their oath of allegiance* and were clamouring for a new emperor, but that by way of tempering their treason they referred the final choice to the Senate and People of Rome. Galba had already been deliberating and seeking advice from associates as to the adoption of a successor, and this occurrence hastened his plans. During all the preceding months this question had undeniably formed the chief subject of gossip throughout the country. Such discussion was eagerly craved, and went unchecked; Galba's age and exhaustion reinforced it. Few people showed sound judgement or any spirit of patriotism. Many were influenced by foolish hopes and spread self-interested

rumours pointing to some friend or patron, thereby also gratifying their hatred for Titus Vinius, whose unpopularity waxed
daily with his power.

13   Galba's affability only served to strengthen the greedy ambitions of his newly powerful friends; for his weakness and
credulity halved the risk of crime and doubled the reward. The
power of the Emperor was divided between the consul, Titus
Vinius, and Cornelius Laco, the Prefect of the Guards; and an
influence as great was enjoyed by Icelus, one of Galba's freedmen, who had been given the rings of a knight* and was
accordingly called by the name of Marcianus. These three
ordinarily disagreed, and each followed his own interest in
smaller matters: but on the question of the succession they fell
into two camps. Vinius was for Marcus Otho; Laco and Icelus
were agreed not so much on any one candidate as on any
other.

Galba was aware of the friendship between Otho and
Vinius. Otho was a bachelor and Vinius had an unmarried
daughter: the gossip among the rumour-mongers was desig-
nating them the future father- and son-in-law. Galba, one may
suppose, felt some concern for his country, too. Why take the
throne from Nero, if it was to be left to Otho? Otho had led
an irresponsible boyhood and a dissolute youth, and endeared
himself to Nero by aping his sybaritism. Thus it was to Otho,
the person privy to his lusts, that Nero had entrusted the
imperial whore Poppaea Sabina, until he could get rid of
Octavia.* But then he suspected Otho of an attachment to this
same Poppaea, and removed him to the province of Lusitania
under cover of a governorship.

Otho had been popular in his administration of the province, and was the first to join Galba's party. Being a man of
action and the most distinguished of Galba's officers in the
war, he had instantly conceived the hope of succeeding him,
and with each passing day grasped at it more eagerly. Most of
the soldiers were on his side, and the court supported him as
a second Nero.

14   After receiving the news of the German revolt, although
Galba still knew nothing for certain of Vitellius' plans, he was
fearful as to the extent to which the violence of the troops

might spread. He was unable to trust even the troops in the city, so he had recourse to what seemed his sole remedy and held an imperial election.* Besides Vinius and Laco he summoned Marius Celsus,* consul-elect, and the City Prefect* Ducenius Geminus. After prefacing a few words about his own advanced age he ordered Piso Licinianus to be sent for; this was either on his own initiative, or, as some believed, at the insistence of Laco.* Laco had met Piso at Rubellius Plautus'* house and they had formed a friendship, but he cunningly pretended that he was supporting a stranger, and Piso's good repute gave colour to this policy.

Piso was a noble on both sides, being the son of Marcus Crassus and Scribonia. There was an old-world austerity in his face and bearing, and just critics spoke of his strict morality: people who took a less favourable view thought him sour. But this side of his character that the uneasy distrusted was what commended him to the Emperor who was adopting him.

Galba, then, is said to have taken Piso's hand and addressed 15 him as follows:*

'Were I a private citizen, and were I to adopt you in the presence of the pontiffs by the usual formality of a curial statute,* it would be an honour for me to introduce into my family a descendant of Gnaeus Pompey and of Marcus Crassus,* and for you it would be a distinction to add to your noble ancestry the glories of the Sulpician and Lutatian houses.* As it is, I have been called by the consent of gods and men to be an emperor. Your distinguished qualities and your patriotism have persuaded me to offer to you peacefully the throne for which our ancestors fought on the field of battle, and which I too won by war. In so doing I am following the precedent set by the deified Augustus, who raised to a rank second only to his own, first his nephew Marcellus, then his son-in-law Agrippa, then his grandsons, and finally his step-son Tiberius Nero.* However, while Augustus looked for a successor in his own family, I have searched throughout the state. Not that I lack either kinsmen or supporters in war, but it was not through self-interest that I myself came to the throne, and, to prove my policy in this matter, consider how

I have passed over not only my own relatives but yours. You have an elder brother,* as noble as yourself. He would have been worthy of this position, but you are worthier.

'You are old enough to have outlived youthful passions. Your life has been such that you have nothing in your past to excuse. So far you have only experienced misfortune.* Prosperity probes the heart with a keener touch; misery only calls for patience, but there is corruption in success. Loyalty, independence, and affection are the prime virtues of the human heart, and certainly you yourself will have the strength of mind to retain them. But the sycophancy of others will weaken them. Flattery and adulation will break down their defences, and self-interest too, the bane of all sincerity. You and I can talk plainly with each other today; yet others will address themselves not to us but to our fortunes. To persuade an emperor what he ought to do is a laborious task: but on any emperor flattery is successful, even in the absence of devotion.

16   'If the vast bulk of this empire could stand and keep its balance without a guiding hand, I was a suitable person to set in motion a republic. As it is, things have long ago come to such a pass that neither I in my old age can give the Roman people any better gift than a good successor, nor you in your prime anything better than a good emperor. Under Tiberius, Gaius, and Claudius, Rome was the heirloom of a single family. There is a kind of liberty in the free choice we are beginning to exercise. Now that the Julian and Claudian house is extinct, the best man will always be discovered by adoption. Royal birth and ancestry are the gift of fortune, and are only valued as such. In adoption we can use a free judgement, and if we wish to choose well, the voice of the country points the way. Think of Nero, swollen with the pride of his long line of royal ancestry. It was not Vindex with a powerless province at his back, nor I with a single legion, that freed Rome's shoulders of that burden: it was his own barbarity and profligacy. And that was before there was any precedent for the conviction of an emperor.

'We have been called to the throne by the sword, and by those who thought us worthy. Our high state will not escape the eye of envy; but there is no reason for you to feel alarm because in this world-wide upheaval a couple of legions have not yet settled down. I myself did not succeed to a safe and peaceful throne, and, when once the news of your adoption is spread, I shall cease to be charged with my advanced age, which is now the only fault they find in me. Evil men will always miss Nero: you and I must ensure that good citizens do not miss him too.

'A longer sermon would ill befit the time, and I have fulfilled my purpose if I have done right in choosing you. The soundest and easiest criterion of right and wrong policy is to consider what you would have approved or condemned in another emperor. For Rome is not like the nations which are ruled by kings, where one house is supreme and the rest are slaves. Your future subjects are men who cannot endure the extremes either of bondage or of freedom.'

Galba spoke these words and more to the same effect in the tone of one creating an emperor: the others addressed Piso as though he were emperor already. Piso is said to have betrayed 17 no sign of agitation or elation either before those who were then present, or later when everybody's eyes centred upon him. His language to his Emperor and adoptive father was deeply respectful and he spoke modestly of himself. He made no change in his expression or bearing, showing himself more able than anxious to rule.

A discussion then took place whether the adoption should be announced formally before the people, or in the Senate, or in the Guards' camp. They decided in favour of the camp, on the ground that it would be a compliment to the troops, whose goodwill it was immoral to win by bounty and bribery, but was by no means to be despised, if it could be won by good means. Meanwhile the curiosity of the populace, impatient of any important secret, had brought together crowds all round the palace, and when once the rumour began to leak out an attempt at suppression only resulted in spreading it.

The tenth of January was a dreary wet day, and was dis- 18 rupted by an extraordinary storm of thunder and lightning showing the displeasure of Providence. Such phenomena were regarded in old days as a sign for the suspension of elections, but they did not deter Galba from proceeding to the camp. He disregarded such things as the result of pure chance—or perhaps the blows of fate are foretold but not forestalled.

He addressed a crowded assembly of the soldiers with true imperial brevity, stating simply that in adopting Piso he was following the example of the deified Augustus, and the old military custom whereby each man chose another.* He was afraid that by suppressing the news of the German rebellion he might only seem to exaggerate the danger, so he voluntarily declared that the Fourth and Twenty-Second Legions* had been led by a few traitors into seditious murmurings but no further, and would soon return to their allegiance. He made no attempt to enhance his words either by pandering to his audience or by largess. However, the tribunes and centurions and those of the soldiers who stood nearest to him gave well-sounding answers. The rest were sorry and silent, for the war seemed to have lost them the bounty that it had always been essential to grant even in peace. Everybody agrees that they could have been won over had the parsimonious old Emperor made the least display of generosity. He was ruined by his old-fashioned inflexibility and excessive strictness, too rigorous for these degenerate days.

19   From the camp they proceeded to the Senate, and Galba's speech to its members was no fuller or finer than to the soldiers. Piso spoke graciously, and there was no lack of support in the Senate. Many wished him well; those who did not were the more effusive. The majority were indifferent, but displayed a ready servility, intent on their private speculations without thought of the country's good. There was no other public speech or action from Piso during the four days which intervened between his adoption and assassination.

Reports of the German rebellion grew daily more insistent and the public was always ready to hear and believe any news, provided it was bad. Accordingly the Senate had decided that a commission must be sent to the army in Germany. It was discussed in private whether Piso should go himself to add dignity to the commission, since he would carry with him the status of a Caesar, the others the authority of the Senate. It

was also voted to send Laco, the Prefect of the Guards, but he
vetoed the plan. The Senate had allowed Galba to nominate
the commissioners and he showed the most atrocious indecision, now nominating members, now excusing them, now
making exchanges, yielding always to pressure from people
who wanted to go or to stay at home according as they were
determined by their hopes or their fears.

The next question was one of finance.* After investigating 20
all possible sources it seemed most reasonable to recover the
revenue from those quarters where the cause of the deficit
lay. Nero had squandered in lavish presents 2,200 million
sesterces. Galba gave instructions that these moneys should be
recovered from the individual recipients, leaving each a tithe
of their original gift. However, in each case there was scarcely
a tenth part left, for they had run through Nero's money as
freely as they had squandered their own: the most worthless
spendthrifts had no lands or investments left, nothing but the
apparatus of their vices.

Thirty of the knights were entrusted with the duty of recovering the money. This commission, for which there was no
precedent, proved burdensome owing to the numbers to receive bribes. Every quarter was beset with sales and brokers,
and unsettled by lawsuits. And yet lively satisfaction was
caused by the discovery that the beneficiaries of Nero's bounty
were as poor as the victims of his greed.

At this time several military tribunes were cashiered,
Antonius Taurus and Antonius Naso of the Guards, Aemilius
Pacensis of the City Garrison, and Julius Fronto* of the
Watch. However, this proved no remedy. The others only
began to feel alarmed, thinking that Galba's craft and timidity
had sacrificed individuals, while his suspicions rested on them
all.

Meanwhile Otho had nothing to hope from a peaceful 21
settlement: all his plans demanded a disturbance. Many
motives spurred him on: his extravagance would have ruined
an emperor, and his poverty was all but unendurable for a
private person: he was angry with Galba and jealous of Piso.

He also invented fears for his safety, by way of whetting his
ambition: 'I proved a major nuisance to Nero,' he would say,

'and can scarcely expect the compliment of a second exile to Lusitania. Besides, monarchs always hate and suspect the man who is mentioned as "next to the throne". This was what did me harm with the elderly emperor, and it will weigh still more with the youthful Piso, who is naturally savage and has been exasperated by a long period of exile: Otho could well be murdered. I must do and dare while Galba's authority is on the wane and Piso's not yet established. These times of change suit big enterprises. Inaction is more deadly than daring: there is no call for delay. Death is the natural end for all alike, and the only difference is between fame and oblivion afterwards. Seeing that the same end awaits the innocent and the guilty, a man of spirit should at least die with good cause.'

22   Otho's character was by no means so effeminate as his physique. His intimate freedmen and slaves, who were allowed a licence unusual in private households, dangled before him the baits for which he was greedy: the luxuries of Nero's court, the marriages he could make, the adulteries he could commit, and all the other imperial pleasures. They were his, they pointed out, if he had the courage—it was shameful to lie quiet and leave them to others.

He was also incited by the astrologers, who declared that their study of the stars pointed to great changes and a year of glory for Otho. People of this class always betray the powerful and deceive the ambitious; we shall go on for ever proscribing them and keeping them by us.* Poppaea had always had her boudoir full of these astrologers, the worst kind of outfit for a royal marriage. One of them, called Ptolemy, had gone with Otho to Spain and foretold that he would outlive Nero. This came true and Otho believed in him. Now, basing himself on his own calculations, and the gossip of those who reckoned up Galba's age and Otho's youth, he had persuaded him that he would ascend the throne. But Otho accepted the prophecy as if it was the signal of fate revealed by a skilled practitioner: human nature always likes to believe what it cannot understand. Nor was Ptolemy himself slow to incite his master to crime, which lies only a short step from such ambitions.

But it is unclear whether Otho's criminal designs were in 23 fact suddenly conceived. He had long been courting the good-will of the soldiers, either in the hope of being adopted by Galba or to prepare the way for treason. On the road from Spain, while the men were marching or on outpost duty, he would address the longest-serving soldiers by name, remind-ing them how he and they had served together under Nero, and calling them his comrades. He renewed acquaintance with some, asked after others and helped them with money or influence, frequently letting fall complaints and ambiguous remarks about Galba, and using all the other arts which work upon uneducated minds. The soldiers grumbled bitterly at the exertions of the march, the shortage of provisions, and the strict discipline. What they were used to was a journey to the Campanian Lakes or Greek seaports on board ship—they found it hard to struggle over the Pyrenees and Alps, and march immense distances under arms.

While the soldiers were thus already fired with discontent, 24 Maevius Pudens, one of Tigellinus'* intimates, had added fuel to their feelings by luring on all who were naturally unstable or in need of money, and who were consequently rashly eager for a change. Eventually, whenever Galba dined with Otho, Maevius went to the length of presenting 100 sesterces to each of the soldiers on guard, on the pretext of feasting them. This system of public largess Otho extended by making presents in confidence to individuals, and such spirit did he show in bribery that when a member of the Body Guard, Cocceius Proculus, brought an action to claim part of his neighbour's farm, Otho bought the whole property out of his own pocket and gave it to him. He was enabled to do this by the ineffi-ciency of the Prefect Laco, who was no less blind to notorious than to secret scandals.

Otho now put Onomastus, one of his freedmen, in charge 25 of the projected crime, and Onomastus took into his confi-dence Barbius Proculus, an aide-de-camp, and a subaltern named Veturius, both in the Body Guard. Having assured himself in a wide-ranging conversation that they were both bold and cunning, Otho proceeded to load them with bribes and promises, providing them with funds to enable them to test the feelings of the others. So a couple of common soldiers took it upon them to hand over the Roman Empire—and they did it.

A very few were admitted as accomplices. These, by various devices, worked on the indecision of the others. The promoted soldiers who had received preferment from Nymphidius felt themselves under suspicion; the others, the private soldiers, were indignant and in despair at the constant postponement of Galba's largesse; some few were fired by the recollection of Nero's regime and longed for the old days of licence; all in common shared the fear of being drafted out of the Guard.

26   The infection of treason soon spread to the legions and auxiliaries, whose excitement had been aroused as soon as the news had spread that the armies of Germany were wavering in their allegiance. So, as the dishonest were ready for treason, and even the honest shut their eyes to it, they at first determined to hurry Otho off to their barracks as he was returning from dinner on the night of the fourteenth. However, they hesitated: the darkness spelt uncertainty, the troops' quarters were scattered all over the town, and unanimity could scarcely be expected from drunken men. They were not deterred by any affection for their country, which they were clear-headedly preparing to stain with its Emperor's blood, but they were afraid that in the darkness the soldiers of the Pannonian or German legions might come across someone else and mistake him for Otho, who was unknown to the majority.

Some evidence of the brewing plot leaked out, but it was suppressed by the conspirators. Rumours even reached Galba's ears, but the Prefect Laco made light of them, being totally ignorant of the soldiers' thoughts, hostile to any suggestion, however wise, that was not his own, and extremely obstinate with men who knew more than he did.

27   On 15 January, as Galba was sacrificing in front of the Temple of Apollo,* the soothsayer Umbricius* declared the entrails unfavourable: treason was impending, and an enemy within the walls. Otho, who was standing beside Galba, overheard and construed the omen as being from his own point of

view a good one, favourable to his plans.* In a few moments
his freedman Onomastus announced that the architect and
contractors were waiting to see him. This had been agreed
upon as the signal that the troops were assembling and the
conspiracy was ripe. On being asked where he was going,
Otho pretended that he was buying an old property, but
suspected its condition and so had to inspect it first. Thus,
leaning on his freedman's shoulder, he passed through
Tiberius' House into the Velabrum and thence to the Golden
Milestone* at the foot of the Temple of Saturn. There twenty-
three soldiers of the Body Guard saluted him as emperor.
When he showed alarm at the smallness of their number they
put him hastily into a litter, and, drawing their swords, hurried him away. About the same number of soldiers joined
them on the way, some accomplices, most merely curious.
Some marched along shouting and flourishing swords; others
kept silent, intending to take their cue from subsequent events.

Julius Martialis was the tribune on duty in the camp. He led 28
most people to suppose he was in the plot, either because of
the magnitude of this unexpected crime, or else because he
was afraid that the treason was widespread in the camp, and
that he might be killed if he offered any opposition. So too the
other tribunes and centurions all preferred present safety to a
risky loyalty. In fact the general attitude was this: few dared
to undertake so foul a crime, many wished it done, and
everybody would condone it.

Meanwhile Galba, in total ignorance and intent upon his 29
sacrifices, continued to importune the gods of an empire that
had already ceased to be his. First there came a rumour that
some one or other of the senators was being hurried to the
camp, then that it was Otho. Immediately people who had
met Otho came flocking in from all quarters of Rome; some in
their terror exaggerated the truth, some minimized it, remembering even then to flatter. After discussion it was decided that
the temper of the cohort on guard in the palace should be
tested, but not by Galba himself. His authority was held in
reserve for the time when stronger medicine was required.

The troops were summoned. Piso, standing out on the steps
of the palace, addressed them as follows:

'Fellow-soldiers, it is now five days since I was made a Caesar. I knew nothing of the future nor whether the name was more to be desired or feared. It now lies with you to decide whether or not my adoption is to prove a calamity for my house and for my country. In saying this, I do not dread disaster on my own account. I have known misfortune, and I am at this very moment discovering that prosperity is just as dangerous. But for the sake of my adoptive father, of the Senate, and of the whole empire, I deplore the thought that we may have today either to die or—what for good men is as wretched—to kill. In the recent revolution our comfort was that Rome was spared the sight of blood,* and the transfer was effected without disturbance; and we thought that my adoption would be a safeguard against an outbreak of civil war even after Galba's death.

30   'I will make no claims for myself as to rank or respectability. To compare myself with Otho, I need not recite my virtues. His vices are all he has to be proud of. They ruined the empire, even when he was playing the part of an emperor's friend. Why should he deserve to be emperor? For his swaggering demeanour? For his effeminate costume? Extravagance deceives some people: they take it for liberality. They are wrong. He will know how to squander money, but not how to give it away. His mind is full of seductions and debauchery and intrigues with women. These are in his eyes the rewards of the throne. And the lusts and pleasures of these vices would be all his, the blushes of shame would be everybody's. No man has ever ruled well who won the throne in infamy.

'The whole of mankind agreed to give Galba the title of Caesar. Galba with your approval gave that title to me. Even if the "country", the "Senate", the "people", are empty terms, it is in your interest, my fellow-soldiers, to see that it is not the rascals who create an emperor. From time to time one hears of the legionaries being in mutiny against their generals. But your good faith and your good name have stood to this day unimpaired. It was not you who deserted Nero: he deserted you. Are you going to allow less than thirty deserters and renegades to bestow the crown? Why, no one would tolerate their choosing so much as a centurion or a tribune for themselves! Are you going to allow this precedent, and by your acquiescence make their crime your own? You will soon see this lawless spirit spreading to the troops abroad: we will suffer from the treason, you from the war. Besides, innocence wins you as much as the murder of your Emperor: you will get from us as large a bounty for your loyalty* as you would from others for your crime.'

The members of the Body Guard dispersed. The rest of the 31 cohort paid some heed to his speech. Aimlessly, as happens in moments of confusion, they seized their standards, without as yet any fixed plan, and not, as was afterwards believed, to cloak their treachery. Marius Celsus had been dispatched to the select detachments of the Illyrian army, which were quartered in the Vipsanian Arcade,* while instructions had been given to two senior centurions, Amullius Serenus and Domitius Sabinus, to summon the German troops from the Hall of Liberty. They distrusted the legion of marines, who had been alienated by Galba's butchery of their comrades on his entry into Rome. Three officers of the Guards, Cetrius Severus, Subrius Dexter, and Pompeius Longinus, also hurried to the camp in the hope that the mutiny was still in its early stages and might be averted by good advice before it came to a head. The soldiers attacked Subrius and Cetrius with threats and forcibly seizing Longinus disarmed him, because his loyalty to his Emperor was in virtue not of his military rank, but of his personal friendship for Galba, and consequently the rebels suspected him all the more. The marines without any hesitation joined the Guards. The select Illyrian detachments drove Celsus away at the point of their javelins. The German detachments wavered for some time. They were still in poor condition physically, and inclined to be passive.* Nero had dispatched them as an advance guard to Alexandria; the long voyage back again had damaged their health, and Galba was restoring their strength with lavish care.

The whole populace of Rome was now crowding into the 32 palace together with a good sprinkling of slaves. With discordant shouts they demanded the death of Otho and the destruction of the conspirators. They might have been in the circus or the theatre, clamouring for entertainment. There was neither sense nor sincerity in their behaviour: on that same day they were going to clamour for the opposite with equal zeal. But it is an established custom to flatter any emperor with unbridled cheering and meaningless enthusiasm.

Meanwhile, Galba was torn between two opinions. Titus Vinius maintained that they ought to remain within the palace, employ the slaves to offer resistance, and block up all the doors, instead of going out to face the angry troops. 'This will give time', he urged, 'for the disloyal to repent and the loyal to unite their forces. Crimes profit by haste, good counsels by delay. Besides, if need be, we shall have the same chance of leaving the palace later: if we leave and repent of it, our return will depend upon other people.'

33   All the others voted for immediate action before the conspiracy, still weak in strength and numbers, could expand. 'Otho', they argued, 'will soon panic. He crept away by stealth and was carried to a parcel of strangers, and now because we dally and waste time he has leisure to rehearse his part of emperor. What is the good of waiting until he sets his camp in order, invades the Forum, and approaches the Capitol, while Galba looks on? Our Emperor is distinguished and his friends gallant—as long as they do not step over the threshold. Are they to close up the house, as if they were anxious to endure a siege? Much help may we hope from slaves, when once the vast crowd loses its unity, and its first indignation, which counts for so much, begins to cool. No, cowardice is too risky. Or if we must fall, let us meet the danger halfway, and cover Otho with disgrace, ourselves with honour.'

When Vinius resisted this proposal, Laco assailed him with threats, prompted by Icelus, who persisted in his private quar-
34 rel to the ruin of his country. Galba without further delay supported those whose plan would look best. However, Piso was first dispatched to the camp. The young man had a great name, his popularity was still fresh, and moreover he disliked Titus Vinius, or, if he did not, rancour made men hope he did: it is so easy to believe in hatred.

Scarcely had Piso departed, when there arrived a rumour that Otho had been killed in the camp.* At first it was vague

and uncertain, but eventually, as so often happens with daring
lies, people began to assert that they had been present and
seen the deed. Some were glad and some indifferent, so the
news gained easy credence. Many, however, thought that the
report had been concocted and disseminated by friends of
Otho, who now mingled in the crowd and tried to lure Galba
out by spreading this agreeable falsehood.

At this point not only the populace and the ignorant mob, 35
but many of the knights and senators as well, broke out into
applause and unbridled enthusiasm. With their fear they had
lost their caution. Breaking open the palace gates they rushed
in and presented themselves before Galba, complaining that
they had been forestalled in the task of revenge. All the cowards who, as events proved, could show no courage in action,
indulged in bombastic words and defiant language. Nobody
knew, everybody pontificated. At last, for lack of the truth,
Galba yielded to the consensus of error. When he had put on
his breastplate he was lifted in a chair, for he was too old and
infirm to stand against the crowds that kept flocking in. In the
palace he was met by Julius Atticus, of the Body Guard, who
displayed a bloody sword and shouted out that he had killed
Otho. 'Comrade,' said Galba, 'who ordered you?' Galba had
a remarkable power of curbing soldiers' presumption, for he
was not afraid of threats nor corrupted by flattery.

Meanwhile, in Otho's camp there was no longer any doubt 36
of the soldiers' unanimity. Such was their enthusiasm that
they were not content with carrying Otho shoulder-high in
procession; they placed him among the standards on the
platform, where shortly before a gilt statue of Galba had
stood, and made a ring round him with their colours. Tribunes and centurions were allowed no approach: the common soldiers even called out, 'Beware of the officers.' The
whole camp resounded with confused shouts of mutual
encouragement.

It was quite unlike the motley shouts and spiritless flattery
of a civilian mob. As new adherents streamed in, directly the
soldiers caught sight of one of them, they grasped him by the
hand, flung their arms round him, kept him at their side, and
dictated the oath of allegiance. Some commended their gen-

eral to his soldiers, and some the soldiers to their general.
Otho, for his part, was not slow to salute the crowd with
outstretched hand and throw kisses to them. In every way he
played the slave to gain a throne.

When the whole legion of the marines had sworn allegiance,
he gained confidence in his strength, and, considering that
those whom he had earlier incited individually needed a few
words of general encouragement, he stood out on the rampart
of the camp and began as follows:

37   'In what guise I come forward to address you, fellow-
soldiers, I cannot tell. Dubbed emperor by you, I dare not call
myself a private citizen: yet "emperor" I cannot say with
another on the throne. And what am I to call you? That too
will remain in doubt until it is decided whether you have here
in your camp an enemy or an emperor of Rome. You hear
how they clamour at once for my death and your punishment?
So clear is it that we must fall or stand together.

'Doubtless Galba—such is his clemency—has already
promised our destruction. Is he not the man who entirely
unbidden butchered thousands of utterly innocent soldiers? I
shudder whenever I recall his ghastly entry into the city, when
before the face of Rome he ordered the decimation of the
troops who had surrendered, had pleaded for mercy, and
had been taken under his protection. That is Galba's only
"victory". These were the auspices under which he made his
entry; and what glory has he brought to the throne he occu-
pies, save the murder of Obultronius Sabinus and Cornelius
Marcellus in Spain, of Betuus Cilo in Gaul, of Fonteius Capito
in Germany, of Clodius Macer in Africa, of Cingonius on his
march to Rome, of Turpilianus in the city, and of Nymphidius
in the camp? What province is there in the empire, what
military camp, that has not been polluted with massacre? He
calls it "salutary correction". For his "remedies" are what
other people call crimes: his cruelty is disguised as "strictness", his avarice as "economy", while by "discipline" he
means punishing and insulting you.

'It is but seven months since Nero's death, and already
Icelus alone has embezzled more than all the depredations of
the Polyclituses and Vatiniuses and Aegialuses* put together.

Vinius would have been less greedy and lawless in his rapacity had he been emperor himself. As it is, he has kept us in subjection as if we belonged to him, yet has despised us as the property of another. His own fortune alone could provide the largess which they daily cast in your teeth but never pay into your pocket.

'Nor in Galba's successor either is there any hope for you. 38 Galba has seen to that. He has recalled from exile the man whose avarice and sour temper he judged most like his own. You witnessed for yourselves, my comrades, the extraordinary storm which signified even Heaven's abhorrence at that ill-starred adoption. The Senate and People of Rome feel the same. They are counting on your courage. You alone can give strength to the right policy: it is powerless without you, however good it be.

'It is not to war and danger that I call you. All the troops are with us. That single plain-clothes cohort* is no longer a defence to Galba, but his gaoler. When once they have caught sight of you, when once they come to take their orders from me, the only quarrel between you will be who can do most to put me in their debt. There is no room for delay in plans which cannot be commended until they are put into action.'

Otho then gave orders to open the arsenal.* The soldiers immediately seized their arms in such haste that all the ordinary distinctions of the service were neglected: neither Guards nor legionaries carried their own arms: in the confusion they took the helmets and shields of the auxiliaries. There were no tribunes or centurions to encourage them: each man was his own leader and motivator, and villains found their chief incentive in the consternation of the good.

As the riot increased, Piso, alarmed by the din of their 39 shouts, which echoed even in the city, had overtaken Galba, who had meanwhile left the palace and was approaching the Forum. Marius Celsus had also brought back no good news. Some were for returning to the palace, others for seeking the shelter of the Capitol, many for seizing the Rostra.* The majority merely disagreed with other people's proposals, and, as so often happens in disasters, the best course always seemed the one for which it was now too late.

It is said that Laco, without Galba's knowledge, proposed the assassination of Titus Vinius, either with the idea that his execution would be a sop to the soldiers, or because he believed him Otho's accomplice, or, as a last alternative, hatred may have been his motive. However, the time and the place both bred misgivings. When killing once begins it is difficult to set a limit: besides, their plans were upset by the arrival of terrified messengers, by the desertion of their supporters, and by a general waning of enthusiasm among those who at first had been the keenest to display their loyalty and courage.

40   Galba was driven hither and thither by the tide of the surging mob. Everywhere the temples and public buildings were crowded with spectators, who viewed a sorry scene. No shouts came from the common people: astonishment was on their faces, and their ears open to every sound. There was neither uproar nor quiet, but the silence of strong anger and alarm.

However, a report reached Otho that the populace was arming. He bade his men fly headlong to forestall the danger. Off went the Roman soldiers as if they were going to drag Vologaeses or Pacorus from the ancestral throne of the Arsacids*—and not to butcher their own Emperor, a helpless old man. Savage and armed, they broke at a full gallop into the Forum, scattering the populace and trampling senators under foot. Neither the sight of the Capitol nor the sanctity of the temples towering above them, nor the thought of Roman emperors past and to come, deterred them from committing that crime which the next successor always avenges.

41   Seeing the armed ranks now close at hand, the standard-bearer of the cohort on guard over Galba—tradition says his name was Atilius Vercilio—tore off the effigy of Galba* and flung it to the ground. This signal clearly showed that all the troops were for Otho: the people fled, deserting the Forum, and swords were drawn against any who lingered. Near the Lacus Curtius* Galba was precipitated from his chair by the panic of the bearers and flung to the ground. The accounts of his last words vary according as they are prompted by hatred or admiration. Some say that he begged and asked what harm he had deserved, imploring for a few days' respite to pay the

troops their largess. The majority say that he deliberately offered his neck to the blow and bade them, 'Come, strike, if it serves the country's need.' Whatever he said mattered little to his assassins.

As to the actual murderer there is a difference of opinion. Some say it was Terentius, a reservist, others that his name was Laecanius. The most common account is that a soldier of the Fifteenth Legion, by name Camurius, pierced his throat with a sword-thrust. The others foully mutilated his arms and legs (his breast was protected) and with bestial savagery continued to stab the headless corpse.

Then they made for Titus Vinius. Here, too, there is a doubt 42 whether the immediate fear strangled his voice, or whether he called out that they had no mandate from Otho to kill him. He may have invented this in his terror, or it may have been a confession of his complicity in the plot. His whole life and reputation give reason to suppose that he was an accomplice in the crime of which he was the cause. He was brought to the ground in front of the temple of the deified Julius by a blow on the back of the knee, and afterwards a common soldier named Julius Carus ran him right through with a sword.

However, Romans now can look to one hero that day. This 43 was Sempronius Densus, a centurion of the Praetorian Guards, who had been assigned by Galba to protect Piso.* Drawing his dagger he faced the armed assassins, flinging their treason in their teeth, and by his shouts and gestures turned their attention upon himself, thus enabling Piso to escape despite his wounds.

Piso, reaching the Temple of Vesta, was mercifully sheltered by the public slave, who hid him in his lodging. There his immediate death was postponed, but thanks to his concealment rather than any reverence shown towards religious observances. Eventually Otho, who was burning to have him killed, dispatched expressly for that purpose Sulpicius Florus of the British auxiliaries, whom Galba had recently enfranchised, and Staius Murcus of the Body Guard. They dragged Piso forth and butchered him on the threshold of the temple.

None of his murders pleased Otho so much as this. On 44 Piso's head, as on no other, they say, he gazed with insatiable

eyes. This was possibly the first moment at which he felt
relieved of all anxiety, and free to indulge his glee. Or perhaps,
in the case of Galba and of Vinius, the recollection of his
treason to the one and his friendship with the other had
troubled even his unfeeling heart with gloomy thoughts;
whereas Piso being an enemy and a rival, he considered it a
pious duty to gloat over his murder.

Their heads were fixed on poles and carried along with the
standards of the cohorts side by side with the eagle of the
legion. Those who had done the deed and those who had
witnessed it vied with each other in displaying their bloody
hands, all boasting of their share, some falsely, some truly, as
if it were a fine and memorable exploit. Vitellius subsequently
discovered more than 120 petitions demanding rewards for
distinguished services rendered on that day. He gave orders to
search out all the petitioners and put them to death. This was
not out of respect for Galba: he merely followed the traditional custom by which emperors secure their present safety
and posthumous vengeance.

45   You would have thought the Senate and people different
men. There was a general rush for the camp, every one push-
ing ahead of his neighbour and trying to overtake those in
front. They heaped insults on Galba, praised the prudence
of the troops, and covered Otho's hand with kisses, their
extravagance in inverse proportion to their sincerity. Otho
rebuffed no one, and succeeded by his words and looks in
moderating the soldiers' greed and menaces. They loudly demanded the execution of Marius Celsus, the consul-elect, who
had remained Galba's faithful friend to the last. They were as
much offended at his efficiency and honesty as if these had
been criminal qualities. What they obviously wanted was to
find a first excuse for plunder and murder and the destruction
of all decent citizens. But Otho had as yet no influence to
prevent crimes: he could only order them. So he simulated
anger, giving instructions for Celsus' arrest, and, by promising
that he should meet with a worse penalty, rescued him from
immediate death.

46   The will of the soldiers was henceforward supreme.* The
Praetorian Guards chose their own Prefects, Plotius Firmus, a

man who had risen from the ranks to the post of Chief of the
Watch, and joined Otho's side before Galba's fall, and
Licinius Proculus, an intimate friend of Otho, and therefore
suspected of furthering his plans. They made Flavius Sabinus
City Prefect, therein following Nero's choice, under whom
Sabinus had held that post;* besides, most of them had an eye
to the fact that he was Vespasian's brother.

An urgent demand arose that the customary fees to
centurions for granting exemptions from duties should be
abolished, for they constituted a sort of annual tax upon the
common soldier. The result had been that a quarter of each
company could be scattered on leave, or else lounge idly about
the barracks, so long as they paid the centurion his fee. Nor
was there anyone to care about either the amount of this
impost or the means by which the soldiers raised the money:
they purchased leisure by highway robbery or menial service.
Then, again, a soldier who had money was savagely burdened
with work until he should buy exemption. Thus he became
impoverished, and moreover enervated by idleness, and returned to his company no longer a man of means and energy
but penniless and lazy. So the process went on. One after
another they became debased by the same poverty and lax
discipline, rushing blindly into quarrels and mutiny, and, as a
last resource, into civil war.* Otho was afraid that bribing the
rank and file would alienate the centurions, and promised to
pay the annual exemption-fees out of his imperial exchequer.
This was indubitably a sound reform, which good emperors
have since established as a regular institution in the army.

The Prefect Laco, Otho pretended to banish to an island;
but he was stabbed by a reservist who had been sent ahead
to murder him.* Marcianus Icelus, as a freedman, Otho
sentenced to public execution.

Thus the day was spent in crimes; but the ultimate evil was   47
the joy they caused. The Senate was summoned by the Urban
Praetor. The other magistrates all vied in flattery. The senators
arrived post-haste. They decreed to Otho the powers of the
tribunate, the title of Augustus, and all the imperial preroga-
tives. They all strove to blot out their former insults and abuse
of him; but, as these had been hurled equally from all sides,

they did not, as far as anyone could see, stick in his memory. Whether he had laid aside his resentment or only postponed punishment, his reign was too short to show.

He was then carried through the still blood-drenched Forum among the piles of dead bodies to the Capitol, and thence to the palace. He granted permission to burn and bury the bodies of his victims. Piso's wife Verania and his brother Scribonianus laid out his body, and this was done for Vinius by his daughter Crispina. They had to search for the heads and buy them back from the murderers, who had preserved them for sale.

48   Piso was nearly 31. His reputation was better than his fortune. His brothers had been executed,* Magnus by Claudius, Crassus by Nero. He himself after being long in exile was a Caesar for four days. Hastily adopted in preference to his elder brother, the only advantage he reaped was to be killed first.

Titus Vinius in his fifty-seven years* had displayed strange contrasts of character. His paternal ancestors included praetors; his mother's father was one of the proscribed.* A scandal* marked his first military service under the command of Calvisius Sabinus. The commander's wife suffered from an untoward desire to inspect the site of the camp, which she entered by night disguised in soldier's uniform. There she brazenly tried her hand at the guard and other military duties, and then had the effrontery to commit adultery in the commander's own quarters. In this scandal Titus Vinius was convicted as the guilty man. He was therefore put in irons by order of Gaius Caesar. However, times soon changed, and he was set at liberty.

After mounting the ladder of office without check, he was as an ex-praetor given the command of a legion, and proved successful. But soon again he soiled his reputation with the ignoble charge that he had stolen a gold cup from Claudius' dinner-table. Claudius on the next day gave orders that Vinius alone of all his guests should be served on earthenware. However, Vinius' governorship of Narbonese Gaul was strict and honest. Subsequently his friendship with Galba drew him over the precipice. He was bold, cunning, and efficient, with equal power for industry or for corruption, according to his mood. Vinius' will was annulled because of his great wealth. Piso was poor, so his last wishes were respected.

Galba's body lay long neglected, and under cover of dark- 49 ness was subjected to numerous insults. Eventually his stew-ard Argius, one of his former slaves, gave it a humble funeral in Galba's private garden. His head, which the camp-followers and servants had mangled and carried on a pole, was found next day in front of the tomb of Patrobius (one of Nero's freedmen whom Galba had executed) and buried with the body which had already been cremated.

Such was the end of Servius Galba, who for seventy-three years had enjoyed prosperity under five different emperors, happier in their reign than his own. He came of an old and noble family and possessed great wealth. His own character was mediocre, rather free from vices than rich in virtues. Though not indifferent to fame, he did not flaunt it. Not greedy of other people's money, he was careful of his own, and a miser with public funds. Towards friends and freedmen, if they happened to be honest, he was irreproachably tolerant; when they were not, he was culpably blind. But his distin-guished origin and the perils of the time disguised his apathy, which passed as prudence. In the flower of his youth he served with distinction in Germany. As pro-consul he governed Africa wisely, and in later years showed the same fairness in Nearer Spain.* When he was a commoner he seemed too big for his station: the universal view was that he had the qualifications to be a ruler—if only he had not ruled.

The city was in a panic. The alarm aroused by the recent 50 atrocious crime and by Otho's well-known proclivities was further increased by the fresh news about Vitellius. This news had been suppressed before Galba's murder, and it was be-lieved that only the army of Upper Germany had revolted. Now when they saw that the two men in the world who were most notorious for immorality, indolence, and extravagance had been, as it were, appointed by Providence to ruin the empire, not only the senators and knights who had some stake and interest in the country, but the masses as well, openly deplored their fate. Their talk was no longer of the recent specimens of bloody peace: they reverted to the records of the civil wars, the taking and retaking of Rome by her own troops, the devastation of Italy, the pillage of the provinces, the battles of Pharsalia, Philippi, Perusia, and Mutina,* those bywords of national disaster. 'The world was turned upside down', they mused, 'even when good men fought for the throne: yet the Roman Empire survived the victories of Julius Caesar and of Augustus, as the Republic would have survived had Pompey and Brutus been victorious. But now—are we to go into temples and pray for Otho or for Vitellius? To pray for either would be impious. It would be wicked to offer vows for the success of either in a war of which we can only be sure that the winner will prove the worse.'

Some predicted the intervention of Vespasian* and the armies of the East. He was preferable to either of the others; still they shuddered at the thought of a fresh war and fresh bloodshed. Besides, Vespasian's reputation was doubtful. He was the first emperor who ever changed for the better.

51   I must now explain the origin and causes of the rising of Vitellius. After the slaughter of Julius Vindex and his whole force, the troops were in high spirits at the fame and booty they had acquired. Without toil or danger they had won a most profitable victory. So they were all for marching against the enemy: plunder seemed better than pay. They had endured a long and unprofitable service, rendered the more irksome by the country and climate and by the strict discipline observed. But discipline, however relentless in time of peace, is always relaxed in civil wars, when temptation stands on either hand and treachery goes unpunished.

Men, armour, and horses they had in abundance for use and for show. But, whereas before the war the soldiers only knew the men of their own company or troop, and the provincial frontier* separated the armies, now, having once joined forces against Vindex, they had gained a knowledge of their own strength and of the Gallic provinces, and were looking for more fighting and fresh quarrels, calling the Gauls no longer allies, as before, but 'our enemies' or 'the vanquished'. They had also the support of the Gallic tribes on the banks of the Rhine, who had espoused their cause and were now the

most eager to rouse them against 'the Galbians', as they now
called them, despising the name of Vindex. So, cherishing
hostility against the Sequani and Aedui,* and against all the
other communities in proportion to their wealth, they drank
in dreams of sacking towns and pillaging fields and looting
houses, inspired partly by the peculiar failings of the strong—
greed and vanity—and partly also by a feeling of irritation at
the insolence of the Gauls, who boasted, to the chagrin of the
army, that Galba had remitted a quarter of their tribute and
had made grants to their community.*

Further fuel was added by a rumour, cunningly circulated
and rashly credited, that the legions were being decimated and
all the most enterprising centurions discharged. From every
side came alarming news and sinister reports from the city.
The colony of Lyons was up in arms, and its stubborn attachment to Nero* made it a hotbed of rumour. But in the camp
itself the soldiers' hatreds and fears, and (when once they had
realized their strength) their feeling of security, furnished the
richest material for lies and won them easy credence.

In the preceding year, shortly before the beginning of 52
December, Aulus Vitellius had entered Lower Germany and
held a careful inspection of the winter quarters of the legions.
He had restored many to their rank, remitted degrading penalties, and relieved those who had suffered disgrace, acting
mainly from ambitious motives, but partly also upon sound
judgement. Amongst other things he had showed impartiality
in remedying the injustices due to the mean and rapacious way
in which Fonteius Capito had issued promotions and reduc-
tions. The soldiers did not judge Vitellius' actions as those of
a consular governor: they took him for something more, and,
while the strict found him undignified, his supporters spoke of
his affability and beneficence, because he showed neither
moderation nor judgement in making presents out of his own
money and squandering other people's. Besides, they were so
greedy for power that they took even his vices for virtues.

In both armies there were plenty of quiet, law-abiding men,
as well as many who were unprincipled and energetic. But for
sheer reckless cupidity none could match two of the legionary
commanders, Alienus Caecina and Fabius Valens. Valens was

hostile to Galba, because, after unmasking Verginius' hesitation and thwarting Capito's designs, he considered that he had been treated with ingratitude: so he incited Vitellius by pointing out to him the enthusiasm of the troops. 'You', he would say to him, 'are famous everywhere, and you need find no obstacle in Hordeonius Flaccus. Britain will join and the German auxiliaries will flock to your standard. Galba cannot trust the provinces; the old man holds the empire on sufferance; the transfer can be soon effected, if only you will spread open your cloak and go to welcome your good fortune. Verginius was quite right to hesitate. He came of a family of knights, and his father was a nobody. He would have failed, had he accepted the empire: his refusal saved him. Your father was thrice consul, and he was censor with an emperor for his colleague. That long ago gave you imperial dignity, and makes it unsafe for you to remain a private citizen.'

These promptings spurred on Vitellius' sluggish nature to form desires, but hardly hopes.

53   Caecina, on the other hand, in Upper Germany, was a handsome youth, whose big build, imperious spirit, clever tongue, and upright carriage had enticed the soldiers to his side. While quaestor in Baetica he had promptly joined Galba's party, and in spite of his youth had been given command of a legion. Later he was found to have misappropriated public funds, and, on Galba's orders, was prosecuted for peculation. Highly indignant, Caecina determined to embroil the world, and veil the injuries he had sustained with the ruin of his country.

Nor were seeds of dissension lacking in the army. The entire force had taken part in the war against Vindex, nor was it until after Nero's death that they joined Galba's side, and even then they had been anticipated in swearing allegiance by the detachments of Lower Germany. Then again the Treviri and Lingones,* and the other communities which Galba had punished by issuing harsh edicts and confiscating part of their territory, were in close communication with the winter quarters of the legions. They began to talk treason: the soldiers degenerated in civilian society. All that was wanted was

someone to avail himself of the support they had offered to
Verginius.

Following an ancient custom, the tribe of the Lingones had 54
made a present of a pair of silver hands to the legions as a
symbol of hospitality. Assuming the squalid appearance of
one in mourning, their envoys made the round of the officers'
quarters and the soldiers' tents complaining of their own
wrongs and of the rewards lavished on neighbouring tribes.
Finding the soldiers ready to listen, they made inflammatory
allusions to the army itself, bewailing its dangers and
humiliation.

Mutiny was almost ripe, when Hordeonius Flaccus ordered
the envoys to withdraw, and, in order to secure the secrecy of
their departure, gave instructions to them to leave the camp by
night.* This gave rise to an alarming rumour. Many declared
that the envoys had been killed, and that, if they did not look
out for themselves, the leading spirits among the soldiers, who
had complained of the present state of things, would be murdered in the dark, while their comrades knew nothing about
it. So the legions formed a secret compact. The auxiliaries
were also taken into the plot, although at first they had been
distrusted, because their infantry and cavalry had been posted
all round as though an attack on the legion were meditated.
However, they soon showed themselves the keener conspirators. Evil men achieve unanimity more easily for war than for
harmony in peacetime.

In Lower Germany, however, the legions on 1 January 55
swore the usual oath of allegiance* to Galba, though with
much hesitation. Few voices were heard even in the front
ranks; the rest were silent, each waiting for his neighbour to
take some bold step. Human nature is always ready to follow
where it hates to lead. However, the feelings of the legions
varied. The First and Fifth were already so mutinous that
some soldiers threw stones at Galba's statues. The Fifteenth*
and Sixteenth dared not venture beyond muttered threats, but
they were watching to see the outbreak begin.

In Upper Germany, on the other hand, on the very same
day, the Fourth and the Twenty-Second Legions, who were

quartered together, smashed their statues of Galba. The Fourth took the lead, the Twenty-Second at first holding back, but eventually making common cause with them. They did not want it to be thought that they were shaking off their allegiance to the empire, so in taking the oath they invoked the obsolete names of the Senate and People of Rome. None of the senior officers made any movement for Galba, and indeed some of them, as happens in such outbreaks, were prominent in the rebellion. However, nobody mounted the platform to make a general address, for there was no one as yet with whom to curry favour.

56   The consular governor Hordeonius Flaccus stood by and watched their treachery. He had not the courage to check the storm or even to rally the waverers and encourage the faithful. Sluggish and cowardly, it was mere indolence that kept him loyal. Four centurions of the Twenty-Second Legion, Nonius Receptus, Donatius Valens, Romilius Marcellus, and Calpurnius Repentinus, who tried to protect Galba's statues, were swept away by the rush of the soldiers and put under arrest. No one retained any loyalty, or remembered their former oath of allegiance; and, as happens in mutinies, they were all on the side of the majority.

On the night of 1 January the standard-bearer of the Fourth Legion came to Cologne, and brought the news to Vitellius at his dinner that the Fourth and Twenty-Second Legions had flung down Galba's statues and sworn allegiance to the Senate and People of Rome. As this oath appeared meaningless, it seemed best to seize the critical moment and offer them an emperor. Vitellius dispatched messengers to inform his own troops and generals that the army of Upper Germany had revolted from Galba; so they must either make war on the rebels immediately, or, if they preferred peace and unity, make an emperor for themselves; and there was less danger, he reminded them, in choosing an emperor than in looking for one.

57   The quarters of the First Legion* were nearest at hand, and Fabius Valens was the most enterprising of the generals. On the following day he entered Cologne with the cavalry of his legion and auxiliaries, and saluted Vitellius as emperor. The

other legions of the province followed suit, vying with each
other in enthusiasm; and the army of Upper Germany, drop-
ping the fine-sounding titles of the Senate and People of Rome,
joined Vitellius on 3 January, which clearly showed that on
the two previous days they were not really at the disposal of
a republican government. The inhabitants of Cologne and the
Treviri and Lingones, rivalling the zeal of the troops, made
offers of assistance, horses, arms, or money, each according to
the measure of their strength, wealth, or enterprise. And these
offers came not only from the civil and military leaders, men
who had plenty of money to spare and much to hope for from
victory, but also whole companies or individual soldiers
handed over their savings, or, instead of money, their belts
and medals, and the handsome silver ornaments on their
uniforms, acting from enthusiasm, impulse, or greed.

Vitellius accordingly commended the zeal of the troops. He   58
distributed among Roman knights the court offices which had
been usually held by freedmen,* paid the centurions their
furlough fees* out of the imperial purse, and for the most part
conceded the soldiers' savage demands for one execution after
another, though he occasionally cheated them by pretending
to imprison their victims. Thus Pompeius Propinquus,* the
procurator in Belgica, was promptly executed, while Julius
Burdo, who commanded the fleet on the Rhine, was adroitly
rescued. The indignation of the army had broken out against
him, because he was supposed to have concocted a false
accusation against Fonteius Capito, and then to have laid a
trap for him. Capito's memory was dear to the army, and
where violence reigned murder might show its face, but pardon had to be stealthy. So Burdo was kept in confinement and
only released after victory had allayed the soldiers' rancour.
Meanwhile a centurion named Crispinus was offered as a
scapegoat. He had actually stained his hands with Capito's
blood, so his guilt seemed more obvious to those who clamoured for his punishment, and Vitellius felt he was a cheaper
sacrifice.*

Julius Civilis was the next to be rescued from danger. He   59
was all-powerful among the Batavi,* and Vitellius did not
want to alienate so spirited a people by punishing him.

Besides, eight cohorts of Batavian troops were stationed in the country of the Lingones. They had been an auxiliary force attached to the Fourteenth, and in the general disturbance had deserted the legion. Their decision for one side or the other would be of the first importance. Nonius, Donatius, Romilius, and Calpurnius, the centurions mentioned above, were executed by order of Vitellius. They had been convicted of loyalty, a heinous offence among deserters.

His party soon gained the support of Valerius Asiaticus, governor of Belgica, who subsequently married Vitellius' daughter, and of Junius Blaesus, governor of the Lyons division of Gaul, who brought with him the Italian Legion* and the 'Taurian' regiment of cavalry, which had been quartered at Lyons. The forces in Raetia lost no time in joining his standard, and even the troops in Britain showed no hesitation.

60   Trebellius Maximus,* the governor of Britain, had earned by his meanness and cupidity the contempt and hatred of the army. This was further inflamed by Roscius Coelius, who commanded the Twentieth Legion;* they were old enemies, but had seized the opportunity of the civil war to break out into a more violent quarrel. Trebellius blamed Coelius for the mutinous temper and insubordination of the army: Coelius complained that Trebellius had robbed his men and impaired their efficiency. Meanwhile the commanders' unseemly quarrel ruined the discipline of the forces, whose insubordination soon came to a head. The auxiliaries joined in the attacks on the governor and ostracized him, and infantry and cavalry companies rallied round Coelius: Trebellius, thus abandoned, took refuge with Vitellius. The province remained quiet, despite the removal of the ex-consul. The government was carried on by the legionary commanders, who were equal in authority, though Coelius' audacity increased his power.

61   Thus reinforced by the army from Britain, Vitellius, who now had an immense force and vast resources at his disposal, decided on an invasion by two routes under two separate generals. Fabius Valens was ordered to lure the Gauls to his standard, or, if they refused, to devastate their country, and then to invade Italy by way of the Cottian Alps. Caecina was to follow the shorter route and descend into Italy over the

Pennine Pass.* Valens' column comprised some picked detachments from the army of Lower Germany, along with the
'eagle' of the Fifth Legion, and auxiliary horse and foot,
amounting in all to about 40,000 men. Caecina's troops from
Upper Germany numbered 30,000, their main strength consisting in the Twenty-First Legion.* Both columns were reinforced by German auxiliaries, whom Vitellius also recruited to
fill up his own army, intending to follow with his full military
strength.

Strange was the contrast between Vitellius and his army. 62
The soldiers were all eagerness, clamouring for battle while
Gaul was still frightened and Spain still undecided. Winter,
they said, was no obstacle; peace and delay were for cowards:
they must invade Italy and seize Rome. Haste was the safest
course in civil war, where action was needed rather than
deliberation. Vitellius was dully apathetic, anticipating his
imperial status by indulging in idle luxury and lavish banquets. At midday he would be drunk and drowsy with
overeating. However, such was the zeal and energy of the
soldiers that they even did the general's duties themselves, and
behaved exactly as if the Emperor had been present to encourage the alert and threaten the laggards. They promptly fell in
and began to clamour for the signal to start. The title of
Germanicus* was then and there conferred on Vitellius:
Caesar he refused to be called, even after his victory.

On the very day of departure a happy omen greeted Fabius
Valens and the army he led to war. As the column advanced,
an eagle flew serenely ahead and seemed to lead the way. Mile
after mile the soldiers cheered loudly, mile after mile the bird
flew calm and undismayed: this was taken for a sure omen of
success.

They entered confidently the country of the Treviri, who 63
were allies. At Divodurum,* the chief town of the
Mediomatrici, although they were welcomed with all courtesy, the troops fell into a sudden panic. Hastily seizing their
arms, they began to massacre the innocent citizens. Their
object was not plunder; they were seized by a mad frenzy,
which was the harder to allay as its cause was a mystery.
Eventually the general's entreaties prevailed, and they refrained from destroying the town. However, nearly 4,000

people had already been killed.* This spread such alarm
throughout Gaul that, as the army approached, whole towns
flocked to meet them, with their magistrates at their head
and prayers in their mouths. Women and boys prostrated
themselves along the roads, and they resorted to every possible means by which an enemy's anger may be appeased,
petitioning for peace, though war there was none.

64   It was in the country of the Leuci* that Fabius Valens heard
the news of Galba's murder and Otho's elevation. The soldiers
showed no emotion, neither joy nor fear; their thoughts were
all for war. The Gauls' doubts were now removed. They hated
Otho and Vitellius equally, but Vitellius they also feared.

They next reached the Lingones, faithful adherents of their
party. There the courtesy of the citizens was equalled by the
good behaviour of the troops. But their joy was short-lived,
thanks to the disorderly conduct of the Batavian auxiliaries
who, as narrated above, had detached themselves from the
Fourteenth Legion and been drafted into Valens' column. A
quarrel between some Batavians and legionaries led to blows:
the other soldiers quickly took sides, and a fierce battle would
have flared up, had not Valens punished a few of them to
remind the Batavians of the discipline they had forgotten.

Coming to the Aedui, they in vain sought an excuse for
fighting. For when the natives were ordered to contribute
money and arms, they in addition presented them with provisions free of charge. Lyons did gladly what the Aedui had
done from fear. But the town was deprived of the Italian
Legion and the 'Taurian' cavalry regiment; Valens decided to
leave the Eighteenth Cohort there in its old winter quarters.
Manlius Valens, who was in command of the Italian Legion,
never received any distinction from Vitellius, although he
deserved well of the party, the reason being that Fabius had
slandered him, making accusations against him behind his
back, while to avert his suspicions he praised him in public.

65   The recent war had served to inflame the long-standing
quarrel between Lyons and Vienne. Much damage was done
on both sides, and the frequency and animosity of their con-
flicts proved that they were not merely fighting for Nero and
Galba. Galba had made his displeasure an excuse for confis-

cating to the Treasury the revenues of Lyons, while on Vienne he had conferred various distinctions. The result was a bitter rivalry between the towns, and the Rhone between them only formed a bond of hatred.

Consequently the inhabitants of Lyons began to work on the feelings of individual Roman soldiers, and to urge them to crush Vienne. They reminded them how the Viennese had laid siege to Lyons, a Roman colony, had assisted the efforts of Vindex, and had lately raised troops to defend Galba. Having supplied a pretext for bad feeling, they went on to point out the rich opportunity for plunder. Not content with private persuasion, they presented a formal petition that the army would march to avenge them, and destroy the headquarters of the Gallic war. Vienne, they urged, was thoroughly un-Roman and hostile, while Lyons was a Roman colony, part of the army* and sharing in its victories and reverses. They besought them in the event of adverse fortune not to leave their city to the fury of its enemies.

By these arguments and others of the same nature they 66 brought matters to such a pass that even the generals and party leaders despaired of cooling the army's indignation. However, the Viennese realized their danger. Arrayed with olive-branches and ritual headbands, they met the approaching column and, seizing the troops' weapons, knees, and feet in supplication,* succeeded in appeasing them. Valens moreover made each of the soldiers a present of 300 sesterces. They were thus persuaded to respect the antiquity and high standing of the colony, and to listen with patience to their general's speech, in which he commended to them the lives and property of the Viennese. Nevertheless, the town was disarmed, and private individuals had to assist the army with various kinds of provisions. There was, however, a persistent rumour that Valens himself had been bought with a heavy bribe. He had long been in mean circumstances and ill concealed his sudden accession of wealth. Prolonged poverty had inflamed his inordinate desires, and the needy youth grew into an extravagant old man.

He next led the army by slow stages through the country of the Allobroges and Vocontii,* bribes to the general determining the length of each day's march and the choice of a camp. For Valens struck disgraceful bargains with the landowners and municipal authorities, often applying violent threats, as, for instance, at Lucus,* a township of the Vocontii, which he threatened to burn, until he was appeased with money. Where it was impossible to get money, he was won over with women for fornication and adultery. And so it went on until the Alps were reached.

67   There was even more looting and bloodshed on Caecina's march. The Helvetii* were a Gallic tribe distinguished formerly as fighting men, but later only in the memory of their past; having heard nothing of Galba's murder, they refused to acknowledge the authority of Vitellius. This exasperated Caecina's headstrong nature. Hostilities broke out owing to the greed and impatience of the Twenty-First Legion, who had seized a sum of money which was being sent to pay the garrison of a fort in which the Helvetii used to keep native troops at their own expense. The Helvetii, highly indignant at this, intercepted a dispatch* from the German army to the Pannonian legions, and kept a centurion and some men in custody. Greedy for battle, Caecina hastened to take vengeance on the nearest culprit without giving them time for second thoughts. Promptly breaking up his camp, he proceeded to harry the country, and sacked a charming and much-frequented watering-place, which had grown during the long peace into the size and importance of a town.

Instructions were sent to the Raetian auxiliaries to attack the Helvetii in the rear, while their attention was occupied
68   with the legion. Full of spirit before the crisis, the Helvetii were terrified in the face of danger. At the first alarm they had chosen Claudius Severus general, but they knew nothing of fighting or discipline and were incapable of combined action. An engagement with the Roman veterans would be disastrous; and the walls, dilapidated by time, could not stand a siege. They found themselves between Caecina and his powerful army on the one side, and on the other the Raetian auxiliaries, both horse and foot, and the whole fighting force of Raetia as well, trained soldiers well used to fighting. Their country was given over to plunder and massacre. Flinging away their arms,

they wandered miserably between the enemy armies. Wounded and scattered, most of them took refuge on Mount Vocetius.* But some Thracian auxiliaries were promptly sent to dislodge them. The German army, aided by the Raetians, pursued them through the woods, and cut them to pieces in their hiding-places. Many thousands were killed and many sold as slaves.

Having completed the work of destruction, the army advanced in hostile array against Aventicum,* their capital town, and were met by envoys offering surrender. The offer was accepted. Caecina executed Julius Alpinus, one of their chief men, as the prime instigator of the revolt. The rest he left to the clemency or cruelty of Vitellius.

It is hard to say whether the Helvetian envoys found 69 Vitellius or the army the more implacable. The soldiers clamoured for the destruction of the town, and shook their fists and weapons in the envoys' faces: even Vitellius indulged in threatening language. Ultimately, however, Claudius Cossus, one of the envoys, a noted speaker who greatly enhanced the effect of his eloquence by concealing his skill under a well-timed affectation of nervousness, succeeded in softening the hearts of the soldiers. A mob is always liable to sudden changes of feeling, and the men were as sensible to pity as they had been extravagant in their brutality. Thus with streams of tears and importunate prayers for a better answer the envoys procured a free pardon for Aventicum.

Caecina halted for a few days in Helvetian territory until he 70 could get news of Vitellius' decision. Meantime, while carrying on his preparations for crossing the Alps, he received from Italy the joyful news that 'Silius' Cavalry', stationed near the Po, had taken the oath of allegiance to Vitellius. The members of this troop had served under Vitellius when governor in Africa.* They had subsequently been detached under orders from Nero to be sent ahead to Egypt, and had then been recalled, owing to the outbreak of the war with Vindex. They were now in Italy. Their officers, who knew nothing of Otho and were attached to Vitellius, extolled the strength of the approaching column and the fame of the German army. At their prompting the troop went over to Vitellius, bringing their new Emperor a gift of the four strongest towns of the Transpadane district, Milan, Novaria, Eporedia, and Vercellae.* Of this they informed Caecina themselves.

But one troop of horse could not garrison the whole of the widest part of Italy. Caecina accordingly hurried forward the Gallic, Lusitanian, and British auxiliaries, and some German detachments, together with 'Petra's Cavalry', while he himself hesitated for a little whether he should not change course, cross the Raetian Alps into Noricum, and attack the governor, Petronius Urbicus, who, having raised a force of irregulars and broken down the bridges, was supposed to be a faithful adherent of Otho. However, he was afraid of losing the infantry and cavalry forces whom he had already sent on ahead, and at the same time he considered that there was more glory in holding Italy, and that, wherever the theatre of the war might be, Noricum was sure to be among the spoils of victory. So he chose the Pennine route and led his reserves and the heavy marching column of regular troops across the Alps, although they were still deep in snow.

71   Meanwhile, contrary to all expectation, Otho was not stagnating in idle luxury. He postponed his pleasures and disguised his extravagance, suiting all his behaviour to his imperial dignity. But people knew they had not seen the last of his vices, and his virtuous hypocrisy only increased their alarm.

He gave orders to summon Marius Celsus to the Capitol. This was the consul-elect whom he had rescued from the savage clutches of the soldiers by pretending to put him in prison. Otho now wanted to earn a name for clemency by pardoning a well-known man who had fought against his party.* Celsus was firm. Pleading guilty to the charge of fidelity to Galba, he voluntarily claimed credit for setting an example. Otho treated him as if there was nothing to pardon. Calling on heaven to witness their reconciliation, he then and there admitted him to the circle of his intimate friends, and subsequently gave him an appointment as one of his generals. Celsus remained faithful to Otho too, doomed apparently to the losing side. His acquittal delighted the upper classes and was the subject of much popular comment, and even earned the approval of the soldiers, who admired the very qualities which aroused their indignation.

Equal rejoicing, though for different reasons, followed the 72 fulfilment of the request for Ofonius Tigellinus' destruction. Born of obscure parentage, he had grown from an immoral youth into a vicious old man. He rose to the command of the Watch and the Praetorian Guard, finding that vice was a short-cut to these and other rewards of virtue. Here he practised the vices of manhood—first cruelty, then greed. He corrupted Nero and introduced him to every kind of depravity; then ventured on some villainies behind his back, and finally deserted and betrayed him. Thus in his case, as in no other, those who hated Nero and those who wished him back agreed, though from different motives, in calling persistently for his execution. During Galba's reign he had been protected by the influence of Titus Vinius, on the plea that he had saved his daughter. Saved her he had, not out of clemency (he had killed too many for that), but to secure a refuge for the future. For all such villains, distrusting the present and fearing a change of fortune, prepare for themselves a shelter against public indignation by obtaining the favour of private persons. So they rely to escape punishment not on their innocence but on a system of mutual insurance. People were all the more incensed against Tigellinus, since the recent feeling against Vinius was added to their old hatred for him. From all quarters of Rome they flocked, flooding into the palace and the squares, into the circus and the theatre (where the mob enjoys complete licence), and broke out into riotous uproar. Eventually Tigellinus at Sinuessa Spa received the news* that his last hour was inevitably come. There, after a cowardly delay for couplings and embraces with his prostitutes, he cut his throat with a razor, and blackened the infamy of his life by a belated and shameful death.

About the same time there arose a demand for the punish- 73 ment of Calvia Crispinilla. But she was saved by various prevarications, and Otho's connivance brought him some discredit. This woman had tutored Nero in vice, and afterwards crossed to Africa to incite Clodius Macer to civil war.* While there she openly schemed to start a famine in Rome.

However, she secured herself by marrying an ex-consul, and lived to enjoy a wide popularity in the country. She escaped harm under Galba, Otho, and Vitellius, and eventually wielded a great influence due to her being both rich and childless, considerations of the first importance in good times as much as in bad.

74   During this time Otho wrote to Vitellius constant letters deformed with various effeminate inducements: he offered him money or an influential position, or any retreat he liked to select for a life of luxury. Vitellius made similar offers. At first both wrote in the mildest tone, though the insincerity on either side was stupid and unseemly. But they soon struck a quarrelsome note, and accused each other of lechery and crime—here neither lied.

Otho recalled the commission which Galba had sent out to Germany, and, using the pretext of senatorial authority, sent fresh commissioners to both the armies in Germany, and also to the Italian Legion and the troops quartered at Lyons. However, the commissioners remained with Vitellius with a readiness which showed they were under no compulsion; and the Guards whom Otho had attached to them, ostensibly as a mark of honour, were sent back before they had time to mix with the legionaries.

Further to this, Fabius Valens sent letters in the name of the German army to the Guards and the City Garrison, extolling the strength of his own side and offering to join forces. He even went so far as to reproach them with having transferred to Otho the title which had long before been conferred on 75 Vitellius.* Thus they were assailed with threats as well as promises, and told that they were not strong enough to fight, and had nothing to lose by making peace. But, in spite of all, the fidelity of the Guards remained unchanged.

However, Otho dispatched assassins to Germany, Vitellius to Rome. Neither met with success. Vitellius' assassins were lost in the crowds of Rome, where nobody knows anybody, and thus escaped detection and punishment: Otho's were betrayed by their strange faces, since the troops all knew each other by sight. Vitellius then composed a letter to Otho's brother Titianus, threatening his life and his son's in the event

that Vitellius' mother and children were in any way harmed.
As it happened, neither household suffered. Fear was perhaps
the reason in Otho's time, but Vitellius, after his victory, could
certainly claim credit for clemency.

The first news which gave Otho confidence was the an- 76
nouncement from Illyricum that the legions of Dalmatia and
Pannonia and Moesia had sworn allegiance to him. Similar
news arrived from Spain, and Cluvius Rufus was commended
in a special decree, but it was found out immediately afterwards that Spain had gone over to Vitellius. Even Aquitania
soon fell away, although Julius Cordus had sworn in the
province for Otho. Loyalty and affection were dead: men
changed from one side to the other through fear or compulsion. It was fear which gave Vitellius the province
of Narbonese Gaul, for it is easy to go over when the big
battalions are so near.

The distant provinces and the troops across the sea all
remained at Otho's disposal, but not from any enthusiasm for
his cause; what weighed with them was the name of Rome and
the aura surrounding the Senate. Besides, Otho had got the
first hearing. Vespasian swore in the Jewish army for Otho,
and Mucianus the legions in Syria; Egypt too and all the
provinces towards the East were held for him. He also received the submission of Africa, where Carthage had taken the
lead, without waiting for the sanction of the governor,
Vipstanus Apronianus. Crescens, one of Nero's freedmen—in
evil days even these creatures make themselves into part of the
state—had given the common people of the town a gala
dinner in honour of the new Emperor, with the result that the
inhabitants hurried into various excesses. The other African
communities followed the example of Carthage.

The provinces and their armies being thus divided, Vitellius 77
could only win the throne by fighting. Otho meanwhile was
carrying on the government as if the time were one of pro-
found peace. Sometimes he took into account the country's
dignity, though more often the exigencies of the moment
forced him into unseemly haste. He held the consulship himself with his brother Titianus as colleague until 1 March. For
the next two months* he appointed Verginius, as a sort of sop

to the army in Germany. As colleague he gave him Pompeius Vopiscus, ostensibly because he was an old friend of his own, but it was generally understood as a compliment to Vienne. For the rest of the year the nominations which Nero or Galba had made were allowed to stand. Caelius Sabinus and Flavius Sabinus were consuls until 1 July, Arrius Antoninus* and Marius Celsus until 1 September; even Vitellius after his victory did not cancel their appointment.

To the pontifical and augural colleges* Otho either nominated old men who had already held high office, as the final crown of their career; or else by way of recompense installed young aristocrats, newly returned from exile, in the priesthoods which their fathers or grandfathers had held. He restored Cadius Rufus, Pedius Blaesus, and Saevinus Propinquus* to their seats in the Senate. They had been convicted during Claudius' and Nero's reigns of extortion in the provinces. In pardoning them the name of their offence was changed, and their greed appeared as 'treason'. For so unpopular was the law of treason that it sapped the force of better statutes.

78   Otho moreover tried to win over the municipalities and provinces by similar bribes. At Hispalis and Emerita* he enrolled new families of settlers, he granted Roman citizenship* to the whole community of the Lingones, and made over certain Moorish towns as a gift to the province of Baetica. For Cappadocia and Africa he devised new legislation, as showy as it was short-lived. All these grants are excused by the exigences of the moment and the impending crisis, but he even found time to remember his old amours, and passed a measure through the Senate restoring Poppaea's statues. He is believed also to have thought of celebrating Nero's memory as a means of attracting public support. Some persons actually erected statues of Nero, and there were even times when the populace and the soldiers saluted Otho as Nero Otho, as though thereby enhancing his fame and dignity. However, he refused to commit himself. He was afraid to ban the title—or else ashamed to accept it.*

79   While people were intent upon the civil war, foreign affairs were neglected. Consequently a Sarmatian tribe called the Rhoxolani, who had slaughtered two cohorts of auxiliaries in

the previous winter, now formed the still more daring scheme
of invading Moesia. They assembled nearly 9,000 mounted
men, all, thanks to their impetuosity and earlier success, more
intent on plunder than on fighting. While they were riding
about aimlessly and off their guard, they were suddenly attacked by the Third Legion and its native auxiliaries. On the
Roman side everything was ready for a battle: the Sarmatians
were scattered over the country; some in their greed for plunder were heavily laden, and the slippery roads deprived them
of their horses' speed. They were cut to pieces as surely as if
they had been in fetters.

It is quite extraordinary how all a Sarmatian's courage is, so
to speak, outside himself. Fighting on foot, no one is more
cowardly; but their cavalry charge would break almost any
troops. But on this occasion it was raining and the ice had
thawed; their pikes and their swords, which were extremely
long and needed both hands to wield, were useless; their
horses slipped and they were encumbered by the heavy coat of
mail which all their chiefs and nobles wear. Being made of
iron plates and very hard leather, it is impenetrable to blows,
but most inconvenient for any one who is knocked down by a
charge of the enemy and tries to get up. Besides, they sank into
the deep, soft snow. The Roman soldiers, whose cuirasses
gave them easy movement, armed with javelin and lance, and
using when necessary their light swords, sprang on the undefended Sarmatians (they never carry shields) and stabbed them
at close quarters. A few, surviving the battle, hid themselves in
the marshes, and there perished from the severity of the winter
and their wounds.

When the news of this reached Rome, Marcus Aponius, the
governor of Moesia, was granted a triumphal statue,* while
the commanding officers of the legions, Aurelius Fulvus,
Tettius Julianus,* and Numisius Lupus, received the insignia
of consular rank. Otho was delighted and took all the credit
to himself, as if he had been the successful general, and
had himself employed his officers and armies to enlarge the
empire.

In the mean time a riot broke out in an unexpected quarter, 80
and, though trivial at first, nearly ended in the destruction of
Rome. Otho had given orders that the Seventeenth Cohort

should be summoned from the colony of Ostia to the city, and
Varius Crispinus, a tribune of the Guards, was instructed to
provide them with arms. Anxious to carry out his instructions
undisturbed while the camp was quiet, he arranged that the
arsenal was to be opened and the cohort's wagons loaded at
nightfall. The hour aroused suspicion; the motive was questioned; his quest for a quiet moment developed into an uproar. The mere sight of swords made the drunken soldiers
long to use them. They began to murmur and accuse their
tribunes and centurions of treachery, suggesting that the senators' slaves were going to be armed against Otho. Some of
them were ignorant and fuddled by wine; the worst element
saw a chance of plunder; the mass of them, as usual, were
eager for any change; and those who were better the night had
kept from their duty. When Crispinus tried to check them,
the mutineers killed him together with the strictest of the
centurions, seized the weapons, bared their swords, and
mounting the horses, made for Rome and the palace.

81   It so happened that a large party of upper-class women and
men was dining with Otho. In their alarm they wondered
whether the soldiers' outbreak was coincidental or a ruse of
the Emperor's: would it be safer to fly in all directions or to
stay and be arrested? At one moment they would make a show
of firmness, at the next their terror betrayed them. All the time
they were watching Otho's face; and, as happens with minds
prone to suspicion, Otho's fears inspired fear in others. But
feeling no less alarm for the senators than for himself, he had
promptly dispatched the Prefects of the Guards to appease the
anger of the troops, and told all his guests to leave immediately. Then on all sides officials threw away their insignia and
avoided their massed entourages of attendants and slaves. Old
gentlemen and their wives roamed the dark streets of the city
in all directions. Few went home, most of them fled to friends,
or sought an obscure refuge with the humblest of their
clients.*

82   The soldiers' onrush could not be stopped even by the gates
of the palace. They invaded the banquet hall, demanding to
see Otho. Julius Martialis, a tribune, and Vitellius Saturninus,
a prefect of the legion,* were wounded while endeavouring to

stem the flood. On every side were swords and threats, now against their centurions and tribunes, now against the whole Senate; and since they could not select any one victim for their wrath, in a blind frenzy of panic they clamoured for a free hand against all. At last Otho, abandoning imperial dignity, stood up on a couch and with great difficulty restrained them by means of prayers and tears. They returned to their camp unwillingly, and with a guilty conscience.

The next day Rome was like a captured city. The houses were shut, the streets almost deserted, the people sombre. The soldiers, too, hung their heads, more through sulkiness than contrition. Their Prefects, Licinius Proculus and Plotius Firmus, harangued them by companies, the one mildly, the other harshly, according to their different characters. They concluded by announcing that the men were to receive 5,000 sesterces apiece. After that Otho ventured to enter the camp. The tribunes and centurions, each flinging away the insignia of his rank, crowded round him begging for a safe discharge. Stung by the disgrace of this, the troops settled down to obedience, and themselves demanded that the ringleaders should be punished.

In the general disturbance Otho's position was difficult. The 83 soldiers were by no means unanimous. The better sort wanted him to put a stop to the prevalent insubordination, but the great bulk of them liked insurrection and emperors who had to court their favour, and the prospect of rioting and plunder made it easier still to press them into civil war. He realized, also, that one who wins a throne by violence cannot keep it by suddenly trying to enforce the rigid discipline of earlier days.* However, the danger of the crisis for both the city and the Senate seriously alarmed him, so he finally delivered the following speech:

'Fellow-soldiers, I have not come to fan the fire of your affection for me, or to instil courage into your hearts: in both those qualities you are more than rich. No, I have come to ask you to moderate your valour and to set some bounds to your devotion towards me. These recent disturbances did not origi- nate in greed or hatred, which so often cause dissension in an army; nor was it even that you feared danger and tried to shirk it. The motivation was your excessive loyalty, which you displayed with more ardour than judgement. For honourable motives, when combined with a lack of discretion, often land men in disaster.

'We are preparing for war. Do you imagine that we could publish all our dispatches, and discuss all our plans in the presence of the whole army, when we have to devise a systematic campaign and keep up with the rapid changes of the situation? There are things a soldier ought to know, but there is much of which he must be ignorant. It is necessary for the maintenance of strict discipline and of the general's authority that even his tribunes and centurions should often obey blindly. If individuals are permitted to question why orders are given, obedience is done for, and authority falls to the ground.

'In actual warfare, are men to take up arms at dead of night? Shall a few drunken blackguards—for I cannot believe that many lost their heads in the recent panic—go and stain their hands with the blood of centurion and tribune, and then
84 break into their general's tent? Now, I know you did it to protect me, but the riot and the darkness and the general confusion might also have provided an opportunity to kill me. Suppose Vitellius and his henchmen had their choice of the state of mind they would pray to find us in: what more could they desire than mutiny and dissension, the men insubordinate to the centurions, the centurions to the tribunes, and the whole force, cavalry and infantry alike, rushing in headlong confusion to their ruin? Good soldiering, my comrades, consists in obedience, not in scrutinizing the general's orders; and the army which is most orderly before the emergency is most courageous when actually in it. Let yours be the swords and the courage: leave it to me to plan the campaign and to direct your valour.

'The culprits were but few, and only two are to be punished; the rest of you must blot out all memory of that discreditable night. No army anywhere must hear those words you spoke against the Senate, the fount of the empire and the glory of all the provinces. Why, in Heaven's name, the very Germans themselves, whom Vitellius is stirring up with all his might

against us, would not dare to advocate the condemnation of
its members! Shall it be said that Italy's own sons, the real
soldiery of Rome, are clamouring to murder and massacre the
very senators through whose lustre and glory we throw into
the shade the obscure and squalid adherents of Vitellius?
Vitellius has captured a few tribes and raised a sort of shadow
of an army: but the Senate is with us. Therefore on our side
stands Rome: they are her foes.

'Do you imagine that the stability of this beautiful city
consists in houses and edifices built of stone upon stone? They
are dumb inanimate things; it is of no consequence whether
they fall to pieces or are rebuilt. The eternity of our empire,
the peace of the world, your welfare and mine, all depend
upon the safety of the Senate.* Instituted with solemn
ceremony by the father and founder of Rome, the Senate has
come down in undying continuity from the kings to the
emperors: and as we have received it from our ancestors, so let
us hand it on to our posterity. From your ranks come the
senators, and from the Senate come the emperors of Rome.'

This speech was well calculated to reprimand and soothe 85
the soldiers' minds; both it and Otho's moderation—for he
had only ordered the punishment of two men—were well
received. He had calmed for the moment troops who could
not be controlled. Yet peace and quiet were not restored in
Rome. Amid the clash of arms the city displayed the face of
war. Refraining from organized riot, the soldiers now dispersed to private houses and lived in disguise, paying malevo-
lent attention to all whom nobility of birth or wealth or any
other distinction made a mark for scandal. Many, besides,
believed that some of Vitellius' soldiers had come to Rome to
study the state of party feeling.

Everywhere suspicion was rife, and terror invaded even the
privacy of the home. But far greater was the alarm displayed
in public places. With every fresh piece of news that rumour
brought, men's feelings and the expression on their faces
changed. They were afraid to be found short of confidence
when things looked doubtful for Otho, or lacking in joy when
they went well. Above all, when the Senate was summoned to
the House, they found it extraordinarily hard always to strike

the right note. Silence would argue arrogance; plain speaking would arouse suspicion; yet flattery would be detected by Otho, who had so lately been a private citizen practising the art himself. So they had to turn and twist their sentences. Vitellius they called enemy and traitor, the more far-sighted confining their insults to such vague generalities. A few engaged in more accurate abuse, but always chose a moment of uproar when a great many people were shouting, or else drowned their own words in a torrent of language.

86   Another cause of alarm was the portents reported by various separate sources. In the entrance to the Capitol, it was said, the figure of Victory had let the reins of her chariot slip from her hands: an apparition of superhuman size had suddenly burst out of the chapel of Juno: a statue of the deified Julius on the island in the Tiber had, on a fine, still day, turned round from the west and faced the east:* an ox had spoken in Etruria: animals had given birth to strange monsters. Still other phenomena were seen, of the sort which in primitive ages were observed even in time of peace, though now we only hear of them in time of panic.*

But the greatest damage at the moment, and the greatest alarm for the future, was caused by a sudden rising of the Tiber. Immensely swollen, it wrecked the Pile Bridge,* and, its current being stemmed by the heavy ruins, it flooded not only the flat, low-lying portions of the city, but also districts that seemed safe from inundation. Many people were swept away in the streets, still more were overtaken by the flood in shops or in their beds. The result was a famine among the poor, since food was scarce and they were deprived of their means of livelihood. Blocks of flats, the foundations of which had rotted in the standing water, collapsed when the river sank. No sooner had the panic caused by the flood subsided than it was found that, although Otho planned an expedition, his army's route over the Campus Martius and up the Flaminian Way* was blocked. Though its causes were accidental or natural, this mishap was turned into a miraculous omen of impending disaster.

87   Otho had held a purification of the city* and meditated his plans for the war. Recognizing that the Pennine and Cottian

Alps and all the other passes into Gaul were held by Vitellius'
troops, he decided to invade Narbonese Gaul by sea. His fleet
was strong, and devoted to his cause; for he had enrolled the
survivors of the Mulvian Bridge massacre, whom Galba's
cruelty had kept in prison, into a legion, and to the remaining
marines likewise he had held out hopes of promotion into a
more prestigious regiment. To the fleet he attached the cohorts
of the City Garrison and a large force of Guards. These were
the flower of the army and its chief strength, well able to
advise and protect the generals.

The command of the expedition was entrusted to Antonius
Novellus and Suedius Clemens, both senior centurions, and to
Aemilius Pacensis, to whom Otho had restored the rank of
tribune, of which Galba had deprived him. In charge of the
fleet he still retained the freedman Moschus* to keep an eye on
his betters. In command of the cavalry and infantry he placed
Suetonius Paulinus,* Marius Celsus, and Annius Gallus, but
the man in whom he put most faith was the Prefect of the
Guards, Licinius Proculus. This officer had shown himself
efficient in garrison service, but was without any experience
of warfare. He maligned the individual virtues of his colleagues—Paulinus' power of influence, Celsus' energy, Gallus'
ripe judgement—and being a knave and no fool, he easily
got the better of men who were both honest and
restrained.

It was about this time that Cornelius Dolabella was ban-   88
ished to the colonial town of Aquinas,* though not kept in
close or dishonourable confinement. There was no charge
against him: the stigma upon him was his ancient name and
kinship to Galba.*

Otho issued orders that several of the magistrates and most
of the ex-consuls were to join the expedition, not to take part
in the campaign or to assist in any way, but apparently as a
friendly escort. Among these was even Lucius Vitellius, whom
he treated neither as an emperor's brother nor as the brother
of an enemy, but just like anybody else.

As a result, much anxiety was aroused for the safety of the
city, where all classes were afraid and at risk. The leading
members of the Senate were old and infirm, and enervated by

a long period of peace: the aristocracy were inefficient and had
forgotten how to fight: the knights knew nothing of military
service. The more they tried to conceal or suppress their
alarm, the more obvious it became. Some of them, on the
other hand, were led by crass ostentation to purchase beautiful armour and fine horses; others procured as provisions of
war elaborate dinner services or some other stimulants for
their appetites. Prudent men were concerned for the country's
peace; the frivolous, without a thought for the future, were
inflated by empty hopes; a good many, whose loss of credit
made peace unwelcome, were delighted at the general unrest,
feeling safest among uncertainties.

89   Though cares of state are too vast to arouse any interest in
the masses, yet as the whole revenue was devoted to military
purposes, and the price of food rose, the common people
gradually began to realize the evils of war. During the revolt
of Vindex they had not suffered so much. Being carried on in
the provinces between the legionaries and the natives of Gaul,
it was in effect a foreign war, and the city had not been
affected. For from the time when the deified Augustus organized the rule of the Caesars, the wars of the Roman people had
been fought in distant countries: all the anxiety and all the
glory fell to the emperor alone. Under Tiberius and Gaius the
country only suffered from the evils of peace. Scribonianus'
rising* against Claudius was no sooner heard of than crushed.
Nero had been dethroned more by rumours and dispatches
than by force of arms. But now not only the legions and the
fleet but, as had seldom happened before, the Guards and the
City Garrison were called out for the campaign. Behind them
were the East and the West and all the forces of the empire,
material for a long war—under any other generals.

An attempt was made to delay Otho's departure by pointing out the impiety of his not yet having replaced the sacred
shields.* But delay had ruined Nero: Otho would have none
of it. And the knowledge that Caecina had already crossed the
90 Alps acted as a further stimulus. Accordingly, on 14 March he
commended the government of the country to the Senate, and
granted to the restored exiles all the rest of the property
confiscated by Nero which had not yet been sold for the

imperial Treasury. The gift was a just one, and made a fine impression, but in practice it was futile: such was the haste with which for a long time the money had been confiscated.

Otho then summoned a public meeting, and, after extolling the majesty of Rome and praising the whole-hearted adherence of the Senate and people to his cause, he used very moderate language against the Vitellian party, criticizing the legions more for folly than treason, and making no mention of Vitellius himself. This may have been due to his own moderation, or it may be that the writer of the speech felt some qualms for this own safety, and therefore refrained from insulting Vitellius. For it was generally believed that as in strategy he took the advice of Suetonius Paulinus and Marius Celsus, so too in political matters he employed the talents of Galerius Trachalus.* Some people even thought they could recognize Trachalus' style of oratory, expansive and sonorous, well adapted to the ears of the crowd: and his style was well known through his frequent speeches in court.

The crowd's loud shouts of applause were typical of the flatterer, excessive and insincere. Men vied with each other in their enthusiasm and prayers for his success, much as though they were sending off the dictator Caesar or the Emperor Augustus. Their motive was neither fear nor affection, but a sheer passion for servility. One can see the same in households of slaves, where each obeys his own interest: public dignity counts for nothing. On his departure Otho entrusted the peace of the city and the interests of the empire to his brother Salvius Titianus.

BOOK TWO

Meanwhile, on the other side of the world, Fortune was 1 already sowing the seeds of a dynasty, the varying fortunes of which were destined to bring happiness and misery to the country, and success and destruction to the rulers themselves.

Before Galba's fall Titus Vespasianus had been dispatched by his father from Judaea to Rome. The ostensible reason of his journey was to show respect to the new Emperor, and to solicit some post for which his years now fitted him.* However, the popular passion for invention had suggested that he had been summoned to be adopted. This rumour was based on the fact that Galba was old and childless: the public never wearies of appointing successors until the choice is made. The character of Titus gave still more colour to it. He was capable of filling any position. His appearance lacked neither charm nor dignity. Vespasian's successes also, and the utterances of oracles, further endorsed the rumour, to say nothing of the chance occurrences which pass for omens when people are predisposed to believe in them.

It was at Corinth in Achaia that Titus received reliable reports of Galba's murder, and was assured by people in the town that Vitellius had declared war. In great perplexity he summoned a few of his friends and considered all the possibilities on either side. If he continued his journey to Rome he would earn no gratitude for homage intended for another sovereign, and would be held as a hostage either for Vitellius or for Otho: on the other hand, if he returned to Judaea he would inevitably offend the victor. However, the struggle was still undecided, and his father's support for the successful party would excuse the conduct of the son. Or if Vespasian himself assumed sovereignty,* they would have to plan war and forget all about giving offence.

Such considerations kept him wavering between hope and 2 fear; but ultimately hope prevailed. Some people believed that his longing to get back to Queen Berenice* fired him to return. True, the young man's fancy was attracted by Berenice, but he did not allow this to interfere with business. Still, his youth was a time of happy self-indulgence, and he showed more restraint in his own reign than in his father's.

Accordingly, he sailed along the coasts of Achaia and Asia Minor, and, skirting the shore which lay upon his left, reached the islands of Rhodes and Cyprus, whence he made a bolder crossing to Syria. On his way he conceived a desire to go and see the Temple of Venus at Paphos, which is famous among all the inhabitants and visitors.

It may be of some interest to give here a short account of the origin of this worship,* the ritual of the cult, and the shape— unparalleled elsewhere—in which the goddess is depicted.

3 According to an old tradition, the temple was founded by King Aerias, and some people maintain that the goddess bears the same name. A more modern version states that the temple was consecrated by Cinyras, on the spot where the goddess landed when the sea gave her birth.* The knowledge and method of divination, however, according to this account, was imported from elsewhere by the Cilician Tamiras,* and an arrangement was made that the descendants of both fami- lies should preside over the rites. Later, however, it seemed wrong that the royal line should not outrank a foreign clan, so the newcomers resigned the practice of the art which they had themselves introduced, and now the priest whom you consult is always of the line of Cinyras.

They accept whatever victim has been vowed, providing males are selected. They put most faith in kids' entrails. Blood must not be poured on the altar, at which they offer only prayers and pure fire. Although the altar stands in the open air it is never wetted by rain. The goddess is not represented in human form; the idol is cone-shaped, rising from a broad circular base to a narrow circumference at the top. The reason for this is unknown.

4 Titus inspected the temple treasures and the offerings made by various kings, and other objects which the Greeks, in their national passion for antiquarianism, attribute to a dim and distant past. He then consulted the oracle first about his voyage. Learning that the sea was calm, and that no obstacles stood in his way, he sacrificed a large number of victims, and

put covert questions about his own fortunes. The priest, whose name was Sostratus, seeing that the entrails were uniformly favourable, and that the goddess assented to Titus' ambitious schemes, returned for the moment a brief and ordinary reply, but afterwards sought a private interview and revealed the future to him. So Titus returned to his father with heightened hopes, and amid the general anxiety of the provinces and their armies his arrival spread boundless confidence of success.

Vespasian had already broken the back of the Jewish War. Only the siege of Jerusalem remained.* That this proved a difficult and laborious task was due rather to the nature of the town's mountain site and the stubborn superstition of its inhabitants than to any adequate provision enabling them to endure the hardships of the siege. Vespasian had, as stated above, three legions well tried in war. Four others were under Mucianus' command. Although these had never seen war, yet their envy of the neighbouring army's fame had banished sloth. Indeed, the former were hardened by work and danger, but just as powerful was the latter's drive, a result of their unbroken inaction, and their passion for the warfare that they had never experienced.

Both generals had auxiliary infantry and cavalry, fleets and allied princes, and a fame that rested on widely differing claims. Vespasian was an indefatigable campaigner. He 5 headed the column, chose the camping-ground, never ceasing by night or day to use strategy and, if need be, the sword to thwart the enemy. He ate what he could get, and dressed almost like a common soldier. Indeed, save for his avarice, he matched the generals of old days. Mucianus, on the other hand, was distinguished by his grandeur and wealth, and his general superiority to the standards of a private person. He was the better speaker, a skilful administrator and prescient statesman. Their combined qualities would have made a fine emperor, if one could have blended their virtues and omitted their vices.

Governing as they did the neighbouring provinces of Judaea and Syria, jealousy had at first led to quarrels. However, on the death of Nero, they forgot their dislike and joined hands.

It was their friends who first brought them together, and subsequently Titus became the chief bond of union and for the common good suppressed their misguided rivalry. His natural and studied qualities combined to fascinate even such a man as Mucianus. They recruited tribunes, centurions, and common soldiers, each according to his character, by his industry or indulgence, playing on his probity or his pleasures.

6   Before the arrival of Titus both armies had sworn allegiance to Otho. News travels fast in such cases, but civil war is a slow and serious undertaking, and the East, after its long and harmonious repose, was now for the first time beginning to arm for it. In earlier times all the fiercest civil wars had broken out in Italy or Gaul, among the forces of the West. Pompey, Cassius, Brutus, and Antony all courted disaster by carrying the war overseas. Syria and Judaea often heard of Caesars, but seldom saw one.* There were no mutinies among the soldiers; they merely made threats against Parthia with varying success. Even in the last civil war the peace of these provinces had been untroubled by the general confusion. Later they were loyal to Galba. But when it became common knowledge that Otho and Vitellius were engaged in a wicked contest to seize the Roman world, the troops began to chafe at the thought that the prizes of empire should fall to others, while their own lot was merely the constraints of slavery. They began to take stock of their strength. Syria and Judaea had seven legions on the spot with a vast force of auxiliaries. Next to them on one side came Egypt with two legions: on the other lay Cappadocia and Pontus, and all the forts along the Armenian frontier. Asia and the remaining provinces were rich and thickly populated. The islands were girdled by sea, and the sea itself was safe from the enemy and aided the intervening preparations for war.

7   The generals were well aware of the soldiers' feelings, but decided to await the issue between the other warring parties. 'In civil war', they reckoned, 'there are no sure ties to unite victor and vanquished. It matters little whether Vitellius or Otho chances to survive. Even good generals grow arrogant through success: this pair's troops are quarrelsome, lazy, and hedonistic, and they are both the victims of their own

vices. One will fall on the field and the other succumb to his success.'

So Vespasian and Mucianus postponed their attack until the time was right. They were themselves recent converts to the project of war, which the others had long fostered from various motives. The better sort were animated by patriotism, many by the delights of plunder, some by the uncertainty of their own fortunes. Thus, though their motives differed, all, good and bad alike, agreed in their eager desire for war.

About this time Achaia and Asia were thrown into a 8 groundless panic by a rumour that 'Nero was at hand'.* The accounts of his death being many and various, people were all the more inclined to allege and to believe that he was still alive. I shall mention in the course of this work the attempts and the fate of the other pretenders. This time it was a slave from Pontus, or, according to other traditions, a freedman from Italy. His skill as a singer and harpist, combined with his facial resemblance to Nero, gave him some credentials for imposture. He bribed some penniless and vagabond deserters by dazzling promises to join him, and they all set out to sea. A storm drove them on to the island of Cythnus, where he found some troops homeward bound on leave from the East. Some of these he enrolled, ordering all who resisted to be killed, and then he proceeded to plunder merchants and arm all the sturdiest of their slaves. Finding a centurion named Sisenna carrying home a pair of silver hands as a token of alliance from the army in Syria to the Guards, he tried by various devices to work upon him, until Sisenna took fright and escaped secretly from the island in fear of violence. Thus the panic spread. The great name of Nero attracted many who pined for revolution and hated the existing state of things.

The rumours waxed daily, until a chance dispelled them. Galba had entrusted the government of the provinces Galatia 9 and Pamphylia to Calpurnius Asprenas, who had been granted an escort of two triremes from the fleet at Misenum.* It so happened that with these he touched at Cythnus, where men were at hand to issue invitations to the ships' captains in the name of Nero. The pretender, assuming an air of melancholy, appealed to 'the loyalty of his former soldiers', and begged them to convey him to Syria or Egypt. The captains, either from indecision or guile, asserted that they must talk to their men, and would come back when they had got their minds prepared. However, they faithfully made a full report to Asprenas, on whose instructions they boarded the ship and killed the impostor, whoever he was. The man's eyes and hair and ferocious look were so remarkable that the body was carried into Asia and thence to Rome.

10   In a country so divided, whose frequent changes of rulers left it wavering between liberty and anarchy, even small events caused serious disturbance. Vibius Crispus,* a man whose wealth, influence, and ability had won him a reputation that was great rather than good, impeached before the Senate a man of equestrian rank called Annius Faustus, who had been a professional informer under Nero. The Senate had recently in Galba's principate passed a resolution authorizing the prosecution of informers. This resolution had been applied inconsistently, and its strength or weakness varied according to whether the defendant was helpless or influential. But it still retained some terrors. Crispus, moreover, had exerted all his powers to secure the ruin of the man who had informed against his brother. He had, in fact, induced a large proportion of the Senate to demand that Faustus should be sent to execution undefended and unheard. However, in the eyes of others the defendant's greatest advantage was his prosecutor's undue influence. 'We must give him time,' they argued, 'the charges must be published: however hateful the criminal, his case must be properly heard.'

At first this advice prevailed: the trial was postponed for a few days. But then came Faustus' conviction, which aroused in the country less satisfaction than his vile character warranted. People recalled the fact that Crispus himself had similarly turned informer for pecuniary profit. It was not the penalty but the prosecutor that was unpopular.

11   Meanwhile the war opened successfully for Otho. At his order the armies of Dalmatia and Pannonia started from their base. They comprised four legions, each of which had sent forward detachments 2,000 strong. The rest followed at a short interval: the Seventh Legion raised by Galba; and those

composed of veteran troops—the Eleventh and Thirteenth, and the Fourteenth, which had won great distinction by crushing the rebellion in Britain.* Nero had further increased their glory by choosing them as his crack troops, which accounts for their lasting loyalty to him and their keen support of Otho. But the mightier their strength, the greater their self-confidence and the slower their march. The auxiliary cavalry and infantry preceded the main body of the legions. From Rome itself came no mean force, five cohorts of Guards with some detachments of cavalry and the First Legion.* To these were added an irregular force of 2,000 gladiators: during the civil wars even strict generals availed themselves of this shameful support.* Annius Gallus was placed in command of these forces with Vestricius Spurinna,* and they were sent forward to hold the banks of the Po. Their first plans had failed: Caecina, whom Otho had hoped to contain within the Gallic provinces, had already crossed the Alps.

Under Otho's personal command marched picked detachments of his Body Guard and the rest of the Praetorian Guard, together with veterans of the latter and a large force of marines. He let no luxury either delay or disgrace his march. In an iron breastplate* he marched on foot at the head of his troops, looking rough and dishevelled, quite unlike his reputation.

Fortune smiled on his first efforts. Through his fleet and 12 control of the sea he held most of Italy right up to the border with the Maritime Alps. To assault this province and attack Narbonese Gaul he had placed in command Suedius Clemens, Antonius Novellus, and Aemilius Pacensis. Pacensis, however, was made a prisoner by his mutinous troops: Antonius Novellus had no authority: Suedius Clemens was in charge, but used his command to curry favour, and was as greedy for battle as he was criminally blind to insubordination.

No one could have imagined they were in Italy, on the soil of their native land. As though on foreign shores and among an enemy's towns, they burnt, ravaged, plundered, with results all the more horrible since no precautions had been taken against danger. The fields were full, the houses open. The inhabitants ran to meet them with their wives and children, and were lured by the security of peace into all the horrors of war.

The governor of the Maritime Alps at that time was Marius Maturus. He summoned the inhabitants, whose fighting strength was ample, and proposed to resist at the frontier the Othonians' invasion of the province. But at the first onslaught the mountain people were cut down and scattered. They had assembled in random haste; they knew nothing of military camps or commanders, nothing of the glory of victory or the disgrace of flight.

13   Enraged by this engagement, Otho's troops visited their indignation on the town of Albantimilium.* The battle had brought them no booty, for the peasants were poor and their armour worthless, and being swift of foot, with a good knowledge of the country, they had escaped capture. However, the soldiers sated their greed at the expense of the innocent town. A Ligurian woman afforded a fine example of courage which made their conduct the more odious. She had concealed her son, and when the soldiers, who believed that she had hidden money with him, demanded from her under torture where she was keeping him concealed, she pointed to her womb and replied, 'He hides here.' No subsequent terrors nor even death itself could bring her to change that resolute and noble answer.

14   Panic-stricken couriers brought to Fabius Valens the news that Otho's fleet was threatening the province of Narbonese Gaul, which had sworn allegiance to Vitellius. Representatives from the Roman colonies also arrived beseeching his aid. He dispatched two cohorts of the Tungri* and four troops of horse, together with the entire cavalry regiment of the Treviri. This force was put under the command of Julius Classicus, and part of it was kept back in the colony of Forum Julii,* since, if the whole force marched inland and the seaboard were left unprotected, Otho's fleet would swoop down at once. Twelve troops of cavalry and a picked body of auxiliaries marched against the enemy: these were reinforced by a Ligurian cohort which had long garrisoned this district, and 500 Pannonian recruits who had not yet joined their legion.

The engagement began promptly. Otho's line was so arranged that some of the marines, reinforced by local civilians, held the rising ground by the sea, while the Guards filled the level space between the hills and the shore. On the sea itself the fleet, acting in conjunction with the land force, was ready for the battle, and extended a threatening front facing the coast. The Vitellians were weaker in infantry; their strength lay in cavalry. The mountain people were posted on the neighbouring heights, and the auxiliary foot-soldiers massed in close order behind the cavalry.

The Treviran cavalry rashly charged the enemy, and meeting Otho's veterans in front were simultaneously assailed in the flank by the civilians, flinging stones. This they could do well enough; and, interspersed among the regulars, they all, bold and timid alike, showed the same courage in the hour of victory. Additional panic struck the defeated Vitellians when the fleet began to harass their rear. They were now surrounded, and would have been entirely destroyed had not the darkness of night hampered the victorious army and sheltered the losers' flight.

But though beaten the Vitellians were not cowed. Calling 15 up reinforcements, they suddenly attacked while the unsuspecting enemy were taking their ease after the victory. They killed the sentries, broke into the camp, and terrified the sailors. In time the panic gradually subsided. The Othonians seized a nearby hill, defended their position, and eventually assumed the offensive. The slaughter was frightful. The officers commanding the cohorts of Tungri, after long maintaining their battle-formation, fell beneath a shower of weapons. Nor was victory bloodless even for the Othonians, for the enemy's cavalry rallied and cut off all who rashly ventured too far in pursuit. So they agreed to a sort of armistice. As a safeguard against sudden alarms caused either by the fleet on the one side or the cavalry on the other, the Vitellians retired to Antipolis,* a town in Narbonese Gaul, and the Othonians to Albingaunum,* away from the front in Liguria.

The news of this naval victory kept Corsica and Sardinia 16 and the other adjacent islands faithful to Otho's cause. However, Decumus Picarius, the governor, nearly ruined Corsica by an act of indiscretion, which in a war of such dimensions could not possibly have affected the issue, and only ended in his own destruction. He hated Otho and determined to aid Vitellius with all the forces of Corsica; a useless assistance, even if it had been forthcoming. He summoned the chief men of the island and disclosed his project. Claudius Pyrrhicus, who commanded the Liburnian cruisers* stationed there, and a Roman knight named Quintius Certus ventured to oppose him. He ordered their execution. Their deaths frightened those present into swearing allegiance to Vitellius; the general mass of ignorant people did the same, blindly sharing the others' fear. However, when Picarius began to enlist them and to harass his undisciplined men with military duties, their loathing for the unwonted labour set them thinking of their weakness. They lived on an island; Vitellius' legions were in Germany, a long way off; Otho's fleet had already sacked and plundered even districts that had auxiliary infantry and cavalry to protect them.

The revulsion was sudden, but did not issue in overt resistance. They chose a moment suitable for treachery. Waiting till Picarius' retinue had gone, they murdered him in his bath, stripped and helpless, and slaughtered his comrades too. The killers themselves brought to Otho the heads, like those of public enemies. They received neither reward from Otho nor punishment from Vitellius: in the vast cesspool of the age their deed was overshadowed by more heinous crimes.

17 I have already described how 'Silius' Cavalry' had opened up Italy and taken the war into its heart. No one there either supported Otho or preferred Vitellius. But prolonged peace had crushed their spirits into utter servility.* They were an easy prey to the first comer and cared little who was the better man. As the auxiliaries sent forward by Caecina had also arrived, all the fields and cities between the Alps and the Po, the most prosperous district in Italy, were held by the Vitellian forces. One of the Pannonian cohorts had been captured at Cremona: 100 cavalry and 1,000 marines had been cut off between Placentia and Ticinum.* After this success the river and its banks were no longer a barrier to the Vitellian troops: indeed the Batavians and the Germans from across the Rhine

found the Po a positive temptation. Crossing suddenly opposite Placentia, they captured a handful of scouts and created
such a panic that the others in terror spread the false report
that Caecina's whole army was upon them.

Spurinna, who was holding Placentia, had made up his 18
mind that Caecina had not yet arrived, and that his own men
must be kept within the city's defences if Caecina should
approach. He could not send three cohorts of Guards, 1,000
troops on special detachment, and a few cavalry to face
Caecina's veteran army. But his men were unruly and ignorant
of war. Seizing the standards and colours they broke out,
threatening with their weapons the general who tried to check
them, and paying no heed to their centurions and tribunes.
They even clamoured that Otho was being betrayed, and that
Caecina was there by invitation. Their recklessness was foreign to Spurinna; yet he accompanied them, at first under
compulsion, later with a pretence of willingness. He was
anxious that his advice should carry greater influence in the
event that the mutiny cooled.

At nightfall, with the Po in sight,* Spurinna decided to 19
entrench his camp. The unaccustomed hard work crushed the
enthusiasm of his town-bred troops. The older men began to
curse their credulity, and to point out the fearful danger to
their small force of being surrounded by Caecina's army in the
open country. More sober language by now had pervaded the
camp. The tribunes and centurions mingled with the men, and
everyone talked with admiration of Spurinna's foresight in
selecting a powerful and wealthy colony as a strong base for
their operations. Finally Spurinna himself explained to his
troops his plans instead of reproaching their faults, and, leaving patrols behind, led the rest of the men back to Placentia in
a quieter and more submissive frame of mind. There the walls
were strengthened, outworks built, and the turrets increased
in height and number, while Spurinna provided for and
prepared not only arms but also obedience and willing discipline. This was all his party lacked, for their courage was
unimpeachable.

Caecina, meanwhile, seemed to have left his cruelty and 20
profligacy on the other side of the Alps. He marched through

Italy with a well-disciplined force. The people in the country towns and colonies took offence at his costume as showing arrogance: while they wore the plain toga, Caecina addressed them attired in a parti-coloured plaid and trousers.* Moreover, his wife Salonina rode on a fine horse with purple trappings, and though this did no one any harm, they grumbled and seemed hurt. It is an ineradicable human trait to turn critical eyes on new-found fortune, and to insist upon moderation most of all in those who used to be our equals.

Crossing the Po, Caecina tried to undermine the loyalty of the Othonians by negotiations and promises. They retaliated with the same weapons, and when they had finished bandying empty and fine-sounding phrases about Peace and Concord, Caecina devoted all his attention and plans to an assault on Placentia in terrifying force. He knew that his future reputation rested on the result of the initial fighting.

21   But the first day's work savoured more of impatience than of the skills of a veteran army. The men ventured under the walls without cover or precaution, drunk and overfed. Meanwhile the amphitheatre, a fine building outside the walls, was burnt down: it was set on fire either by the attacking force hurling torches and heated shot and firebrands against the besieged, or by the besieged in returning their fire. The common people of the town, typically suspicious, believed that fuel for the fire had been surreptitiously introduced by inhabitants of the neighbouring colonies out of envy and jealousy, since no building in Italy could hold so many people. However the disaster happened, they thought little of it while worse threatened: once safety was restored, they bewailed it as the worst calamity they could have suffered.

To return, however, to Caecina: he was repulsed with heavy losses, and the night was spent in preparing siege-equipment. The Vitellians produced screens, fascines, and mantlets, to protect the assailants while undermining the walls: the Othonians procured stakes and huge masses of stone, lead, and brass, to destroy the enemy and crush them to pieces. Both parties were actuated by feelings of pride and ambition. However, the encouragements used were different, one side praising the strength of the legions and the German army, the other the reputation of the Guards and the City Garrison. The Vitellians decried their enemy as lazy idlers who had been corrupted by the circus and the theatre: in response they vilified the Vitellians as a pack of foreigners and barbarians. Meanwhile, Otho and Vitellius were lauded or blamed, mutual insults providing the more fruitful stimulus.

Hardly had day dawned before the walls of Placentia bris- 22 tled with defenders, and the fields glittered with the soldiers' armour. The Vitellian legions advancing in close order with their auxiliaries in scattered bands assailed the higher portions of the walls with arrows and stones: where the walls were in disrepair or crumbling from age they attacked from close quarters. The Othonians above, poising and aiming their weapons with surer effect, rained them down on the Germans, who came rashly charging under the walls, naked, as is their national custom, chanting fiercely and brandishing their shields over their heads. Meanwhile, the legionaries under cover of their screens and fascines undermined the walls, built up a mound, and assailed the gates, while Otho's Guards rolled onto them with terrific crashes huge millstones, which they had arranged for this purpose along the walls. Of those beneath, some were crushed by the stones; others were pierced through and left mangled and bleeding to death. Panic redoubled the slaughter, and the missiles from the walls came all the fiercer and more disabling. They retreated, their party's reputation ruined.

Caecina, ashamed of his rash attempt at assault, was afraid of looking ridiculous and useless if he sat still in the same camp. So he recrossed the Po and made for Cremona. As he was retiring, Turullius Cerialis with a large force of marines, and Julius Briganticus with a few cavalry, surrendered to him. The latter, a Batavian by birth, had held a cavalry command: the former was a senior centurion, who was known to Caecina, as he had commanded a company in Germany.

Spurinna, learning the enemy's route, informed Annius 23 Gallus by letter of all that had happened, the defence of Placentia and Caecina's plans. Gallus was leading the First

Legion to the relief of Placentia, for he doubted the ability of so few cohorts to resist a long siege and the full strength of the German army. Hearing that Caecina was defeated and making for Cremona, he halted at Bedriacum, though he found it hard to restrain his troops, whose zeal for battle nearly broke into mutiny. The village of Bedriacum lies between Verona and Cremona, and two Roman disasters have now given it a sinister notoriety.

Around the same time Martius Macer gained a victory in the neighbourhood of Cremona. With great enterprise he had transported his gladiators over the Po in boats, and suddenly unleashed them onto the opposite bank. There they routed the Vitellian auxiliaries and killed all who offered resistance, the rest taking flight to Cremona. But Macer checked their victorious ardour, in case the enemy acquired reinforcements and reversed the fortune of the battle.

This aroused suspicion among the Othonians, who put a bad construction on all that their generals did. All the least courageous and most impudent of the troops vied with each other in assailing with various accusations Annius Gallus, Suetonius Paulinus, and Marius Celsus (for the two latter had also been placed in command by Otho). The most energetic in promoting mutiny and dissension were Galba's murderers, who, maddened by fear and guilt, created endless disorder, sometimes talking open sedition, sometimes sending secret letters to Otho. As he always believed the lowest sort of man, and feared the virtuous, he now wavered nervously, being always irresolute in success and firmer in the face of danger. He therefore sent for his brother Titianus and gave him the chief command.

24   Meanwhile, success attended the generalship of Paulinus and Celsus. Caecina was tortured by his constant failure and the waning reputation of his army. Repulsed from Placentia, he had lately seen his auxiliaries slaughtered, and even his patrols constantly worsted in skirmishes more frequent than memorable. Now that Fabius Valens was close at hand, he determined not to let all the glory of the war fall to him, and hastened with more greed than prudence to retrieve his reputation. About twelve miles distant from Cremona, at a place

called Castores,* he carefully concealed his most aggressive
auxiliaries in a wood overlooking the road. The cavalry were
ordered to ride further forward and provoke an engagement.
They were then to feign flight and lure the enemy into an
impetuous pursuit, until they fell into the ambush.

This plan was betrayed to Otho's generals. Paulinus took
charge of the infantry, Celsus of the horse. A detachment of
the Thirteenth Legion, four auxiliary cohorts, and 500 cavalry
were stationed on the left flank. Three cohorts of the Guards
in column occupied the raised high road. On the right flank
marched the First Legion, two auxiliary cohorts, and 500
cavalry. Besides these they moved out 1,000 cavalry drawn
from Guards and auxiliaries, as a reserve to crown their
success, or assist them in difficulties.

Before they came to close quarters, the Vitellians began to 25
retire. Celsus, forewarned of the ruse, halted his men. Whereupon the Vitellians impatiently rose from their ambush and,
while Celsus slowly retired, followed him further and further
until they plunged headlong into an ambush themselves. The
auxiliaries were on their flanks; the legions faced them in
front; and the cavalry had suddenly divided and closed in on
their rear. However, Suetonius Paulinus did not immediately
give the signal for his infantry to join battle. He was by nature
dilatory, the sort who prefers cautiously reasoned measures to
accidental success. He kept on issuing orders about filling up
the ditches, clearing the fields, and extending the line, convinced that it was soon enough to begin his victory when he
had taken every precaution against defeat. This delay gave the
Vitellians time to take refuge in the vineyards, where the
interlaced vine-stems made it hard to follow. Adjoining these
was a little wood, under cover of which they took heart anew
and killed the foremost of the Guards' cavalry. There Prince
Epiphanes* was wounded, while vigorously rallying Otho's
forces.

At this point Otho's infantry charged, crushed the opposing 26
line, and even routed the troops who were hurrying up in
support. For Caecina had brought up his auxiliaries not all at
once but in separate detachments. These, arriving in scattered
units, and never in sufficient force, only added to the confu-

sion, since they were caught up in the panic of the rout. In the camp, moreover, the troops mutinied over the failure to lead the entire army into battle. Julius Gratus, the camp prefect, was put in irons on the charge of planning to betray the army to his brother,* who was fighting on Otho's side: the Othonians had arrested the brother, the tribune Julius Fronto, on the same charge.

But such was the universal panic among the pursued and their assailants, on the field and before the camp, that it was commonly said on both sides that, if Suetonius Paulinus had not sounded the retreat, Caecina's whole army might have been destroyed. Paulinus maintained that he avoided any excessive strain of work or marching, for fear of exposing his exhausted troops to a counterattack from the Vitellians in the camp, who were still fresh for battle: besides, he had no reserves to fall back on in case of defeat. A few approved of the general's strategy, but the common opinion was against him.

27 This reverse reduced the Vitellians not to despair but to discipline. Not only was this the case in the camp of Caecina, who blamed his men as being readier for mutiny than for battle, but the troops under Fabius Valens, who had now reached Ticinum, lost their contempt for the enemy, conceived a desire to retrieve their glory, and offered their general a more respectful and steady obedience.

There had, all the same, been a serious outbreak of mutiny. It had begun at an earlier point in the story, to which I shall now revert—it seemed wrong to break the narrative of Caecina's operations. The Batavian cohorts, who had left the Fourteenth Legion during the war against Vindex, heard of Vitellius' rising while on their way to Britain, and, as I have already described, joined Fabius Valens in the country of the Lingones. There they grew insolent. Whenever they passed the tents of the Roman soldiers, they boasted that they had kept the Fourteenth under control, had deprived Nero of Italy, and held the whole issue of the war in the palm of their hand. This insulted the soldiers and galled the general; brawls and quarrels ruined good discipline. Ultimately Valens began to suspect that their insubordination meant treachery.

Accordingly, on receiving the news that Otho's fleet had 28
defeated the Treviran cavalry and the Tungri, and was now
blockading Narbonese Gaul, he determined to assist his allies,
and at the same time by a stroke of generalship to separate
contingents that were so undisciplined and, if united, so
strong. He therefore ordered a section of the Batavians to
march to the rescue. Immediately this order became generally
known, the auxiliaries began to complain and the legionaries
to chafe. They were, they said, being deprived of their strongest support. Here were these veterans, so often victorious in
war—but directly the enemy came in sight they were being
withdrawn virtually from the battle-line. If the province was
more important than the safety of Rome and the empire, why
was everybody not following them there? But if Italy was
the corner-stone of victory, the Batavians ought not to be
severed from the army—it would be like amputating a body's
strongest limbs.

In answer to this fierce criticism, Valens loosed his lictors 29
upon them and set to work to check the mutiny: but they
attacked him, stoned him, and chased him out of the camp,
shouting that he was concealing the spoils of Gaul and the
gold from Vienne, the due reward of their labours. They
looted the baggage, ransacked the general's quarters, and even
rummaged in the ground with javelins and lances; Valens, in
slave's dress, took refuge with a cavalry officer. Gradually the
disorder began to die down, aided by the policy of Alfenus
Varus, the camp prefect: the centurions were forbidden to
inspect the sentries, and no bugle sounded to summon the men
to their martial duties. As a consequence all were paralysed:
they eyed each other in astonishment, dismayed above all at
having no one to command them. By silence, by submission,
but at last with tearful prayers, they sought pardon. Valens
appeared, squalid and in tears, but unexpectedly safe and
sound—such delight, sympathy, and cheers. Mobs oscillate
between extremes of emotion; theirs had now changed to joy.
They made a ring round him with the eagles and standards,
and carried him to the Tribunal platform with praises and
congratulations. With prudent moderation he demanded no
punishment for anyone, but, to disarm suspicion of his good

faith, he criticized one or two of them severely. He was well aware that in civil war the men are allowed more licence than their generals.

30   While they were entrenching themselves at Ticinum they heard the news of Caecina's defeat, and the mutiny nearly broke out afresh:* Valens, they thought, had treacherously delayed in order to keep them out of the battle. They refused rest, would not wait for the general, marched on in front of the standards, hurrying on the bearers, and swiftly marched to join Caecina.

Valens had a bad name with Caecina's army. They complained that despite their greatly inferior numbers he had exposed them to the full force of the enemy. At the same time, for fear of being despised as defeated cowards, they excused themselves and flattered the new arrivals by exaggerating their strength. In fact, though Valens' numbers were larger, and he had almost twice as many legionaries and auxiliaries as Caecina, yet it was Caecina who enjoyed the confidence of the men. Apart from his kindness, in which he seemed much readier than Valens, they admired him for his youthful vigour and commanding stature; but some of their partiality was also quite irrational.

So there was rivalry between the generals. Caecina mocked at Valens for his dirty and dishonest ways, Valens at Caecina's pompous vanity. But they smothered their dislike and worked together for a common end, writing frequent letters in which they sacrificed all hope of pardon and heaped abuse on Otho. Otho's generals refrained from retaliating upon Vitellius,
31 though his character offered richer scope. Certainly before their respective deaths, in which Otho earned a noble name and Vitellius a most infamous one, people were more afraid of Otho's burning passions than of Vitellius' listless luxury. Moreover, the murder of Galba had made Otho feared and hated, while no one attributed to Vitellius the outbreak of the war. It was felt that Vitellius' gluttony was a personal disgrace: Otho's self-indulgence, cruelty, and recklessness spelt more danger to the country.*

Now that Caecina and Valens had combined forces, the Vitellians had no longer anything to delay them from joining

battle with their entire army. Otho held a council to decide
whether he should prolong the war or put his fortune to the
test. Suetonius Paulinus, who was considered the cleverest 32
general of his day, now felt that he owed it to his reputation
to deliver his views on the general conduct of the war. His
contention was that the enemy's interests were best served by
haste, Otho's by delay.

'The whole of Vitellius' force', he argued, 'has now arrived
and he has few reinforcements in his rear, for the Gallic
provinces are in a ferment, and it would be imprudent to
abandon the Rhine with tribes so hostile ready to swarm
across it. The troops in Britain are obstructed by their own
foes and the sea: the Spanish provinces can scarcely spare
any troops: the Narbonese are seriously alarmed by their
recent reverse and the inroads of our fleet. Italy north of the
Po is shut in by the Alps and denied all supplies by sea, and,
besides, the passage of their army has left it a wasteland.
Nowhere can they get grain, and without supplies no army
can be kept together. The German troops are their fiercest
fighting arm, but their constitutions will not be strong enough
to stand the change of climate and weather, if we protract the
war into summer. Often a force that is powerful when on the
offensive has dwindled to nothing through the tedium of
inaction.

'On the other hand, our resources are rich and reliable. We
have on our side Pannonia, Moesia, Dalmatia, and the East:
the armies there are fresh and strong. We have Italy and
Rome, the capital of the world, and the Roman Senate and
People: those titles are never obscure, though their glory may
sometimes be veiled. We have large public and private resources, and in civil war a vast quantity of money is stronger
than the sword. Our soldiers are inured to the Italian climate
or, at any rate, to heat. We are entrenched behind the Po: its
cities are protected by their walls and inhabitants, and the
defence of Placentia has shown that none of them will yield to
the enemy.'

Therefore, he said, Otho should prolong the war. In a few
days the Fourteenth Legion would arrive: its fame alone was
great, and the Moesian forces would be with it. He should, at

any rate, postpone his deliberations until then, and if he determined on battle, they would fight with augmented strength.

33   Marius Celsus supported Paulinus. Annius Gallus had been hurt a few days before by a fall from his horse, but messengers were sent to inquire his views, and they reported that he too agreed. Otho inclined to a decisive engagement. His brother Titianus and Proculus, the Prefect of the Guards, with all the impatience of inexperience, stoutly maintained that fortune, the gods, and Otho's divine power inspired his policy, and would inspire its performance. They had descended to flattery* by way of checking opposition.

When it was decided to take the offensive, the question arose whether Otho in person should take part in the battle or hold himself in reserve. Those bad counsellors again carried their point. Otho was to retire to Brixellum,* and, by withdrawing from the hazards of the field, reserve himself for the supreme control of the campaign and of the empire. To this Paulinus and Celsus offered no further opposition, for fear of seeming to endanger the person of their Emperor.

From this day dates the decline of Otho's party. Not only did he take with him a considerable force of the Guards, Body Guard, and cavalry, but the spirit of the troops who remained behind was broken. The men trusted no one but Otho, and Otho no one but the men. His generals were under suspicion and their authority left in doubt.

34   None of these arrangements failed to reach the ears of the Vitellians. Desertions were frequent, as they always are in civil war, and the scouts in their eagerness to discover the enemy's plans failed to conceal their own. Caecina and Valens, counting on the fatal impatience of the enemy, remained quietly on their guard to await another's folly—a good substitute for wisdom. Feigning an intention of crossing the Po, they began to construct a bridge, partly against the gladiators on the opposite bank, partly to find something for their idle troops to do.* Boats were placed at equal intervals with their heads upstream and fastened together by strong wooden planks. They also cast anchors from them to ensure the solidity of the bridge, but they allowed the hawsers to drift slack, so that

when the river rose the boats might all rise with it without the
line being broken. To enclose the bridge a tower was built
on it, and extended out to the end boat; from it they could
repulse the enemy with engines and catapults. Meanwhile the
Othonians had built a tower on the bank and kept up a steady
shower of stones and torches.

In midstream there was an island, to which the gladiators 35
struggled in boats, while the Germans swam to it floating
downstream. It happened that the latter were across in some
numbers: Macer manned Liburnian cruisers and attacked
them with the keenest of his gladiators. But in battle gladiators are less steadfast than soldiers, and from their unsteady
boats they could not shoot so well as the others, who had a
firm footing on the bank. Swaying this way and that in their
alarm, the sailors and the marines were beginning to get in
each other's way, when the Germans took the initiative, leapt
into the shallows, caught hold of the sterns, and either clambered up by the gangways or sunk them bodily with their own
hands. All this took place before the eyes of both armies, and
the greater the joy of the Vitellians, the fiercer the curses of
the Othonians against Macer, the author and cause of their
disaster.

The remainder of the boats were dragged off, and the battle 36
ended in flight. The army demanded Macer's execution. He
had already been wounded by a lance that had been flung at
him, and the soldiers were rushing on him with drawn swords
when the tribunes and centurions intervened and rescued
him. Soon after this, Vestricius Spurinna, on Otho's orders,
brought up a reinforcement of the Guards, leaving behind a
small garrison at Placentia; then Otho sent the consul-elect,
Flavius Sabinus, to take command of Macer's force. This
change of generals pleased the soldiers, but the frequent mutinies made the generals unwilling to assume such a perilous
command.

In some of my authorities I find a statement that either fear 37
of war or scorn for the two emperors, whose scandalous
misconduct grew daily more notorious, led the armies to
wonder whether they should not give up the struggle and
either negotiate jointly among themselves or refer the choice

of an emperor to the Senate. This, it is suggested, was the motive of Otho's generals in advising delay, and Paulinus in particular had high hopes, since he was the senior ex-consul, and a distinguished general who had earned a brilliant reputation by his operations in Britain. For my own part, while I am ready to admit that a few people may have tacitly wished for peace instead of civil war, or for a good and virtuous emperor instead of two who were the worst of criminals, yet I imagine that Paulinus was much too wise* to hope that in a time of universal corruption the mob would show such moderation. Those who had sacrificed peace in a passion for war were not likely to stop the war from any affection for peace. Nor was it possible that armies whose language and characteristics differed so widely should ever come to such an agreement. As for the officers and generals, hedonism, bankruptcy, and crimes had left nearly all of them with guilty consciences: they would not put up with any emperor who was not corrupt and under an obligation for their services.

38   The old ingrained human passion for power has matured and burst into prominence with the growth of the empire. With straiter resources equality was easily preserved. But when once we had brought the world to our feet and exterminated every rival state or king, we were left free to covet wealth without fear.* It was then that strife first flared up* between patricians and plebeians: at one time arose seditious tribunes, at another over-mighty consuls: in the Forum at Rome they had trial runs for civil war. Before long, Gaius Marius, rising from the lowest ranks of the people, and Lucius Sulla,* the most cruel of all the nobles, crushed our liberty by force of arms and substituted a despotism. Then came Gnaeus Pompey, whose aims, though less patent, were no better. From that time onwards the one end sought was autocracy. Even at Pharsalia and Philippi the citizen armies did not lay down their arms. How then can we suppose that the troops of Otho and Vitellius would have willingly stopped the war? The same anger of heaven, the same human frenzy, the same criminal motives drove them into discord. True, these wars were each settled by a single blow, but that was due to the generals' lack of spirit. However, my reflections on the ancient

and the modern character have carried me too far: I must now resume the thread of the narrative.

When Otho started for Brixellum, he left his brother 39 Titianus in nominal command, but power and control lay with the Prefect Proculus. As for Celsus and Paulinus, no one made use of their sagacity; their rank as general was a sham, enabling them only to act as a screen for other people's faults. The tribunes and centurions were in two minds, since the better ones had been slighted, and the worst were in charge. The men were full of spirit, but preferred commenting upon their officers' orders to carrying them out.

It was decided to advance and encamp four miles from Bedriacum—but it was done so ineptly that, though it was spring, and rivers abounded, the men suffered from want of water. Here they were in doubt whether to join battle, for Otho kept sending dispatches urging haste, but the soldiers kept clamouring for their Emperor to be present at the fight. Many demanded that the troops stationed across the Po should be brought up. It is not so easy to decide what was the best thing to do, as to be sure that what they did do was the worst.

They set out as if going on a campaign, not to a fight. Their 40 objective was the confluence of the Po and the Addua,* sixteen miles away. Celsus and Paulinus refused to expose their troops, fatigued by the march and heavily kitted out, to the assault of an enemy who was battle-ready, had barely four miles to cover, and who would certainly attack them, either while they were in the disorder of a marching column, or when they had broken up to build the ramparts. However, Titianus and Proculus, worsted in argument, appealed to their authority: and it is true that there had arrived post-haste a Numidian with a savage directive from Otho, inveighing against his generals' inaction, and ordering them to bring matters to a head. He was sick of delay and too impatient to live on hope.

On that same day, while Caecina was busy with the bridge- 41 building operations, two tribunes of the Guards came and demanded an interview. He was preparing to hear and answer their proposals, when some scouts burst in with the news that the enemy were close at hand. The tribunes' conversation was thus interrupted, and it was left uncertain whether they were broaching a trick or a piece of treachery, or some honourable plan. Caecina, dismissing the tribunes, rode back to the camp, where he found that Fabius Valens had given orders to sound for battle, and the troops were already under arms.

While the legions were balloting for their places in the marching order, the cavalry rode out and charged. Strange to say, they would have been hurled back upon the ramparts by a smaller force of Othonians, had not the Italian Legion bravely stopped them by drawing their swords and forcing the retreating troops to go back and resume the fight. The Vitellian legions formed without any disorder, for though the enemy were close at hand, thick plantations hid the approaching force. In the Othonian army the generals were nervous and the men ill-disposed towards them: they were hindered by carts and camp-followers, and the road, with its steep ditches on either side, was too narrow even for a peaceful march. Some of the men formed round their standards, others went searching for their place: on every side there was an uproar as men ran about shouting to each other: the boldest kept pressing on to the front, while the tide of the timid ebbed to the rear.

42   Amid the confusion of this sudden panic some people invented a story that Vitellius' army had abandoned his cause: whereupon an unwarrantable glee relaxed the Othonians' efforts. It was never fully known whether this report was spread by Vitellian scouts or whether it was started on Otho's own side, either by treachery or chance. Losing all their thirst for battle, the Othonians broke into a spontaneous cheer. The enemy answered with angry muttering, and most of Otho's soldiers, having no idea what caused the cheering, feared treachery.

At this point the Vitellian line charged, their ranks unbroken; they were stronger and more numerous. However, the Othonians, despite their disorder, fewer numbers, and fatigue, offered fierce resistance. The area was encumbered with trees and vines, and the character of the battle varied. They fought now from a distance, now at close quarters, and charged sometimes in detachment, sometimes in column. On the high road they fought hand to hand, using the weight of their bodies and their shields. They gave up throwing their javelins and cut through helmet and breastplate with sword and axe. Each man knew his foe; they were in view of their comrades; they fought with the outcome of the whole war depending on them.

It happened that two legions met in the open fields between 43 the road and the Po. These were: for Vitellius the Twenty-First, commonly called Rapax, a regiment of old renown; and for Otho the First Adiutrix, which had never been in battle before,* but was full of spirit and eager to win its first laurels. The First overthrew the front ranks of the Twenty-First, and they carried off its eagle. Fired with indignation, the Twenty-First rallied and charged the enemy, killing the commanding officer, Orfidius Benignus, and capturing many of their colours and standards.

Elsewhere in the battle, the Fifth drove the Thirteenth off the field. The Fourteenth was attacked by superior numbers and surrounded. Otho's generals had long ago fled. Caecina and Valens began to bring up the reserves to the support of their men, and, as a fresh reinforcement, there arrived Alfenus Varus with his Batavians. They had routed the gladiators by confronting them and cutting them to pieces in the river before their transports could land, and flushed by their victory came charging in upon the flank of the enemy.

Their centre broken, the Othonians fled in disorder, making 44 for Bedriacum. The distance was immense; the roads encumbered with heaps of dead. This made the slaughter all the greater, for in civil war captives cannot be turned to profit. Suetonius Paulinus and Licinius Proculus, going by different routes, avoided the camp. Vedius Aquila, who commanded the Thirteenth Legion, panicked irrationally and so fell into the hands of his indignant troops. It was still broad daylight when he entered the ramparts. Immediately a crowd of mutinous fugitives came clamouring round him. They spared neither abuse nor violence, assailing him as a deserter and a traitor. They could bring no special charge against him, but the mob always accuses others of its own transgressions.

84   THE HISTORIES   [2, 45]

Night came to the aid of Titianus and Celsus, for Annius Gallus had already placed sentinels on guard and got the men under control. By words of advice, by prayers, by his personal authority, he had induced them not to add to the disaster of their defeat by brutally murdering their own friends. Whether the war was over, or whether they wanted to fight again, union, he told them, was the one thing that mitigated defeat.

All the other troops were crushed by the blow. The Guards complained that they had been beaten, not by the enemy's valour, but by sheer treachery. 'Why,' they said, 'even the Vitellians have won no bloodless victory. We beat their cavalry and captured a eagle from one of their legions. We still have Otho left and all the troops with him on the other side of the Po. The Moesian legions are on their way. A large part of the army was left behind at Bedriacum. These, at any rate, have not been defeated yet: they would, if need be, die more honourably in battle.' These reflections made them savage or else nervous: but their state of blank despair more often aroused their anger than their fear.

45   The Vitellian army bivouacked at the fifth milestone on the road from Bedriacum. Their generals would not venture to storm the camp that same day, and hoped the enemy would consent to surrender. However, although they had marched out equipped only with what they needed for battle, their weapons and their victory acted as their fortifications.

On the next day there was no doubt about the wishes of the Othonians. Even those who showed most spirit had now changed their minds. So they sent a deputation. The Vitellian generals had no hesitation in granting terms.* However, they detained the deputation for a short time, which caused some qualms to those who did not know whether it had been successful. At length the envoys returned, and the camp was opened up. Then both victors and vanquished burst into tears, and with sorrowful satisfaction cursed their fate of civil war. Sitting in the same tents, they nursed wounded brothers or other relatives. Their hopes of recompense were doubtful: all that was certain was bereavement and grief, for no one was so fortunate as to mourn no loss. They searched for the body of the fallen commander, Orfidius, and burnt it with due solemnity. Of the other dead, a few were buried by their relatives, the great mass were left lying on the ground.

Otho was awaiting news of the battle with perfect confidence and firm resolve.* First came a disquieting rumour. Soon fugitives from the field revealed the ruin of his cause. But the soldiers in their zeal did not wait to hear their Emperor speak. 'Keep a good heart,' they said, 'you still have fresh forces left, and, as for us, we are ready to risk everything and suffer everything.' Nor was this flattery. In a wild passion of enthusiasm they burned to march to the field and restore the fortunes of their party. Those who were near him clasped his knees, while those who stood further off stretched out their arms to him. The most eager of all was Plotius Firmus, the Prefect of the Guards, who besought Otho again and again not to desert a supremely faithful army, men who had done him such great service. He told him that it showed more courage to bear misfortune than to desert it, that men of vigour and courage cling to their hopes even in the face of disaster: it is only cowards and faint-hearts who let their terror hurry them into despair. Amid all these appeals the soldiers now cheered, now groaned, according as Otho's expression relaxed or hardened. Nor were these feelings confined to the Guards, Otho's own troops. The first arrivals from Moesia assured him that the spirit of the advancing force was just as firm, and that the legions had already entered Aquileia. There is no room for doubt that it was still possible to revive this cruel and pitiable war,* so full of uncertainty to both victors and vanquished.

But Otho himself disliked the policy of fighting. 'Am I', he said, 'to expose all your splendid courage and valour to further risks? That would, I think, be too great a price to pay for my life. Your high hopes of succeeding, if I were minded to live, will only swell the glory of my death. We have learnt to know each other, Fortune and I. Do not merely count length of time. Self-control is all the harder when a man knows that his fortune cannot last. It was Vitellius who began the civil war: he initiated our contest* for the throne. But one battle is enough. This is the precedent that I will set: let posterity judge Otho by it. I do not grudge Vitellius his brother, or wife, or

46

47

children. I want neither revenge nor consolation. Others may
have held the sceptre longer, but no one can ever have laid it
down so bravely. Am I the man to allow the flower of Rome
in all these famous armies to be mown down once again and
lost to the country? Let me take with me the consciousness
that you would have died for me. But you must stay and live.
I must no longer interfere with your chance of pardon, nor
you with my resolve. It is a sort of cowardice to go on talking
about the end. Here is your best proof of my determination: I
complain of no one. To blame gods or men is the mark of one
who desires to live.'

48   After some such speech, he addressed each courteously in
turn, according to their age and position. He urged them to
hurry away and not to exasperate the victor by their hesitation, using his authority with the young and persuasion with
his elders, while his quiet looks and firm speech helped to
control their ill-timed tears. He gave orders for boats and
carriages to be provided for their departure. All petitions and
letters containing any marked compliments to himself, or
insults to Vitellius, he destroyed, and distributed his money
carefully,* not like a man at the point of death. He then went
out of his way to comfort the sorrowful fears of his brother's
young son Salvius Cocceianus, by praising his attachment and
chiding his alarm.

'Do you imagine', he said, 'that Vitellius will be so hard-
hearted as not to show me some gratitude for saving his whole
household? By promptly putting an end to myself, I deserve to
earn some mercy from the victor. For it is not in blank despair,
but with my army clamouring for battle, that I have saved my
country from the last calamities. I have won enough fame for
myself and ennoblement for my posterity; for, after the line of
the Julians, Claudians, and Servians,* I have been the first to
bring the principate into a new family. So go on with your life
with a lofty heart. Never forget that Otho was your uncle—
and never remember it overmuch.'*

49   After this he made them all retire, and rested for a while.
But his last preparations were interrupted by a sudden distur-
bance and the news of a mutinous outbreak among the troops.
They were threatening to kill those who were leaving, and

turned with especial violence against Verginius, whose house was in a state of siege. Otho rebuked the ringleaders and returned, consenting to receive the adieux of those who were going, until they were able to depart in safety.

As the day deepened into evening he quenched his thirst with a drink of iced water. Two daggers were brought to him and, after trying them both, he put one under his pillow. Being assured on enquiry that his friends had started, he spent a peaceful night, not, it is said, without sleep. At break of day he fell upon his dagger.* Hearing his dying groan, his slaves and freedmen entered with Plotius Firmus, the Prefect of the Guards, and found a single wound in his breast.

The funeral was hurried forward out of respect for his own earnest entreaties, for he had been afraid his head might be cut off and subjected to outrage. The Guard carried the body, sounding his praises with tears in their eyes, and covering his hands and wounded breast with kisses. Some of the soldiers killed themselves beside the pyre, not through servility or fear, but from love of their Emperor, and to follow his noble example. Similar suicides became common afterwards at Bedriacum and Placentia, and in other encampments. An inconspicuous tomb was built for Otho, as being less likely to be disturbed: and thus he ended his life in his thirty-seventh year.

Otho came originally from the town of Ferentium.* His 50 father had been consul and his grandfather praetor. His mother's family was inferior, but not without distinction. His boyhood and youth were such as I have indicated. By two acts, one most criminal and the other heroic, he earned in equal measure the praise and the reprobation of posterity.

I am of the view that it is beneath the dignity of my task to collect fictions and fables for the amusement of my readers, but there are certain popular traditions which I cannot venture to contradict. On the day of the battle of Bedriacum, according to the account of the locals, a bird of unprecedented appearance was seen in a much-frequented grove near Regium Lepidum.* There it sat, unterrified and unmoved, either by the crowds of people or by the birds which fluttered round it, until the moment at which Otho killed himself. Then it vanished. A calculation of the time showed that the prodigy's appearance and disappearance coincided with Otho's death.

51   At his funeral the rage and grief of the soldiers broke out into another mutiny. This time there was no one to control them. They turned to Verginius and begged him with threats now to accept the principate, now to head a deputation to Caecina and Valens. However, Verginius escaped them, slipping out by the back door of his house just as they broke in at the front. Rubrius Gallus* carried a petition from the Guards at Brixellum, and obtained immediate pardon. Flavius Sabinus surrendered to the victor the troops under his command.

52   Now that the war was everywhere ended, a large number of senators, who had quitted Rome with Otho and been left behind at Mutina, found themselves in a critical position. When the news of the defeat reached Mutina, the soldiers paid no heed to what they took for a baseless rumour, and, believing the senators to be hostile to Otho, they treasured up their conversation and put the worst interpretation on their looks and behaviour. In time they broke into abusive reproaches, seeking a pretext for starting a general massacre, while the senators suffered at the same time from another source of alarm, for they were afraid of seeming to be slow in welcoming the victory of the now predominant Vitellian party.

Terrified at their double danger, they held a meeting. For no one dared to form any policy for himself; each felt safer in sharing his guilt with others. The town council of Mutina, too, kept adding to their anxiety by offering them arms and money, styling them with ill-timed respect 'Conscript Fathers'.*

53   A remarkable quarrel arose at this meeting. Licinius Caecina attacked Eprius Marcellus* for the ambiguity of his language. Not that the others disclosed their sentiments, but Caecina, who was still a nobody, recently raised to the Senate, sought to distinguish himself by quarrelling with someone of importance, and selected Marcellus, because the memory of his career as an informer made him an object of loathing.

They were parted by the prudent intervention of their betters, and all then retired to Bononia,* intending to continue the discussion there, and hoping for more news in the meantime.

At Bononia they dispatched men along the roads in every direction to question all newcomers. From one of Otho's freedmen they inquired why he had come away, and were told he was carrying his master's last instructions: the man said that when he had left, Otho was still indeed alive, but had renounced the pleasures of life and was devoting all his thoughts to posterity. This filled them with admiration. They felt ashamed to ask any more questions—and in their hearts unanimously favoured Vitellius.

Vitellius' brother Lucius was present at their discussion, 54 and now displayed his willingness to receive their flattery; but one of Nero's freedmen, called Coenus, suddenly startled them all by inventing the atrocious falsehood that the Fourteenth Legion had joined forces with the troops at Brixellum, and that their sudden arrival had turned the fortune of the day: the victorious army had been cut to pieces. He hoped by inventing this good news to regain some authority for Otho's safe-conducts,* which were beginning to be disregarded. He did, indeed, thus ensure for himself a quick journey to Rome, but was punished by order of Vitellius a few days later.*

However, the Senate's danger was augmented because Otho's soldiers believed the news. Their fears were the more acute, because it looked as if their departure from Mutina was an official move, by which they had deserted Otho's party. So they refrained from holding any more meetings, and each looked after himself, until a letter arrived from Fabius Valens which quieted their fears. Besides, the news of Otho's death travelled all the more quickly because it excited admiration.

At Rome, however, there was no sign of panic. The festival 55 of Ceres was being celebrated with the usual spectacle. When it was reported in the theatre* on reliable authority that Otho had ended his life, and that Flavius Sabinus, the City Prefect, had made all the troops in Rome swear allegiance to Vitellius, the audience cheered Vitellius. The populace decked busts of Galba with laurel-leaves and flowers, and carried them round from temple to temple. The garlands were eventually piled up into a sort of tomb near the Lacus Curtius, on the spot which Galba had stained with his life-blood.

In the Senate the distinctions devised during the long reigns of other emperors were all conferred on Vitellius at once. To these was added a vote of thanks and congratulation to the German army, and a deputation was dispatched to express the Senate's satisfaction. Letters were read which Fabius Valens had addressed to the consuls in very moderate terms. But Caecina's moderation was still more gratifying: he had not written at all.*

56   However, Italy found peace a more ghastly burden than the war. Vitellius' soldiers scattered through all the boroughs and colonial towns, indulging in plunder, violence, and rape. Impelled by greed or venality, they cared nothing for right and wrong: kept their hands off nothing sacred or profane. Even civilians put on uniform and seized the opportunity to murder their enemies. The soldiers themselves, knowing the country-side well, marked down the richest fields and wealthiest houses for plunder—or murder, if anyone offered resistance. Their generals were too much in their debt to venture any opposition. Of the two Caecina was driven less by greed, more by ambition. Valens had earned a bad name by his own ill-gotten gains, and was therefore bound to shut his eyes to others' shortcomings. The resources of Italy had long been exhausted; all these thousands of infantry and cavalry, all this violence and damage and outrage was almost more than the country could bear.

57   Meanwhile Vitellius knew nothing of his victory. With the remainder of his German army he continued to advance as though the war had just begun. A few of the veterans were left in winter quarters, and troops were hurriedly enlisted in the Gallic provinces, to fill up the vacancies in the legions left behind. Leaving Hordeonius Flaccus to guard the line of the Rhine, Vitellius advanced with a picked detachment from the army in Britain, 8,000 strong.

After a few days' march he received news of the victory of Bedriacum and the collapse of the war on the death of Otho. He summoned a meeting and heaped praise on the courage of the troops. When the army demanded that he should confer equestrian rank on his freedman Asiaticus, he checked their shameful flattery. Then with characteristic instability he granted at a private banquet what he had refused in public. This Asiaticus, who was thus decorated with the gold rings, was an infamous menial who sought to rise by his vices.*

During these same days news arrived that Albinus, the 58 governor of Mauretania, had been murdered, and both provinces had declared for Vitellius. Appointed by Nero to the province of Mauretania Caesariensis, Lucceius Albinus* had further received from Galba the governorship of Tingitana, and thus commanded a very considerable force of auxiliaries: nineteen cohorts of infantry, five regiments of horse, and an immense horde of Moors, well trained for war by their practice in brigandage and plunder. After Galba's murder he inclined to Otho's side and, not contented with Africa, began to threaten Spain on the other side of the narrow strait. Cluvius Rufus, alarmed at this, moved the Tenth Legion down to the coast as though for a crossing. He also sent some centurions ahead to gain the sympathies of the Moors for Vitellius. The great reputation of the German army throughout the provinces facilitated this task, and they also spread a rumour that Albinus was not contented with the title of 'Procurator', and wanted to adopt a regal style under the name of Juba.* So the 59 sympathies of the army shifted. Asinius Pollio, who commanded the cavalry, one of Albinus' most loyal friends, was assassinated. The same fate befell Festus and Scipio, who were in command of the infantry. Albinus himself was journeying from Tingitana to Mauretania Caesariensis, and was murdered as he landed. His wife confronted the assassins and was murdered too. How all this happened Vitellius never inquired. He passed by events of the highest importance after a few moments' attention, being quite unable to cope with serious matters.

On reaching the Arar,* Vitellius ordered his army to march overland while he sailed down the river. Travelling with no imperial state, he had nothing but his original poverty to make him conspicuous, until Junius Blaesus, governor of the Lyons division of Gaul, a member of an eminent family,* whose liberality matched his wealth, provided the Emperor with a retinue and escorted him in lavish style, which earned him no thanks, although Vitellius concealed his malice under servile flattery.

At Lyons he found the generals of the victorious and vanquished parties awaiting him. Valens and Caecina were openly commended at a public meeting, and given places on either side of the Emperor's throne. He then sent the whole army out to meet his infant son,* and when they brought him wearing a general's cloak, Vitellius took him up in his arms and named him Germanicus, at the same time decorating him with all the insignia of his imperial position. The exaggerated honours of these days of prosperity proved a consolation in the evil times which followed.

60   The most energetic of Otho's centurions were now executed, which did more than anything else to alienate the armies of Illyricum. The other legions also caught the infection, and their dislike of the German troops made them harbour thoughts of war. Suetonius Paulinus and Licinius Proculus were left in misery and squalor while their case was adjourned. When at last it was heard, their pleas savoured more of necessity than honour. They positively claimed credit for treachery, alleging that the long march before the battle, the fatigue of their troops, the confusion created by the wagons in their lines, and various chance events, were due to their own deceit. Vitellius believed their protestations of treason, and acquitted them of all suspicion of loyalty. Otho's brother Salvius Titianus was in no danger. His affection for his brother and his personal inefficiency excused him. Marius Celsus was allowed to keep his consulship. But it was rumoured, and believed, that Caecilius Simplex had tried to purchase the consulship and to secure Celsus' destruction (Simplex later was charged with this in the Senate). Vitellius, however, refused, and afterwards allowed Simplex to hold the consulship without detriment to his conscience or his purse. Trachalus was protected against his accusers by Galeria, Vitellius' wife.

61   With so many of the great in danger of their lives, I am ashamed to say that a certain Mariccus, a commoner of the tribe of the Boii, boldly endeavoured to thrust himself into

greatness and to challenge the armies of Rome, pretending to
be divine.* This champion of Gaul, and god, as he had entitled
himself, had already gathered a force of 8,000 men, and was
beginning to influence the neighbouring Aeduan cantons. But
the chief community of the Aedui wisely sent out a picked
force, and Vitellius provided auxiliaries in support; they
scattered the mob of fanatics. Mariccus was captured in
the engagement, and later thrown to wild beasts. As they
refused to devour him, the common people stupidly believed
him invulnerable, until he was executed in the presence of
Vitellius. There was no further brutality against the rebels, or   62
against anyone's property. The estates of those who had fallen
fighting for Otho were allowed to devolve by will or else by
the law of intestacy.

Indeed, if Vitellius had set limits to his luxury, there was no
need to fear his greed for money. It was his foul and insatiable
gluttony. Rome and Italy were scoured for dainties to tickle
his palate: from shore to shore the high roads rang with the
traffic. The leading provincials were ruined by having to
provide for his feasts. The very towns were impoverished.
Meanwhile the soldiers were acquiring luxurious habits,
learning to despise their general, and gradually losing their
former efficiency and courage.

Vitellius forwarded an edict to Rome, in which he declined
the title of Caesar, and postponed calling himself Augustus
without giving up any portion of his power. All astrologers
were exiled from Italy, and rigorous provision was made to
restrain Roman knights from the disgrace of appearing at the
games in the arena.* Previous emperors had paid, or more
often compelled, them to take part, and many of the provincial towns vied with one another to lure the most profligate
young aristocrats with gold.

The arrival of his brother, and the influence of those worm-   63
ing themselves in as his tutors in tyranny, made Vitellius more
haughty and cruel. He gave orders for the execution of
Dolabella, whom Otho, as we have seen, had exiled to the
colonial town of Aquinas. On hearing of Otho's death, he
had ventured back to Rome. Whereupon an ex-praetor,
named Plancius Varus,* one of Dolabella's closest friends, laid

information before the City Prefect, Flavius Sabinus, maintaining that he had broken from custody to put himself at the
head of the defeated party. He added that Dolabella had tried
to tamper with the cohort stationed at Ostia. Varus had no
proof of these very serious charges; he then repented and
begged for his friend's forgiveness. But it was too late: the
crime was committed. While Flavius Sabinus was hesitating
what to do in such a serious matter, Lucius Vitellius' wife
Triaria, whose cruelty was altogether unwomanly, terrified
him by suggesting that he was trying to get a reputation for
mercy at the expense of his Emperor's safety. Sabinus was
naturally of a kindly disposition, but easily changed under the
influence of fear. Though it was not he who was in danger, he
was alarmed for himself, and hastened Dolabella's impending
64 ruin for fear of being supposed to have helped him. Vitellius,
accordingly, from motives both of fear and of hatred
(Dolabella had married his divorced wife Petronia), summoned him by letter, and ordered that Dolabella was to avoid
the crowded thoroughfare of the Flaminian Way and to turn
off to Interamna,* where he was to be murdered. The assassin
thought this tedious; he flung his victim to the floor at a
wayside inn, and cut his throat. This gave the new government
a very bad name. People took it as a symbol of what to expect.
Triaria's shameless behaviour was further emphasized by being set beside the exemplary moderation of Galeria, the Emperor's wife, who kept clear of these dreadful doings. Equally
admirable was the character of the mother of the Vitellii,
Sextilia, a woman of the old school. It was even on record
that, on receiving her son's first letters, she said, 'It was no
Germanicus, but a Vitellius that I brought into the world.'
From that time neither the attractions of her high station nor
the flattery of Rome could win her over to complacence. She
shared only the sorrows of her house.
65   When Vitellius left Lyons, Cluvius Rufus, who had abandoned Spain, caught up with him. He knew that accusations
had been made against him, and his smiling congratulations
hid an anxious heart. A freedman of the imperial court,
Hilarus by name, had given evidence against him, alleging
that, when Cluvius heard of the rival claims of Otho and

Vitellius, he had endeavoured to set up an independent authority of his own in Spain, and to this end had issued safe-conducts with no emperor's name at the head. Certain phrases in his speeches were also construed as insulting to Vitellius and as a bid for his own popularity. However, Cluvius' influence carried the day, and Vitellius even had his own freedman punished. Cluvius was given a place in the Emperor's entourage, while still retaining Spain, of which he was absentee governor, following the precedent of Lucius Arruntius.* In Arruntius' case, however, the Emperor Tiberius' motive had been fear, whereas Vitellius detained Cluvius without any such qualms. Trebellius Maximus was not allowed the same privilege. He had fled from Britain to escape the fury of his troops. Vettius Bolanus, who was then about the court, was sent out to take his place.

The soldiers of the defeated legions still gave Vitellius a 66 good deal of anxiety. Their spirit was by no means broken. They were distributed all over Italy, mingling with the victors and talking treason. The most uncompromising of all were the Fourteenth, who refused to acknowledge their defeat. At the battle of Bedriacum, they argued, it was only a detachment that had been beaten: the main strength of the legion was not present. It was decided to send them back to Britain, whence Nero had summoned them, and meanwhile they were to share their quarters with the Batavian cohorts, because of the long-standing feud between them.

Quartered as they were under arms, their strong mutual hatred soon broke out into disorder. At Turin one of the Batavians was cursing a workman for having cheated him, when a legionary, who lodged with the workman, took his part. Each quickly gathered his fellow-soldiers round him, and from abuse they came to bloodshed. Indeed, a fierce battle would have broken out, had not two cohorts of Guards sided with the Fourteenth, thus giving them confidence and frightening the Batavians.

Vitellius gave orders that the Batavians should be attached to his army as a mark of their fidelity, while the legion was to be marched over the Graian Alps by a detour which would avoid Vienne (its inhabitants were another cause for alarm).

On the night on which the legion started they left fires burning all over Turin, and part of the town was burnt down. This disaster, like so many others in the war, has been obliterated by the greater calamities which befell other cities. No sooner were the Fourteenth across the Alps than the most mutinous spirits started off to march for Vienne, but they were stopped by the unanimous action of the better men, and the legion was shipped across to Britain.

67   Vitellius' next cause of anxiety was the Guards. At first they were quartered apart, and then, appeased by an honourable discharge, they gave up their arms to their tribunes. But when the war started by Vespasian intensified, they enlisted again and formed the main strength of the Flavian party.

The First Legion of marines was sent to Spain to cultivate docility in peace and quiet. The Eleventh and the Seventh were sent back to their winter quarters. The Thirteenth was set to work to build amphitheatres. For Caecina at Cremona and Valens at Bononia were each preparing to give a gladiatorial show. Vitellius never let his anxieties interfere with his pleasures.

68   Vitellius had shown restraint in dispersing the losing party; but disorder broke out in the victorious camp. It originated in sport, but the number of deaths increased the feeling against Vitellius. He had invited Verginius to a feast at Ticinum, and had settled down to eat. The conduct of senior officers is always determined by the behaviour of their generals: whether they imitate his austerity or enjoy elaborate banquets. This again determines whether the troops are alert or undisciplined. In Vitellius' army disorder and drunkenness were universal: it was more like a midnight orgy than a properly disciplined camp. So it happened that two of the soldiers, one belonging to the Fifth Legion, the other to the Gallic auxiliaries, in an unruly frolic were excited into a wrestling match. The legionary fell; and when the Gaul began to exult over him, the soldiers who had gathered round took sides; the legionaries broke out against the auxiliaries with murderous intent, and cut to pieces a couple of cohorts. This commotion was only cured by another. A cloud of dust and the glitter of arms appeared on the horizon. Suddenly a cry arose that the

Fourteenth had turned back and were marching on them. However, it was the army's own rearguard; this discovery quieted their alarm.

Meanwhile, coming across one of Verginius' slaves, the soldiers charged him with intending to assassinate Vitellius, and rushed off to the banquet clamouring for Verginius' head. No one really doubted his innocence, not even Vitellius, who always quailed at a breath of suspicion. Yet, though it was the death of an ex-consul, their own former general, which they demanded, it was with difficulty that they were quieted. No one was the target of every mutinous act as regularly as Verginius. He still retained the admiration and esteem of the men, but they hated him for disdaining them.

On the next day Vitellius granted an audience to the depu- 69 tation of the Senate, which he had told to await him at Ticinum. He then entered the camp and spontaneously complimented the troops on their devotion to him. This made the auxiliaries grumble at the extensive impunity* and arrogance now enjoyed by the legions. So, to keep the Batavian cohorts from desperate acts of still greater savagery, they were sent back to Germany: this was to be the origin, contrived by Fate, of a war that was at once both civil and foreign.

The Gallic auxiliaries were also sent home. Their numbers were very large, and had been used at the first outbreak of the rebellion for an empty parade of force. Indeed, the imperial finances were already embarrassed by the distribution of largess, to meet the expenses of which Vitellius gave orders for depleting the strength of the legions and auxiliaries. Recruiting was forbidden, and discharges offered without restriction. This policy was disastrous for the country and unpopular among the soldiers, who found that their turn for work and danger came round all the more frequently, now that there were so few to share the same duties. Besides, their energy was being corroded by luxury, the reverse of the old-fashioned discipline and the good rules of our ancestors, who preferred to base the security of Rome on character than on money.

Leaving Ticinum, Vitellius turned off to Cremona. There he 70 witnessed Caecina's games and conceived a wish to stand upon the field of Bedriacum, and to see the traces of the recent victory with his own eyes. Within forty days of the battle, it was a disgusting and horrible sight; mangled bodies, mutilated limbs, rotting carcasses of men and horses, the ground foul with clotted blood. Trees and crops all trampled down: the countryside a miserable waste. No less heartless was the stretch of road which the people of Cremona had strewn with laurel-leaves and roses, erecting altars and sacrificing victims as if in honour of an Oriental despot. The rejoicings of the moment soon turned to their destruction.

Valens and Caecina were in attendance and showed Vitellius over the battlefield: this was where their legions had charged: the cavalry launched their attack from here: this was where the auxiliaries had outflanked the enemy. The various officers each magnified his own exploits, adding a few false or, at any rate, exaggerated touches. The common soldiers, too, turned gaily shouting from the high road to inspect the scene of the struggle, gazing with wonder at the huge pile of arms and heaps of bodies. There were a few who reflected with tears of pity on the shifting chances of life. But Vitellius never took his eyes off the field: never shuddered at the sight of all these thousands of Roman citizens lying unburied. On the contrary, he was very well pleased,* and, unconscious of his own impending doom, he offered a sacrifice to the local deities.

71   They next came to Bononia, where Fabius Valens gave a gladiatorial show, for which he had all the apparatus brought from Rome. The nearer they drew to the city, the greater became the depravity of the march, which was now joined by troops of actors, eunuchs, and the like, all in the true spirit of Nero's court. For Vitellius always had a great personal admiration for Nero. He used to follow him about to hear him sing, not under compulsion—many a decent man suffered that fate—but because he was the slave of his stomach, and had sold himself to luxury.

To secure a few months of office for Valens and Caecina, the other consuls of the year had their terms shortened, while Martius Macer's claim was ignored on the grounds that he was a leader of Otho's party. Valerius Marinus, who had been nominated by Galba, had his term postponed, not for any offence, but because he was a mild creature and too lazy to resent an injury. The name of Pedanius Costa* was omitted altogether. Vitellius had never forgiven him for rising against Nero and instigating Verginius; however, he alleged other reasons. They all moreover observed the servile custom of the time, and offered their thanks to Vitellius.

An imposture, received at first with great excitement, failed 72 to last more than a few days. A man had appeared who gave out that he was Scribonianus Camerinus,* and that during Nero's reign of terror he had taken refuge in Histria, where the Crassi still had their old connections and estates, and their name was much respected. He accordingly took all the rascals he could find and cast them for parts. The credulous mob and some of the soldiers, who were either victims of the imposture or anxious for a riot, eagerly flocked to join him. However, he was taken before Vitellius and questioned as to his identity. When it was found that there was no truth in his story, and his master recognized him as a runaway called Geta, he suffered the execution of a slave.*

When his couriers brought news from Syria and Judaea that 73 the East had sworn allegiance to him, Vitellius' vanity and indolence reached a pitch which is almost incredible. For already, though the rumours were still vague and unreliable, Vespasian's name was in everybody's mouth, and the mention of him generally shocked Vitellius. But now he and his army seemed to reck of no rival: they at once broke out into the unbridled cruelty, debauchery, and oppression more usual among foreigners.

Vespasian, on the other hand, was meditating war* and 74 reckoning all his forces both distant and near at hand. He had so much attached his troops to himself, that when he dictated to them the oath of allegiance and prayed that 'all might be well' with Vitellius, they listened in silence. Mucianus' feelings were not hostile to him, and were even more sympathetic to Titus. Tiberius Alexander, the governor of Egypt, had made common cause with him. The Third Legion,* since it had crossed into Moesia from Syria, he could reckon as his own, and there was good hope that the other legions of Illyria would follow its lead. The whole army, indeed, was incensed at the arrogance of Vitellius' soldiers: truculent in action and rough of tongue, they scoffed at all the other troops as their inferiors.

But a war of such magnitude usually causes hesitation. High as were his hopes, Vespasian would sometimes calculate his risks. He realized that it would be a critical day for him when he committed his sixty summers and his two youthful sons* to the chances of war. In his private ambitions a man may feel his way and rely less or more on fortune according as he feels inclined; but when one covets a throne there is no middle way

75 between the zenith of success and headlong ruin. Moreover, as a soldier he realized the strength of the German army, and always kept it in view. His own legions, he knew, had no experience of civil war, while Vitellius' troops were fresh from victory: and the defeated party were richer in grievances than in troops. Civil strife had undermined the loyalty of the troops: there was danger in each single man. What would be the good of all his horse and foot regiments, if one or two traitors should seek the reward the enemy offered and assassinate him then and there? It was thus that Scribonianus had been killed in Claudius' reign, and his murderer, Volaginius, raised from a common soldier to the highest rank. It is easier to move men in the mass than to take precautions against them singly.

76 These anxieties made Vespasian hesitate. Meanwhile the other generals and his friends continued to encourage him. At last Mucianus, after several private interviews, went so far as to address him in public, as follows:*

'Everybody', he said, 'who plans some great exploit is bound to consider whether his project serves both the public interest and his own reputation, and whether it is easily practicable or, at any rate, not impossible. He must also weigh the advice which he gets. Are those who offer it ready to run the risk themselves? And, if fortune favours the undertaking, who gains the supreme glory? I myself, Vespasian, call you to the throne. How that may bring benefit to the country, and grandeur to you, lies with you—under Providence—to decide.

'You need not be afraid that I may seem to flatter you. It is more of an insult than a compliment to be chosen to succeed Vitellius. It is not against the powerful intellect of the deified Augustus that we are rising in revolt; not against the cautious prudence of the old Tiberius; nor even against a long-established imperial family like that of Gaius, Claudius, or Nero. You even gave way to Galba's ancient lineage. To remain inactive any longer, to leave your country to ruin and pollution, that would appear sheer sloth and cowardice, even if such slavery were as safe for you as it would be dishonourable. The time is long past when you could look unambitious: the throne is now your only refuge. Have you forgotten Corbulo's murder?* He was a man of better family than we, I admit, but so was Nero more nobly born than Vitellius. A man who is feared is always illustrious enough for the one who fears him.

'That an army can make an emperor Vitellius himself has proved. He had neither experience nor military reputation, but merely rose on Galba's unpopularity. Even Otho fell not by the generalship of his opponent or the might of his army, but by his own precipitate despair. And today he seems a great and desirable emperor, when Vitellius is disbanding his legions, disarming his Guards, and daily sowing fresh seeds of civil war. Why, any spirit or enthusiasm which his army had is being dissipated in carouses in cookshops: for they imitate their Emperor. But you, in Judaea, in Syria, in Egypt, you have nine fresh legions. War has not weakened nor mutiny demoralized them. The men are trained to discipline and have already won a foreign war. Besides these, you can rely on the strength of your fleet, and of your auxiliaries both horse and foot, on the faithful allegiance of foreign princes, and on your own unparalleled experience.

'For myself I make but one claim. Let me not rank below 77 Valens and Caecina. Nor must you despise Mucianus' help because you do not encounter his rivalry. I rank myself above Vitellius and below you. Your house has received the insignia of a triumph.* You have two youthful sons, one of whom already has the qualifications to be a ruler, and in his first years of service made a name for himself in the German armies. It would be absurd for me not to give way to one whose son I should adopt, were I emperor myself. Apart from this, we shall stand on a different footing in success and in failure, for if we succeed I shall have such honour as you grant me: of the risk and the dangers we shall share the burden equally. Or rather, do what is better still. Dispose your armies yourself and leave me the conduct of the war, and the uncertainties of battle.

'At this moment the defeated are more strictly disciplined than their conquerors: indignation, hatred, the passion for revenge, all serve to fire their courage. The Vitellians are dulled by pride and mutiny. The course of the war will soon bring to light and reopen the hidden and festering sores of the victorious party. I rely on your vigilance, your economy, your wisdom, and still more on the indolence, ignorance, and cruelty of Vitellius. Above all, our cause is far safer in war than in peace: for to plan rebellion is to have rebelled already.'

78   At the end of Mucianus' speech the others all pressed round with new confidence, offering their encouragement and quoting the answers of soothsayers and the movements of the stars. Nor was Vespasian uninfluenced by such superstition. In later days, when he was master of the world, he made no secret of keeping an astrologer called Seleucus to help him by his advice and prophecy. Early omens began to recur to his memory. A tall and conspicuous cypress on his estate had once suddenly collapsed: on the next day it had risen again on the same spot to extend its verdure high and broader than ever. The soothsayers had agreed that this was an omen of great success, and augured the height of fame for the still youthful Vespasian. At first his triumphal honours, his consulship, and the name he won by his Jewish victory seemed to have fulfilled the promise of this omen.* But having achieved all this, he began to believe that it portended his rise to the throne.

On the frontier of Judaea and Syria lies a hill called Carmel.* A god of the same name is there worshipped according to ancient ritual. There is no image or temple: only an altar where they reverently worship. When Vespasian was sacrificing on this altar, brooding on his secret ambition, the priest,

Basilides, after repeatedly inspecting the omens said to him: 'Whatever it is which you have in mind, Vespasian, whether it is to build a house or to enlarge your estate, or to increase the number of your slaves, there is granted to you a great habitation, vast acres, and a multitude of men.'

Rumour had immediately seized on this riddle and now began to solve it. Nothing was more talked of, especially in Vespasian's presence: conversation increases with hope. Having come to a definite decision they departed, Mucianus to Antioch, Vespasian to Caesarea—the former is the capital of Syria, the latter of Judaea.

The move to confer the throne on Vespasian began at 79 Alexandria, where Tiberius Alexander with great promptitude administered the oath of allegiance to his troops on 1 July. This was later celebrated as his day of accession, although it was not until the third* that the Jewish army took the oath in his presence. So eager was their enthusiasm that they would not even wait for the arrival of Titus, who was on his way back from Syria, where he had been conducting the negotiations between his father and Mucianus.

What happened was all due to the impulse of the soldiers: there was no parade, no formal assembly of the troops. The 80 time and the place were still under discussion, as was the hardest point of all—who should speak first. While minds were still busy with hopes and fears, reasons and chances, Vespasian happened to come out of his quarters. A few of the soldiers, forming up in the usual way to salute him as commander, saluted him as emperor. The others promptly rushed up calling him Caesar and Augustus, and heaping on him all the imperial titles. Fears at once gave way to confidence. Vespasian himself, unchanged by the change of fortune, showed no sign of vanity or arrogance. His sudden elevation made his eyes mist over; but the instant he recovered he addressed the troops in simple soldier fashion, and received a shower of congratulations from every quarter.

Mucianus, who had been waiting for this, administered the oath of allegiance to his eager troops, and then entered the theatre at Antioch, where the Greeks ordinarily hold their debates. There he addressed the fawning crowd as it came flocking in. For he could speak quite elegantly, even in Greek, and had the art of making the most of all he said or did. What most served to inflame the province and the army was his statement that Vitellius had determined to transfer the German legions to peaceful service in the rich province of Syria, and to send the Syrian legions to endure the rigorous climate and toils of a winter in Germany. The provincials were accustomed to the soldiers' company and liked to have them quartered there, and many were bound to them by ties of intimacy and kinship, while the soldiers in their long term of service had come to know and love their old camp like a home.

81   Before 15 July the whole of Syria had sworn allegiance. The party also gained the support of Sohaemus, with all the resources of his kingdom and a considerable force, and of Antiochus, the richest of the subject princes, who owed his importance to his ancestral treasures. Before long Agrippa,* too, received a secret summons from his people, and leaving Rome without the knowledge of Vitellius, sailed as fast as he could to join Vespasian. His sister Berenice showed equal enthusiasm for the cause. She was then in the flower of her youth and beauty, and her munificent gifts to Vespasian quite won the old man's heart too.* Indeed, every province on the seaboard as far as Asia and Achaia, and inland to Pontus and Armenia, swore allegiance, but their governors were without troops, for as yet no legions had been assigned to Cappadocia.

A meeting was held at Beirut to discuss the general situation. To this came Mucianus with all his senior officers and the most distinguished of his centurions and soldiers, besides the impressive élite of the Jewish army. All this pageant of cavalry and infantry, and of subject princes vying with each other in splendour, gave the meeting an air of imperial grandeur.

82   The first step was to levy new troops and to recall the veterans to the standards. Some strong towns were designated for the manufacture of arms. New gold and silver were coined at Antioch. All these works were promptly carried out, each in the proper place, by competent officials. Vespasian came and

inspected them himself, encouraging good work by his praises and rousing the inefficient by example rather than compulsion, always more ready to conceal the faults than the merits of his friends. Many were rewarded by being made prefects or procurators. A number were raised to senatorial rank: they were mostly men of distinction who soon rose high, and with others success atoned for their lack of merit. A donation for the troops had been mentioned by Mucianus in his first speech, but only a modest one. Even Vespasian offered for the civil war no more than others gave in time of peace, for he had set his face with admirable firmness against largess to the soldiers, and his army was the better for it.

Envoys were dispatched to Parthia and Armenia to ensure that the legions, while engaged in the civil war, should not be exposed to attack in the rear. It was arranged that Titus should carry on the war in Judaea, while Vespasian held the keys of Egypt.* Against Vitellius it seemed sufficient to send a part of their forces under the command of Mucianus. He would have Vespasian's name behind him and the irresistible force of destiny. Letters were written to all the armies and their generals with instructions that they should try to win over those of the Guards who were hostile to Vitellius by promising them renewal of service.

Meanwhile Mucianus, who acted more as the Emperor's 83 partner than his subordinate,* moved forward with troops ready for action, neither marching so slowly as to look like holding back, nor so rapidly that rumours would not have time to spread. He realized that his force was small, and that things are magnified by those who cannot see them. However, he had a solid column following in support, composed of the Sixth Legion and some special detachments numbering 13,000 men. He had ordered the fleet to move from the Black Sea to Byzantium, for he was half-minded to leave Moesia and instead attack Dyrrachium* with infantry and cavalry, at the same time using his warships to blockade the Adriatic. He would thus secure Greece and Asia in his rear, which would otherwise be at the mercy of Vitellius, unless furnished with troops. Vitellius also would himself be in doubt what points of the Italian coast to defend, if Mucianus with his ships threatened both Brundisium* and Tarentum and the whole coastline of Calabria and Lucania.

84   Thus the provinces rang from end to end with the preparations for ships, soldiers, and arms. But the heaviest burden was the raising of money. 'Funds', said Mucianus, 'are the sinews of civil war,'* and in his assessments he cared for neither equity nor truth, but solely for the amount of the sum. Informers abounded, and pounced on every rich man as their prey. This intolerable oppression, excused by the necessities of war, was allowed to continue even in peace. It was not so much that Vespasian at the beginning of his reign had made up his mind to maintain unjust decisions, but later fortune spoilt him; he learnt in a bad school and made a bold use of his lessons.* Mucianus also contributed to the war-effort from his private means, of which he was generous, as he hoped to get a high rate of interest out of the country. Others followed his example in making contributions, but very few had his opportunity of recovering their money.

85   In the mean time Vespasian's progress was accelerated by the enthusiasm with which the Illyrian army espoused his cause.* The Third set the example to the other legions of Moesia, the Eighth and the Seventh Claudian, both supporters of Otho through and through, although they had not been present at the battle. On their arrival at Aquileia they had mobbed the couriers who brought the news of Otho's fall, and torn to pieces the colours bearing Vitellius' name, finally looting the camp-chest and dividing the money among themselves. These were hostile acts. Alarmed at what they had done they began to reflect that, while their conduct needed excuse before Vitellius, they could make a merit of it with Vespasian. Accordingly, the three Moesian legions addressed letters to the Pannonian army, inviting their co-operation, and meanwhile prepared to meet refusal with force.

Amid this upheaval, Aponius Saturninus, the governor of Moesia, attempted an abominable crime. He sent a centurion to murder Tettius Julianus, who commanded the Seventh Legion, cloaking a personal quarrel by claiming that it was in the interests of his party. Julianus heard of his danger and, taking some guides who knew the country, escaped into the wilds of Moesia and got beyond Mount Haemus. After that he meddled no more in civil war; he prolonged his journey to Vespasian by various expedients, retarding or hastening his pace according to the nature of the news he received.

In Pannonia, however, the Thirteenth Legion and the 86 Seventh Galbian had not forgotten their resentment and fury after the battle of Bedriacum. They lost no time in joining Vespasian's cause, being chiefly instigated by Antonius Primus.* This man was a criminal who had been convicted of fraud during Nero's reign. Among the many evils of the war had been his recovery of senatorial rank. Galba gave him command of the Seventh Legion, and he was believed to have written repeatedly to Otho offering his services as general to the party. But, as Otho took no notice of him, he played no part in the war. When Vitellius' cause began to decline, he joined Vespasian and proved a significant acquisition. He was a man of great physical energy and a ready tongue; an artist in calumny, invaluable in riots and sedition; light-fingered and free-handed, abominable in peace, but by no means contemptible in war.

The union of the Moesian and Pannonian armies soon attracted the troops in Dalmatia to the cause. Tampius Flavianus and Pompeius Silvanus, the two ex-consuls who governed respectively Pannonia and Dalmatia, were wealthy old gentlemen who had no thought of rising. But the procurator, Cornelius Fuscus,* a vigorous young man of good family, was close at hand. In his early youth a lack of ambition had led him to resign his senatorial rank. He had headed the men of his colony in declaring for Galba, and his services had won him a position as procurator. Then he joined Vespasian's party, giving a fierce stimulus to the war; for, being attracted more by danger itself than by its prizes, he disliked what was certain and long established, preferring everything that was new and dangerous and doubtful.

So the Vespasian party used all their efforts to fan every spark of discontent throughout the empire. Letters were sent to the Fourteenth Legion in Britain and to the First Legion in Spain, since both had stood for Otho against Vitellius. In Gaul, too, letters were scattered broadcast. All in an instant a mighty war was in full flame. The armies of Illyricum openly revolted, and all the others were ready to follow the first sign of success.

87   While Vespasian and his generals were showing such activity in the provinces, Vitellius grew more contemptible and indolent every day.* Halting at every town or country house that offered any attractions, he made his way to Rome with a heavy marching column of 60,000 troops, ruined by loose discipline, and an even greater number of soldiers' servants, as well as those camp-followers who are more impudent than any slaves. Besides these he had the vast retinue of his generals and friends, whom not even the strictest discipline could have kept under control. This mob was further encumbered by senators and knights, who came from Rome to meet him, some from fear, many from servility; and gradually all the others followed, so as not to be left behind by themselves. There flocked in, too, a crowd of low-bred buffoons, actors, and chariot-drivers, who had gained Vitellius' acquaintance by various dishonest services. He took remarkable delight in such discreditable connections. To furnish supplies for this host not only were the colonies and country towns laid waste, but the farmers as well. The crops were just ripe and the fields were ravaged like an enemy country.

88   Many murderous affrays took place among the soldiers, for after the mutiny at Ticinum there were ceaseless quarrels between the legions and the auxiliaries. They only united to harry the villagers. But the worst bloodshed took place at the seventh milestone from Rome. Here Vitellius had ready-cooked food served to each of the soldiers, as if he were fattening up gladiators,* and the common people had flocked out from Rome and wandered all over the camp. Some of these visitors indulged in a cheap practical joke, and robbed the soldiers, quietly cutting their belts while their attention was diverted. Then they kept asking them, 'Have you got your sword on?' The troops were not used to being laughed at, and refused to tolerate it. They attacked the defenceless crowd with their swords. Amongst others, the father of one of the soldiers was killed while in his son's company. When it was

discovered who he was, and the news spread, they shed no more innocent blood.

Still, there was some panic in the city as the first soldiers rushed in on all sides. They mostly made for the Forum, anxious to see the spot where Galba had fallen. They themselves were a sufficiently grim sight with their rough skin coats and long pikes. Unused to towns, they failed to pick their way in the crowd: or they would slip on the greasy streets, or collide with someone and tumble down, whereupon they took to abuse and before long to fists and swords. Their officers, too, terrified the city by swarming along the streets with their bands of armed men.

After crossing the Mulvian Bridge, Vitellius himself rode on 89 a conspicuous horse, wearing his sword and general's uniform, with the Senate and people trooping in front of him. However, as this looked too much like an entry into a captured city, his friends persuaded him to change into civilian dress and walk on foot at the head of his column. The eagles of four legions led the way, surrounded by the colours belonging to four other legions. Next came the standards of twelve cavalry regiments, then the files of infantry and the cavalry behind them. Then came thirty-four cohorts of auxiliaries, arranged according to their nationality or the nature of their weapons. In front of the eagles came the camp prefects and tribunes, and the senior centurions, all dressed in white. The other centurions marched each at the head of his company, glittering with their armour and decorations. Gaily, too, shone the soldiers' medals and their chains of honour. It was a noble spectacle, an army worthy of a better emperor. Thus Vitellius entered the Capitol, where he embraced his mother and conferred on her the title of Augusta.

On the following day Vitellius delivered a grandiloquent 90 eulogy on his own merits. He might have been addressing the Senate and people of some other state, for he extolled his own industry and self-control, although each member of his audience had seen his infamy for himself, and the whole of Italy had witnessed during his march the shameful spectacle of his sloth and luxury. However, the irresponsible crowd could not

discriminate between truth and falsehood. They had learnt the
usual flatteries by heart and chimed in with loud shouts of
applause. In the face of his protests they forced him to take the
title of Augustus. But neither his refusal nor their insistence
made any difference.

91   In Rome nothing passes without comment, and it was regarded as a fatal omen that Vitellius took office as Chief
Pontiff, and issued an ordinance on public worship, on 18
July, which, as the anniversary of the disasters on the Cremera
and the Allia,* had long been considered an unlucky day. But
his ignorance of all civil and religious precedent was only
equalled by the incapacity of his freedmen and friends. He
seemed to live in a society of drunkards. However, he conducted the consular elections in the presence of the candidates
according to the law; and in everything strove for a good
report among the lowest classes, attending performances in
the theatre and backing his favourite at the races. This would
undoubtedly have made him popular had his motives been
good, but the memory of his former life made his conduct
seem cheap and discreditable.

He constantly attended the Senate, even when the debates
were on trivial matters. It once happened that Helvidius
Priscus, then praetor-elect, opposed Vitellius' policy. At first
the Emperor showed annoyance, but was content to appeal to
the tribunes of the people to come to the rescue of his slighted
authority.* Afterwards, when his friends, fearing that his resentment might be deep-seated, tried to smooth matters,
he replied that there was nothing strange in two senators
disagreeing on a question of public policy: he himself had
often even opposed Thrasea.* Most people laughed at the
impudence of this comparison; others were gratified that he
had selected Thrasea, and not some mighty politician, as an
example of real distinction.

92   Vitellius had given the command of the Guards to Publilius
Sabinus, who had commanded an auxiliary cohort, and Julius
Priscus, hitherto only a centurion. Priscus owed his prominence to Valens' support, Sabinus to that of Caecina. The
rivalry between Valens and Caecina left Vitellius no authority
at all. They managed the government between them. They had

long felt the strain of mutual hatred. During the war they had
concealed it imperfectly; lately it had been fanned by dishonest friends and by life at Rome, which so easily breeds quarrels. They were constant rivals, comparing their respective
popularity, the number of their retinue, the size of the crowds
that came to wait upon them. Vitellius let his favour alternate
between them, for excessive power is never to be relied upon.
Meanwhile, they both feared and despised the Emperor himself, who veered between sudden brusqueness and unseasonable flattery. However, they were not in the least deterred
from seizing on the houses, gardens, and imperial funds, while
the crowd of miserable and needy nobles, whom Galba had
recalled from exile with their children, derived no assistance
or compassion from the Emperor. He earned the approval
both of the upper classes and of the people by granting to the
restored exiles full rights over their freedmen.* But the latter
employed all their slavish cunning to invalidate the edict. They
would hide their money in the pocket of someone obscure or
influential. Some, indeed, passed into the imperial household
and became more powerful than their masters.

As for the soldiers, the barracks were crowded, and the 93
overflow spread through the city, finding shelter in colonnades
and temples. They ceased to observe the roll-call, to go on
guard, or to keep themselves in training, but fell victims to the
attractions of city life and its unmentionable vices, until they
deteriorated both physically and morally through idleness and
debauchery. Many of them even imperilled their lives by set-
tling in the pestilent Vatican quarter, thus increasing the rate
of mortality. They were close to the Tiber, and the Germans
and Gauls, who were peculiarly liable to disease and could ill
stand the heat, ruined their constitutions by their passion for
the river. Moreover, the rules of the service were tampered
with, the result of perversity or bribery. Sixteen cohorts of
Guards* were enrolled, and four for the City Garrison, each
composed of 1,000 men. In enlisting these troops Valens was
more brazen than Caecina, whose life he claimed to have
saved. It is true, indeed, that his arrival had consolidated the
party, and by his successful engagement he had silenced the
criticism of his slow marching. Besides which, the whole of

the army of Lower Germany was attached to Valens, and this is said to be the reason why Caecina's loyalty first wavered.

94   Whatever indulgence Vitellius showed to his generals, he allowed still more licence to the troops. Each man chose his duties. However unfit, he might enlist in the City Garrison, if he preferred it. On the other hand, good soldiers were allowed, if they wished, to remain in the legions or the auxiliary cavalry. Many wished to do this who suffered from ill health and complained of the climate. However, the best soldiers were withdrawn from the legions and from the cavalry; and the prestige of the City Garrison was shattered when 20,000 men were not so much selected for service with them as drafted at random from the whole army.

While Vitellius was addressing the troops, they demanded the execution of three Gallic chieftains, Asiaticus, Flavus, and Rufinus, on the ground that they had fought for Vindex. Vitellius never checked such outcries. For, apart from his innate sloth, he knew that his donation to the soldiers was nearly due, and that he had no money for it; so he freely granted all their other demands. The imperial freedmen were forced to contribute a sort of tax, proportionate to the number of their slaves. Meanwhile, his one occupation was extravagance. He built stables for chariot-drivers, filled the arena with shows of gladiators and wild beasts, and fooled away his money as though he had more than he wanted.

95   Moreover, Valens and Caecina celebrated Vitellius' birthday* by holding gladiatorial shows in every quarter of Rome on a scale of magnificence hitherto unknown. Vitellius then gratified the vile rabble and scandalized all decent people by building altars in the Campus Martius, and holding a funeral service in honour of Nero. Victims were killed and burnt in public: the torch was applied by the Augustales, members of the college which Tiberius Caesar had founded in honour of the Julian family, just as Romulus had similarly commemorated King Tatius.*

It was not yet four months* since Vitellius' victory, and yet his freedman Asiaticus was as bad as a Polyclitus or a Patrobius, or any of the favourites whose names were hated in

earlier days. At this court no one strove to rise by honesty or
industry. There was only one road to power. By lavish banquets, costly profusion, and feats of gastronomy, you had to
try and satisfy Vitellius' insatiable gluttony. He himself, without thought for the morrow, was well content to enjoy the
present. It is believed that he squandered 900 million sesterces
in these brief months. Truly it shows Rome's greatness and
misfortune, that she endured Otho and Vitellius both in the
same year, and suffered humiliation of every kind at the hands
of men like Vinius and Fabius, Icelus and Asiaticus, until at
last they gave way to Mucianus and Marcellus—a change of
men but not of manners.

The first news of rebellion which reached Vitellius came 96
from Aponius Saturninus, who, before himself going over to
Vespasian's side, wrote to announce the desertion of the Third
Legion. But a sudden crisis makes a man nervous: Aponius did
not tell the whole story. So the Emperor's flattering friends
began to explain it all away: what was the defection of a
single legion, while the loyalty of the other armies remained
unshaken? Vitellius himself used the same language to the
soldiers. He accused the men who had been recently discharged from the Guards of spreading false rumours, and kept
assuring them there was no fear of civil war. All mention of
Vespasian was suppressed, and soldiers were sent round the
city to frighten the public into silence—which did more than
anything else to make them talk.

Vitellius, nevertheless, sent for reinforcements from Ger- 97
many, Britain, and the Spanish provinces, though lethargi-
cally and concealing his straits. The provinces and their
governors showed the same want of enthusiasm. Hordeonius
Flaccus' suspicions of the Batavi left him uneasy that he would
have a war of his own,* while Vettius Bolanus never had
Britain under complete control: nor was the loyalty of either
beyond doubt. The Spanish provinces, where there was at the
time no governor, were equally slow. The three legionary
commanders held an equal authority, and if Vitellius' cause
had prospered, would have each outbid the other for his
favour: but they all shared the resolve to leave his misfortunes
alone.

In Africa the legion and auxiliaries enlisted by Clodius
Macer, and subsequently disbanded by Galba, mobilized
again at Vitellius' orders, and at the same time the remaining
young men of the province eagerly enlisted. Vitellius had been
an honest and popular governor in Africa, while Vespasian
had been distrusted and disliked.* The provincials took this
as a foretaste of their reigns; but experience proved them
wrong.

98   The commander Valerius Festus* at first loyally seconded
the enthusiasm of the province. After a while he began to
waver. In his official letters and edicts he still acknowledged
Vitellius, while in secret communication with Vespasian and
ready to support whichever party proved successful.

In Raetia and the Gallic provinces some soldiers and
centurions carrying letters and edicts from Vespasian were
taken prisoner and sent to Vitellius, who had them executed.
But most of these envoys escaped capture either by their own
ingenuity or by the loyal help of friends. Thus, while Vitellius'
plans were known, Vespasian's were for the most part still a
secret. This was partly due to Vitellius' negligence, but also to
the fact that the garrisons on the Pannonian Alps stopped all
messengers. By sea, too, the Etesian winds* favoured ships
sailing eastward, but hindered the voyage from the East.

99   It was the enemy invasion and the alarming news that
reached him from all quarters that at last terrified Vitellius
into instructing Caecina and Valens to prepare for war.
Caecina was sent on ahead, Valens, who was just recovering
from a serious illness, being delayed by his weak state of
health. Great, indeed, was the change in the appearance of the
German army as it marched out of Rome. There was neither
energy in their muscles nor fire in their hearts. Slowly the
column straggled on, their horses spiritless, their weapons
dangling. The men grumbled at the sun, the dust, the weather,
and their readiness to quarrel grew as their capacity to endure
toil was dulled.*

To these disadvantages were added Caecina's inveterate
self-seeking and his newly acquired indolence. An overdose of
success had made him slack and self-indulgent, or, if he was
plotting treachery, this may have been one of his devices

for demoralizing the army. It has often been believed that Caecina's loyalty was shaken by the strategy of Flavius Sabinus who, using Rubrius Gallus as his agent, promised that, if Caecina came over, Vespasian would ratify any conditions. Caecina was also reminded of his hatred and rivalry with Fabius Valens: as he did not stand first with Vitellius, he had better acquire credit and influence with a new emperor.

Caecina's departure was marked by warm embraces and 100 tremendous accolades from Vitellius; he then dispatched a body of cavalry to occupy Cremona. Detachments of the First, Fourth, Fifteenth, and Sixteenth Legions soon followed; then the Fifth and Twenty-Second; and in the rear of the column came the Twenty-First Rapax and the First Italian Legion, with detachments from the three legions of Britain and a select force of auxiliaries.

When Caecina had started, Fabius Valens wrote instructions to the army of which he had been general to await him on the march, saying that he and Caecina had arranged this. Caecina, however, took advantage of being on the spot, and pretended that this plan had been altered so as to enable them to meet the first outbreak of the war with their full strength. So some legions were ordered to hurry forward to Cremona, others to head for Hostilia.* Caecina himself turned aside to Ravenna on the pretext of giving instructions to the fleet. But soon it became apparent that he in fact sought secrecy for his treacherous designs. For Lucilius Bassus,* who had been a cavalry commander, and whom Vitellius had raised to the supreme command of the two fleets at Ravenna and Misenum, felt aggrieved at not being immediately given the Prefectship of the Guards, and sought in vile treachery the remedy for his unjustifiable annoyance. It can never be known whether he influenced Caecina or whether one was as dishonest as the other (there is seldom much to choose between rascals). The 101 historians who compiled the records of this war in the days of the Flavian dynasty perverted their explanation of this betrayal for the sake of flattery: they attributed it to patriotism and the interests of peace.* We cannot think them right. Apart from the innate fickleness of the rebels and the worthlessness of fidelity after Galba's betrayal, they seem to have been led by jealousy and rivalry into destroying Vitellius himself for fear that they might lose the first place in his favour.

After Caecina joined his army, he used every device to undermine the staunch fidelity of the centurions and soldiers to Vitellius. Bassus found the same task less difficult, for the fleet remembered that they had lately been in Otho's service, and were liable to slip towards rebellion.

BOOK THREE

On the Flavian side the generals arranged their plans for the 1
war with greater loyalty and greater success. They had met at
Poetovio* at the winter quarters of the Thirteenth Legion,
where they debated whether they should block the passage of
the Pannonian Alps and wait until their whole strength came
up to reinforce them, or whether they should take a bolder
line and go to join battle and fight for Italy. Those who were
in favour of waiting for reinforcements and prolonging the
war dwelt on the strength and reputation of the German
legions, and pointed out that the flower of the British army
had lately arrived in Rome with Vitellius; their own forces
were numerically inferior and had recently suffered defeat;*
moreover, conquered troops, however fierce their language,
never show the same courage. On the other hand, if they
occupied the Alps, Mucianus would soon arrive with the
forces from the East. Besides, Vespasian still commanded the
sea and the fleets, and could count on the support of
the provinces, where he could set in motion what was virtually
a colossal second war. A salutary delay would bring them
fresh forces without in any way prejudicing their present
position.

In answer to these arguments Antonius Primus, who was 2
the most enthusiastic instigator of war, maintained that
prompt action would help them and ruin Vitellius. 'Their
victory', he said, 'has not served to inspirit but to enervate
them.'* The men are not held in readiness in camp, but are
loitering in towns all over Italy. No one but their hosts has any
call to fear them. The more ferocious they showed themselves
before, the greater the greed with which they now indulge in
unwonted draughts of pleasure. The circus, the theatre, and
the charms of the capital have ruined their hardness and their
health. But if we give them time to train for war they will
regain their energy. It is not far to Germany, whence they
draw their main strength. Britain is only separated by a narrow channel. Close at hand they have Gaul and Spain, from

the provinces of which they can get men, horses, and subsidies. Then again, they can rely on Italy itself and all the resources of the capital, while, if they want to take the offensive, they have two fleets and full command of the Illyrian Sea. What good to us will the barrier of the mountains be then? Why should we drag on the war into another summer? Where can we get funds and supplies in the meanwhile? No, let us seize our opportunity. The Pannonian legions are burning to rise in revenge. They were not defeated but deceived.* The Moesian army has not yet lost a man. If you count not legions but men, our forces are stronger and untouched by licentiousness. The very shame of our defeat makes for good discipline. And even then our cavalry was not beaten. For though we lost the day, they shattered Vitellius' line.

'And what was the force that broke through the Vitellians? Two regiments of cavalry from Pannonia and Moesia. What have we now? Sixteen regiments. Will not their combined forces, as they roar and thunder down upon the enemy, burying them in clouds of dust, overwhelm these horses and horsemen that have forgotten how to fight? I have given you my plan, and, unless I am stopped, I will put it in operation. Some of you have not yet burnt your boats. Well, you can keep back the legions. Give me the auxiliaries in light marching order. They will be enough for me. You will soon hear that the door of Italy is open and the power of Vitellius overthrown. You will be glad enough to follow in the footsteps of my victory.'

3   All this and much else of the same tenor Antonius poured out with flashing eyes and savage voice, so as to reach the centurions and some of the soldiers who had gathered round to share in their deliberations. He carried away even the more cautious and far-seeing, while the rest, and the common soldiers, were filled with contempt for the sloth of the other generals, and cheered their one and only leader to the echo. He had already established this reputation at the original meeting, when Vespasian's letter was read. Most of the generals had then taken an ambiguous line, intending to interpret their language in the light of subsequent events. But Antonius seemed to have taken the field without any disguise, and this

carried more weight with the men, who saw that he must share their guilt or their glory.

Next to Antonius in influence stood Cornelius Fuscus, the 4 procurator. He, too, always attacked Vitellius in no mild terms, and had left himself no hope in case of failure. Tampius Flavianus was a man whose disposition and advanced years made him dilatory, and he aroused the suspicion of the soldiers, who felt he had not forgotten his kinship with Vitellius. Besides this, when the legions first rose, he had fled, and subsequently returned of his own free will, which looked like meditating treachery. Having given up his province of Pannonia and returned to Italy, he was out of the reach of danger, but the passion for revolution had induced him to resume the title of governor and meddle in the civil war. It was Cornelius Fuscus who had persuaded him to this—not that he needed the energy of Flavianus, but because he felt that, especially at the outset of the rising, the prestige of an ex-consul would give the party an honourable veneer.

In order to make their march across into Italy safe and 5 effective, letters were sent to Aponius Saturninus to bring the Moesian army up as quickly as possible. To prevent the exposure of the defenceless provinces to the attacks of foreign tribes, the chiefs of the Sarmatian Iazyges,* who formed the government of the tribe, were enlisted in the service. They also offered their tribal force, consisting entirely of cavalry, but were excused from this contribution for fear that the civil war might give them the opportunity to work in foreign interests, or that an offer of higher pay from the enemy might tempt them to sacrifice their duty and their honour. Sido and Italicus, two princes of the Suebi,* were induced to join Vespasian's side. They had long acknowledged Roman sovereignty, and their tribe preferred being trusted to being commanded. Some auxiliaries were stationed on the flank towards Raetia, where hostilities were expected, since its governor Porcius Septiminus remained incorruptibly loyal to Vitellius. Sextilius Felix was therefore dispatched with Aurius' Cavalry and eight cohorts of auxiliary infantry, together with the native levies of Noricum, to hold the bank of the River Inn, which forms the frontier of Raetia and Noricum. But neither side provoked a battle: the fortune of the rival parties was decided elsewhere.

6   Meanwhile, at the head of a picked band of auxiliaries and part of the cavalry, Antonius hurried on to invade Italy. He took with him an energetic soldier named Arrius Varus, who had made his reputation while serving under Corbulo in his Armenian victories. He was also supposed to have sought a private interview with Nero, at which he maligned Corbulo's character. His infamous treachery brought him the Emperor's favour and a post as senior centurion. This ill-gotten prize delighted him now, but ultimately proved his ruin.

After occupying Aquileia, Antonius and Varus found a ready welcome at Opitergium and Altinum* and all the other towns in the neighbourhood. At Altinum a garrison was left behind to guard against an attack by the fleet at Ravenna, for the news of its desertion* had not as yet arrived. Pressing forward, they won Padua and Ateste* for the party. At the latter place they learnt that three Vitellian auxiliary cohorts and a regiment known as Sebosus' Cavalry were established at Forum Alieni, where they had constructed a bridge. The report added that they were off their guard, so this seemed a good opportunity to attack them. They accordingly rushed the position at dawn, and cut down many of the men without their weapons. Orders had been given that, after a few had been killed, the rest should be terrorized into desertion. Some surrendered at once, but the majority succeeded in destroying the bridge, and thus checked the enemy's pursuit. The first bout had gone in the Flavians' favour.

7   When the news of the victory had spread, the Seventh Galbian and the Thirteenth Gemina hurried in high spirits to Padua under the command of Vedius Aquila. At Padua they were given a few days' rest, during which Minicius Justus, the camp prefect of the Seventh Legion, who endeavoured to enforce a standard of discipline too severe for civil war, had to be rescued from the fury of his troops and sent to Vespasian.

Antonius conceived that his party would gain in prestige if they showed approval of Galba's government, and stood for the revival of his cause. So he gave orders that all the statues of Galba, which had been thrown down during the civil war, should be replaced for worship throughout the country towns. This was a thing that had long been desired, but the creditable construction placed on it meant that it assumed an undue importance.

The question then arose where they should choose their 8 base for the war. The best place seemed to be Verona. The open country round it was suited for a cavalry battle, in which the Flavian strength lay: and they would gain both prestige and profit by wresting from Vitellius a powerful and wealthy town. On the road they occupied Vicetia.* In itself this was a very small matter, since the town had only moderate resouces, but it gained considerable importance when one reflected that it was Caecina's birthplace: the enemy's general had thus lost his native town.* But Verona was well worth while. The inhabitants aided the party by their example and their funds: and the army was thrust midway between Raetia and the Julian Alps, and had thus blocked all passages by that route for the German armies.

This move had been made either without the knowledge or against the orders of Vespasian. His instructions were to suspend operations at Aquileia and wait for the arrival of Mucianus. He had additionally set out his plan: that so long as he held Egypt, the key to the corn supply, as well as the revenue of the richest provinces, he could reduce Vitellius' army to submission from sheer lack of money and provisions. Mucianus had sent letter after letter with the same advice, pointing to the prospect of a victory without bloodshed or bereavement, and using other similar pretexts to conceal his real motive: ambition.* He wanted to keep all the glory of the war to himself. However, the distance was so great that events outran his instructions. Antonius accordingly made a sudden 9 sally against the enemy's outposts, and after a slight skirmish, in which they tested each other's nerve, both sides withdrew without advantage.

Soon after, Caecina entrenched a strong position between a Veronese village called Hostilia and the marshes of the River Tartaro. Here he was safe, with the river in his rear and the marsh to guard his flanks. Had he added loyalty to his other advantages, he might have employed the full strength of the

Vitellian forces to crush the enemy's two legions before they were reinforced by the Moesian army, or at least have forced them to retire in ignominious flight and abandon Italy. But Caecina used various pretexts for delay, and at the outset of the war treacherously yielded all his advantages to the enemy. While it was open to him to rout them by force of arms, he preferred to pester them with letters and to wait until his intermediaries had settled the terms of his treason.

In the mean time, Aponius Saturninus arrived with the Seventh Claudian Legion, commanded by the tribune Vipstanus Messala, a distinguished member of a famous family,* and the only man who brought any honesty to this war. To these forces, still only three legions and no match for the Vitellians, Caecina addressed his letters. He criticized their rash attempt to sustain a lost cause, and at the same time praised the courage of the German army in the highest terms. His allusions to Vitellius were few and casual, and he refrained from insulting Vespasian. In fact he used no language calculated either to seduce or to terrorize the enemy. The Flavian generals made no attempt to explain away their former defeat. They proudly championed Vespasian, showing their loyalty to the cause, their confidence in the army, and their hostile prejudice against Vitellius. To the tribunes and centurions they held out the hope of retaining all the favours they had won from Vitellius, and they urged Caecina himself in plain terms to desert. These letters were both read before a meeting of the Flavian army, and served to increase their confidence, for while Caecina wrote humbly and seemed afraid of offending Vespasian, their own generals had answered contemptuously and apparently scoffed at Vitellius.

10   When two more legions arrived, the Third commanded by Dillius Aponianus and the Eighth by Numisius Lupus, Antonius decided to enclose Verona with ramparts and make a demonstration in force. It so happened that the Galbian Legion, who had been told to work on the rampart facing the enemy, catching sight of some of their allies' cavalry in the distance, took them for the enemy, and fell into a groundless panic. Fearing treachery, they seized their arms and visited their fury on Tampius Flavianus. They could prove no charge

against him, but he had long been unpopular, and a blind impulse made them clamour for his head. He was Vitellius' kinsman, they howled; he had betrayed Otho; he had embezzled their donative. They would listen to no defence, although he implored them with outstretched hands, repeatedly grovelling flat upon the ground, his clothes all torn, his face and chest shaken with sobs. This only served to inflame the soldiers' hostility. His very excess of terror* seemed to prove his guilt.

Aponius tried to address them, but his voice was drowned in their shouts. The others, too, were contemptuously howled down. They would give no one a hearing except Antonius, who had the power of authority as well as the arts of eloquence necessary to quiet a mob. When the riot grew worse, and they began to pass from insulting speeches to murderous violence, he gave orders that Flavianus should be put in chains. Realizing that this was a farce, the soldiers broke through the guards round the general's platform, prepared to resort to extreme violence. Whereupon Antonius, drawing his sword, bared his breast and vowed that he would die either by their hands or his own. Whenever he saw a soldier whom he knew and was wearing military decorations, he called on him by name to come to the rescue. At last he turned towards the standards and the gods of war,* and prayed incessantly that they would rather inspire the enemy's army with this mad spirit of mutiny. At last the riot died away, and at nightfall they all dispersed to their tents. Flavianus left that same night, and on his way met letters from Vespasian which delivered him from danger.

The infection seemed to spread among the legions. They 11 next attacked Aponius Saturninus, who was in command of the Moesian army. This fresh disturbance was caused by the circulation of letters which Saturninus was supposed to have written to Vitellius, and it was all the more brutal since it broke out not when they were tired by their labours but in the middle of the day. Once soldiers had vied with each other in courage and discipline: now they were rivals in ribaldry and riot. They were determined that the fury with which they demanded the execution of Aponius should not fall short of their outcry against Flavianus. The Moesian legions remembered that they had helped the Pannonian army to take their revenge; while the Pannonian troops, feeling that their comrades' mutiny acquitted them of blame, were glad enough to repeat the crime. They made for the country house in which Saturninus was living. He escaped, however, aided not so much by the efforts of Antonius, Aponianus, and Messala, who did everything in their power to rescue him, but rather by the security of his hiding-place, for he concealed himself in the furnace of some baths* that were fortuitously not in use. Eventually he gave up his lictors* and retired to Padua.

The departure of both the governors left Antonius in supreme command of the two armies. His colleagues deferred to him and the men gave him enthusiastic support. It was even supposed by some that he had cunningly promoted both outbreaks, to secure for himself the full profit of the war.

12   Vitellius' party was likewise a prey to disquiet, and there the dissension was the more fatal, since it was aroused not by the men's suspicions but by the treachery of the generals. The sailors of the fleet at Ravenna were mostly drawn from the provinces of Dalmatia and Pannonia, which were both held by Vespasian, and while they were still wavering, the commander, Lucilius Bassus, decided them in favour of the Flavian party. Choosing the night-time for their treason, the conspirators assembled at headquarters without the knowledge of the other sailors. Bassus, who was either ashamed or uncertain of their success, awaited developments in his house. Amid great disturbance the ships' captains attacked the images of Vitellius and cut down the few men who offered any resistance. The rest of the fleet were glad enough of a change, and their sympathies soon came round to Vespasian. Then Lucilius appeared and publicly claimed responsibility. However, the fleet appointed Cornelius Fuscus as their commander, and he came hurrying onto the scene. Bassus was put under honourable arrest and conveyed with an escort of Liburnian cruisers to Atria,* where he was imprisoned by Vibennius Rufinus, who commanded a cavalry regiment in garrison there. However, he was soon set free on the interven-

tion of Hormus, one of the imperial freedmen. For he, too, ranked as a general.

When the news that the navy had gone over became known, 13 Caecina, carefully selecting a moment when the camp was deserted, and the men had all gone to their various duties, summoned to headquarters the senior centurions and a few of the soldiers. He then proceeded to praise the spirit and the strength of Vespasian's party: they themselves had been deserted by the fleet; they were cramped for supplies; Spain and Gaul were against them; Rome could not be trusted. In every way he exaggerated the weakness of Vitellius' position. Eventually, when some of his accomplices had given the cue and the rest were dumbfounded by his change of front, he made them all swear allegiance to Vespasian. Immediately the portraits of Vitellius were torn down and messengers dispatched to Antonius.

However, when rumours of the treason got abroad in the camp, and the men returning to headquarters saw Vespasian's name on the standards and Vitellius' portraits scattered on the ground, at first there was an ominous silence: then everything broke out at once. Had the pride of the German army sunk so low that without a battle and without a blow they should let their hands be shackled and render up their arms? What had they against them? None but defeated troops. The only solid legions of Otho's army, the First and the Fourteenth, Vespasian had not got, and even those they had routed and cut to pieces on that very field.* And all for what? That these thousands of fighting men should be handed over like a drove of slaves to Antonius, the convict! 'Eight whole legions are to follow the lead of one miserable fleet. Such is the pleasure of Bassus and Caecina. They have robbed the Emperor of his home, his estate, his wealth, and now they want to rob the troops of their Emperor. We have not lost a man nor shed a drop of blood. Even the Flavians will despise us. What answer can we give when we are questioned about our victory or our defeat?'

Thus they shouted one and all as their indignation urged 14 them. Led by the Fifth Legion, they replaced the portraits of

Vitellius and put Caecina in irons. They selected Fabius Fabullus, commanding the Fifth Legion, and the camp prefect, Cassius Longus, to lead them. Some marines who arrived at this point from three Liburnian cruisers, quite innocent and unaware of what had happened, were promptly butchered. Then the men deserted their camp, broke down the bridge, and marched back to Hostilia, and thence to Cremona to join the two legions, the First Italian and Twenty-First Rapax, which Caecina had sent ahead with some of the cavalry to occupy Cremona.*

15   When Antonius heard of this he determined to attack the enemy while they were still at variance and their forces divided. The Vitellian generals would soon recover their authority and the troops their discipline, and confidence would return if the two divisions were to unite. He guessed also that Fabius Valens had already started from Rome and would hasten his march when he heard of Caecina's treachery. Valens was loyal to Vitellius and an experienced soldier. There was good reason, besides, to fear an attack on the side of Raetia from an immense force of Germans. Vitellius had already summoned auxiliaries from Britain, Gaul, and Spain in sufficient numbers to blight their chances utterly, had not Antonius in fear of this very prospect seized the victory by hurriedly forcing an engagement. In two days he marched his whole force from Verona to Bedriacum. On the next day he left his legions behind to fortify the camp, and sent out his auxiliary cohorts into territory belonging to Cremona, to taste the joys of plundering their compatriots under pretext of collecting supplies. To secure greater freedom for their depredations, he himself advanced at the head of 4,000 cavalry eight miles along the road from Bedriacum. The scouts, as is usual, sped on ahead.

16   About eleven in the morning a mounted scout galloped up with the news that the enemy were at hand; there was a small body in advance of the rest, but the noise of an army in movement could be heard over the countryside. While Antonius was debating what he ought to do, Arrius Varus, who was greedy for action, rushed out with the keenest of the troopers and charged the Vitellians, inflicting only slight loss;

for reinforcements arrived, the tables were turned, and those who had been hottest in pursuit were now hindmost in the rout.

Their haste had no sanction from Antonius, who had foreseen what would happen. Encouraging his men to engage the enemy with brave hearts, he drew off the cavalry onto each flank and left a free passage in the centre to receive Varus and his troopers. Orders were sent to the legions to arm and signals were displayed to the foraging party, summoning them to cease plundering and join the battle by the quickest possible path. Meanwhile, Varus came plunging in terror into the middle of their ranks, spreading confusion among them. The fresh troops were swept back along with the wounded, sorely discomfited by their own panic and the narrowness of the road.

In all the confusion of the rout Antonius never for a moment forgot what befitted a determined general and a brave soldier.* Staying the panic-stricken, checking the fugitives, wherever the fight was thickest, wherever he saw a gleam of hope, he schemed, he fought, he shouted, always conspicuous to his own men and a mark for the enemy. At last, in the heat of his impatience, he thrust through with a lance a standard-bearer, who was in full flight, then seized the standard and turned it to face the enemy. Whereupon for very shame a few of his troopers, not more than a hundred, made a stand. The nature of the ground helped them. The road there was narrower; a stream barred their way, and the bridge was broken; the riverbed was treacherous and the steep banks checked their flight. Thus necessity or chance restored their fallen fortunes. Forming in close order, they received the Vitellians' reckless and disordered charge, and flung them into confusion. Antonius pressed hard on their shattered ranks and cut down all who blocked his path. The others followed each his own inclination, rifling the dead, capturing prisoners, seizing arms and horses. Meanwhile, summoned by their shouts of triumph, those who had just now been in full flight across the fields came hurrying back to share the victory.

Four miles from Cremona the standards of the Rapax and 18 Italian Legions gleamed in the sun. They had marched out

thus far during their cavalry's original success. When fortune
turned against them, they neither opened their ranks to receive
the routed troops nor marched out to attack the enemy,* who
were wearied with fighting and their long pursuit. The
Vitellians had no systematic leadership; but in the hour of
danger they realized their loss. The victorious cavalry came
charging into their wavering line, and at the same time the
tribune Vipstanus Messala arrived with the Moesian auxiliaries and a good number of men from the legions, who had
kept up with the pace of their forced march. This combined
force of infantry and cavalry broke the opposing column, and
the proximity of Cremona's walls gave the Vitellians more
hope of refuge and less stomach for resistance.

Antonius did not follow up his advantage. He realized that,
although the issue had been successful, the battle had long
been doubtful, and had cost the troopers and their horses
19 many wounds and much hard fighting. As evening fell, the
whole strength of the Flavian army arrived. They had
marched among heaps of corpses and the still reeking traces of
slaughter, and now, feeling that the war was over, they clamoured to advance at once on Cremona and either receive its
submission or take it by storm. This sounded well for public
utterance, but each man in his heart was thinking that they
could easily rush a city on the plain: in a night assault men
were just as brave and had a better chance of plunder. But if
they waited for day it would be all peace and petitions; what
then would they get for their wounds and their labours? A
reputation for mercy—there was no money in that. All the
wealth of Cremona would find its way into the commanders'
pockets. Storm a city, and the plunder goes to the soldiers: if
it surrenders, the generals get it. They refused to listen to their
centurions and tribunes and drowned their voices in a rattle of
arms, swearing they would break their orders unless they were
led out.

20   Antonius then went round among the companies. When his
authoritative bearing had obtained silence, he assured them
that he had no wish to rob them of the glory and the reward
they so well deserved. 'But', he said, 'an army and a general
have different functions. It is right that soldiers should be

greedy for battle, but the general more often does good by foresight, deliberation, and delay than by temerity. I have done all I could to aid your victory with sword in hand: now I will serve you by the general's proper arts of calculation and strategy. The risks that face us are obvious. It is night; we know nothing of the lie of the city; the enemy are behind the walls; everything favours an ambush. Even if the gates were open, we cannot safely enter except by day and after due reconnoitring. Are you going to begin storming the town when you cannot possibly see where the ground is level and how high the walls are? How do you know whether to assault it with engines and showers of missiles, or with siege-works and mantlets?' Then he turned to individuals, asking one after another whether they had brought hatchets and pickaxes and other implements for storming a town. When they answered no, 'Well,' he said, 'could any troops possibly break through walls or undermine them with swords and javelins? Suppose it proves necessary to construct a mound and to shelter ourselves with screens and fascines, are we going to stand idle like a lot of helpless idiots, gaping at the height of the enemy's towers and ramparts? Why not rather wait one night till our siege-engines arrive and then carry the victory by force?'*

So saying, he sent the camp-followers and servants with the freshest of the troopers back to Bedriacum to bring up supplies and whatever else was wanted. The soldiers indeed 21 chafed at this, and mutiny was imminent, when some of the mounted scouts, who had ridden right up to the walls, captured a few Cremonese stragglers, and learnt from them that six Vitellian legions and the whole army that had been at Hostilia had that very day covered thirty miles, and, hearing of their comrades' defeat, were already arming for battle and would be on them immediately. This alarming news cured their obstinate deafness to the general's advice. He ordered the Thirteenth Legion to take up their position on the actual embankment of the Postumian Way. In touch with them on the left wing in the open country were the Seventh Galbian, beside whom stood the Seventh Claudian, with their front protected by one of the local drainage ditches. On the right wing were the Eighth, drawn up along an open path, and next to them the Third, distributed among some thick clumps of trees. Such, at any rate, was the order of the eagles and standards. In the darkness the soldiers were confused and took their places at random. The band of Guards was next to the Third, and the auxiliaries on the wings, while the cavalry were disposed in support round the flanks and the rear. The Suebi Sido and Italicus with a picked band of their compatriots fought in the front line.

22   For the Vitellians, the right course was to rest at Cremona and recuperate their strength with food and sleep, and then on the next day to extirpate and annihilate the Flavians when they were weak from cold and hunger. But they had no general; they had no plan. Though it was nearly nine at night they flung themselves upon the Flavians, who were standing steady in their places to receive them. In their fury and the darkness the Vitellian line was so disordered that I should hardly dare vouch for the disposition of their troops. However, it has been stated that the Fourth Macedonian Legion were on the right flank; in the centre were the Fifth and Fifteenth with the detachments of the Ninth, the Second, and the Twentieth from Britain; the Sixteenth, the Twenty-Second, and the First formed the left wing. The men of the Rapax and Italian Legions were distributed among all the companies. The cavalry and auxiliaries picked their own positions.

All night the battle raged with varying fortune, never decided, always savagely contested. Disaster threatened now one side, now the other. Courage, strength were of little use: their eyes could not even see in front of them. Both sides were armed alike; the watchwords, constantly demanded, soon became known; the standards were all in confusion, as they were captured and carried off from one band to another. The Seventh Legion, raised recently by Galba,* suffered most severely. Six of the senior centurions fell and several standards were lost. They nearly lost their eagle too, but it was rescued by the senior centurion Atilius Verus, who after great slaughter of the enemy fell finally himself.

23   Antonius called up the Guards to reinforce his wavering line. Taking up the fight, they repulsed the enemy, only to be

repulsed in their turn. For the Vitellian artillery, which had at first scattered its fire, discharging upon the bushes without hurting the enemy, was now massed upon the high road, and swept the open space in front. One immense catapult in particular, which belonged to the Fifteenth,* mowed down the Flavian line with huge stones. The slaughter thus caused would have been enormous, had not two of the Flavian soldiers performed a memorable exploit. Concealing their identity by snatching up shields from the enemy's dead, they cut the ropes which suspended the weights of the engine. They fell immediately, riddled with wounds, and so their names have perished; but of their deed there is no doubt.

Fortune had favoured neither side when, as the night wore on, the moon rose, revealing and deceiving the armies. Shining from behind the Flavians the moon was in their favour. It magnified the shadows of their men and horses so that the enemy took the shadow for the substance, and their missiles were misdirected and fell short. The Vitellians, on the other hand, had the moon shining full on them and were unaware that they were exposed to the Flavians, shooting as it were out of cover.

Antonius was thus enabled to recognize his own men, and 24 to be recognized by them. He fired some by taunting their honour, many by words of praise and encouragement, all by promising hope of reward. He asked the Pannonian legions why they had drawn their swords again. Here on this field they could regain their glory and wipe out the stain of their former disgrace. Then turning to the Moesian troops, he called on them as the chief promoters of the war: it was no good challenging the Vitellians with verbal threats, if they could not bear to face their looks and blows. Thus he addressed each legion as he reached it. To the Third he spoke at greater length, reminding them of their victories both old and new. Had they not under Mark Antony defeated the Parthians and the Armenians under Corbulo?* Had they not but lately crushed the Sarmatians? Then he turned in fury on the Guards. 'Peasants that you are,' he shouted, 'have you another emperor, another camp waiting to shelter you, if you are defeated? There in the enemy's line are your standards and your arms: defeat means death. You have drained disgrace already to the dregs.'

25   These words roused cheers on all sides, and the Third, following the Syrian custom,* saluted the rising sun. From this there arose a casual rumour—or possibly it was deliberately concocted by the general—that Mucianus had arrived, and that the two armies were cheering each other. On they pressed, feeling they had received fresh reinforcements. The Vitellian line was more ragged now, for, having no general to marshal them, their ranks now filled, now thinned, according to each individual's passion or fear. As soon as Antonius saw them crumble, he kept thrusting at them in massed column. The line disintegrated and then broke, and the inextricable confusion of wagons and engines prevented their rallying. The victorious troops scattered them along the straight road in headlong pursuit.

The massacre was especially noteworthy, because during it a son killed his father. I give the facts and names on the authority of Vipstanus Messala. One Julius Mansuetus, a Spaniard who had joined the Rapax Legion, had left a young son at home. This boy subsequently grew up and enlisted in the Seventh Legion, raised by Galba. Chance now sent his father in his way, and he felled him to the ground. While he was ransacking the dying man, they recognized each other. Flinging his arms round the now lifeless corpse, in a piteous voice he implored his father's spirit to be appeased and not to turn against him as a parricide. The crime was his country's, he cried; what share had a single soldier in these civil wars? Meanwhile he lifted the body and began to dig a grave and perform the last rites for his father. Those who were nearest noticed this; then the story began to spread, till there ran through the army astonishment, complaints, and curses against this most brutal war. Yet they never ceased busily killing and plundering relatives, in-laws, and brothers; and while they talked of the crime they were committing it themselves.

26   When they reached Cremona a fresh task of vast difficulty awaited them. During the war with Otho the German army

had entrenched their camp round the walls of Cremona and then erected a rampart round the camp; and these fortifications had been further strengthened. The sight of them brought the victors to a halt, and their generals were uncertain what instructions to give. The troops had had no rest for a day and a night. To storm the town at once would be an arduous and, in the absence of reserves, a perilous task. On the other hand, a retreat to Bedriacum would involve the intolerable fatigue of a long march, and destroy the value of their victory. Again, it would be dangerous to entrench themselves so close to the lines of the enemy, who might at any minute sally forth and rout them while they were dispersed and digging trenches.

But the chief anxiety lay in the temper of their own men, who were much more ready to face danger than delay. To them discretion was disagreeable and hazard spelt hope. Their thirst for plunder outweighed all fears of slaughter, wounds, and bloodshed.

Antonius also inclined to this view* and gave orders for 27 them to surround the rampart. At first they stood back and exchanged volleys of arrows and stones, suffering themselves the severer loss, for a storm of missiles rained down from the walls. Antonius then assigned each legion to assault a different part of the rampart and gates, hoping that by thus separating their tasks he could distinguish the cowards from the brave and inflame them with a spirit of honourable rivalry. The Third and Seventh took the position nearest the road to Bedriacum; the Eighth and Seventh Claudian assaulted the right-hand side of the rampart; the Thirteenth swept up to the Brixian Gate. A brief delay was caused while some fetched mattocks and pickaxes from the nearby fields, and others hooks and ladders. Then holding their shields above their heads in close 'tortoise' formation,* they advanced under the rampart.

Both sides employed Roman tactics. The Vitellians rolled down huge masses of stones, and, as the 'tortoise' parted and wavered, they thrust at it with lances and poles, until at last the whole structure of shields was broken up and they mowed down the torn and bleeding soldiers beneath with terrible slaughter. The men began to hesitate; but the generals, realiz-

ing that they were too tired to respond to encouragements that
28 seemed futile, pointed significantly to Cremona. Whether this
was Hormus' idea, as Messala records, or whether we should
rather follow Gaius Pliny,* who accuses Antonius, it is not
easy for me to determine. This one may say: however abominable the crime, in committing it neither Antonius nor
Hormus belied their reputation or their lives.

After this neither wounds nor bloodshed could stay the
Flavian troops. They demolished the rampart, shook the
gates, climbed up on each other's shoulders and over the re-
formed 'tortoise', and caught hold of the enemy's weapons
and limbs. Thus the wounded and unwounded, the half-dead
and the dying, all came rolling down and perished together by
every imaginable kind of death.

29 The fight raged fiercest round the Third and Seventh Legions, and the general, Antonius, came up with a picked band
of auxiliaries to support their assault. The Vitellians, finding
themselves unable to resist the attack of troops stubbornly
vying with each other, and seeing their missiles all glide off the
'tortoise', at last sent their catapult crashing down upon their
heads. For the moment it scattered and crushed beneath it the
men on whom it fell, but it dragged with it the battlements
and the top of the rampart. At the same moment an adjoining
tower gave way under a shower of stones. While the men of
the Seventh struggled up to the breach in close column, the
Third hewed down the gate with hatchets and swords. All the
authorities agree that Gaius Volusius of the Third Legion was
the first man in. Emerging on the top of the rampart, he hurled
down those who barred his path; and, attracting attention by
his gestures and shouts, yelled that the camp was taken. The
others poured through, while the Vitellians in panic flung
themselves down from the rampart, and the whole space
between the camp and the walls became a seething scene of
carnage.

30 Here, once again, a new type of task appeared to the
Flavians. Here were high walls, stone towers, iron-barred
gates, and soldiers hurling javelins. The citizens of Cremona
were numerous and devoted to the cause of Vitellius, and half
Italy had gathered there for the fair which fell just at that time.

Their numbers were a help to the defenders, but the prospect of plundering them offered an incentive to their assailants. Antonius ordered his men to bring fire and apply it to the most beautiful of the buildings outside the walls, hoping that the loss of their property might induce the citizens to turn traitor. The houses that stood nearest to the wall and overtopped them he crowded with his bravest troops, who dislodged the defenders with showers of beams and tiles and flaming torches.

Meanwhile, some of the legionaries were collecting for a 31 'tortoise' formation, while others kept up a steady fire of javelins and stones. Gradually the spirit of the Vitellians ebbed. The higher their rank, the more easily they gave way to misfortune. For they were afraid that if Cremona too was demolished, there would be no hope of pardon; the victors' fury would fall not on the common poor but on the tribunes and centurions, whom it would pay to kill. The common soldiers felt safe in their obscurity, and, careless of the future, continued to offer resistance. They roamed the streets or hid themselves in houses, and though they had given up the war, refused even so to sue for peace. Meanwhile the tribunes and centurions did away with the name and portraits of Vitellius. They released Caecina, who was still in irons, and begged his help in pleading their cause. When he turned from them in haughty contempt they besought him with tears. It was the ultimate evil that all these brave men should invoke a traitor's aid.

They then hung olive-branches and ritual bands* out on the walls, and when Antonius had given the order to cease firing, they carried out their standards and eagles, followed by a miserable column of disarmed soldiers, dejectedly hanging their heads. The victors had at first crowded round, heaping insults on them and threatening violence, but when they found that the vanquished had lost all arrogance, but turned to face the taunts and endured every indignity, they gradually began to recollect that these were the men who had made such a moderate use of their recent victory at Bedriacum. But when the crowd parted, and Caecina advanced in his consular robes, attended by his lictors in full state, their indignation

broke into flame. They charged him with insolence and
cruelty, and they even—so hateful is crime—flung his treachery in his teeth. Antonius restrained them and sent Caecina
under escort to Vespasian.

32   Meanwhile the citizens of Cremona suffered sorely from the
violence of the troops, and it was only when the soldiers were
on the point of a general massacre that the entreaties of their
generals calmed them down. Antonius summoned a mass
meeting where he eulogized his victorious army, promised
mercy to the vanquished, but spoke non-committally of
Cremona. Besides the troops' natural passion for plunder,
there was an old grudge which urged them to annihilate the
Cremonese. The town was believed to have given assistance to
the Vitellian cause* before this in the war with Otho; and
again, when the Thirteenth had been left behind to build an
amphitheatre, the populace had shown its town-bred imperti-
nence by assailing them with insolent ridicule. Other causes
increased this bad feeling: it was here that Caecina had given
his show of gladiators; the town had become for a second time
the theatre of the war; the citizens had conveyed food to the
Vitellians during the battle; some women had been killed,
whose enthusiasm for the cause had led them to the battlefield. Besides all this, the fair had filled the rich city with an
even greater display of wealth than usual.

All eyes were now centred on Antonius, whose fame and
good fortune overshadowed all the other generals. He hurried
off to the baths to wash off the stains of blood. Finding fault
with the temperature of the water, he was heard to quip, 'It
will not be long before it is hot.' This vulgar joke brought on
him all the odium, as it was taken to be his signal to set fire to
Cremona, which was already in flames.

33   Forty thousand soldiers* burst into the town, with a yet
larger crowd of servants and sutlers even more depraved in
their readiness for cruelty and lust. Without any respect for
age or for authority they added rape to murder and murder to
rape. Aged men and decrepit old women, who were worthless
as booty, were hustled off to make sport for them. Any grown
girl or handsome youth who fell into their clutches was torn to
pieces by the violence of rival rapists, leaving the plunderers

themselves to cut each other's throats. Whoever carried off
money or the solid gold offerings in the temples was cut to
pieces, if he met others stronger than himself. Some, disdaining easy finds, hunted for hidden hoards, and dug out buried
treasure, flogging and torturing the householders. They held
torches in their hands and, having once secured their prize,
would fling them wantonly into the empty houses and bare
temples. Composed as the army was of citizens, allies, and
foreign troops, differing widely in language and customs, the
objects of the soldiers' greed differed also. But while their
views of what was right might vary, they all agreed in thinking
nothing wrong. Cremona lasted them four days. While all
other buildings sacred and secular sank in the flames, only the
Temple of Mefitis* outside the walls was left standing, saved
either by its position or by the power of the deity.

Such was the end of Cremona, 286 years after its founda- 34
tion. It had been originally built in the consulship of Tiberius
Sempronius and Publius Cornelius,* while Hannibal was
threatening Italy, to serve as a bulwark against the Gauls
beyond the Po, and to resist any other power that might break
in over the Alps. And so it grew and flourished, aided by its
large number of settlers, its conveniently situated rivers, the
fertility of its territory, and its connections through intermar-
riage with local tribes. Foreign invasions had left it untouched
only to become the victim of civil war.

Antonius, ashamed of his crime, and realizing the growing
odium against him, proclaimed that no citizen of Cremona
was to be kept prisoner; and, indeed, the unanimous feeling in
Italy against buying such slaves had already frustrated the
soldiers' hope of profit. So they began to kill their captives,
whose relatives and in-laws, when this became known, covertly bought their release. After a while, the surviving inhabitants returned to Cremona, and the squares and temples were
rebuilt by the munificence of the Italian towns and under
Vespasian's direct patronage.

However, the soil was so foully infected that it was impos- 35
sible for the Flavians to encamp for long on the ruins of the
buried city. They advanced along the road to the third milestone, and mustered the Vitellians, still straggling and panic-

stricken, each under his own standard. The defeated legions were then distributed through Illyricum, for the civil war was still in progress and their fidelity could not be relied on. They then dispatched couriers to carry the news to Britain and the Spanish provinces. To Gaul they sent a tribune named Julius Calenus, to Germany Alpinius Montanus, who had commanded an auxiliary cohort. Montanus was a Treviran and Calenus an Aeduan; both had fought for Vitellius and thus served to advertise Vespasian's victory. At the same time garrisons were sent to hold the passes of the Alps, for fear that Germany might gird herself to support Vitellius.

36   When Caecina had left Rome,* Vitellius, after an interval of a few days, sent Fabius Valens hurrying to the front, and then proceeded to mask his cares with self-indulgence. He neither made any provision for the war, nor fortified his troops either by haranguing or by drilling them. He did not keep himself in the public eye, but retired into the pleasant shade of his gardens, regarding past, present, and future with equal indifference, like one of those listless animals which lie sluggish and torpid so long as you supply them with food. While he thus loitered languid and indolent in the woods of Aricia,* he was startled by the news of Lucilius Bassus' treachery and the disaffection of the fleet at Ravenna. Soon afterwards he heard with mixed feelings of distress and satisfaction that Caecina had deserted him, but had been imprisoned by the army. On his insensate nature joy had more effect than concern. He returned triumphantly to Rome and at a crowded meeting praised the devotion of the troops in extravagant terms. He gave orders for the imprisonment of Publilius Sabinus, the Prefect of the Guards, on the ground of his intimacy with Caecina, and appointed Alfenus Varus in his place.

37   He next delivered in the Senate a speech constructed to appear grand, and was eulogized with studied obsequiousness by the senators. Lucius Vitellius rose to propose a harsh sentence against Caecina. The rest of the house inveighed with assumed indignation against the consul who had betrayed his country, the general who had betrayed his commander-in-chief, the friend who had betrayed his benefactor to whom he owed all his riches and distinction. But in their protestations

of sympathy with Vitellius they really voiced their personal
vexation. None of the speeches contained any disparagement
of the Flavian generals. They threw the blame on the misguided and impolitic action of the armies, and with anxious
circumlocution avoided all direct mention of Vespasian.
Caecina's consulship had still one day to run, and Rosius
Regulus actually made humble petition for this one day's
office, Vitellius' offer and his acceptance exciting widespread
derision. Thus on 31 October he entered and abdicated his
office. Men who were learned in constitutional history
pointed out that no one before had ever filled a vacancy when
no bill had been passed rescinding the magistracy;* there was,
however, precedent for the one-day consulship in the case of
Caninius Rebilus* when Julius Caesar was dictator and the
civil war necessitated prompt rewards.

   It was at this time that the news of the death of Junius 38
Blaesus gave rise to much talk. I give the story as I find it.
Vitellius was lying seriously ill at his house in the Servilian
Park,* and noticed that a neighbouring mansion was bril-
liantly illuminated at night. On asking the reason, he was told
that Caecina Tuscus* was giving a large dinner party, at
which Junius Blaesus was the chief guest. To this was added
an exaggerated account of their extravagance and dissipation.
Then informants appeared with accusations against Tuscus
and others, but especially slandering Blaesus for spending his
days in revelry while his Emperor lay ill. There are people who
keep a sharp eye on every sign of an emperor's displeasure.
They soon made sure that Vitellius was furious and that
Blaesus' ruin would be an easy task, so they cast Lucius
Vitellius in the role of informer. He had a mean and jealous
hatred of Blaesus, whose spotless reputation far outshone his
own, which was tainted with every kind of infamy. Bursting
into the Emperor's apartment, he caught up Vitellius' young
son* in his arms and fell at his feet. When asked the reason for
his consternation, he said it was due to no personal fear or
anxiety for himself; all his prayers and tears were for his
brother and his brother's children. Their fears of Vespasian
were idle: between him and Vitellius lay all the legions of
Germany, all those brave and loyal provinces, and an immeas-

urable space of land and sea. 'It is here in Rome,' he cried, 'in our very bosom that we have an enemy to fear, one who boasts that the Junii and Antonii are his ancestors,* one who shows himself affable and munificent to the troops, posing as a descendant of imperial stock. It is to him that Rome's attention turns, while you, careless who is friend or foe, cherish a rival, who sits feasting and watches his Emperor suffering. You must requite his unseasonable gaiety with a night of deadly sorrow, in which he may both know and feel that Vitellius lives and is emperor, and, if anything should happen, has a son to be his heir.'

39   Vitellius hesitated anxiously between his criminal desires and his fear that, if he deferred Blaesus' death, he might hasten his own ruin, or by giving official orders for it might raise a storm of indignation. He decided to proceed by poison. He made his culpability credible by going to see Blaesus and showing obvious satisfaction. Moreover, he was heard to make the savage boast that he had, to quote his own words, 'feasted his eyes on his enemy's death-bed'.

Blaesus, besides his distinguished origin and refined character, was steadfastly loyal. Even before the decline of Vitellius' cause he had been canvassed by Caecina and other party leaders, who were turning against the Emperor, and had met them with a persistent refusal. He was a man of quiet and blameless life, with no ambition for the principate or, indeed, for any sudden distinction, but he could not escape the danger of being considered worthy of it.

40   Meanwhile Fabius Valens, with a long and languid train of harlots and eunuchs, was conducting a leisurely advance,* most unlike a march to the front, when couriers arrived post-haste with the news that Lucilius Bassus had surrendered the Ravenna fleet. If he had hurried forward on his march he might have been in time to save Caecina's faltering loyalty, or to have joined the legions before the critical engagement was fought. Some, indeed, advised him to avoid Ravenna and with his most reliable troops to make his way by obscure by-roads to Hostilia or Cremona. Others wanted him to send to Rome for the Guards and to break through the enemy's lines with a strong force. Valens himself, with futile indecision, let the time

for action go by while he took advice; and then rejecting the advice he was offered, chose the middle course, which is always the worst in a crisis, and thus failed both in courage and in caution. He wrote to Vitellius demanding reinforce- 41 ments, and there arrived three cohorts of Guards and a regiment of cavalry from Britain, too many to slip through unobserved and too few to force a passage.

But even in such a crisis as this Valens' reputation was as unsavoury as ever. He was still believed to be grabbing illicit pleasures and defiling the homes of his hosts by seducing their wives and families. He had power and money to help him, and the lustful impatience of one whose star is on the wane.

At last the arrival of the infantry and cavalry revealed the perversity of his strategy. He had too few men to take the road through the enemy, even if they had been unquestionably loyal—and their loyalty was under grave suspicion. However, their sense of decency and respect for the general restrained them for a while, though such ties are soon broken when troops are scared of danger and indifferent to disgrace. Fearing trouble, he sent the cohorts forward to Ariminum* with the cavalry to secure the rear. Valens himself, with a few companions, whose loyalty had survived misfortune, turned off into Umbria and thence to Etruria, where he learnt the result of the battle of Cremona. Thereupon he formed a plan, which was far from cowardly and would have had alarming consequences, if it had succeeded. This was to seize ships and cross to some point on the coast of Narbonese Gaul, whence he could rouse the provinces of Gaul, the armies, and the German tribes for a fresh outbreak of war.

As Valens' departure had dispirited the troops at 42 Ariminum, Cornelius Fuscus advanced his force and, sending Liburnian cruisers along the adjoining coast, invested the town by land and sea. The Flavians thus occupied the Umbrian plain and the Adriatic seaboard of Picenum; and the Apennines now divided Italy between Vitellius and Vespasian. Valens, embarking from the Bay of Pisa, was either becalmed on a slow sea or caught by an unfavourable wind and had to put in at the harbour of Hercules Monoecus.*

Stationed in the neighbourhood was Marius Maturus, the governor of the Maritime Alps, who had remained loyal to Vitellius, and, though surrounded by enemies, had so far been faithful to his oath of allegiance. He gave Valens a friendly welcome and strongly advised him not to venture rashly into Narbonese Gaul: this alarmed Valens, who found also that his 43 companions' loyalty was yielding to their fears. For Valerius Paulinus, the procurator in Narbonese Gaul, was an energetic soldier who had been friendly with Vespasian before his elevation, and had lately sworn the surrounding communities to his cause. Having summoned to his flag all the Guards discharged by Vitellius, who needed no persuasion to resume the war, he was now holding the colony of Forum Julii, the key to the command of the sea. His influence carried the more weight since Forum Julii was his native town and, having once been tribune of the Guards, he was respected by the men. Besides this, the inhabitants supported their fellow-citizen, and in the hope of future aggrandizement rendered enthusiastic service to the party.

The news of these efficient preparations, somewhat exaggerated by rumour, dinned in the ears of the Vitellians, who were already in some doubt; Fabius Valens returned to the ships with four men of the Body Guard, three of his friends, and three centurions, while Maturus and the rest preferred to remain and swear allegiance to Vespasian. As for Valens, though he felt safer at sea than among the cities on the coast, he was still full of doubts for the future, since he was more clear about what he had to avoid than whom he could trust. Eventually a gale drove him upon the Stoechades,* some islands belonging to Marseilles, and there he was caught by the cruisers which Paulinus had sent in pursuit.

44   With the capture of Valens the tide had now fully turned in favour of Vespasian. The movement began in Spain with the First Legion Adiutrix, whose reverence for Otho's memory made them hate Vitellius. They carried the Tenth and the Sixth with them. The provinces of Gaul soon followed suit. Britain tended to support Vespasian's cause, since he had been sent there by Claudius* in command of the Second Legion, and had fought there with great distinction. But the adherence

of the province was to some extent opposed by the other legions, in which many of the centurions and soldiers had been promoted by Vitellius. They were used to their Emperor and felt some doubt about the change.*

This quarrel between the legions, and the constant rumours 45 of civil war, encouraged the Britons to take heart. Their chief instigator was one Venutius. He was of a ferocious disposition and hated the name of Rome, but his strongest motive was a private quarrel with Queen Cartimandua, a member of a powerful family, who ruled the Brigantes.* Her authority had lately increased, since she had betrayed King Caratacus* into the hands of the Romans, and was thus considered to have provided the Emperor Claudius with his triumph. Thus she had grown rich, and with prosperity came dissipation. She threw over Venutius, who was her husband, and gave her hand and kingdom to his squire Vellocatus. This scandal soon proved the ruin of her house. The husband was backed by popular zeal: the lover by the queen's brutal lusts. Venutius therefore summoned assistance and, aided by the simultane- ous revolt of the Brigantes, brought Cartimandua into dire straits. She petitioned for troops from Rome. Our auxiliaries, both horse and foot, then fought several engagements with varying success, but eventually rescued the queen. The king- dom was left in Venutius' hands—and the war in ours.

Almost simultaneously a disturbance broke out in 46 Germany, where the inefficiency of the generals, the disaffec- tion of the troops, the strength of the enemy, and the treachery of our allies all combined to bring the Roman government into serious danger. The causes and history of this protracted struggle—for such it proved—we must leave to a later chapter.

Amongst the Dacians also there was trouble. They could never be trusted, and now that the army was moved from Moesia they were no longer restrained by fear. At first they remained quiet and awaited developments. But when they saw Italy in the flames of war, and found the whole world divided into hostile camps, they fell upon the winter quarters of the cohorts and cavalry and began to occupy both banks of the Danube. They were on the point of storming the legionary

camp as well, when Mucianus, who knew of the victory at
Cremona, sent the Sixth Legion* against them. For the empire
was in danger of a double foreign invasion, if the Dacians and
the Germans had broken in from opposite directions. But
here, as so often, Rome's good fortune saved her by bringing
Mucianus on the scene with the forces of the East just at the
moment when we had settled matters at Cremona. Fonteius
Agrippa,* who had for the last year been governor in Asia,
was transferred to the government of Moesia. His forces were
strengthened by a draft from the defeated Vitellian army, for
in the interest of peace and prudence these troops were distributed over the provinces and had their hands tied by foreign
war.

47   The other peoples soon made their voices heard. Pontus*
had suddenly risen in a general rebellion at the instigation of
a foreign menial, who was in command of what had once been
the royal fleet. He was one of Polemo's freedmen, by name
Anicetus, who had formerly been influential and resented the
change which had converted the kingdom into a province of
the Roman Empire. He accordingly enlisted in Vitellius' service the tribes neighbouring on Pontus, attracting with promises of plunder all the most needy. At the head of no mean
force he suddenly fell upon Trapezus,* an ancient and famous
city, founded by Greek settlers at the eastern end of the Pontic
coast. There he cut to pieces a cohort that had once formed
the king's Body Guard, and, after receiving the Roman fran-
chise, had adopted our ensigns and equipment, while still
retaining all the inefficiency and insubordination of Greek
troops. Anicetus also set fire to the fleet and thus had free play
on an empty sea, since Mucianus had moved the pick of his
cruisers and all his troops to Byzantium.

The sea was insolently overrun by natives too, who had
hurriedly built themselves boats. These, which they call 'arks',
are broad-bottomed boats that narrow above the waterline,
built without any brass or iron rivets. In a rough sea, as the
waves rise higher and higher, the height of the sides is raised
by the addition of planks which, in the end, enclose the whole
boat under a sort of roof. They are thus left to toss up and
down on the waves. They have bows at both ends and can be

rowed either way, since it is as easy and as safe to land in one direction as in the other.

This state of things attracted Vespasian's attention. He sent 48 out a picked force of detachments from the legions under Virdius Geminus, a soldier of experience. He attacked the enemy while they were dispersed in all directions in quest of plunder, and drove them back to their ships. He then had some Liburnian cruisers hurriedly constructed and ran Anicetus to ground in the mouth of the River Chobus,* where he had taken refuge with the king of the Sedochezi tribe, whose alliance he had purchased by bribes. At first, indeed, the king endeavoured to protect his petitioner by using violent threats, but he soon saw that it was a choice between making war or being paid for his treachery. As usual, the barbarian sense of honour dissolved. He arranged for Anicetus' death and surrendered the other fugitives, and thus put an end to the slaves' war.

This victory delighted Vespasian: everything was succeeding beyond his hopes, and to crown all the news of the battle of Cremona now reached him in Egypt. He hurried forward all the faster towards Alexandria with the object of bringing starvation upon Vitellius' defeated troops and the inhabitants of Rome, who were in need of imports: he was at the same time making preparations for an invasion of the adjacent province of Africa by land and sea. By cutting off their corn supply he hoped to reduce the enemy to famine and disunion.

Thus a world-wide convulsion marked the passing of the 49 imperial power into new hands. Meanwhile, after Cremona, the behaviour of Antonius Primus was not so blameless as before. He had settled the war, he felt; the rest would be plain sailing. Or perhaps in such a nature as his success only brought to light his greed and arrogance and all his other dormant vices. While harrying Italy like a conquered country, he courted the goodwill of his troops as if they were his own, and he used every word and every action to pave his way to power. He allowed his men to appoint centurions themselves in place of those who had fallen, and thus gave them a taste for insubordination; for they voted for the most turbulent spirits. The generals no longer controlled the men, but were dragged along by their violence. This revolutionary system, utterly fatal to good discipline, was exploited by Antonius for his own profit. Of Mucianus' approach he had no fears, and thus made a mistake even more fatal than despising Vespasian.*

50   As winter was at hand, however, and the Po had inundated the meadows, his column marched unencumbered by heavy baggage. The main body of the victorious legions was left behind at Verona: the soldiers who were incapacitated by wounds or old age, and many besides who were still in good condition. Having already broken the back of the campaign, Antonius felt strong enough with his auxiliary cohorts, horse regiments, and some picked detachments from the legions. The Eleventh* had voluntarily joined the advance. They had held back at first, but, seeing Antonius' success, were distressed to think they had had no share in it. The column was also accompanied by a force of 6,000 Dalmatian troops, which had been recently raised. The ex-consul Pompeius Silvanus commanded the column, but the actual control was in the hands of the legionary commander Annius Bassus.* Silvanus was quite ineffective as a general, and wasted every chance of action in talking about it. Bassus, while showing all due respect, managed him completely, and was always ready with quiet efficiency to do anything that had to be done. Their force was further increased by enlisting the best of the marines from the Ravenna fleet, who were clamouring for service in the legions; the vacancies in the fleet were filled by Dalmatians.

The army and its generals halted at Fanum Fortunae,* still hesitating what policy to adopt, for they had heard that the Guards were on the move from Rome, and supposed that the Apennines were held by troops. And they had fears of their own. Supplies were scarce in a district devastated by war. The men were mutinous and demanded 'boot-money', as they called the donative. No provision had been made either for money or for stores. The precipitate greed of the soldiers made further difficulties, for they looted what they could otherwise have been given.

In some famous authorities, I find evidence which shows 51
how wickedly careless were the victorious army of all considerations of right and wrong. They tell how a trooper declared
that he had killed his brother in the last battle, and demanded
a reward from his generals. Common morality forbade them
to remunerate such a murder, but in the interests of civil war
they dared not punish it. They had put him off with the plea
that they could not at the moment reward his service ad-
equately. And there the story stops. However, a similar crime
had occurred in earlier civil wars. In the battle which
Pompeius Strabo fought against Cinna at the Janiculum,* one
of his soldiers killed his own brother and then, realizing what
he had done, committed suicide. This is recorded by Sisenna.*
Our ancestors had a livelier sense than we have both of the
glory of good deeds and the shame of bad. I may appropri-
ately cite these and other such instances from past history,
whenever the subject demands either an example of good
conduct or some consolation for a crime.

Antonius and his fellow generals decided to send the cavalry 52
ahead to explore the whole of Umbria and to see whether the
summit of the Apennines was accessible by a gentler route.
They would summon the main body of the forces and all the
remaining troops at Verona, and fill the Po and the sea with
supply ships.

Some of the generals contrived to delay progress; Antonius,
they felt, had grown too big for his place, and they had surer
hopes of reward from Mucianus. Mucianus was distressed
that victory had come so soon, and felt that, if he was not
present when Rome was taken, he would lose his share in the
war and its glory. So he kept on writing to Antonius and
Varus in ambiguous terms, sometimes urging them to 'press
forward on their path', sometimes expatiating on 'the manifold value of delay'. He thus managed to arrange that he could
disclaim responsibility in case of a reverse, or acknowledge
their policy as his own if it succeeded.

To Plotius Grypus, whom Vespasian had lately raised to
senatorial rank and put in command of a legion, and to his
other trusty friends he sent less ambiguous instructions, and

they all wrote back criticizing the haste with which Antonius and Varus acted. This was just what Mucianus wanted. He forwarded the letters to Vespasian with the result that Antonius' plans and deeds were not appreciated as highly as Antonius had hoped.

53   This Antonius took very ill; he threw the blame on Mucianus, whose charges, he conceived, had cheapened his perilous exploits. Being little accustomed to control his tongue or to obey orders, he was most unguarded in his conversation. He composed a letter to Vespasian in presumptuous language which ill befitted a subject, making various covert charges against Mucianus. 'It was I', he wrote, 'who brought the legions of Pannonia into the field: it was I who goaded into activity the officers in Moesia: it was by my persistence that we broke through the Alps, seized hold of Italy, and cut off the German and Raetian auxiliaries. When Vitellius' legions were all scattered and disunited, it was I who routed them, flinging the cavalry on them like a whirlwind, and then pressing home with the infantry all day and all night. That victory is my greatest achievement and it is entirely my own. As for the mishap at Cremona, that was the fault of the war. In old days the civil wars cost the country far more damage and involved the destruction of more than one town. It is not with couriers and dispatches that I serve my master, but with my sword in my hand. Nor can it be said that I have interfered with the glory of the men who have meanwhile settled matters in Dacia. What peace in Moesia is to them, the safety and welfare of Italy are to me. It was my encouragement which brought the provinces of Gaul and of Spain, the strongest parts of the whole world, over to Vespasian's side. But my labours will prove useless,* if the reward for the dangers I have run is to fall to those who were not there to share them.'

All this reached the ears of Mucianus and a serious quarrel resulted. Antonius fostered it in a frank spirit of dislike, while Mucianus showed a cunning which was far more implacable.

54   After the crushing defeat at Cremona Vitellius stupidly suppressed the news of the disaster, thus postponing not the evil itself but only its cure. Had he admitted the facts and

sought advice, hope and strength were still left to him: his pretence that all went well only made matters worse. In his presence there prevailed an extraordinary silence about the war, and in Rome all discussion of the subject was forbidden. This only increased the number of people who, if permitted, would have told the truth, but in the face of this prohibition spread grossly exaggerated rumours. Nor were the Flavian leaders slow to foster these stories. Whenever they captured Vitellian spies they escorted them round the camp to show them the strength of the winning army, and sent them back again. Vitellius cross-examined each of them in secret and then had them murdered.

A centurion named Julius Agrestis, after many interviews, in which he endeavoured in vain to fire Vitellius' courage, at last with remarkable and heroic persistence induced the Emperor to send him to inspect the enemy's forces and discover what had really happened at Cremona. He made no attempt to deceive Antonius by concealing the object of his mission, but openly avowed the Emperor's instructions, stated his intentions, and demanded to be shown everything. He was given guides, who showed him the field of battle, the ruins of Cremona, and the captured legions. Back went Agrestis to Vitellius. Finding that the Emperor disbelieved his report and even suggested that he had been bribed, he said, 'You want some certain evidence: since you have no further use for me either alive or dead, I will give you evidence that you can believe.' Going straight from the Emperor's presence, he corroborated his report by committing suicide.* Some say he was killed by order of Vitellius, but they give the same account of his heroic devotion.

Vitellius was like a man roused from sleep. He dispatched 55 Julius Priscus and Alfenus Varus with fourteen cohorts of Guards and all his available cavalry to hold the Apennines; a legion levied from the marines was sent after them. This large army of picked men and horses was strong enough to have even taken the offensive—if it had had another general. His other cohorts were given to his brother Lucius Vitellius, for the protection of the city. The Emperor himself gave up none of his habitual luxuries, but pessimism made him hasty. He hurried on the elections and nominated consuls for several years in advance. He lavished treaties on allied communities and extended Latin rights* to foreign towns: he remitted taxation here, granted immunities there. In fact, he took no thought for the future and crippled the empire. However, the mob accepted these munificent grants with open mouths. Fools paid money for them, but wise men held them invalid, since they could be neither given nor received without destroying the state. At last he yielded to the demands of the army and joined the camp at Mevania,* where they had taken up their position. A long train of senators followed him, many moved by their ambition, but most by their fears. Here he was still undecided and at the mercy of treacherous advice.

56   During one of his speeches a portent occurred. A black cloud of ill-omened birds flew over his head, and its density obscured the daylight. To this was added another omen of disaster. A bull broke from the altar, scattered the utensils for the ceremony, and was impaled a distance away instead of being sacrificed according to the proper ritual. But the chief portent was Vitellius himself. He was ignorant of soldiering, incapable of forethought: knew nothing of marching order or scouting, or how far operations should be pressed forward or protracted. He always had to ask someone else. At every fresh piece of news his expression and gait betrayed his alarm. And then he would get drunk.

At last he found camp life too tedious, and on learning of a mutiny in the fleet at Misenum he returned to Rome. Every fresh blow terrified him, but of the real crisis he was insensible. For it was open to him to cross the Apennines and with his full strength unimpaired to attack the enemy while they were worn out with cold and hunger. But by breaking up his forces he sent his keenest soldiers, stubbornly loyal to the last, to be killed or taken prisoner. The more experienced of his centurions disapproved of this policy and would have told him the truth, if they had been consulted. But Vitellius's intimates refused them admittance. The Emperor had, indeed, formed a habit of regarding wholesome advice as unpleasant, and listening only to what was agreeable—and ultimately fatal.

In civil war individual enterprise counts for much. The 57
mutiny of the fleet at Misenum had been engineered by
Claudius Faventinus, a centurion whom Galba had dismissed
in disgrace. To obtain his object he had forged a letter from
Vespasian, promising rewards for treachery. The admiral,
Claudius Apollinaris, was neither a staunch loyalist nor an
enthusiastic traitor. Accordingly Apinius Tiro, an ex-praetor
who happened to be at Minturnae, volunteered to lead the
rebels. They proceeded to win over the colonies and country
towns. Puteoli in particular was strong for Vespasian, while
Capua remained loyal to Vitellius, for they dragged their local
jealousies into the civil war.

To pacify the excited troops Vitellius chose Claudius
Julianus, who had lately been in command of the fleet at
Misenum and had allowed lax discipline. He was given to
back him up one cohort of the City Garrison and the force of
gladiators already serving under him. The two parties encamped close to one another, and it was not long before
Julianus came over to Vespasian's side. They then occupied
Tarracina,* which owed its strength more to its walls and
situation than to the character of its new garrison.

When news of this reached Vitellius, he left part of his force 58
at Narnia* with the Prefects of the Guards, and sent his
brother Lucius with six cohorts and 500 horse to cope with
the threatened outbreak in Campania. His own nervous de-
pression was somewhat relieved by the enthusiasm of the
troops and of the populace, who clamoured loudly for arms.
For he dignified this poor-spirited mob, which would never
dare to do anything but shout, by the specious titles of 'the
army' or 'his legions'. His friends were all untrustworthy in
proportion to their eminence; but on the advice of his freedmen he held a tribal assembly and swore in all who gave their
names. As their numbers were too great, the consuls handled
the conscription jointly. From each of the senators he levied a
fixed number of slaves and a weight of silver. The knights
offered money and personal service, while even freedmen
volunteered similar assistance. Indeed, feigned loyalty
prompted by fear had changed into real sympathy. People
began to feel pity, not so much for Vitellius as for the throne

and its misfortunes. He himself by his looks, his voice, his tears made ceaseless demands upon their compassion, promising rewards lavishly and, as men do when they are frightened, beyond all limits. He had hitherto refused the title of Caesar, but he now expressed a wish for it. He had a superstitious respect for the name, and in moments of terror one listens as much to gossip as to sound advice. However, while an undertaking that is based on irrational emotion may prosper at the outset, in time it always begins to flag. Gradually the senators and knights deserted him. At first they hesitated and waited till his back was turned, but soon they ceased to care and openly showed their disrespect. At last Vitellius grew ashamed of the failure of his efforts and excused them from the services which they refused to render.

59   The occupation of Mevania had terrified Italy: there was the sense that the war had begun afresh. But now Vitellius' cowardly retreat perceptibly strengthened the popularity of the Flavian party. The Samnites, Paelignians, and Marsians were jealous of Campania for stealing a march on them, and the change of masters, as so often happens, made them perform all their military duties with the utmost alacrity. But in crossing the Apennines Antonius' army suffered severely from the rough December weather. Though they met with no opposition, they found it hard enough to struggle through the snow, and realized what danger they would have had to face if Vitellius had not happened to turn back. Chance helped the Flavian generals quite as often as strategy.

Here they came across Petillius Cerialis,* who had been enabled by his knowledge of the country to elude Vitellius' outposts, disguised as a peasant. As he was a near relative of Vespasian and a distinguished soldier he was given a place on the staff. Several authorities say that Flavius Sabinus and Domitian were also afforded facilities for escape, and Antonius sent messengers who contrived by various tricks to get through to them, and made arrangements for an interview and safe conduct. Sabinus, however, pleaded that his health was unequal to the fatigue of such a bold step. Domitian was quite ready to venture, but he had been detained on Vitellius' orders; the guards promised that they would share his flight, but he was afraid they might be laying a trap for him. As a matter of fact, Vitellius was too anxious for the safety of his own relatives to plot any harm against Domitian.

The Flavian generals arrived at Carsulae, took a few days' 60 rest, and awaited the arrival of the main legionary force. The place suited them admirably for an encampment. It commanded a wide view, and with so many prosperous towns in the rear their supplies were safe. The Vitellians too were only ten miles away, and they had hopes of negotiating treason with them. The soldiers chafed at this delay, preferring victory to peace. They did not even want to wait for their own legions, for there would be more plunder than peril to share with them.

Antonius accordingly summoned a meeting of the men and explained to them that Vitellius still had troops at his command. Reflection might make them waver, despair would steel their hearts. In civil war, he told them, the first steps may be left to chance; nothing but careful strategy can win the final victory. The fleet at Misenum and the richest part of the Campanian coastline had already deserted Vitellius, and in the whole world nothing was left to him now except the country between Tarracina and Narnia. The battle of Cremona had brought them credit enough, the destruction of Cremona more than enough discredit. Their desire must be not to take Rome but to save it. They would gain richer rewards and far the highest glory if they sought to save the Senate and People of Rome without shedding a drop of blood.

Such considerations as these calmed their excitement, and it 61 was not long before the legions arrived. Alarmed by the report of this enlarged army, Vitellius' cohorts began to waver. There was no one to encourage them to fight, while many urged them to desert and competed to hand over their companies or squadrons to the enemy and by such a gift to secure the victor's gratitude for the future. From them the Flavians learned that the camp on the nearby plains at Interamna had a garrison of 400 cavalry. Varus was promptly sent off with a light marching force, and the few who offered resistance were killed—the majority threw away their arms and begged for quarter. Some escaped to the main camp and spread universal panic by exaggerating the strength and prowess of the enemy, in order to mitigate the disgrace of losing the fort.

In the Vitellian camp all offences went unpunished: desertion met with sure reward. Their loyalty soon gave way and a competition in treachery began. Tribunes and centurions deserted daily, but not the common soldiers, who had grown stubbornly faithful to Vitellius. At last, however, Priscus and Alfenus abandoned the camp and returned to Vitellius, releasing all the others from any obligation to blush for their treachery.

62 About the same time Fabius Valens was executed in his prison at Urbinum,* and his head was exhibited to Vitellius' Guards to show them that further hope was vain. For they cherished a belief that Valens had made his way into Germany, and was there mustering armies old and new. This evidence of his death threw them into despair. The Flavian army was vastly inspirited by it and regarded Valens' death as the end of the war.*

Valens had been born at Anagnia* of an equestrian family. He was a man of loose morality, not without intellectual gifts, who by indulging in frivolity posed as a wit. In Nero's time he had acted in a farce at the Juvenalian Games,* at first pleading compulsion, but afterwards voluntarily; his performances were clever rather than respectable. Rising to the command of a legion, he supported Verginius and then defamed his character. He murdered Fonteius Capito when he had corrupted him—or perhaps it was because he had failed to corrupt him. He betrayed Galba and remained faithful to Vitellius, a merit given lustre by the treachery of others.

63 Now that their hopes were crushed on all sides, the Vitellians prepared to go over to the enemy. But even now they saved their honour by marching down with their standards and colours to the plains below Narnia, where the Flavian army was drawn up in full array ready for battle in closed ranks on either side of the road. The Vitellians marched in between and were surrounded. Antonius then spoke to them kindly and told them to remain, some at Narnia and some at Interamna. He also left behind some of the victorious

legions, which were strong enough to quell any outbreak but
would not molest them so long as they remained quiet.

During these days Antonius and Varus kept sending messages to Vitellius, in which they offered him his life, a gift of
money, and the choice of a safe retreat in Campania, if he
would stop the war and surrender himself and his children to
Vespasian. Mucianus wrote him letters to the same effect.
Vitellius usually took these offers seriously and talked about
the number of slaves he would have and the choice of a seaside
place. He had sunk, indeed, into such mental torpor that, if
other people had not remembered that he was an emperor, he
would have forgotten it himself.

However, it was to Flavius Sabinus, the City Prefect, that 64
the leading men at Rome addressed themselves. They urged
him secretly not to lose all share in the glory of victory. They
pointed out that the City Garrison was under his own command, and that he could count on the Watch and their own
bands of slaves, to say nothing of the good fortune of the
party and all the advantage that victory gives. He must not
leave all the glory to Antonius and Varus. Vitellius had nothing left but a few cohorts of Guards, who were seriously
alarmed at the bad news which came from every quarter. As
for the populace, their feelings soon changed, and if he put
himself at their head, they would be just as loud in their
flattery of Vespasian. Vitellius himself could not even cope
with success, and disaster had positively paralysed him. The
credit of ending the war would go to the man who seized
the city. It was eminently fitting that Sabinus should secure the
throne for his brother, and that Vespasian should hold him
higher than any one else.

Age had enfeebled Sabinus,* and he showed no alacrity to 65
listen to such talk as this. Some people covertly insinuated that
he was jealous of his brother's success and was trying to delay
its realization. And in fact Flavius Sabinus was the elder
brother and, when they were both private citizens, he had
been the richer and more influential. It was also believed that
when Vespasian's finances were in jeopardy, Sabinus had
begrudged him assistance, and had taken a mortgage on his

house and estates. Consequently, though they remained openly friendly, there were suspicions of a secret enmity between them.

The more charitable explanation is that Sabinus' gentle nature shrank from the idea of bloodshed and massacre, and that this was his reason for so constantly discussing with Vitellius the prospects of peace and a capitulation on terms. After several interviews at their homes they finally came to a settlement—so the report went—at the Temple of Apollo. To the actual conversation there were only two witnesses, Cluvius Rufus and Silius Italicus,* but their faces were watched from a distance. Vitellius was said to look abject and ignoble: Sabinus showed less sign of mockery than of pity.

66 Had Vitellius found it as easy to persuade his friends as to make his own renunciation, Vespasian's army would have marched into Rome without bloodshed.* But as it was, the greater their loyalty, the more they persisted in refusing terms of peace. They pointed to the danger and disgrace. Would their conqueror keep his promises any longer than he liked? However great Vespasian's arrogance, he could not allow Vitellius to live as a private citizen; nor would even the losers agree to it. So appealing to mercy brings peril. 'Of course,' they said, 'you are an old man.* You have had your fill of fortune, good or bad. But what name or position will your son Germanicus enjoy? At present they are promising you money and a household, and the pleasant shores of Campania. But when once Vespasian has seized the throne, neither he nor his friends nor even his army will feel their safety assured until the rival claimant is dead. They imprisoned Fabius Valens and meant to make use of him if a crisis occurred, but they found him too great an incubus. You may be sure that Antonius and Fuscus, and that typical representative of the party, Mucianus, will have no choice but to kill you. Julius Caesar did not let Pompey live unmolested, nor Augustus Antony.* Do you suppose that Vespasian's is a loftier disposition? Why, he was dependant of a Vitellius when that Vitellius was Claudius' colleague.* No, think of your father's censorship, his three consulships, and all the honour your great house has won. You must not disgrace them. Despair, at least, should nerve

you to audacity. The troops are steadfast; you still enjoy the people's favour. Indeed, nothing worse can happen to you than what we are rushing into of our own free will. If we are defeated, we must die; if we surrender, we must die. All that matters is whether we breathe our last amid mockery and insult or bravely and with honour.'

But Vitellius was deaf to all courageous counsel. His mind 67 was obsessed with pity for his wife and children, and anxiety that obstinate resistance might make the conqueror merciless towards them. He had also a mother, very old and infirm, but she forestalled the ruin of her house, opportunely dying* a few days before. All she had got out of her son's principate was sorrow and a fine reputation.

On 18 December he heard the news that the legion and the cohorts at Narnia had deserted him and surrendered to the enemy. He at once put on sombre garments and left the palace, surrounded by his sorrowful household. His small son was carried in a little litter, as though this had been his funeral. The populace uttered untimely flatteries: the soldiers kept an ominous silence.

No one could have been so indifferent to the tragedy of 68 human life as to be unmoved by this spectacle. A Roman emperor, yesterday master of the inhabited world, had left the seat of his authority, and was now passing through the streets of the city, through the crowding populace, quitting the throne. Such a sight had never been seen or heard of before. The dictator, Caesar, had been the victim of sudden violence; Gaius of a secret conspiracy. Nero's* had been a stealthy flight to some obscure country house under cover of night. Piso and Galba might almost be said to have fallen on the field of battle. But here was Vitellius—before the assembly of his own people, his own soldiers around him, with even women look-ing on—uttering a few sentences suitable to his miserable situation. He said it was in the interest of peace and of his country that he now resigned. He begged them only to retain his memory in their hearts and to take pity on his brother, his wife, and his innocent little children. As he said this, he held out his son to them and commended him, now to individuals, now to the whole assembly. At last tears choked his voice.

Turning to the consul Caecilius Simplex, who was standing by, he unstrapped his dagger from his side, and offered to surrender it as a symbol of his power over the life and death of his subjects. The consul refused, and the people standing by shouted 'No'. So he left them with the intention of depositing the imperial regalia in the Temple of Concord and then going to his brother's house. But he was faced with a still louder uproar. They refused to let him enter a private house, and shouted to him to return to the palace. They blocked every other way and only left open the road leading into the Sacred Way.* Not knowing what else to do, Vitellius returned to the palace.

69   A rumour of his abdication had preceded him, and Flavius Sabinus had sent written instructions to the officers of the cohorts to keep the men under control. Thus the whole empire seemed to have fallen into Vespasian's lap. The chief senators, the majority of the knights, and the whole of the City Garrison and the Watch came flocking to the house of Flavius Sabinus.* There they heard the news of the popular enthusiasm for Vitellius and the threatening attitude of the German Guards. But Sabinus had gone too far to draw back, and when he showed hesitation, they all began to urge him to fight, each being afraid for his own safety if the Vitellians were to fall on them when they were disunited and consequently weaker. However, as so often happens on these occasions, everyone offered advice but few exposed themselves to danger.

While Sabinus' armed escort were marching down by the Fundane Pool they were attacked by the most determined Vitellians. The trouble was unforeseen, but the Vitellians got the best of an unimportant skirmish. In the panic Sabinus chose what was at the moment the safest course, and occupied the summit of the Capitol,* where his mixture of troops were joined by a few senators and knights. It is not easy to record their names, since after Vespasian's victory crowds of people claimed credit for this service to the party. There were even some women who endured the siege, the most famous being Verulana Gratilla,* who was drawn there neither by children nor relatives, but by the war itself.

The Vitellians blockading them kept a half-hearted watch, and Sabinus was thus enabled to send for his own children and his nephew Domitian at dead of night, and to dispatch a courier by an unguarded route to tell the Flavian generals that he and his men were under siege, and would be in great straits unless they were rescued. All night, indeed, he was quite unmolested, and could have escaped with perfect safety. The Vitellian troops could face danger with spirit, but were much too careless in the task of keeping guard; besides which a sudden storm of chilly rain interfered with their sight and hearing.

At daybreak, before the two sides commenced hostilities, 70 Sabinus sent Cornelius Martialis, who had been a senior centurion, to Vitellius with instructions to complain that the conditions were being violated; that he had evidently made a mere empty show of abdication, meant to deceive a number of eminent gentlemen. Why else had he gone from the meeting to his brother's house, which caught the eye from a conspicuous position overlooking the Forum, and not rather to his wife's home on the Aventine?* That was the proper course for a private citizen, anxious to avoid all pretension to supreme authority. But no, Vitellius had returned to the palace, the very stronghold of imperial majesty. From there he had launched a column of armed men, who had strewn with innocent dead the most crowded quarter of Rome, and even laid violent hands upon the Capitol. As for Sabinus himself, he was only a civilian, a mere member of the Senate. While the issue was being decided between Vespasian and Vitellius by the engagement of legions, the capture of towns, the capitulation of cohorts, even when the provinces of Spain, of Germany, of Britain, had risen in revolt, he, though Vespasian's brother, had still remained faithful to his allegiance, until Vitellius, unasked, invited him to a conference. Peace and union serve the interest of the losers, but only the reputation of the winners. If Vitellius regretted their compact, he ought not to take arms against Sabinus, whom he had treacherously deceived, or against Vespasian's son, who was all but a boy. What was the good of killing one youth and one old man? He ought rather to march out against the legions and fight for the empire one the field. The result of the battle would decide all other questions.

Greatly alarmed, Vitellius replied with a few words in which he tried to excuse himself and throw the blame on his soldiers. 'I am too unassuming', he said, 'to cope with their overpowering impatience.' He then warned Martialis to make his way out of the building by a secret passage, for fear that the soldiers should kill him as an ambassador of the peace to which they were so hostile. Vitellius himself was not in a position to issue orders or prohibitions; no longer an emperor, merely an excuse for war.*

71   Martialis had hardly returned to the Capitol when the furious soldiery arrived. They had no general to lead them: each was a law to himself. Their column marched at full speed through the Forum and past the temples overlooking it. Then they advanced up the hill in front of them, until they reached the lowest gates of the fortress on the Capitol. In those days there was a series of colonnades at the side of this slope, on the right as you go up. Emerging onto the roof of these, the besieged overwhelmed the Vitellians with showers of stones and tiles. The attacking party carried nothing but swords, and it seemed a long business to send for siege-engines and missiles. So they flung torches into a projecting colonnade and, following in the wake of the flames, would have burst through the burnt gates of the Capitol, if Sabinus had not torn down all the available statues—the monuments of our ancestors' glory—and built a sort of barricade on the very threshold. They then attacked the Capitol by two opposite approaches, one near the 'Grove of Refuge'* and the other by the 100 steps which lead up to the Tarpeian Rock.* This double assault came as a surprise; but that by the Refuge was the closer and more vigorous. Nothing could stop the Vitellians, who climbed up by some adjoining buildings, which in the days of prolonged peace had been raised to such a height that their roofs were level with the floor of the Capitol. It is uncertain whether the houses at this point were fired by the assailants or—the most common account*—by the besieged in trying to dislodge their enemies who had struggled up so far. The fire spread to the colonnades adjoining the temple;* and then the gables supporting the roof, which were made of very old

wood, caught the flames and fed them. And so the Capitol, with its doors fast shut, undefended and unplundered, was burnt to the ground.

Since the foundation of the city no such deplorable and 72 horrible disaster had ever befallen the people of Rome. It was no case of foreign invasion. Had our own wickedness allowed, the country might have been enjoying the blessings of a benign Providence; and yet here was the seat of Jupiter Optimus Maximus—the temple solemnly founded by our ancestors as the guarantee of their imperial greatness, which not even Porsenna, when Rome surrendered, nor the Gauls, when they took it, could have defiled*—being brought utterly to ruin by the mad folly of rival emperors! The Capitol had been burnt before in civil war,* but that was the crime of private persons. Now it had been openly besieged and openly burnt. And what was the military justification? What recompense for such disaster?

While we fought for our country, the temple stood firm. King Tarquinius Priscus had vowed to build it in the Sabine war, and had laid the foundations on a scale that suited rather his hope of the city's future greatness than the still moderate fortunes of the Roman people. Later Servius Tullius, with the support of Rome's allies, and Tarquinius Superbus,* with the spoils of the Volscians after the capture of Suessa Pometia,* continued the building. But the glory of completing it was reserved for the days of freedom. After the expulsion of the kings, Horatius Pulvillus in his second consulship* dedicated this monument on such a magnificent scale that in later days, with all her boundless wealth, Rome was able to embellish but never to enlarge it. After an interval of 415 years, in the consulship of Lucius Scipio and Gaius Norbanus,* it was burnt and rebuilt on the same foundations. Sulla after his victory undertook the task of restoring it, but did not dedicate it: this one thing his famous 'Fortune'* denied him. Much as the emperors did to it, the name of Lutatius Catulus* still remained upon it up to the time of Vitellius. This was the temple that was now ablaze.

The besieged suffered more panic than their assailants. The 73 Vitellian soldiers lacked neither cunning nor steadiness in moments of crisis. But on the other side the troops were terrified, the general inert and apparently so paralysed that he was deaf and dumb. He neither adopted others' plans nor formed any of his own, but only drifted about from place to place, attracted by the shouts of the enemy, banning what he had commanded and commanding what he had banned.* The result was what always happens in a hopeless disaster: everybody gave orders and nobody obeyed them. At last they threw away their weapons and began to look round for a way of escape or some means of hiding. Then the Vitellians came bursting in, and with blood, fire, and sword made havoc. A few good soldiers dared to show fight and were cut to pieces: of these the most notable were Cornelius Martialis, Aemilius Pacensis, Casperius Niger, and Didius Scaeva. Flavius Sabinus, who stood unarmed and made no attempt to escape, was surrounded together with the consul Quintius Atticus, who was a marked man thanks to his empty title, as well as his fatuous vanity, which had led him to distribute manifestos full of encomia of Vespasian and insults against Vitellius. The rest escaped by various means. Some disguised themselves as slaves: some were sheltered by faithful clients and hid among the baggage. Others, again, overheard the password by which the Vitellians recognized each other, and actually went about demanding it and giving it when challenged, thus escaping under a cloak of effrontery.

74   When the enemy first broke in, Domitian had taken refuge with the sacristan, and was enabled by the ingenuity of a freedman to escape among a crowd of worshippers disguised in a linen mantle,* and took refuge near the Velabrum with Cornelius Primus, one of his father's clients. When his father came to the throne, Domitian pulled down the sacristan's lodging and built a little chapel to Jupiter the Saviour with an altar, on which his adventures were depicted in marble relief. Later, when he became emperor, he dedicated a huge temple to Jupiter the Guardian with a statue of himself in the lap of the god.

Sabinus and Atticus were loaded with chains and taken to Vitellius, who received them without any hostility in language or looks, despite the protests of those who wanted to see them punished with death and themselves rewarded for their successful labours. When those who stood nearest started an outcry, the dregs of the populace soon began to demand Sabinus' execution with mingled threats and flatteries. Vitellius came out onto the steps of the palace prepared to plead for him: but they forced him to desist. Sabinus was stabbed and mutilated: his head was cut off and the trunk dragged away to the Gemonian Steps.*

Such was the end of a man who certainly merits no con- 75 tempt. He had served his country for thirty-five years, and won credit both as civilian and soldier. His integrity and fairness were beyond criticism. He talked too much, but this is the one charge which rumour could hint against him in the seven years when he was governor of Moesia, and the twelve years during which he was Prefect of the City. At the end of his life some thought he showed a lack of enterprise, but many believed him a moderate man, who was anxious to save his fellow-citizens from bloodshed.* In this, at any rate, all would agree, that before Vespasian became emperor the reputation of his house rested on Sabinus. It is said that Mucianus was delighted to hear of his murder, and many people maintained that it actually served the interests of peace by putting an end to the jealousy of two rivals, one of whom counted on the fact that he was the Emperor's brother, the other that he was his partner in the empire.

When the people demanded the execution of the consul, Vitellius withstood them. He had forgiven Atticus, and felt that he owed him a favour. For Atticus, when asked who had set fire to the Capitol, had taken the blame on himself, and by this avowal—or well-timed falsehood—he had apparently fixed all the guilt and odium on himself and exonerated the Vitellian party.

About this same time Lucius Vitellius, who had pitched his 76 camp at the Temple of Feronia,* made every effort to destroy Tarracina, where he had shut in the gladiators and sailors, who did not venture to leave the shelter of the walls or to face death in the open. The gladiators were commanded, as I have already said, by Julianus, and the sailors by Apollinaris, men whose dissolute inefficiency better suited gladiators than generals. They set no watch, and made no attempt to repair the weak places in the walls. Day and night they idled loosely; the soldiers were dispatched in all directions to find them luxuries; that beautiful coast rang with their revelry; and they spoke of war only in their cups. A few days earlier, Apinius Tiro had started on his mission, and, by cruelly requisitioning gifts of money in all the country towns, was winning more unpopularity than assistance for the cause.

77   In the mean time, one of Vergilius Capito's* slaves deserted to Lucius Vitellius, and promised that, if he were provided with men, he would put the abandoned citadel into their hands. Accordingly, at dead of night he established a few lightly armed cohorts on the top of the hills which overlooked the enemy. Thence the soldiers came charging down more to butchery than battle. They cut down their victims standing helpless and unarmed or groping for their weapons, or newly startled from their sleep—all in a bewildering confusion of darkness, panic, bugle-calls, and savage cries. A few of the gladiators resisted and sold their lives dearly. The rest rushed to the ships; and there the same panic and confusion reigned, for the villagers were all mixed up with the troops, and the Vitellians slaughtered them without distinction. Just as the first uproar began, six Liburnian cruisers slipped away with the commander Apollinaris on board. The rest were either captured on the beach or overweighted and sunk by the crowds that clambered over them. Julianus was taken to Lucius Vitellius, who had him humiliatingly flogged and then slaughtered before his eyes. Some upbraided Lucius Vitellius' wife Triaria for putting on a soldier's sword and behaving with insolent cruelty among the misery and horrors of captured Tarracina.

    Lucius himself sent a laurel wreath to his brother in token of his success, and inquired whether he wished him to return at once or to continue subjugating Campania. This delay saved not only Vespasian's party but the state as well. Had he marched on Rome while his men were fresh from their victory, with the flush of success added to their natural stead-fastness, there would have been a tremendous struggle, which must have involved the city's destruction. For Lucius Vitellius, for all his evil repute, was a man of action. Good men owe

their power to their virtues; he was one of that worst sort who
derive it from their vices.

While this was happening on Vitellius' side, the Flavian   78
army after leaving Narnia spent the days of the Saturnalian
holiday* quietly at Ocriculum.* The object of this misguided
delay was to wait for Mucianus. Antonius has been suspected
of delaying treacherously after receiving a secret communication from Vitellius; he was in fact offered as the price of
treason the consulship, Vitellius' young daughter's hand, and
a rich dowry. Others hold that this story was invented to
gratify Mucianus. Some people consider that the policy of all
the Flavian generals was rather to threaten the city than to
attack it. They realized that Vitellius had lost his strongest
cohorts, and now that all his forces were cut off they expected
he would abdicate. But this prospect was spoilt first by
Sabinus' precipitation and then by his cowardice, for, after
rashly taking arms, he failed to defend against three cohorts
the powerful fortress of the Capitol, which ought to have been
impregnable even to a large army.

However, it is not easy to assign to any one man the blame
which they all share. Mucianus helped to delay the victors'
advance by the ambiguity of his dispatches, while Antonius
was also to blame for his compliance, which was wrong-
headed—or aimed at deflecting popular resentment.* The
other generals thought the war was over, and thus gave its
final scene all the more notoriety. Petillius Cerialis was sent
forward with 1,000 cavalry to make his way across country
through Sabine territory, and enter the city by the Salarian
Way.* But even he failed to make sufficient haste, and at last
the news of the siege of the Capitol brought them all at once
to their senses.

Marching up the Flaminian Way, it was already deep night   79
when Antonius reached 'The Red Rocks'.* His help had come
too late. There he heard that Sabinus had been killed, and the
Capitol burnt; the city was in panic; everything looked black;
even the populace and the slaves were arming for Vitellius.
Petillius Cerialis, too, had been defeated in a cavalry engagement: he had pushed on without caution, thinking the enemy
already beaten, and the Vitellians with a mixed force of horse

and foot had caught him unawares. The engagement had taken place near the city among buildings, gardens, and winding lanes, with which the Vitellians were familiar, while the Flavians were terrified by their ignorance. Besides, the troopers were not all of one mind; some of them belonged to the force which had recently surrendered at Narnia, and were waiting to see which side won. Julius Flavianus, who commanded a regiment of cavalry, was taken prisoner. The rest fell into a disgraceful panic and fled, but the pursuit was not continued beyond Fidenae.*

80   This success served to increase the popular excitement. The city rabble now took arms. A few had service shields: most of them snatched up any weapons they could find and clamoured to be given the sign for battle. Vitellius expressed his gratitude to them and bade them sally forth to protect the city. He then summoned a meeting of the Senate, at which envoys were appointed to go to the two armies and, supposedly for the sake of the country, urge them to accept peace.

The fortunes of the envoys varied. Those who approached Petillius Cerialis found themselves in dire danger, for the soldiers indignantly refused their terms. The praetor, Arulenus Rusticus,* was wounded. Apart from the wrong done to a praetor and an envoy, the man's own acknowledged worth made this all the more scandalous. His companions were beaten up, and the lictor nearest to him was killed for venturing to make a way through the crowd. Indeed, if the guard provided by the general had not intervened, the sanctity of ambassadors, which even foreign nations respect, in the mad rage of civil strife would have been violated by murder under the very walls of Rome.

Those who went to Antonius met with a more reasonable reception; not that the soldiers were less violent, but the
81 general had more authority. A knight named Musonius Rufus* had attached himself to the envoys. He was a student of philosophy and an enthusiastic advocate of Stoicism. He mingled with the companies, offering the armed soldiers advice and discoursing on the advantages of peace and the perils of war. This amused many of them and bored still more. Some, indeed, wanted to knock and trample him down, but

the advice of the more sober spirits and the threats of others persuaded him to cut short his ill-timed lecture. The Vestal Virgins,* too, came in procession to bring Antonius a letter from Vitellius, in which he demanded one day's postponement of the final crisis, saying that everything could easily be settled if only they would grant this respite.

Antonius sent the Virgins away with all respect, and wrote in answer to Vitellius that with the murder of Sabinus and the burning of the Capitol all negotiations were terminated. How- 82 ever, he summoned the legions to a meeting and endeavoured to mollify them, proposing that they should pitch their camp near the Mulvian Bridge and enter the city on the following day. His motive for delay was a fear that the troops, when once their blood was up after a skirmish, would have no respect for civilians or senators, or even for the temples and shrines of the gods. But they suspected every postponement as a hindrance to their victory. Moreover, some colours which were seen glittering along the hills gave the impression of a hostile force, although none but inexperienced civilians accompanied them.

The Flavian attack was made in three columns. One advanced from its original position on the Flaminian Way, one kept near the bank of the Tiber, and the third approached the Colline Gate* along the Salarian Way. The cavalry rode into the mob and scattered them. But the Vitellian troops faced the enemy, themselves, too, in three separate divisions. Again and again they clashed before the walls with varying success. But the Flavians had the advantage of being well led and thus more often won success. Only one of the attacking parties suffered at all severely, that which had made its way along narrow, greasy lanes to Sallust's Gardens* on the left side of the city. Standing on the garden walls, the Vitellians hurled stones and javelins down upon them and held them back until late in the day. But at last the cavalry forced an entrance by the Colline Gate and encircled the defenders. Then the opposing forces met on the Campus Martius itself. Fortune and the awareness of their many victories favoured the Flavians. The Vitellians charged simply through despair, but, though driven back, they gathered again in the city.

83   The people came and watched the fighting, cheering and applauding now one side, now the other, like spectators at a gladiatorial contest. Whenever one side gave ground, and the soldiers hid in shops or sought refuge in some private house, they clamoured for them to be dragged out and slaughtered. In this way they got the greater part of the plunder for themselves: for while the soldiers were busy with the bloody work of massacre, the spoil fell to the crowd.

The scene throughout the city was cruel and distorted: on the one side fighting and wounded men, on the other baths and restaurants: here lay heaps of bleeding dead, and close at hand were harlots and their ilk. All the vice and licence of luxurious peace, and all the crime and horror of a captured town. You would have thought the city mad with fury and riotous with pleasure at the same time. Armies had fought in the city before this, twice when Sulla mastered Rome, once under Cinna;* nor were there less horrors then. What was now so inhuman was the people's indifference. Not for one minute did they interrupt their life of pleasure. The fighting was a new amusement for their holiday.* Caring nothing for either party, they enjoyed themselves in riotous dissipation and took pleasure in their country's disaster.

84   The storming of the Guards' camp* was the most troublesome task. It was still held by the bravest Vitellians, who saw in it their final hope; this made the victors all the more eager to take it, especially those who had previously served in the Guards. They employed against it every means ever devised for the storming of the most strongly fortified towns, a 'tortoise', artillery, earthworks, firebrands. This, they cried, was the crown of all the toil and danger they had undergone in all their battles. They had restored the city to the Senate and People of Rome, and the temples to the gods. But the soldier's pride is his camp, it is his country and his home. If they could not regain it at once, they must spend the night in fighting. The Vitellians, for their part, had numbers and fortune against them, but by marring their enemy's victory, by postponing peace, by fouling houses and altars with their blood, they embraced the last consolations that the conquered can enjoy. Many lay half-conscious on the towers and ramparts of the

walls and there expired. When the gates were torn down, the remainder faced the conquerors in a body. And there they fell, every man of them facing the enemy with all his wounds in front: even as they died they took care to make an honourable end.

When the city was taken, Vitellius left the palace by a back way and was carried in a litter to his wife's house on the Aventine. If he could lie hidden during the day, he hoped to make his escape to the cohorts with his brother at Tarracina. But it is in the very nature of terror that, while any course looks dreadful, one's current situation seems worst of all. In his endemic restlessness he returned to the vast, deserted palace. Even the lowest of his menials had slipped away, or at least avoided meeting him. The solitude and hushed silence of the place terrified him; he tried locked doors, he shuddered at the emptiness. At last, wearied with his miserable search, he crept into some shameful hiding-place.* There Julius Placidus, a tribune of the Guards, found him and dragged him out. His hands were tied behind his back, his clothes were torn, and he was led forth—a disgraceful spectacle at which many hurled insults, no one shed a single tear of pity. The ignominy of his end had wiped out all compassion. On the way a soldier of the German army* either aimed an angry blow at him, or tried to put him out of his shame, or meant, perhaps, to strike the tribune—it is unclear which. At any rate, he cut off the tribune's ear and was immediately stabbed to death.

With the points of their swords they forced Vitellius to hold up his head and face their insults, then to watch his own statues hurtling down, but above all to look at the Rostra and the site of Galba's murder.* At last he was thrust along to the Gemonian Steps, where the body of Flavius Sabinus had lain. Just one thing that he was heard to say had a ring of true nobility. When some tribune jeered at him, he answered, 'And yet I was once your Emperor.' After that he fell under a shower of wounds; and the mob in their perversity abused him in his death, just as they had flattered him in his lifetime. 85

Vitellius' father* . . . Vitellius' home was at Luceria.* He was 57 years old, and had won the consulship, priesthoods, and a name and position among Rome's greatest men, all of 86

which he owed to no efforts of his own, but solely to his
father's eminence. Those who offered him the throne did not
know him; and yet his slothful cowardice won from his soldiers an enthusiasm which the best of generals have rarely
evoked. Nevertheless, he was candid and generous, although
these qualities in excess will prove disastrous. He believed that
friendship is maintained not by moral stamina, but by extravagant presents; thus though he deserved friends, he had
few. It was indubitably good for the country that Vitellius
should be beaten. But those who betrayed him to Vespasian
can hardly make a merit of their perfidy, for they were the
very men who had deserted Galba for Vitellius.*

The day was already sinking into evening. The magistrates
and senators in terror had slipped out of the city, or were still
in hiding at clients' houses: it was therefore impossible to call
a meeting of the Senate. When all fear of violence was at an
end,* Domitian emerged and presented himself to the generals
of his party. The crowds of soldiers hailed him as Caesar, and,
still in full armour, escorted him to his father's house.

BOOK FOUR

The death of Vitellius had ended the war without inaugurat- 1
ing peace. The victors remained under arms, and the defeated
Vitellians were hunted through the city with implacable
hatred, and butchered indiscriminately wherever they were
found. The streets were choked with corpses; squares and
temples ran with blood. Soon the riot knew no restraint; they
began to hunt for those who were in hiding and to drag them
out. All who were tall and of youthful appearance were cut
down, without distinction between soldiers and civilians.
While their rage was fresh they sated their savage cravings
with blood; but now the instinct of greed had prevailed. On
the pretext of hunting for hidden enemies, they would leave
no door unopened and respect no privacy. Thus they began to
burst into private houses or else made resistance an excuse for
murder. There were plenty of needy citizens, too, and villainous slaves, who without prompting betrayed their wealthy
masters. Others were denounced by their friends. From all
sides came cries of mourning and misery. Rome was like a
captured city. People even longed to have the insolent soldiers
of Otho and Vitellius back again, much as they had been
hated. The Flavian generals, who had fanned the flame of civil
war with such energy, were incapable of acting temperately in
victory. In riot and disorder the worst characters take the lead;
peace and quiet call for the highest qualities.

Domitian had secured the title and the official residence of 2
a Caesar, but did not as yet busy himself with serious matters.
Instead, he played the role of emperor's son by devoting
himself to rape and adultery. Arrius Varus took command of
the Guards, but the supreme authority rested with Antonius
Primus. He removed money and slaves from the Emperor's
house as though he were plundering Cremona.* The other
generals, through their excess of modesty or humble origins,
shared neither the distinctions of the war nor its profits.

People in Rome were now so nervous and so resigned to
despotism that they demanded that Lucius Vitellius and his

force of Guards should be surprised on their way back from Tarracina, and the last sparks of the war stamped out. Some cavalry were sent forward to Aricia, while the column of the legions halted short of Bovillae. Vitellius, however, lost no time in surrendering himself and his Guards to the conqueror's discretion, and the men flung away their unlucky swords more in anger than in fear. The long line of prisoners filed through the city between ranks of armed guards. None looked like begging for mercy. With sad, set faces they remained sternly indifferent to the applause or the mockery of the ribald crowd. A few tried to break away, but were surrounded and overpowered. The rest were put in prison. Not one of them uttered an unseemly word. Through all their misfortunes they preserved their reputation for courage. Lucius Vitellius was then executed. He was as flawed as his brother, though during his principate he showed himself more alert. Without sharing his brother's success, he was carried away on the flood of his disaster.

3   At this time Lucilius Bassus was sent off with a force of light horse to quell the disquiet in Campania, which was caused more by the mutual jealousy of the townships than by any arrogant opposition to the Emperor. The sight of the soldiers restored order. The smaller colonies were pardoned, but at Capua the Third Legion was left in winter quarters and some leading families suffered severely. Tarracina, on the other hand, received no relief. It is always easier to requite an injury than a service: gratitude is a burden, but revenge is found to pay. Their only consolation was that one of Vergilius Capito's slaves, who had, as we have seen, betrayed the town, was hanged on the gallows with the very rings on his fingers which Vitellius had given him to wear.

At Rome the Senate decreed to Vespasian all the usual powers of the principate. They were now happy and confident. Seeing that the civil war had broken out in the provinces of Gaul and Spain, and, after causing a rebellion first in Germany and then in Illyricum, had spread to Egypt, Judaea, Syria, and in fact to all the provinces and armies of the empire, they felt as if the world had been purged of guilt and that all was now over. Their satisfaction was still further enhanced by a letter from Vespasian, which at first sight seemed to be phrased as if the war was still going on. Still his tone was that of an emperor: he portrayed himself as a simple citizen, and spoke with high esteem for the state. The Senate for its part showed no lack of deference. They decreed that Vespasian himself should be consul with his son Titus for his colleague, and on Domitian they conferred the praetorship with the powers of a consul.*

Mucianus had also addressed a letter to the Senate which 4 gave rise to a good deal of talk. If he were a private citizen, why adopt the official tone? He could have expressed the same opinions a few days later from his place in the House. Besides, his attack on Vitellius came too late to prove his independence, and what seemed particularly humiliating for the country and insulting to the Emperor was his boast that he had held the empire in the palm of his hand, and had given it to Vespasian. However, they concealed their ill-will and made a great show of flattery, decreeing to Mucianus in the most complimentary terms full triumphal honours, which were really given to him for his success against his fellow-countrymen, though they trumped up an expedition to Sarmatia as a pretext.* On Antonius Primus they conferred the insignia of the consulship; and those of the praetorship on Cornelius Fuscus and Arrius Varus. Then came the turn of the gods: it was decided to restore the Capitol.*

These proposals were all moved by the consul-elect, Valerius Asiaticus.* The others signified assent by their expressions and gestures, though a few, who were particularly distinguished, or especially practised in the art of flattery, delivered set speeches. When it came to the turn of Helvidius Priscus, the praetor-elect, he expressed himself in terms which, while doing honour to a new emperor,* were frank and honest. The Senate showed their keen approval, and it was this day above all that was the start of his great disfavour and great distinction.

Since I have had occasion to make a second allusion to a 5 man whom I shall often have to mention again, it may be well to give here a brief account of his character and ideals, and of his fortune in life.* Helvidius Priscus came from the country town of Cluviae. His father had been a senior centurion in the army. From his early youth Helvidius devoted his great mental powers to intellectual studies, not as many people do, with the idea of using a philosopher's reputation as a cloak for indolence, but rather to fortify himself against the caprice of fortune when he entered public life. He became a follower of that school of philosophy* which holds that morality is the one good thing in life and vice the only evil, while power and rank and other things that are not qualities of character are neither good nor bad. He had risen no higher than the rank of quaestor when Thrasea Paetus chose him for his son-in-law, and of Thrasea's virtues he absorbed none so much as his independence. As citizen, senator, husband, son-in-law, friend, in every sphere of life he was thoroughly consistent, always showing contempt for money, stubborn persistence in

6 the right, and courage in the face of danger. But some people thought him too ambitious, for even with philosophers the passion for fame is the last weakness to be discarded.

After Thrasea's fall Helvidius was banished, but he returned to Rome under Galba and proceeded to prosecute Eprius Marcellus,* who had informed against his father-in-law. This attempt to secure a revenge, perhaps no less pointless than justified, divided the Senate into two parties, for the fall of Marcellus would involve the ruin of a whole army of similar offenders. At first the struggle was full of recrimination, as the outstanding speeches on either side testify; but after a while, finding that Galba's attitude was doubtful and that many of the senators begged him to desist, Helvidius dropped the prosecution. On his action in this matter men's comments varied with their character, some praising his moderation, others asking what had become of his tenacity.

To return to the Senate: at the same meeting at which they voted powers to Vespasian they had also decided to send a deputation to address him. This gave rise to a sharp altercation between Helvidius Priscus and Eprius Marcellus. The former thought that the members of the delegation ought to be nominated by magistrates acting under oath; Marcellus demanded their selection by lot. The consul-elect had already

7 spoken in favour of the latter method, but Marcellus' motive

was fear of personal disgrace, for he was afraid that if others were chosen he would seem slighted.

Their exchange of views gradually grew into a formal and acrimonious debate. Helvidius inquired why it was that Marcellus was so afraid of the magistrates' judgement, seeing that he himself had great advantages of wealth and of eloquence over many others. Could it be the memory of his misdeeds that so oppressed him? The fall of the lot could not discern character; but the whole point of submitting people to the vote and to scrutiny by the Senate was to get at the truth about each man's life and reputation. In the interest of the country, and out of respect to Vespasian, it was important that he should be met by men whom the Senate considered beyond reproach, men who would give the Emperor a taste for the language of integrity. Vespasian, Helvidius pointed out, had been a friend of Thrasea, Soranus, and Sentius,* and even though there might be no need to punish their prosecutors, still it would be wrong to put them forward. Moreover, the Senate's selection would be a sort of hint to the Emperor whom to approve and whom to avoid. 'Good friends', he concluded, 'are the most effective instruments of good government. Marcellus ought to be content with having driven Nero to destroy so many innocent people. Let him enjoy the impunity and the profit he has won from that, and leave Vespasian to more honest advisers.'

Marcellus replied that the opinion which was being impugned was not his own. The consul-elect, he said, had already advised them to follow the established precedent, which was that deputations should be chosen by lot, so that there should be no room for intrigue or personal animosity. Nothing had happened to justify them in setting aside such an ancient system. Why turn a compliment to the Emperor into a slight upon someone else? Anybody could do homage. What they had to avoid was the possibility that some people's obstinacy might irritate the Emperor at the outset of his reign, while he was hesitating and still busy watching everybody's face and listening to what was said.

'I have not forgotten', he went on, 'the days of my youth or the constitution which our fathers and grandfathers established. But while admiring a distant past, I support the existing state of things. I pray for good emperors, but I take them as they come. As for Thrasea, it was not my speech but the Senate's verdict which ruined him. Nero took a savage delight in farces like that trial, and the friendship of such an emperor cost me as much anxiety as banishment did to others.

'To conclude, Helvidius may be as brave and as firm as any Brutus or Cato;* I am but a senator, and we have all been slaves together. Besides, I advise him not to try and get an upper hand with our Emperor or to force his tuition on a man of Vespasian's age,* who wears the insignia of a triumph and is the father of grown sons. Bad rulers like absolute sovereignty, and even the best of them must set some limit to their subjects' independence.'

This heated interchange of arguments found supporters for both views. The party which wanted the deputies chosen by lot eventually prevailed, since even the moderates were anxious to observe the precedent, and all the most prominent members tended to vote with them, for fear of encountering ill-feeling if they themselves were selected.

9   This dispute was followed by another. The Praetors, who in those days administered the Treasury,* had complained that the exchequer was impoverished, and demanded some restriction on expenditure. The consul-elect said that, as the responsibility was so vast and the remedy so difficult, he was in favour of leaving it for the Emperor. Helvidius maintained that it ought to be settled by the Senate's decision. When the consuls began to take each senator's opinion, Vulcacius Tertullinus, one of the tribunes, interposed his veto,* on the ground that they could not decide such an important question in the Emperor's absence. Helvidius had previously moved that the Capitol should be restored at the public cost, and with the assistance of Vespasian. The moderates all passed over this suggestion in silence and soon forgot it, but there were others who took care to remember it.*

10   Then Musonius Rufus attacked Publius Celer* on the ground that it was only by perjury that he had secured the conviction of Barea Soranus. It was felt that an inquiry would

rekindle the loathing felt for professional accusers. But the defendant was worthless and guilty, and could not be sheltered, and, moreover, Barea's memory was sacred. Celer had set up as a teacher of philosophy and then committed perjury against Barea, thus treacherously violating the very principles of friendship which he professed to teach. The case was put down for the next meeting. But now that a taste for revenge was aroused, people were waiting not so much for Musonius and Publius as for Priscus and Marcellus and the rest.

Thus the Senate quarrelled; the defeated party nursed their 11 grievances; the winners had no power to enforce their will; law was in abeyance and the Emperor absent. This state of things continued until Mucianus arrived in Rome and took everything into his own hands. This shattered the supremacy of Antonius Primus and Arrius Varus, for, though Mucianus tried to show a friendly face towards them, he was not very successful in concealing his dislike. But the people of Rome were skilful in detecting signs of displeasure, and had already transferred their allegiance. Mucianus was now the sole object of their flattering attentions, and he lived up to them. He surrounded himself with an armed escort, and kept changing his house and gardens. His display, his parades, his bodyguard, all showed that he had adopted the power of an emperor* while forgoing the title.

The greatest alarm was aroused by his execution of Calpurnius Galerianus, son of Gaius Piso.* He had attempted no treachery, but his distinguished name and handsome presence made the youth a subject of common talk, and the country was full of turbulent spirits who delighted in revolutionary rumours and idly talked of his coming to the throne. Mucianus gave orders that he should be arrested by the soldiers, and to avoid a conspicuous execution in the heart of the city, they marched him forty miles along the Appian Way, where they severed his veins and let him bleed to death. Julius Priscus, who had commanded the Guards under Vitellius, committed suicide, more from shame than of necessity. Alfenus Varus survived the disgrace of his cowardice. Asiaticus, who was a freedman, paid for his malign influence by dying the death of a slave.

12   The growing rumour of a reverse in Germany had not as yet caused any alarm in Rome. People alluded to the loss of armies, the capture of the legions' winter quarters, the defection of the Gallic provinces as matters of indifference. I must now go back and explain the origin of this war, and of the widespread rebellion of foreign and allied tribes which now broke into flame.

The Batavi were once a tribe of the Chatti,* living beyond the Rhine. But an outbreak of civil war had driven them out, and they settled in a still unoccupied district on the frontier of Gaul and also in the neighbouring island,* enclosed on one side by the ocean and on the other three sides by the Rhine. There they fared better than most tribes who ally themselves to a stronger power. Their resources remained intact, and they had only to contribute men and arms for the imperial army. After a long training in the German wars, they increased their reputation still further in Britain, where their troops had been sent, commanded according to an ancient custom by some of the noblest chiefs. There still remained behind in their own country a picked troop of horsemen with a peculiar knack of swimming, which enabled them to cross the Rhine in unbroken ranks without losing control of their horses or their weapons.

13   Of their chieftains two far outshone the rest. These were Julius Paulus* and Julius Civilis, both of royal stock. Paulus had been executed by Fonteius Capito on a false charge of rebellion; Civilis was sent in chains to Nero. Galba, however, set him free, and under Vitellius he again ran great risk of his life, when the army clamoured for his execution. This gave him a motive for hating Rome, and our misfortunes fed his hopes. He was, indeed, far cleverer than most barbarians, and professed to be a second Sertorius* or Hannibal—all three had the same physical defect. He was afraid that if he openly rebelled against the Roman people they would treat him as an enemy, and march on him at once, so he pretended to be a friend of Vespasian and keen supporter of his party. This much was true, that Antonius Primus had written instructing him to divert the auxiliaries whom Vitellius had summoned, and to delay the legions on the pretence of a rising in

Germany. Moreover, Hordeonius Flaccus had given him the
same advice in person, for Flaccus was inclined to support
Vespasian and was anxious for the safety of Rome, which was
threatened with utter disaster if the war were to break out
afresh and all these thousands of troops come pouring into
Italy.

Having thus made up his mind to rebel, Civilis concealed in 14
the mean time his ulterior design, intending to guide his ultimate policy by future events, and proceeded to initiate the
rising as follows. The young Batavians were by Vitellius'
orders being pressed for service, and this burden was being
rendered even more irksome than it need have been by the
greed and depravity of the recruiting officers. They took to
enrolling elderly men and weaklings so as to get bribes for
excusing them: or, as most of the Batavian children are tall,
they would drag off and rape the handsomest boys. This
caused bitter feeling; an insurrection was organized, and the
Batavians were persuaded to refuse service.

On the pretext of giving a banquet, Civilis summoned the
chief nobles and the most determined of the commoners to a
sacred grove. Then, when he saw them excited by their night-
time revelry, he began to speak of the glorious past of the
Batavi, then enumerated the injustices, extortions, and all the
other evils of their servitude. 'We are no longer treated',
he said, 'as we used to be, like allies, but like slaves. Why, we
are never even visited by a governor—irksome and arrogant
though his staff would be. We are given over to prefects* and
centurions; and when these subordinates have had their fill of
extortion and bloodshed replacements come seeking new
pockets to ransack and a new language of plunder.

'Now conscription is upon us: children are to be torn from
parents, brother from brother, never, perhaps, to meet again.
And yet the Roman state has never been weaker. Their can-
tonments contain nothing but loot and old men. Lift up your
eyes and look at them: there is nothing to fear from legions
that exist in name alone. And we are strong. We have infantry
and cavalry: the Germans are our kinsmen: the Gallic provinces share our ambition. Even the Romans will be grateful if
we go to war—if it ends in stalemate, we will acquire credit

with Vespasian: if we succeed, there will be no one to call us to account.'

15   His speech was received with great approval, and he swore them all to union, using barbarous ceremonies and traditional imprecations. Envoys were then sent to the Canninefates to make common cause with them. This tribe inhabits part of the Island,* and though inferior in numbers to the Batavi, they are of the same race and language and the same courageous spirit. Civilis next sent secret messages to win over the Batavian troops, which after serving as Roman auxiliaries in Britain had been sent, as we have already seen, to Germany and were now stationed at Mogontiacum.*

One of the Canninefates, Brinno by name, was a man of distinguished family and foolhardy recklessness. His father had often ventured acts of hostility, and had with complete impunity shown his contempt for Gaius' farcical expeditions.* To belong to such a family of rebels was in itself a recommendation. He was accordingly after the fashion of the tribe placed on a shield, swung up on the shoulders of his friends, and thus elected leader. Summoning to his aid the Frisii*—a tribe from beyond the Rhine—he fell upon two cohorts of auxiliaries whose camp lay close to the shore. The attack was unexpected, and the troops, even if they had foreseen it, were not strong enough to offer resistance: so the camp was taken and looted. They then fell on the Roman camp-followers and traders, who had wandered off in all directions as if peace were assured. Finding the forts now threatened with destruction, the commanders of the Roman cohorts set fire to them, as they had no means of defence. The remaining troops with their standards and colours retired in a body to the upper end of the Island, led by Aquilius, a senior centurion. But they were an army in name only, not in strength, for Vitellius had withdrawn all the efficient soldiers and had replaced them by a useless mob drawn from the neighbouring Nervian* and German villages and loaded up with armour.

16   Civilis thought it best to proceed by guile, and pre-empted the Romans by himself blaming their commanders for abandoning the forts. He could, he told them, with the

cohort under his command, suppress the outbreak of the Canninefates without their assistance: they could all go back to their winter quarters. However, it was plain that treachery underlay his advice: it would be easier to crush the cohorts if they were separated, and Civilis, not Brinno, was at the head of this war. Evidence of this gradually leaked out, as the Germans loved war too well to keep the secret for long. Finding his artifice unsuccessful, Civilis tried force instead, forming the Canninefates, Frisii, and Batavi into three separate columns. The Roman line faced them, positioned near the Rhine bank. They had brought their ships there after the burning of the forts, and these were now turned with their prows towards the enemy.

Soon after the engagement began a Tungrian cohort deserted to Civilis, and the Romans were so startled by this unexpected treachery that they were cut to pieces by their allies and their enemies combined. Similar treachery occurred in the fleet. Some of the rowers were Batavians, and, feigning clumsiness, tried to impede the sailors and marines in the performance of their functions; then they openly resisted them and steered the ships towards the enemy's bank. Finally, they killed the pilots and centurions who refused to join them, and thus all the twenty-four ships of the flotilla either deserted to the enemy or were captured by them.

This victory made Civilis immediately famous, and subse- 17 quently proved very useful. Having now got the ships and the weapons which they needed, he and his followers were enthusiastically proclaimed as champions of liberty throughout Germany and Gaul. The German provinces immediately sent envoys with offers of help, while Civilis endeavoured by diplomacy and bribery to secure an alliance with the Gauls. He sent back the auxiliary commanders whom he had taken prisoner, each to his own tribe, and offered the cohorts the choice of either going home or remaining with him. Those who remained were given an honourable position in his army: and those who went home received presents out of the Roman spoil.

At the same time Civilis talked to them confidentially, reminding them of the miseries they had endured for all these years, in which they had disguised their wretched slavery under the name of peace. 'The Batavi', he would say, 'were excused from taxation, and yet they have taken arms against the common tyrant. In the first engagement the Romans were routed and beaten. What if Gaul throws off the yoke? What forces are there left in Italy? It is with the blood of provincials that their provinces are won.

'Don't think of the defeat of Vindex. Why, it was Batavian cavalry which trampled underfoot the Aedui and Arverni,* and there were Belgic auxiliaries in Verginius' force. Thinking it through properly, we see that Gaul succumbed to her own armies. But now we are all united in one party, fortified, moreover, by the military discipline which once prevailed in Roman camps: and we have on our side the veterans before whom Otho's legions lately bit the dust. Let Syria and Asia play the slave: the East is used to tyrants:* but there are many still living in Gaul who were born before the days of tribute.* Indeed, it is only the other day that Quintilius Varus was killed,* when slavery was driven out of Germany, and they were challenging not the Emperor Vitellius but Caesar Augustus himself. Why, liberty is the natural prerogative even of dumb animals: courage is the peculiar attribute of man. Heaven helps the brave. Come, then, fall upon them while your hands are free and theirs are tied, while you are fresh and they are weary. Some of them are for Vespasian, others for Vitellius; now is your chance to crush both parties at once.'

18   Civilis thus had his eye on Gaul and Germany and aspired, had his project prospered, to become king of the strongest and wealthiest countries of the world.

Hordeonius Flaccus at first furthered Civilis' schemes by shutting his eyes to them. But when messengers kept arriving in panic with news that a camp had been stormed, cohorts wiped out, and not a Roman left in the Batavian Island, he instructed Munius Lupercus, who commanded the two legions in winter quarters, to march against the enemy. Lupercus lost no time in crossing the river, taking with him some of his legionaries, some Ubii* who were close at hand, and the Treviran cavalry who were stationed not far away. To this force he added a regiment of Batavian cavalry, who,

though their loyalty had long ago succumbed, still concealed
the fact, because they hoped their desertion would fetch a
higher price if they actually betrayed the Romans on the field.

Civilis set the standards of the defeated cohorts round him
in a ring to keep before the eyes of his men their new-won
glory, and to terrify the enemy by reminding them of their
disaster. He also gave orders that his own mother and sisters
and all the wives and small children of his soldiers should be
stationed in the rear* to spur them to victory or shame them
if they were beaten. When his line raised their battle-cry, the
men singing and the women shrieking, the legions and their
auxiliaries replied with a comparatively feeble cheer, for their
left wing had been exposed by the desertion of the Batavian
cavalry, who promptly turned against us. However, despite
the confusion, the legionaries gripped their swords and kept
their places. Then the Ubian and Treviran auxiliaries broke
in shameful flight and scattered all over the country. The
Germans pressed hard on their heels and meanwhile the
legions made good their escape into the camp, which was
called Vetera.*

Claudius Labeo, who commanded the Batavian cavalry,
had opposed Civilis as a rival in some petty municipal dispute.
Civilis was afraid that, if he killed him, he might offend his
countrymen, while if he spared him his presence would give
rise to dissension; so he had him taken away to the Frisii.

It was at this time that Civilis' messenger caught up with the 19
cohorts of Batavians and Canninefates on their way to Rome
under orders from Vitellius. They promptly fell into a ferment
of unruly insolence and demanded a special grant as payment
for their journey, double pay, and an increase in the number
of their cavalry.* All these things had doubtless been promised
by Vitellius, but they were not attempting to obtain them: they
wanted an excuse for rebellion. Flaccus made many conces-
sions, but the only result was that they redoubled their vigour
and demanded what they knew he would refuse. Paying no
further heed to him they made for Lower Germany, to join
Civilis.

Flaccus summoned the tribunes and centurions and debated
with them whether he should use force to check this defiance

of authority. After a while he gave way to his natural cowardice and the fears of his subordinates, who were anxious because the loyalty of the auxiliaries was doubtful and the levy
by which the legions were reinforced had been rushed. It was
decided, therefore, to keep the soldiers in camp. However, he
soon changed his mind when he found himself criticized by
the very men whose advice he had taken. He now seemed bent
on pursuit, and wrote to Herennius Gallus in command of the
First Legion,* who was holding Bonn, telling him to bar the
path of the Batavians, and promising that he and his army
would follow hard upon their heels. The rebels could certainly
have been crushed had Flaccus and Gallus each advanced their
forces from opposite directions and thus surrounded them.
But Flaccus soon gave up the idea, and wrote another letter to
Gallus, warning him to let the rebels pass untroubled. This
gave rise to a suspicion that the commanders were purposely
promoting the war; and all the disasters which had already
occurred or were feared in the future were attributed not to
the soldiers' inefficiency or the strength of the enemy, but to
the treachery of the generals.

20   On nearing the camp at Bonn, the Batavians sent forward a
messenger to explain their intentions to Herennius Gallus.
Against the Romans, for whom they had fought so often, they
had no wish to make war: but they were worn out after a long
and unprofitable term of service and wanted to go home and
rest. If no one opposed them they would march peaceably by;
but if hostility was offered they would find a way through
with the points of their swords. Gallus hesitated,* but his men
induced him to risk an engagement. Three thousand legionaries, some hastily recruited Belgic auxiliaries, and a mob of
peasants and camp-followers, who were as cowardly in action
as they were boastful before it, came pouring out simultaneously from all the gates, hoping with their superior numbers
to surround the Batavians. But these were experienced veterans. They formed up into columns in deep formation that
defied assault on front, flank, or rear. They thus pierced our
thin line. The Belgae gave way, the legion was driven back and
ran in terror to reach the rampart and gates of the camp. It
was there that they suffered the heaviest losses. The trenches

were heaped with dead, who were not all killed by the blows
of the enemy: for many perished from their fall or on their
own swords. The victorious cohorts avoided Cologne and
marched on without attempting any further hostilities. For the
battle at Bonn they continued to excuse themselves. They had
asked for peace, they said, and when peace was persistently
refused, had merely acted in self-defence.

After the arrival of these veteran cohorts Civilis was now at 21
the head of a respectable army. But being still uncertain of his
plans, and reckoning up the strength of Rome, he made all
who were with him swear allegiance to Vespasian, and sent
envoys to the two legions which after their defeat in the
former engagement had retired into the camp at Vetera, asking them to take the same oath. The answer came back that
they never followed the advice either of a traitor or of an
enemy: Vitellius was their Emperor, and they would keep their
allegiance and their arms for him so long as they had breath in
their bodies. A Batavian deserter need not try to decide the
destiny of Rome; he should rather expect the punishment he
richly deserved. When this was reported to Civilis he flew into
a passion, and called the whole Batavian people to take arms.
They were joined by the Bructeri and Tencteri,* and Germany
was summoned to share the plunder and the glory.

Threatened with this gathering storm of war, Munius 22
Lupercus and Numisius Rufus, who were in command of the
two legions, proceeded to strengthen the rampart and walls.
They pulled down the buildings near the military camp, which
had grown into a small town during the long years of peace,
fearing that the enemy might make use of them. But they
omitted to provide for provisions to be brought into the camp,
and allowed them to be looted, with the result that what
might have supplied their needs for a long time was wantonly
consumed in a few days.

Meanwhile Civilis advanced, himself holding the centre
with the flower of the Batavi: on both banks of the Rhine he
massed large bands of Germans so as to look more savage: the
cavalry charged through the fields, while the ships were simultaneously moved up the stream. Here could be seen the standards of veteran Roman cohorts, there the figures of beasts

which the Germans had brought from their woods and groves, as their tribes do when they go to battle. It seemed a civil and a foreign war at once; and this strange confusion astounded the besieged.

The hopes of the assailants rose when they saw the circumference of the ramparts, for there were barely 5,000 Roman soldiers to defend a camp which had been laid out to hold two legions.* However, a large number of camp-followers had collected there after the disruption of peace, and remained to give what assistance they could to the military operations.

23 Part of the camp was built on the gentle slope of a hill, part was approachable on level ground. Augustus had believed that it would serve as a base of operations and a check upon the German tribes: as for their actually coming to assault our legions, such a disaster never occurred to him. Consequently, no trouble had been taken over the site or defences: the strength of the troops had always seemed sufficient.

The Batavians and the Germans from across the Rhine now formed up tribe by tribe—the separation was designed to show their individual prowess—and opened fire from a distance. Finding that most of their missiles fixed harmlessly in the turrets and pinnacles of the walls, and that they were being wounded by stones hurled from above, they charged with a wild shout and surged up to the rampart, some using scaling-ladders, others climbing over their comrades who had formed a 'tortoise'. But no sooner had some of them begun to scale the wall, than they were hurled down by the besieged, who thrust at them with sword and shield, and buried them under a shower of stakes and javelins.

The Germans are always impetuous at the beginning of an action and over-confident when they are winning; but on this occasion their greed for plunder even steeled them to face difficulties. They actually attempted to use siege-engines, with which they were quite unfamiliar. But though they had no skill themselves, some of the deserters and prisoners showed them how to build a sort of bridge of timber; they fitted wheels onto it and rolled it forward. Thus some of them stood on this platform and fought as though from a mound, while others, concealed inside, tried to undermine the walls. How-

ever, stones hurled from catapults soon destroyed this crude
device. Then they began to get ready fascines and mantlets,
but the besieged shot blazing spears on to them from engines,
attacking the assailants themselves with fire. At last they
gave up all hope of an assault and resolved to try a waiting
policy, being well aware that the camp contained only a few
days' provisions and a large number of non-combatants. They
hoped that famine would breed treason, and counted, besides,
on the wavering loyalty of the slaves and the usual hazards of
war to aid them.

Meanwhile, Flaccus, who had received news of the siege of 24
Vetera, dispatched a party to recruit auxiliaries in Gaul, and
gave Dillius Vocula, in command of the Twenty-Second, a
force of picked soldiers from his two legions. Vocula was to
hurry by forced marches along the bank of the Rhine, while
Flaccus himself was to approach by water, since he was in bad
health and unpopular with his men. Indeed, they grumbled
openly that he had let the Batavian cohorts get away from
Mogontiacum, had shut his eyes to Civilis' schemes, and
invited the Germans to join the alliance. Vespasian, they said,
owed his rise more to Flaccus than to all the assistance of
Antonius Primus or of Mucianus, for overt hatred and violence can be openly crushed, but treachery and deceit cannot
be detected, much less parried. Civilis took the field himself
and arranged his own fighting line; Hordeonius lay on a couch
in his bedroom and gave whatever orders best suited the
enemy's convenience. Why should all these companies of
brave soldiers be governed by one miserable old man's health?
Let them rather kill the traitor and free their brave hearts and
good hopes from this incubus. Having worked on each other's
feelings by these complaints, they were still further incensed
by the arrival of a letter from Vespasian. As this could not be
concealed, Flaccus read it before a meeting of the soldiers, and
the messengers who brought it were sent to Vitellius in chains.

The army was appeased by this, and marched on to Bonn, 25
the headquarters of the First Legion. There the men were still
more indignant with Flaccus, on whom they laid the blame of
their recent defeat. It was by his orders, they argued, that they
had taken the field against the Batavians on the understanding

that the legions from Mogontiacum were in pursuit.* But no reinforcements had arrived, and his treachery was responsible for their losses. The facts, moreover, were unknown to the other armies, nor was any report sent to their Emperor, although this treacherous outbreak could have been nipped in the bud by rapidly bringing aid from numerous provinces.

In answer Flaccus read out to the army copies of all the letters which he had sent all over Gaul and Britain and Spain to ask for assistance, and introduced the disastrous practice of having all letters delivered to the standard-bearers of the legions, who read them to the soldiers before the officers had seen them. He then gave orders that one of the mutineers should be put in irons, more by way of vindicating his authority than because one man was especially to blame.

Leaving Bonn, the army moved on to Cologne, where they were joined by large numbers of Gallic auxiliaries, who at first zealously supported the Roman cause: later, when the Germans prospered, most of the tribes took arms against us, actuated by hopes of liberty and an ambition to establish an empire of their own when once they had shaken off the yoke. Meanwhile the army's indignation steadily increased. The imprisonment of a single soldier was not enough to terrify them, and, indeed, the prisoner actually accused the general of complicity in crime, alleging that he himself had carried messages between Flaccus and Civilis. 'It is because I can testify to the truth', he said, 'that I am being suppressed with a false charge.' Thereupon Vocula, with admirable self-possession, mounted the Tribunal and, in spite of the man's protestations, ordered him to be seized and led away to execution. This alarmed the disaffected, while the better sort obeyed him promptly. The army then unanimously demanded that Vocula should lead them, and Flaccus accordingly resigned the chief command to him.

26   However, there was much to exasperate the disaffected. They were short both of pay and of provisions: the Gauls refused either to enlist or to pay tribute: drought, unfamiliar in that climate, made the Rhine almost too low for navigation, and thus hampered their commissariat: patrols had to be posted at intervals all along the bank to prevent the Germans

fording the river: and in consequence of all this they had less food and more mouths to eat it. To the ignorant the scarcity of water seemed in itself an evil omen, as though the rivers too, the ancient bulwarks of the empire, were now failing us. In peace they would have called it bad luck or the course of nature: now it was 'fate' and 'the anger of heaven'.*

On entering Novaesium* they were joined by the Sixteenth Legion. Their general, Herennius Gallus, now shared with Vocula the responsibility of command. As they could not venture out against the enemy, they encamped . . .* at a place called Gelduba.* Here the soldiers were trained in deployment, in building fortifications and ramparts, and in all the other military manœuvres. To inspire their courage with the further incentive of plunder, Vocula led out part of the force against the neighbouring cantons of the Cugerni, who had accepted Civilis' offers of alliance.

The rest of the troops were left behind with Herennius Gallus, and it happened that a corn-ship with a full cargo, 27 which had run aground close to the camp, was towed over by the Germans to their own bank. This was more than Gallus could tolerate, so he sent an auxiliary cohort to the rescue. The number of the Germans soon increased: both sides gradually gathered reinforcements and a regular battle was fought, with the result that the Germans removed the ship, inflicting heavy losses. The defeated troops followed what had now become their regular custom, and threw the blame not on their own inefficiency but on their commanding officer's treachery. They dragged him from his quarters, tore his uniform and flogged him, bidding him tell them how much he had got for betraying the army, and who were his accomplices. Then their indignation recoiled on Hordeonius Flaccus: he was the real criminal: Gallus was only his tool. At last their threats of murder so terrified Gallus that he, too, accused Flaccus. He was put in irons until the arrival of Vocula, who at once set him free, and on the next day had the ringleaders of the riot executed.

This demonstrated the army's inconsistency: its equal readiness to mutiny and to submit to punishment. The common soldiers' loyalty to Vitellius was beyond question, while the higher ranks inclined towards Vespasian. Thus we find crimes and penalties in succession, frenzied violence joined to obedience: the troops could be punished though not controlled.

28   Meanwhile the whole of Germany was promoting Civilis, sending him vast reinforcements and ratifying the alliance with hostages from their noblest families. He gave orders that the country of the Ubii and Treviri was to be laid waste by their nearest neighbours, and sent another party across the River Maas to harass the Menapii and Morini* and other frontier tribes of Gaul. In both lands they plundered freely, and were especially savage towards the Ubii, because they were a tribe of German origin who had renounced their fatherland and adopted the name of Agrippinenses.* Ubian cohorts were cut to pieces at the village of Marcodurum,* where they were off their guard, trusting to their distance from the Rhine. The Ubii did not take this quietly, nor hesitate to seek reprisals from the Germans, which they did at first with impunity. In the end, however, the Germans caught them: throughout the war the Ubii were always more conspicuous for good faith than good fortune.

    Their collapse strengthened Civilis' position, and, emboldened by success, he now vigorously pressed on the blockade of the legions at Vetera, and redoubled his vigilance to prevent any message creeping through from the relieving army. The Batavians were set to look after the engines and siege-works: the Germans from across the Rhine, who clamoured for battle, were sent to demolish the rampart and renew the fight directly they were beaten off. There were so many of them
29 that their losses mattered little. Nightfall did not see the end of their task. They built huge piles of wood all round the ramparts, kindled them, and sat by feasting; then, as the wine warmed each man's heart, he dashed into the fight with pointless impetuosity. In the darkness their missiles were ineffective, but the barbarian troops were clearly visible to the Romans, and any one whose daring or bright ornaments made him conspicuous at once became a mark for their aim.

    When Civilis realized this, he gave orders to extinguish the fires and plunge the whole scene into a confusion of darkness and weapons. Discordant shouts now arose: men clashed blindly: no one could see to strike or to parry. Wherever a shout was heard, they would wheel round and lunge in that direction. Valour was useless: chance and chaos ruled supreme: and the bravest soldier often fell under a coward's bolt. The Germans fought with blind fury; the Roman troops were more familiar with danger, and hurled down iron-clamped stakes and heavy stones with sure effect. Wherever the sound of siege-work or the clang of a scaling-ladder betrayed the presence of the enemy, they thrust them back with their shields and followed them with a shower of javelins. Many appeared on top of the walls, and these they stabbed with their short swords.

Thus the night wore on; day dawned upon new methods of attack. The Batavians had built a wooden tower of two stories 30 and moved it up to the main gate, the area with the flattest approach. However, the Romans, by using strong poles and hammering it with wooden beams, soon battered it to pieces, with great loss of life to those standing on it. While they were reeling from this, the defenders made a sudden and successful sally. Meanwhile the legionaries, with remarkable skill and ingenuity, invented still further contrivances. The one which caused most terror was a crane with a movable arm suspended over their assailants' heads: this arm was suddenly lowered, snatched up one or more of the enemy into the air before his fellows' eyes, and, as the heavy end was swung round, tossed him into the middle of the camp. Civilis now gave up hope of storming the camp and renewed a leisurely blockade, trying all the time by messages and offers of reward to undermine the loyalty of the legions.

Such was the course of events in Germany up to the date of 31 the battle of Cremona. News of this arrived by letter from Antonius Primus, who enclosed a copy of Caecina's edict;* and Alpinius Montanus, who commanded one of the defeated auxiliary cohorts, came in person to confess that his party had been beaten. The troops were variously affected by the news. The Gallic auxiliaries, who had no feelings of affection or dislike to either party and served without sentiment, promptly took the advice of their commanders and deserted Vitellius. The veterans hesitated; under pressure from their tribunes

they eventually took the oath of allegiance administered by
Flaccus, but it was clear from their faces that their hearts were
not in it, and while repeating the rest of the formula they
balked at the name of Vespasian, either muttering it under
32 their breath or more often omitting it altogether. Their suspicions were further inflamed when Antonius' letter to Civilis
was read out before the meeting; it seemed to address Civilis
as an ally of the Flavian party, and to express hostility to the
German army.

The news was next brought to the camp at Gelduba, where
it gave rise to the same comments and the same scenes.
Montanus was sent to carry instructions to Civilis that he was
to cease from hosilities and not to make war on Rome under
a false pretext; if it was to help Vespasian that he had taken
arms, he had now achieved his object.

Civilis at first replied in guarded terms. Then, as he saw that
Montanus was an impetuous person who would welcome a
revolution, he began to complain of all the dangers he had
endured in the service of Rome for the last twenty-five years.
'A fine reward I have received', he cried, 'for all my labours—
my brother's execution, my own imprisonment, and the
bloodthirsty clamours of this army. Since they have sought my
destruction, I claim satisfaction from them under interna-
tional law. As for you Trevirans and all the rest that have the
souls of slaves, what reward do you hope to gain for shedding
your blood so often, except thankless military service, eternal
taxation, and their rods, axes, and tyrannical caprices? Look
at me! I have only a single cohort under my command, and yet
with the Canninefates and Batavi, a mere fraction of the Gallic
peoples, I have destroyed their great and useless camps, or else
am grinding them down with famine and the sword. In short,
either our venture will end in freedom or, if we are beaten, we
shall be no worse off than before.'

Having thus inflamed Montanus, he told him to take back
a milder answer and dismissed him. On his return Montanus
pretended that his errand had been fruitless, and said nothing
about all the rest: but it soon came to light.

33   Retaining a portion of his force, Civilis sent the veteran
cohorts with the most efficient of the German troops against

Vocula and his army. He gave the command to Julius Maximus and Claudius Victor, his sister's son. After plundering the winter quarters of a cavalry regiment at Asciburgium* on their way, they swept down upon the Roman camp and so completely surprised it that Vocula had no time to address his army or to form it for battle. In the general panic he could only advise them to mass the reserves in the centre; the auxiliaries were scattered all around them.

The Roman cavalry charged, but found the enemy in good order ready to receive them, and came flying back onto their own infantry. What followed was more of a massacre than a battle. The Nervian cohorts, either from panic or treachery, left our flanks exposed; thus the legions had to bear the brunt. They had already lost their standards and were being cut down behind the rampart, when a fresh reinforcement suddenly changed the fortune of the fight. Some Basque auxiliaries, originally levied by Galba and now summoned to Germany, on nearing the camp heard the sound of fighting; while the enemy were occupied, they came charging in on their rear. This caused more consternation than their numbers warranted, the enemy taking them for the whole Roman force, either from Novaesium or from Mogontiacum. This mistake encouraged the Roman troops: their confidence in others restored confidence in themselves. The best Batavians, at least of their infantry, fell. The cavalry made off with the standards and prisoners taken in the first stage of the battle. Though our losses that day were numerically larger, they were of lower-quality fighters, whereas the Germans lost their best troops.

On both sides the generals deserved defeat, and failed to 34 make good use of their success. Their fault was the same. Had Civilis furnished the attacking column with more troops, they could never have been surrounded by such a small force, but would have broken into the camp and destroyed it. Vocula, on the other hand, had not even reconnoitred the enemy's attack, and consequently no sooner sallied out than he was beaten. Then, when he had won the victory, he showed great lack of confidence, and wasted day after day before moving against the enemy. If he had made haste to follow up his success and struck at the enemy at once, he might have raised the siege of Vetera at one blow.

Meanwhile, Civilis had been playing upon the feelings of the besieged by pretending that the Romans had been defeated and success had favoured his army. The captured standards and colours were carried round the walls and the prisoners also displayed. One of these did a deed of outstanding heroism: shouting at the top of his voice, he revealed the truth. The Germans at once struck him dead, which only served to confirm his information; while the besieged saw the harried fields and burning farms and realized that the victorious army was approaching.

When he was in sight of the camp Vocula ordered his men to plant the standards and construct a trench and rampart round them: they were to deposit all their baggage there and fight unencumbered. Instead, this made them shout at the general and demand to fight; and they were now accustomed to use threats. Without even taking time to form their line they started the battle, all tired as they were and in disorder. Civilis was ready waiting for them, trusting quite as much to their mistakes as to the merits of his own men.

The Romans fought with varying fortune. All the most mutinous proved cowards: some, however, remembered their recent victory and stuck to their place, cutting down the enemy, and encouraging themselves and their neighbours. After re-forming the battle-line, they waved their hands and signalled to the besieged not to lose their opportunity. These were watching all that happened from the walls, and now came bursting out at every gate. It chanced that at this point Civilis' horse fell and threw him; both armies believed the rumour that he had been wounded or killed. This caused immense consternation to his army and immense encouragement to the enemy. However, Vocula failed to pursue them when they fled, and merely set about strengthening the rampart and turrets of his camp, apparently in fear of another blockade. His victories were so often botched as to give colour to the suspicion that he preferred war.

35   What chiefly distressed our troops was the lack of supplies. The baggage-train of the legions was sent to Novaesium with

a crowd of non-combatants to fetch grain by land, the enemy being now masters of the river. The first convoy got through safely, while Civilis' control was still shaky. Then he heard that a second foraging-party had been sent to Novaesium under guard of several auxiliary cohorts, and that they were proceeding on their way as if it was a time of perfect peace, few keeping to the standards, their weapons piled in the wagons, all wandering at will. He sent some men forward to hold the bridges and any places where the road was narrow, and then formed up and attacked. The battle was fought on a long straggling line, and the issue was still doubtful when nightfall broke it off. The cohorts made their way through to Gelduba, where the camp remained as it was, garrisoned by the soldiers who had been left behind there.

It was obvious just how much danger the convoy would have to face on the return journey; they would be heavily laden and had already lost their nerve. Vocula accordingly added to his force 1,000 picked men from the Fifth and Fifteenth Legions who had been at Vetera during the siege, all tough soldiers with a grievance against their generals. Against his orders, more than the 1,000 started with him, openly complaining on the march that they would not put up with famine and the treachery of their generals any longer. On the other hand, those who stayed behind grumbled that they were left to their fate now that part of the garrison had been removed. Thus there was a double mutiny, one party calling Vocula back, the others refusing to return to camp.

Meanwhile Civilis laid siege to Vetera. Vocula retired to 36 Gelduba, and thence to Novaesium, shortly afterwards winning a cavalry skirmish just outside Novaesium. The Roman soldiers, however, alike in success and in failure, were as eager as ever to make an end of their generals. Now that their numbers were swelled by the arrival of the detachments from the Fifth and the Fifteenth they demanded their donative, having learnt that money had arrived from Vitellius. Without further delay Flaccus gave it to them in Vespasian's name, and this did more than anything else to promote mutiny. They indulged in wild dissipation, banquets, and nocturnal gatherings, and revived their old grudge against Hordeonius Flaccus.

None of the senior officers ventured to interfere with them—
the darkness had somehow abolished all shame; the mutineers
dragged Flaccus out of bed and murdered him. They were
preparing to do the same with Vocula, but he narrowly
escaped in the darkness, disguised as a slave.

37   When the excitement subsided, their fears returned, and
they sent letters round by centurions to all the Gallic communities, asking for reinforcements and pay. But without a leader
a mob is always rash, timorous, and inactive: on the approach
of Civilis they hurriedly snatched up their arms, and then
immediately dropped them and took to flight. Misfortune
now bred disunion, and the army of the Upper Rhine dissoci-
ated itself from the rest. However, they set up the statues of
Vitellius again in the camp and in the neighbouring Belgic
villages, although by now Vitellius was dead. Soon the soldiers of the First, Fourth, and Twenty-Second repented of
their folly and rejoined Vocula. He made them take a second
oath of allegiance to Vespasian and led them off to raise the
siege of Mogontiacum. The besieging army, a combined force
of Chatti, Usipi, and Mattiaci,* had already retired, having
got sufficient loot and suffered some loss: our troops had
surprised them while they were scattered. Moreover, the
Treviri had built a rampart and breastwork all along their
frontier and fought the Germans with heavy loss to both sides.
Before long, however, they rebelled, and thus sullied their
great services to the Roman people.

38   During these events Vespasian took up his second consulship and Titus his first, both in absence. Rome was depressed
and beset by manifold anxieties. Apart from the real miseries
of the moment, it was plunged into a groundless panic on the
rumour of a rebellion in Africa, where Lucius Piso was supposed to be plotting revolution.* Piso, who was governor of
the province, was far from being a firebrand. But the severity
of the winter delayed the corn-ships, and the common people,
accustomed to buy their bread day by day, whose interest in
politics was confined to the corn supply, soon began to believe
their fears that the coast of Africa was being blockaded and
supplies withheld. The Vitellians, who had retained their par-
tisanship, fostered this rumour, and even the victors were not

entirely displeased at it, for none of their victories in the civil war had ever satisfied their greed, and even foreign wars fell far short.

On 1 January the Senate was convened by the Urban 39 Praetor, Julius Frontinus,* and passed votes of thanks and congratulation to the generals, armies, and foreign princes. Tettius Julianus was deprived of his praetorship; this was supposedly because he had left his legion when it went over to Vespasian, but was in fact so that his office could be conferred upon Plotius Grypus. Hormus was raised to equestrian rank. Frontinus then resigned his praetorship and Domitian Caesar succeeded him. His name now stood at the head of all dispatches and edicts, but the real authority lay with Mucianus, although Domitian, following the promptings of his friends and of his own desires, frequently asserted his independence.

But Mucianus' chief cause of anxiety lay in Antonius Primus and Arrius Varus. The fame of their exploits was still fresh; the soldiers worshipped them; and they were popular in Rome, because they had used no violence off the field of battle. It was even hinted that Antonius had urged Crassus Scribonianus* to seize the throne. He was a man who owed his distinction to famous ancestors and to his brother's memory, and Antonius could promise him adequate support for a conspiracy. However, Scribonianus refused. He had a terror of all risks, and would hardly have been seduced even by the certainty of success.

Being unable to crush Antonius openly, Mucianus showered compliments on him in the Senate and overloaded him in private with promises, hinting at the governorship of Nearer Spain, which the departure of Cluvius Rufus had left vacant. Meanwhile he lavished military commands on Antonius' friends. Then, having filled his empty head with ambitious hopes, he destroyed his influence at one stroke by moving the Seventh Legion,* who were passionately attached to Antonius, into winter quarters. The Third, who were similarly devoted to Arrius Varus, were sent back to Syria, and part of the army was taken out to the war in Germany. Thus, on the removal of all disturbing factors, the city could

resume its normal life under the old regime of law and civil
government.

40   On the day of his first appearance in the Senate Domitian
said a few moderate words regretting the absence of his father
and brother, and concerning his own youth. His behaviour
was most proper, and, as his character was still an unknown
quantity, his repeated blushes were taken for signs of modesty.* He moved from the chair that all Galba's honours
should be restored, to which Curtius Montanus proposed an
amendment that respect should also be paid to the memory of
Piso. The Senate approved both proposals, though nothing
was done about Piso.* Next, various commissions were
appointed by lot to restore the spoils of war to the owners;
to examine and affix the bronze tablets of laws, which
in course of time had dropped off the walls; to lighten the
list of public holidays, which in these days of flattery had
been disgracefully tampered with;* and to introduce some
economy into public expenditure. Tettius Julianus was restored to his praetorship as soon as it was discovered that he
had taken refuge with Vespasian:* but Grypus was allowed to
retain his rank.

It was then decided to resume the hearing of the case of
Musonius Rufus against Publius Celer. Publius was convicted
and the shade of Soranus satisfied. This strict verdict made the
day memorable in the annals of Rome, and credit was also due
to individual enterprise, for everybody felt that Musonius had
done his duty in bringing the action. On the other hand,
Demetrius, a professor of Cynic philosophy,* earned discredit
for defending an obvious criminal, his motive being self-
publicity rather than morality. As for Publius, as danger
threatened courage and fluency alike failed him.

This trial was the signal for further reprisals against
prosecutors. Junius Mauricus* petitioned Domitian that the
Senate might be allowed access to the minutes of the imperial
cabinet, in order to find out who had applied for leave to bring
a prosecution and against whom. The answer was that on
such a question as this the Emperor must be consulted.

41   Accordingly, at the instigation of its leading members, the
Senate framed an oath in these words: 'I call Heaven to

witness that I have never countenanced any action prejudicial
to any man's civil status, nor have I derived any profit or any
office from the misfortune of Roman citizens.' The magistrates vied with each other in their haste to take this oath, and
the other members did the same, when called upon to speak.
Those who had a guilty conscience were alarmed, and managed to alter the wording of the oath by various devices. The
house meanwhile applauded every sign of scruple, and protested against each case of perjury. This kind of informal
censure fell most severely on Sariolenus Vocula, Nonius
Attianus, and Cestius Severus, who were notorious as habitual
informers under Nero. Against Sariolenus there was also a
fresh charge of having continued his practices under Vitellius.
The members went on shaking their fists at him until he left
the House. They next turned on Paccius Africanus and
hounded him out in the same way. He was supposed to
have suggested to Nero the murder of the two brothers
Scribonius,* who were famous for their friendship and their
wealth. Africanus dared not admit his guilt, though he could
not very well deny it. So he swung round on Vibius Crispus,*
who was pestering him with questions, and implicated him in
the charges which he could not rebut, thus deflecting odium
by having an accomplice.

On this occasion Vipstanus Messala, although he had not 42
attained the senatorial age,* gained a great reputation both
for dutiful affection and for eloquence by venturing to inter-
cede for his brother Aquilius Regulus.* Regulus had been
raised to the summit of disfavour for having brought about
the ruin of the noble families of the Crassi and of Orfitus. It
was supposed that, though quite a young man, he had voluntarily undertaken the prosecution, not to escape any danger
which was threatening him, but purely from ambition.
Crassus' wife Sulpicia Praetextata and his four sons were
anxious to secure revenge if the Senate would grant a trial.
Messala therefore made no attempt to defend the case or the
accused, but tried to shelter his brother from peril, and had
already won over some of the senators.

Curtius Montanus opposed him with a fierce speech, and
even went so far as to charge Regulus with having given

money to Piso's murderer after Galba's death, and with having bitten Piso's head. 'That at least', said he, 'Nero did not compel you to do. You purchased neither position nor safety by that savagery. We may put up with the pleas of those wretches who preferred to ruin others rather than endanger their own lives. But your father's banishment had guaranteed your security. His property had been divided amongst his creditors.* You were not of an age to stand for office. Nero had nothing either to hope or to fear from you. Your talents were as yet untried and you had never exerted them in any man's defence, yet your lust for blood, your insatiable rapacity, led you to stain them in the blood of Rome's nobility. At one swoop you caused the ruin of innocent boys, of old and distinguished statesmen, of high-born ladies; and out of the country's disaster you secured for yourself the spoils of consuls, stuffed yourself with seven million sesterces,* and shone with the glory of a priesthood. You blamed Nero's lack of enterprise because he took one household at a time, thus causing unnecessary fatigue to himself and his informers, when he might have toppled the whole Senate at a single word. Why, gentlemen, you must indeed keep and preserve to yourselves a counsellor of such ready resource. Let each generation have its good examples: and as our old men follow Eprius Marcellus or Vibius Crispus, let the rising generation emulate Regulus.

'Villainy finds followers even when it fails. What if it flourish and prosper? If we hesitate to offend a mere ex-quaestor, shall we be any bolder when he has been praetor and consul? Or do you suppose that the race of tyrants came to an end in Nero? That is what the people believed who outlived Tiberius or Gaius, and meanwhile there arose one more infamous and more bloody still. We are not afraid of Vespasian. We trust his years and his natural moderation. But a good precedent outlives a good sovereign. Gentlemen, we have grown effete: we are no longer that Senate which, after Nero had been killed, clamoured for the punishment of his informers and menials according to ancestral law. Once an evil emperor is no more, the first day is the finest.'

The Senate listened to Montanus' speech with such sympa- 43
thy that Helvidius began to hope that even Marcellus might be
brought down. He began with a eulogy of Cluvius Rufus,
who, though his wealth and eloquence were no less celebrated
than Marcellus', had never endangered anyone under Nero;
he went on to attack Marcellus, both by contrasting him with
Rufus and by pressing home the charge against him. Feeling
that the House was warming to this rhetoric, Marcellus got up
as though to leave, exclaiming, 'I am off, Helvidius: I leave
you your Senate: you can tyrannize over it under Caesar's
nose.'* Vibius Crispus began to follow Marcellus, and,
though both were angry, their expressions were very different:
Marcellus with flashing eyes, Crispus with a smile on his face.
Their friends, however, dashed forward and pulled them
back. Thus the struggle grew more and more heated between
a virtuous majority and a small but powerful minority; and
since they were both animated by irreconcilable hatred, the
day was spent in conflict.

At the next sitting Domitian opened by recommending 44
them to forget their grievances and grudges and the unavoid-
able exigences of the recent past. Mucianus then at great
length moved a motion in favour of the prosecutors, issuing
a mild warning, almost in terms of entreaty, to those who
wanted to revive actions which had been begun and dropped.
Seeing that their attempt at independence was being opposed,
the Senate gave it up. However, so that it would not seem as
if the Senate's opinion was being flouted and complete impunity granted for all crimes committed under Nero, Mucianus
forced Octavius Sagitta and Antistius Sosianus,* men of senatorial rank who had returned from exile, to go back to the
islands to which they had been confined. Octavius had seduced Pontia Postumina, and, on her refusal to marry him,
had murdered her in a fit of jealous fury. Sosianus was an
unprincipled scoundrel who had been the ruin of many. The
Senate had found them both guilty, and passed a heavy sentence of exile, and the penalty was now reaffirmed, although
others were allowed to return. However, this failed to allay
the hatred felt for Mucianus, for Sosianus and Sagitta,

whether they returned or not, were of no importance, whereas people were afraid of the professional prosecutors, who were men of wealth and ability, and experts at employing their power for evil.

45   Unanimity was gradually restored in the Senate by the holding of a trial according to ancient precedent, before a court of the whole House. A senator named Manlius Patruitus complained that he had been beaten before a mob of people in the colony of Sena* by order of the local magistrates. Nor had the affront stopped there. They had held a mock funeral before his eyes, and had accompanied their dirges and lamentations with gross insults levelled at the whole Senate. The accused were summoned; their case was tried; they were convicted and punished. A further decree of the Senate was passed warning the commons of Sena to pay more respect to the laws. About the same time Antonius Flamma was prosecuted by Cyrene for extortion, condemned, and exiled for the inhumanity of his conduct.

46   Meanwhile, a mutiny almost broke out among the soldiers.* The Guards who had been discharged by Vitellius came together again in support of Vespasian, and demanded re-admission. They were joined by the selected legionaries who had also been led to hope for service in the Guards, and they now demanded the pay they had been promised. Even the Vitellians alone could not have been dispersed without serious bloodshed, but it would require immense sums of money to retain the services of such a large number of men. Mucianus accordingly entered the barracks to make a more accurate estimate of each man's term of service. He formed up the victorious troops with their own arms and distinctive decorations, each man a few paces from the next. Then the Vitellians who had surrendered, as we have described, at Bovillae, and all the other soldiers who had been hunted down in the city and its neighbourhood, were marched out almost naked. Mucianus then had them sorted out, and drew up in separate corps the troops of the German army, of the British army, and of any others that were in Rome.

Their first glance at the scene had astounded them. Facing them they saw what looked like a fighting front bristling with

weapons and armour, while they were caught in a trap, naked
and foul with dirt. As soon as they began to be sorted out a
panic seized them all. The German troops in particular were
terrified at their isolation, and felt they were being marked off
for slaughter. They embraced their comrades and clung upon
their necks, asking for one last kiss, begging not to be left
alone, crying out, 'Our cause is the same as yours, why should
our fate be different?' They appealed now to Mucianus, now
to the absent Emperor, and lastly to the powers of Heaven,
until Mucianus came to the rescue of their imaginary terrors
by calling them all 'soldiers under the same oath, and the same
Emperor'—for he found that the victorious army was joining
in and seconding their tears with cheering.

On that day the matter ended there. A few days later, when
Domitian addressed them, they received him with renewed
confidence, refused his offer of lands, and begged for enlistment and pay instead. This was only a petition, but one that
could not be refused: so they were admitted to the Guards.
Subsequently, those who had grown old and completed the
regular term of service* were honourably discharged. Others
were dismissed for misbehaviour, but one by one at different
times, which is always the safest method of weakening a mass
movement.

To return to the Senate; a bill was now passed that a loan 47
of sixty million sesterces should be raised from private individuals and administered by Pompeius Silvanus. This may
have been a financial necessity, or they may have wanted it to
seem so. At any rate the necessity soon ceased to exist, or else
they gave up the pretence. Domitian then carried a proposal
that the consulships conferred by Vitellius should be can-
celled, and that a state funeral should be held in honour of
Flavius Sabinus. These proposals are striking evidence of the
fickleness of fortune, entangling prosperity with catastrophe.

It was about this time that Lucius Piso, the governor of 48
Africa, was killed. To give a true explanation of this murder I
must go back and make a brief survey; this is quite relevant to
the reasons for such crimes.

Under the deified Augustus and Tiberius, the governor of
Africa had in his command one legion and some auxiliaries

with which to guard the frontier of the empire. Subsequently
Gaius Caesar, who was restless by nature and harboured
suspicions of the then governor, Marcus Silanus,* withdrew
the legion from his control and put it under a commander
whom he sent out for the purpose. He deliberately created a
state of friction, giving each man an equal amount of patronage and overlapping functions; this was further aggravated by
regrettable quarrels. The greater permanence of his tenure
strengthened the commander's position—or perhaps because
an inferior is more anxious to vie with his betters. The most
eminent governors, on the other hand, were more careful of
their safety than of their authority.

49   At the present time the legion in Africa was commanded by
Valerius Festus, an extravagant young man, immoderately
ambitious, whose kinship with Vitellius had given him some
anxiety. He had frequent interviews with Piso, and it is impossible to tell whether he tempted Piso to rebel or resisted Piso's
temptations. No one was present at their interviews, which
were held in private, and after Piso's death most people were
inclined to ingratiate themselves with his murderer. Beyond
doubt the province and the garrison were unfavourable to
Vespasian. Besides, some of the Vitellian refugees from Rome
pointed out to Piso that the Gallic provinces were wavering;
that Germany was ready to rebel, and he himself was in
danger, and that if one earns suspicion in peace the safest
course is war.*

Meanwhile, Claudius Sagitta, who commanded 'Petra's
Cavalry', made a good crossing, outstripping the centurion
Papirius, who had been sent out by Mucianus and was com-
missioned, so Sagitta affirmed, to assassinate Piso. Sagitta
further stated that Galerianus, Piso's cousin and son-in-law,
had already been murdered, and told him that while his one
hope lay in taking a bold step, there were two courses open to
him: he might either take up arms on the spot, or he might
prefer to sail to Gaul and offer to lead the Vitellian armies.
This made no impression on Piso.

When the centurion whom Mucianus had sent arrived at
the port of Carthage, he kept on shouting all sorts of congratulations to Piso on becoming emperor. The people he met,

who were astounded at this unexpected miracle, were instructed to take up the cry. With a crowd's usual credulity,
they rushed into the forum calling on Piso to appear, and as
they had a passion for flattery and took no interest in the
truth, they filled the whole place with a confused noise of
cheering. Piso, however, either at a hint from Sagitta, or from
his natural good sense, would not show himself in public or
give way to the excitement of the crowd. He examined the
centurion, and learnt that his object was to trump up a charge
against him and then kill him. He accordingly had the man
executed, more from indignation against an assassin than in
any hope of saving his life. He had found that the man had
been one of the murderers of Clodius Macer: after staining his
hands in the blood of the commander he had now reappeared
to slaughter the civil governor. Piso then reprimanded the
Carthaginians in a nervous edict, and refrained from perform-
ing even the routine of his office, shutting himself up in his
house, for fear that he might by accident provide some pretext
for further demonstrations.

The news of the popular excitement and the centurion's 50
execution reached the ears of Festus, considerably exaggerated and, as usual with rumours, mingling truth with falsehood; he then sent off a party of horsemen to murder Piso.
Riding at full speed, they reached the governor's house in the
twilight of early dawn and broke in with drawn swords. As
Festus had mainly chosen Carthaginian auxiliaries and Moors
to do the murder, most of them did not know Piso by sight.
However, near his bedroom they happened on a slave and
asked him who he was and where they could find Piso. In
answer the slave told them a heroic lie and said he was Piso,
whereupon they immediately cut him down. However, Piso
himself was killed very soon after, for there was one man there
who knew him: Baebius Massa, one of the imperial agents in
Africa, who was already a danger to all the best men in Rome.
His name will recur again and again in this narrative,* as one
of the causes of the troubles which beset us later on.

Festus had been waiting at Adrumetum* to see how things
went, and he now hastened to rejoin his legion. He had the
camp prefect, Caetronius Pisanus, put in irons, alleging that

he was one of Piso's accomplices, though his real motive was personal animosity. He then punished some of the soldiers and centurions and rewarded others; in neither case for their deserts, but because he wanted it to be thought that he had stamped out a war.

His next task was to settle the differences between Oea* and Lepcis. These had had a trivial origin in thefts of crops and cattle by the peasants, but they were now trying to settle them in open warfare. Oea, being inferior in numbers, had called in the aid of the Garamantes,* an untamed tribe who were always a fruitful source of damage to their neighbours. Thus the people of Lepcis were in great straits. Their fields had been wasted far and wide, and they had fled in terror under the shelter of their walls, when the Roman auxiliaries, both horse and foot, arrived on the scene. They routed the Garamantes and recovered all the booty, except what the nomads had already sold among the inaccessible hut-settlements of the far interior.

51   After the battle of Cremona and the arrival of good news from every quarter, Vespasian now heard of Vitellius' death. A large number of people of all classes, who were as lucky as they were adventurous, successfully braved the winter seas to bring him the news. There also arrived envoys from King Vologaeses offering the services of 40,000 Parthian cavalry. It was, indeed, a proud and fortunate situation to be courted with such splendid offers of assistance, and to need none of them. Vologaeses was duly thanked and instructed to send his envoys to the Senate and to understand that peace had been made. Vespasian now devoted his attention to the affairs of Italy and the capital, and received an unfavourable report of Domitian, who seemed to be trespassing beyond the natural sphere of an emperor's youthful son. He accordingly handed over the flower of his army to Titus, who was to finish off the war with the Jews.

52   It is said that before his departure Titus had a long talk with his father and begged him not to be rash and lose his temper at these incriminating reports, but to meet his son in a forgiving and unprejudiced spirit. 'Neither legions nor fleets', he is reported to have said, 'are such sure bulwarks of the throne as

a number of children. Time, chance, and often, too, ambition
and misunderstanding weaken, alienate, or extinguish friendship: a man's own blood cannot be severed from him; and
above all is this the case with a sovereign, for, while others
enjoy his good fortune, his misfortunes only concern his nearest kin. Even brothers are unlikely to remain good friends
unless their father sets them an example.'

These words had the effect of making Vespasian delighted
at Titus' loyalty rather than inclined to forgive Domitian.
'You may ease your mind,' he said to Titus. 'It is now your
duty to increase the prestige of Rome on the field: I will
concern myself with peace at home.'

Though the weather was still very rough, Vespasian at once
launched his fastest corn-ships* with a full cargo: for the city
was teetering on the verge of disaster. Indeed, there were not
more than ten days' supplies in the public granaries at the
moment when Vespasian's convoy brought relief.

The task of restoring the Capitol was entrusted to Lucius   53
Vestinus,* who, though only a knight, yet in reputation and
influence ranked with the highest. He summoned the soothsayers, and they recommended that the ruins of the former
temple should be carried away to the marshes and a new
temple erected on the same foundations: the gods were unwilling, they said, that the original form of the building should be
changed. On 21 June, a day of bright sunshine, the whole
consecrated area of the temple was decorated with chaplets
and garlands. In marched soldiers, all men with names of
good omen, carrying branches of auspicious trees: then came
the Vestal Virgins accompanied by boys and girls, each of
whom had father and mother alive, and they cleansed it all by
sprinkling fresh water from a spring or river. Next, while the
pontiff, Plautius Aelianus,* dictated the proper formulae,
Helvidius Priscus, the praetor, first purified the site by a solemn sacrifice of a pig, a sheep, and an ox,* and then, duly
offering the entrails on an altar of turf, he prayed to Jupiter,
Juno, and Minerva,* the guardian deities of the empire, to
prosper the enterprise, and by divine grace to raise on high
this house of theirs which human piety had here begun. He
then took hold of the chaplets around the foundation-stone,

to which ropes were attached. At the same moment the other magistrates and the priests and senators and knights and large numbers of the populace in joyous excitement with one great effort dragged the huge stone into its place. On every side gifts of gold and silver were flung into the foundations, blocks of virgin ore unscathed by any furnace, just as they had come from the womb of the earth. For the soothsayers had given out that the building must not be desecrated by the use of stone or gold that had been put to any other purpose. The height of the roof was raised. This was the only change that religious scruples would allow, and it was felt to be the only point in which the former temple lacked grandeur.

54   Meanwhile, the news of Vitellius' death had spread through Gaul and Germany and redoubled the vigour of the war. Civilis now dropped all pretence and hurled himself upon the Roman Empire. The Vitellian legions felt that even foreign slavery was preferable to the rule of Vespasian. The Gauls too had taken heart. A rumour had been spread that our winter camps in Moesia and Pannonia were being blockaded by Sarmatians and Dacians: similar stories were fabricated about Britain: the Gauls began to think that the fortune of the Roman armies was the same all the world over. But above all, the burning of the Capitol encouraged them to believe that the empire was coming to an end.* Once in old days the Gauls had captured Rome, but Jupiter's home was left unscathed and the empire stood firm. But now (so the Druids* with superstitious folly kept dinning into their ears) this fatal fire was a sign of Heaven's anger, and meant that the Transalpine tribes were destined now to rule the world. It was also rumoured that the Gallic chieftains, whom Otho had sent against Vitellius, had agreed before they parted that if Rome was shattered by its internal troubles and an unbroken sequence of civil wars, they would not fail the cause of Gallic freedom.

55   Prior to the murder of Hordeonius Flaccus nothing had leaked out to arouse suspicions of a conspiracy, but when he had been assassinated, messages passed between Civilis and Classicus, who commanded the Treviran cavalry. Classicus was far above the rest both in birth and in wealth. He came of

royal line and his ancestors were famous in both peace and war. It was his boast that his family had given Rome more enemies than allies. These two were now joined by Julius Tutor and Julius Sabinus, the one a Treviran, the other a Lingonian. Tutor had been appointed by Vitellius as commander of the bank of the Rhine. Sabinus' natural vanity was further inflamed by spurious pretensions of high birth, for he alleged that his great-grandmother's beauty had caught the fancy of the deified Julius Caesar during the campaign in Gaul, and that they had committed adultery.*

These four tested the temper of the rest in private interviews, and having bound to the conspiracy those who were considered fit, they held a conference at Cologne in a private house, the general feeling in the city being hostile to such plans as theirs. A few of the Ubii and Tungri, indeed, attended, but the Treviri and Lingonians were the backbone of the conspiracy. Nor would they tolerate deliberation or delay. They vied with each other in protesting that the Roman people were crazed with their internal quarrels; legions had been cut to pieces, Italy devastated, the city was on the point of being taken, while all her armies were occupied with wars of their own in different quarters. They need only garrison the Alps and then, when liberty had taken firm root, the Gallic provinces could debate what limits they desired to their power. All 56 this was no sooner spoken than applauded.

About the remnant of Vitellius' army they were in some doubt. Many held that they ought to be killed as being treacherous and insubordinate and stained with the blood of their generals. However, the policy of sparing them carried the day. To destroy all hope of pardon would only steel their obstinacy: it was much better to seduce them into alliance. Only the generals need be killed; a guilty conscience and the hope of pardon would soon bring the common soldiers flocking over to their flag.

Such was the tenor of their first meeting. Agitators were sent all over Gaul to stir up war. The conspirators themselves feigned loyalty to Vocula, hoping to catch him off his guard. There were, indeed, traitors who reported all this to Vocula, but he was not strong enough to crush the conspiracy, his legions being short-handed and unreliable. Caught between suspect troops on one side and secret enemies on the other, it seemed his best course under the circumstances to dissemble in his turn, and thus use their own weapons against them. So he marched down the river to Cologne. There he found Claudius Labeo, who after being taken prisoner, as described above, and exiled to the Frisii, had bribed his guards and escaped to Cologne. He promised that if Vocula would pro-vide him with troops, he would go to the Batavi and win back the better part of their community to the Roman alliance. He was given a small force of horse and foot; but ventured nothing among the Batavi. Instead he attracted a few of the Nervii and Baetasii to his standard, and proceeded to harass the Canninefates and Marsaci* more by stealth than open warfare.

57   Lured by the treachery of the Gauls, Vocula marched out against his enemy. Not far from Vetera, Classicus and Tutor rode forward on the pretext of scouting, and ratified their compact with the German leaders. They now for the first time separated from the legions, and entrenched themselves in a camp of their own. At this, Vocula protested that Rome was not as yet so shattered by civil war as to earn the contempt of tribes like the Treviri and Lingones. She could still rely on loyal provinces and victorious armies, on the good fortune of the empire and the avenging hand of the gods. Thus it was that in former days Sacrovir* and the Aedui, and more lately Vindex and the Gallic provinces, had each been crushed at a single battle. Now again these treaty-breakers must expect to face the same powers of Providence and Destiny. The deified Julius and the deified Augustus had understood these people better: it was Galba's reduction of the tribute* that had clothed them in enmity and pride. The Gauls were enemies today because their yoke was easy: when they had been stripped and plundered they would be friends.

After these spirited words, seeing that Classicus and Tutor still persisted in their treachery, he turned back and retired to Novaesium, while the Gauls encamped a couple of miles away on the plain. There centurions and soldiers flocked to and fro selling their souls. This was, indeed, an unheard of villainy:

that Roman soldiers should swear allegiance to a foreign
power, and offer as a pledge for this heinous crime to kill or
imprison their generals.

Though many urged Vocula to escape, he felt that he must
make a bold stand, so he summoned a meeting and spoke
somewhat as follows:

'Never before have I addressed you with such feelings of 58
anxiety for you, or with such indifference to my own fate.
That plans are being laid for my destruction I am glad enough
to hear: in such a parlous case as this I look for death as the
end of all my troubles. It is for you that I feel shame and pity.
It is not that a field of battle awaits you, for that would only
accord with the laws of warfare and the just rights of combat-
ants, but because Classicus hopes that with your hands he can
make war upon the Roman people, and flourishes before you
an oath of allegiance to All Gaul. What if fortune and courage
have deserted us for the moment: have we not glorious examples in the past? Have not often Roman soldiers chosen to die
rather than be driven from their post? Often our allies have
endured the destruction of their cities, and have given themselves and their wives and children to the flames,* without any
other reward for such an end save the name of honourable
men.

'At this very moment Roman troops are enduring famine
and siege at Vetera, and neither fear nor promises can move
them, while we, apart from arms and men and a magnificently
fortified camp, have grain and supplies enough to last through
any length of war. Money, too—the other day there was
enough even for a donative, and whether you choose to say
that it was given you by Vespasian or Vitellius, at any rate you
got it from a Roman emperor. After all the engagements you
have won, after routing the enemy at Gelduba, at Vetera, it
would to be sure be shameful to shirk battle; but you have
your trenches and your walls, and there are ways of gaining
time until armies come flocking from the neighbouring provinces to your rescue. Granted that you dislike me: well, there
are others to lead you, whether general, tribune, centurion,
and even private soldier. But do not let this portent be trum-
peted over the whole world, that Civilis and Classicus are

going to invade Italy with you in their train. Suppose the
Germans and Gauls lead the way to the walls of Rome, will
you turn your arms upon your fatherland? The mere thought
of such a crime is horrible. Will you stand sentry for Tutor the
Treviran? Shall a Batavian give you the signal for battle? Will
you swell the ranks of German hordes? And what will be the
issue of your crime, when the Roman legions take the field
against you? Desertion upon desertion, treachery upon treachery! You will be drifting miserably between the old allegiance
and the new, with the curse of Heaven on your heads. Jupiter
Optimus Maximus, whom we have worshipped at triumph
after triumph for 820 years; and Quirinus,* Father of the city
of Rome, if it was not your pleasure that under my command
this camp be kept from the stain of dishonour, grant at the
least, I humbly beseech you, that it never be defiled with the
pollution of Tutor or Classicus; and to these soldiers of Rome
give either innocence of heart or a speedy repentance before
the harm is done.'

59   The speech was variously received, with feelings fluctuating
between hope, fear, and shame. Vocula withdrew and began
to prepare for his end, but his freedmen and slaves prevented
him from forestalling by his own hand a dreadful death. As it
was, Classicus dispatched Aemilius Longinus, a deserter from
the First Legion, who quickly murdered him. For the commanders Herennius and Numisius imprisonment was thought
sufficient. Classicus then assumed the uniform and insignia
of a Roman general, and thus entered the camp. Hardened
though he was to every kind of crime, words failed him, and
he could only read out the oath. Those who were present
swore allegiance to the Empire of All Gaul. He then gave high
promotion to Vocula's assassin, and rewarded the others each
according to the villainy of his service.

The command was now divided between Tutor and
Classicus. Tutor at the head of a strong force besieged Cologne and forced the inhabitants and all the soldiers on
the Upper Rhine to take the same oath of allegiance. At
Mogontiacum he killed the tribunes and drove away the camp
prefect, who had refused to swear. Classicus ordered all the
greatest scoundrels among those who had surrendered to go

to Vetera and offer pardon to the besieged if they would yield
to circumstances: otherwise there was no hope for them:
they would suffer famine and sword and every extremity. The
messengers further cited their own example. Torn by a conflict   60
of loyalty and hunger the besieged vacillated between honour
and disgrace. While they hesitated, all their sources of food,
both normal and abnormal, began to fail them. They had
eaten their mules and horses and all the other animals which,
though foul and unclean, necessity had forced them to use. At
last they took to grubbing up the shrubs and roots and the
grass that grew between the stones, and became a model of
endurance in wretchedness—until they sullied their outstanding glory by a shameful conclusion. Envoys were sent to
Civilis begging for their lives. Even then he refused to receive
their petition until they had sworn allegiance to All Gaul.
They agreed that the camp should be plundered; and he sent
guards, some to secure the money, servants, and baggage, and
others to conduct the men themselves out of the camp empty-
handed. About five miles down the road their line was surprised by an ambush of Germans. The bravest fell on the spot;
many were cut down as they scattered; the rest got back to
camp. Civilis, indeed, complained that the Germans had
criminally broken faith and rebuked them for it. There is no
evidence to show whether this was a pretence or whether he
was really unable to restrain his savage troops. The camp was
plundered and torched, and all who had survived the battle
were devoured by the flames.

When Civilis first took up arms against Rome he vowed, as   61
is common with barbarians, to let his ruddled hair grow wild;
now that he had at last accomplished the destruction of the
legions he had it cut. It is said also that he put up some of the
prisoners for his little son to shoot in sport with arrows and
javelins. However, he did not himself swear allegiance to All
Gaul, nor did he force any of the Batavi to do so. He felt that
he could rely on the strength of the Germans, and that if any
quarrel arose with the Gauls* over control of the empire, his
fame would give him an advantage.

Munius Lupercus, one of the legionary commanders,
was sent among other presents to Veleda,* a virgin of the

Bructeran tribe who wielded widespread authority. It is an ancient custom in Germany to consider many women to be prophets and (as superstition grows) goddesses. At this moment Veleda's influence was at its height, for she had prophesied the success of the Germans and the destruction of the Roman army. However, Lupercus was killed on the journey. A few of the centurions and tribunes who had been born in Gaul were detained as a security for good faith. The winter camps of the legions and of the auxiliary infantry and cavalry were all dismantled and burnt, with the sole exception of those at Mogontiacum and Vindonissa.*

62 The Sixteenth Legion and the auxiliary troops who had surrendered with it now received orders to migrate from their quarters at Novaesium to Trier, and a date was fixed by which they had to leave their camp.* They spent the mean time brooding on various anxieties, the cowards all shuddering at the precedent of the massacre at Vetera, the better sort covered with shame at the stigma. What sort of a march would this be? Whom would they have to lead them? Everything would be decided by the will of those into whose hands they had put their life and death. But others were quite indifferent to the disgrace, and simply stowed their money or cherished possessions about their persons, while many got their armour ready and buckled on their swords, as if for battle.

Amidst these reflections the hour struck for their departure, and it proved more bitter than they had expected. Within the rampart their degradation was not so noticeable. The open country and the light of day revealed their depth of shame. The emperors' medallions had been torn down and their standards desecrated, while Gallic ensigns glittered all around them. They marched in silence, like a long funeral procession, led by Claudius Sanctus, a man whose sinister appearance—he had lost one eye—was only surpassed by his weakness of intellect. Their disgrace was doubled when they were joined by the other legion, who had left their camp at Bonn. Moreover, the news of their capture had spread, and all the people who shortly before had trembled at the very name of Rome now came flocking out from fields and houses, and scattered far and wide in transports of joy at this unwonted sight. The mob's insulting glee was too much for the Picenum cavalry regiment. Defying all Sanctus' threats and promises, they turned off to Mogontiacum, and coming by chance upon Longinus, the man who killed Vocula, they slew him with a shower of javelins—and thus made a beginning of future amends. The legions continued without changing their route, and camped before the walls of Trier.

Highly elated by their success, Civilis and Classicus debated 63 whether they should allow their troops to sack Cologne. Their natural savagery and lust for plunder inclined them to destroy the town, but policy forbade it; and they felt that in inaugurating a new empire a reputation for clemency would be an asset. Civilis was also moved by the memory of a past service, for at the beginning of the outbreak his son had been arrested in Cologne, but they had kept him in honourable custody. However, the tribes across the Rhine were jealous of this rich and rising community, and held that the war could only be ended either by throwing the settlement open to all Germans without distinction or by destroying it, thereby dispersing the Ubii. Accordingly the Tencteri, Cologne's nearest neighbours across 64 the Rhine, dispatched a deputation to lay their demands before a public meeting of the town. The most belligerent delegate set them out in some such terms as these:

'We give thanks to the national gods of Germany, and to Mars, supreme among gods,* that you are again incorporated in the German nation and the German name, and we congratulate you that you will now at last become free members of a free community. Until today the Romans had closed to us the rivers,* the earth, and almost the very air of heaven, to prevent all communication or association between us; or else they offered a still fouler insult to born warriors, that we should meet under supervision, unarmed and almost naked, and should pay for the privilege. Now, so that our friendly alliance may be ratified for all eternity, we demand of you that you pull down those bulwarks of slavery, the walls of your town, for even wild beasts lose their spirit if you keep them caged: that you put to the sword every Roman on your soil, since tyrants are incompatible with freedom; that all the property of those killed form a common stock and no one be allowed to conceal anything or to secure any private advantage. It must also be open both for us and for you to live on either river-bank, as our forefathers could in earlier days. As daylight is the natural heritage of all mankind, so every land is free to all brave men. Resume again the customs and manners of your own country and throw off those luxurious habits which enslave Rome's subjects* far more effectively than Roman arms. Then, pure and uncorrupt, you will forget your past slavery and either know none but equals or hold empire over others.'

65   The townspeople took time to consider these proposals, and, feeling that their apprehensions for the future forbade them to assent, while their present nervousness forbade them to return a plain negative, they answered more or less as follows:

'We have seized our first opportunity of freedom with more haste than prudence, because we wanted to be joined with you and all our other German kinsmen. As for our town walls, seeing that the Roman armies are massing at this moment, it would be safer for us to heighten them than to pull them down. All the foreigners from Italy or the provinces who lived on our soil have either perished in the war or fled to their own homes. As for the original settlers, who are united to us by ties of marriage, they and their offspring regard this as their home, and we do not think you are so unreasonable as to ask us to kill our parents and brothers and children. All trade duties and tariffs we remit. You may cross the Rhine without supervision, but you must come in daylight and unarmed until today's novel laws grow into a long-established custom. As arbitrators we will appoint Civilis and Veleda, and we will ratify our compact in their presence.'

Thus the Tencteri were pacified. A deputation was sent with presents to Civilis and Veleda, and obtained all that the people of Cologne desired. They were not, however, allowed to approach and speak to Veleda or even to see her, but were kept at a distance to inspire in them the greater awe. She herself lived at the top of a high tower, and one of her relatives was appointed to carry the questions and answers like a mediator between God and man.

Now that the alliance with Cologne had enhanced his 66
power, Civilis determined to win over the neighbouring communities or to attack any who opposed him. He took control
of the Sunuci* and formed their fighting strength into cohorts,
but then found his advance barred by Claudius Labeo at the
head of a hastily recruited band of Baetasii, Tungri, and
Nervii. He had forestalled the enemy in securing the bridge
over the Maas, and relied on the strength of his position. A
skirmish in this narrow space proved indecisive, until the
Germans swam across* and took Labeo in the rear. At this
point Civilis by a bold move—or possibly by arrangement—
rode into the lines of the Tungri and called out in a loud voice,
'Our object in taking up arms is not to secure empire for the
Batavi and Treviri over other tribes. We are far from any such
arrogance. Take us as allies. I am come to join you; whether
as general or as private it is for you to choose.'

This had a great effect on the common soldiers, who began
to sheathe their swords. Then two of their chieftains,
Campanus and Juvenalis, surrendered the entire tribe. Labeo
escaped before he was surrounded. Civilis also received the
allegiance of the Baetasii and Nervii, and added their forces to
his own. His power was now immense, for all the Gallic
communities were either terrified or ready to offer willing
support.

In the mean time, Julius Sabinus, who had destroyed every 67
memorial of the Roman alliance, assumed the title of Caesar
and proceeded to hurry a large unwieldy horde of his tribesmen against the Sequani, a neighbouring community faithful
to us. The Sequani accepted battle: the good cause prospered:
the Lingones were routed. The terror with which Sabinus fled
the field matched the rash haste with which he had plunged
into battle. Wishing to spread a rumour of his death, he took
refuge in a house and set fire to it, and was thus supposed to
have perished by his own act. I shall, however, relate in due
course the devices by which he lay in hiding* and prolonged
his life for nine more years, and describe also the loyalty of his
friends and the memorable example set by his wife Epponina.

This success on the part of the Sequani removed all momen-
tum from the war. The Gallic communities gradually came to

their senses and began to remember their moral and legal obligations. In this movement the Remi* took the lead. They circulated a notice throughout Gaul, summoning a meeting of delegates to consider whether liberty or peace was the preferable alternative.

68   At Rome, however, everything was exaggerated into a disaster, and Mucianus began to feel anxious. He had already appointed Annius Gallus and Petillius Cerialis to the chief command, and, distinguished officers as they were, he was afraid the conduct of such a war might be too much for them. Moreover, he could not leave Rome without government; he was afraid of Domitian's indomitable passions,* and, as I have said, was suspicious of Antonius Primus and Arrius Varus. Varus, as commanding the Guards, still controlled a powerful military force; Mucianus accordingly displaced him, but, as a compensation, made him director of the corn supply. As he had also to placate Domitian, who was inclined to support Varus, he appointed to the command of the Guards Arrecinus Clemens,* who was connected by marriage with Vespasian and greatly favoured by Domitian. He also impressed it upon Domitian that Clemens' father had filled this command with great distinction under Gaius:* that it would please the troops to have someone of the same name, and that, although he was a member of the Senate, he was quite able to fill both positions.*

Mucianus then chose his staff, some the most eminent men in the country, others recommended by private influence. Meanwhile both he and Domitian made ready to start, but with very different feelings. Domitian was full of the sanguine haste of youth, while Mucianus kept devising delays to check this enthusiasm. He was afraid that if Domitian once seized control of an army, his youthful aggression and his bad advisers would lead him into action prejudicial to both peace and war. Three victorious legions, the Eighth, Eleventh, and Thirteenth; the Twenty-First—one of Vitellius' legions—and the Second,* which had been newly enrolled, all started for the front, some by way of the Pennine and Cottian Alps, others over the Graian Alps. The Fourteenth Legion was summoned from Britain, and the Sixth and First from Spain.

The rumour that this force was on its way, along with their own natural character, inclined the Gallic communities to adopt a sober policy. Their delegates now met in the territory of the Remi, where they found the representatives of the Treviri awaiting them. One of these, Julius Valentinus, who was the keenest instigator of a hostile policy, delivered a set speech, in which he heaped spiteful aspersions on the Roman people, making all the charges which are usually brought against great empires. He was an unruly agitator, whose deranged rhetoric made him popular with the crowd. However, 69 Julius Auspex, a chieftain of the Remi, enlarged upon the power of Rome and the blessings of peace. Any sluggard can begin a war, he said, but in conducting it the risks are run by the energetic: and the legions were already upon them. Thus he restrained them, awakening a sense of respect and duty in all the sager breasts, and appealing to the fears of the younger men. So, while applauding Valentinus' courage, they followed the advice of Auspex.

The Treviri and Lingones were manifestly handicapped in Gaul by the fact that in Vindex's rising they had sided with Verginius. Many, too, were held back by inter-provincial jealousy. Where would the headquarters of the war be? To whom were they to look for authority and auspices? If all went well, which town would be chosen as the seat of government? So without achieving victory, they were already in disunion. Quarrels broke out, as some boasted of their great connections, others of their wealth and strength, others of their ancient lineage, until the future appeared so wearisome that they voted for the existing state of things. Letters were written to the Treviri in the name of Gaul, bidding them cease hostilities, suggesting that pardon might be obtained, and that many were ready to plead their cause if they showed repentance. Valentinus, however, opposed this, and made his tribesmen offer a deaf ear to it; but he was less anxious to organize a campaign than to make speeches on every possible occasion. The result was that neither the Treviri nor the Lingones nor 70 the other rebel tribes behaved as if aware of the serious risks they were undertaking. Even the leaders did not act in concert. Civilis wandered over the wilds of the Belgic country, trying to catch or expel Claudius Labeo. Classicus mainly lived a life of leisure, as if he were enjoying the fruits of empire. Even Tutor seemed in no hurry to garrison the Upper Rhine and block the Alpine passes.

In the mean time, the Twenty-First Legion launched an invasion from Vindonissa, while Sextilius Felix advanced through Raetia with some auxiliary cohorts. These were joined by the 'Select' cavalry regiment that had been raised by Vitellius and then deserted to Vespasian. This was commanded by Julius Briganticus, the son of Civilis' sister: for uncle and nephew hated each other with all the aggravated bitterness of near relatives. Tutor had swelled his force of Treviri with fresh levies from the Vangiones, Triboci, and Caeracates,* and now stiffened it with Roman veterans, both horse and foot, tempting or intimidating some legionaries into joining them. These soldiers first cut up an auxiliary cohort sent forward by Sextilius Felix, but on the advance of the Roman army with its generals they loyally deserted to their old flag, and were followed by the Triboci, Vangiones, and Caeracates. Tutor, accompanied by his Treviri, avoided Mogontiacum and fell back on Bingium,* relying on his position there, as he had broken down the bridge over the River Nava.* However, Sextilius' cohorts followed him up; a traitor showed them a ford; Tutor was routed.

This disaster was a crushing blow to the Treviri. The rank and file dropped their weapons and scattered through the fields, while some of their chieftains, hoping it might be thought that they had been the first to lay down arms, took refuge among tribes who had never repudiated the Roman alliance. The legions which had been moved, as I said above, from Novaesium and Bonn to Trier, now administered to themselves the oath of allegiance to Vespasian. This happened in Valentinus' absence. When he arrived in furious excitement, ready to spread universal ruin and confusion, the legions withdrew into the friendly territory of the Mediomatrici. Valentinus and Tutor then led the Treviri forcibly back into the field, but first they killed the two commanders, Herennius and Numisius. By diminishing the hope of pardon they tried to cement their bond of crime.

Such was the position when Petillius Cerialis reached 71
Mogontiacum. His arrival roused high hopes. He was himself
thirsting for battle, and being always better at despising his
enemy than at taking precautions, he fired his men by deliver-
ing a spirited harangue, promising that directly there was a
chance of joining with the enemy he would engage battle
without delay. He dismissed the Gallic recruits to their homes
with a message that the legions were enough for the empire:
the allies could resume their peaceful occupations, feeling
assured that the war was practically ended, now that Roman
troops had taken it in hand. This action rendered the Gauls all
the more tractable. They made less difficulty about taxation,
now that they had got their men back again, while his disdain
for them only sharpened their sense of duty.

On the other side, when Civilis and Classicus heard of
Tutor's defeat, the destruction of the Treviri, and the universal
success of their enemy's arms, they fell into a panic, hastily
mobilized their own scattered forces, and kept sending messages to Valentinus not to risk a decisive battle. This only
hastened Cerialis' movements. He sent guides to the legions
stationed in the country of the Mediomatrici to lead them
back onto the enemy by the shortest route. Then, assembling
all the troops to be found in Mogontiacum together with his
own force, he marched in three days to Rigodulum.* Here, on
a spot protected by the mountains on one side and the Moselle
on the other, Valentinus had already taken his stand with a
large force of Treviri. His camp had been strengthened with
trenches and stone barricades, but these fortifications had no
terrors for the Roman general. He ordered the infantry to
force the position in front, while the cavalry were to ascend
the hill. Valentinus' hurriedly assembled forces filled him with
contempt, for he felt that whatever advantage their position
might give them, the courage of his men would outweigh it. A
short delay was necessary while the cavalry climbed, exposed
to the enemy's fire. But when the close combat began, the
Treviri tumbled headlong down the hill like a landslide. Some
of our cavalry, who had ridden round by an easier gradient,
captured several Belgic chieftains, including their general,
Valentinus.

72   On the next day Cerialis entered Trier. The troops clamoured greedily for its destruction. It was, they said, the native
town of Classicus and of Tutor: these were the men who had
wickedly entrapped and slaughtered the legions. Its guilt was
far worse than that of Cremona, which had been wiped off the
face of Italy for causing the victors a single night's delay. This
place stood untouched on the German frontier, glorying in the
spoil of Roman armies and the blood of Roman generals. The
plunder could go to the imperial Treasury. It would be enough
for them to see the rebel town in smoking ruins; that would be
some compensation for the destruction of so many camps.
Cerialis was afraid of soiling his reputation if it was said that
he gave his men a taste for cruelty and riot, so he suppressed
their indignation. They obeyed him, too, for now that civil
war was done with, there was less insubordination on foreign
service.

Their thoughts were now distracted by the pitiful appearance of the legions who had been summoned from the country
of the Mediomatrici.* Miserably conscious of their guilt, they
stood with eyes rooted to the ground. When the armies met,
there were no greetings: they had no answer for those who
offered comfort and encouragement: they skulked in their
tents, shunning the light of day. It was not fear of punishment
so much as the shame of their disgrace which thus overwhelmed them. Even the victorious army showed their bewil-
derment: hardly venturing to make an audible petition, they
craved pardon for them with silent tears. At length Cerialis
soothed their alarm. He insisted that all events caused by
dissension between officers and men, or by the enemy's guile,
were to be regarded as acts of destiny. They should count this
as their first day of service and sworn allegiance: neither he
nor the Emperor remembered past misdeeds. He then gave
them quarters in his own camp, and sent orders round the
separate companies that no one in the heat of any quarrel
should taunt a fellow-soldier with mutiny or defeat.

73   Cerialis next summoned the Treviri and Lingones, and
addressed them as follows:

'I am unpractised in public speaking, for it is only on the
field that I have asserted the valour of the Roman people. Yet

since words have so much weight with you, and since you judge good and evil not by their actual qualities but by what agitators tell you, I have decided to make a few remarks, which, as the war is practically over,* are likely to be more profitable to you the audience than to me the speaker.

'Roman generals and emperors originally set foot in your country and the rest of Gaul from no motives of greed, but at the call of your ancestors, who were worn almost to ruin by dissension. The Germans who were summoned to help had forced the yoke of slavery on allies and enemies alike.* You know how often we fought against the Cimbri and the Teutons,* with what infinite pains and with what striking success our armies have undertaken German wars. All that is famous. It was not to protect Italy that we occupied the Rhine, but to prevent some second Ariovistus making himself master of All Gaul. Do you imagine that Civilis and his Batavi and the other tribes across the Rhine care any more about you than their ancestors cared about your fathers and grandfathers? The Germans have always had the same motives for crossing into Gaul—lust, greed, and the desire to change their dwellings. They wanted to leave their marshes and deserts, and to make themselves masters of this magnificently fertile soil and of you who live on it. Of course they use specious pretexts and talk about liberty. No one has ever wanted to enslave others and play the tyrant without making use of the very same phrases.

'Tyranny and warfare were always rife throughout the length and breadth of Gaul, until you accepted Roman government. Often as we have been provoked, we have never imposed upon you any burden by right of conquest, except what was necessary to maintain peace. Tribes cannot be kept quiet without troops. You cannot have troops without pay; and you cannot raise pay without taxation. In every other respect you are treated as our equals. You frequently command our legions yourselves: you govern this and other provinces yourselves.* We have no exclusive privileges. Though you live so far away, you enjoy the blessings of a praiseworthy emperor no less than we do, whereas the tyrant only oppresses his nearest neighbours. 74

'You must put up with depravity and greed* in your masters, just as you put up with bad crops or excessive rain, or any other natural disaster. Vice will last as long as mankind. But these evils are not continual. There are intervals of good government, which make up for them. You cannot surely hope that the tyranny of Tutor and Classicus would mean milder government, or that they will need less taxation for the armies they will have to raise to keep the Germans and Britons at bay. For if the Romans were driven out—which Heaven forbid—what could ensue save universal warfare between all races? During 800 years, by good fortune and good organization, this structure of empire has been consolidated. It cannot be uprooted without destroying the uprooters. And it is you who would run the greatest risk of all, since you have gold and rich resources, which are the prime causes of war. You must learn, then, to love and foster peace and the city of Rome in which we all, vanquished and victors alike, have the same rights. You, who have tried both conditions, should take warning that submission and safety are better than rebellion and ruin.'

By such words as these he quieted and reassured his audience, who had been afraid of more rigorous measures.

75   While the victorious army was occupying Trier, Civilis and Classicus sent a letter to Cerialis, the gist of which was that Vespasian was dead, though the news was being suppressed; Rome and Italy were exhausted by civil war: Mucianus and Domitian were mere names with no power behind them. If Cerialis desired to be emperor of All Gaul, they would be satisfied with the boundaries of their own states: but if he should prefer battle, that, too, they would not deny him. Cerialis made no answer to Civilis and Classicus, but sent the letter and its bearer to Domitian.

The enemy now approached Trier from every quarter in detached bands, and Cerialis was much criticized for allowing them to unite, when he might have cut them off one by one. The Roman army now threw a trench and rampart round their camp, for they had rashly settled in it without seeing to the fortifications.

In the German camp different opinions were keenly de- 76 bated. Civilis contended that they should wait for the tribes from across the Rhine, whose arrival would spread a panic sufficient to crush the enfeebled forces of the Romans. The Gauls, he urged, were simply a prey for the winning side and, as it was, the Belgae, who were their sole strength, had declared for him or were at least sympathetic.

Tutor maintained that delay only strengthened the Roman force, since their armies were converging from every quarter. 'They have brought one legion across from Britain, others have been summoned from Spain, or are on their way from Italy. Nor are they men recruited in haste, but experienced veterans, while the Germans, for whose aid we hope, are subject to no discipline or control but do whatever they like. You can only bribe them with money or presents, and the Romans have the advantage of us there: besides, however keen he is to fight, a man always prefers peace to danger, so long as the pay is the same. But if we engage them at once, Cerialis has nothing but legions created from the remnants of the German army, who have sworn allegiance to the Gallic Empire. The very fact that they have just unexpectedly routed Valentinus' undisciplined band serves to fuel the imprudence of both soldiers and general. They will venture out again and will fall into the hands—not of an inexperienced boy, who is more practised in words and speeches than in sword and steel, but of Civilis and Classicus, at the sight of whom fear, flight, and famine will be reawakened in their minds; and they will remember how often their lives were at their captors' mercy. Nor is it any liking for the Romans that keeps back the Treviri and Lingones: they will fly to arms again, when once their fears are dispelled.'

Classicus finally settled the difference of opinion by declar- ing for Tutor's policy, and they promptly carried it out. The 77 Ubii and Lingones were placed in the centre, the Batavian cohorts on the right, and on the left the Bructeri and Tencteri. Advancing, some by the hills and some by the path between the road and the River Moselle, they took the Romans com- pletely by surprise. So sudden was their onslaught that

Cerialis, who had not spent the night in camp, was still in bed when he heard almost simultaneously that the fighting had begun and that his troops were losing. He cursed the messengers for panicking, until he saw the whole extent of the disaster with his own eyes. The legionary camp had been forced, the cavalry routed, and the intervening bridge over the Moselle, which connects the suburbs with the town, was held by the enemy. But confusion had no terrors for Cerialis. Pulling back fugitives bodily, flinging himself without any armour into the rain of missiles, he succeeded by his inspired imprudence and the assistance of the braver men in retaking the bridge. Leaving a picked band to hold it, he hurried back to the camp, where he found that the companies of the legions which had surrendered at Bonn and Novaesium were all broken up, few men were left at their posts, and the eagles were all but surrounded by the enemy.

He turned on them in blazing anger: 'It is not Flaccus or Vocula that you are deserting. There is nothing treasonable about me. I have done nothing to be ashamed of, except that I was rash enough to believe that you had forgotten your Gallic ties and awakened to the memory of your Roman allegiance. Am I to be numbered with the Numisiuses and Herenniuses? Are all your generals to have fallen either by your hands or the enemy's? Go and tell the news to Vespasian, or rather, to Civilis and Classicus—they are nearer at hand: that you have deserted your general on the field of battle. There will yet come legions who will not leave me unavenged or you unpunished.'

78   All he said was true, and the officers heaped the same reproaches on their heads. The men were drawn up in cohorts and companies, since it was impossible to deploy with the enemy swarming round them, and, the fight being inside the rampart, the tents and baggage were a serious encumbrance. Tutor and Classicus and Civilis, each at his post, were busy rallying their forces, appealing to the Gauls to fight for freedom, the Batavians for glory, and the Germans for plunder. Everything, indeed, went well for the enemy until the Twenty-First Legion, who had rallied in a clearer space than any of the others, first withstood their charge and then repulsed them.

Then, by divine providence, the enemy suddenly lost their nerve: the victors turned tail. They themselves attributed their panic to the appearance of the Roman auxiliaries, who, after being scattered by the first charge, formed again on the hill-tops and were taken for fresh reinforcements. However, what really cost the Gauls their victory was that they let their enemy alone and indulged in ignoble squabbles over the spoil. Thus after Cerialis' carelessness had almost caused disaster, his pluck now saved the day, and he followed up his success by capturing the enemy's camp and destroying it before nightfall.

Cerialis' troops were allowed short respite. Cologne was 79 clamouring for help and offering to surrender Civilis' wife and sister and Classicus' daughter, who had been left behind there as pledges of the alliance. In the mean time the inhabitants had massacred the Germans billeted separately in private house-holds. They were now alarmed at this, and had good reason to implore aid before the enemy could recover their strength and prepare for their desired objective—or at any rate for revenge.

Indeed, Civilis already had designs on Cologne, and he was still formidable, for the most ferocious of his cohorts, composed of Chauci and Frisii, was still in full force at Tolbiacum,* within the territory of Cologne. However, he changed his plans on receiving the bitter news that this force had been entrapped and destroyed by the inhabitants of Cologne. They had entertained the Germans at a lavish ban-quet, drugged them with wine, shut the doors upon them and burned the place to the ground; at the same moment Cerialis hurried his army to relieve the town.

A further anxiety haunted Civilis. He was afraid that the Fourteenth Legion, in conjunction with the fleet from Britain, might harry the Batavians encircled by the North Sea. How-ever, Fabius Priscus, who was in command, led his troops by land into the country of the Nervii and Tungri, who surren-dered to him. The Canninefates made an unprovoked attack upon the fleet and sank or captured the greater number of the ships. They also defeated a mass of Nervian volunteers who had been recruited in the Roman interest. Classicus secured a further success against an advance guard of cavalry which Cerialis had sent forward to Novaesium. These repeated

checks, though unimportant in themselves, served to dim the
lustre of the recent Roman victory.

80   It was about this time that Mucianus gave orders for the
murder of Vitellius' son, on the plea that dissension would
continue until all the seeds of war were stamped out. He also
refused to allow Antonius Primus to go out on Domitian's
staff, being alarmed at his popularity among the troops and
at the man's own vanity, which would brook no equal, much
less a superior. Antonius accordingly went to join Vespasian,
whose reception, though not hostile, proved a disappoint-
ment. The Emperor was drawn two ways. On the one side
were Antonius' services: it was undeniable that his generalship
had ended the war. In the other scale were Mucianus' letters.
Besides which, everyone else raked up the scandals of his past
life and inveighed against his vanity and bad temper. In his
arrogance Antonius himself did his best to provoke hostility
by expatiating to excess on his services, decrying the other
generals as incompetent cowards, and stigmatizing Caecina as
a prisoner who had surrendered. Thus without any open
breach of friendship he gradually declined lower and lower in
the Emperor's favour.

81   During the months which Vespasian spent at Alexandria
waiting for the regular season of the summer winds* to ensure
a safe voyage, there occurred many miraculous events mani-
festing the goodwill of Heaven and a certain favour of Providence towards him. At Alexandria a commoner, whose eyes
were well known to have wasted away, on the advice of
Serapis (whom this superstitious people worship as their chief
god) fell at Vespasian's feet demanding with sobs a cure for
his blindness, and imploring that the Emperor would deign to
moisten his eyes and eyeballs with the spittle from his mouth.
Another man with a maimed hand, also inspired by Serapis,
besought Vespasian to imprint his footmark on it.

At first Vespasian laughed at them and refused, but they
insisted. He half-feared a reputation for gullibility, but was
half-moved to hope by their petition and the flattery of his
courtiers. He eventually told the doctors to form an opinion
whether such cases of blindness and deformity could be
remedied by human aid. The doctors discussed the question

from various angles, saying that in the one case the power of sight was not extinct and would return if the impediments were removed; in the other case the limbs were distorted and could be set right again by the application of an effective remedy: this might be the will of Heaven and the Emperor had perhaps been chosen as the divine instrument. They added that he would gain all the credit if the cure were successful, while, if it failed, the ridicule would fall on the unfortunate patients.

This convinced Vespasian that there were no limits to his destiny: nothing now seemed incredible. To the great excitement of the bystanders, he stepped forward with a smile on his face and did as the men desired him. Immediately the hand recovered its functions and daylight shone once more in the blind man's eyes. Those who were present still attest both miracles today, when there is nothing to gain by lying.

This occurrence deepened Vespasian's desire to visit the 82 holy place and consult Serapis about the fortunes of the empire. He gave orders that no one else was to be allowed in the temple, and then went in. While absorbed in his devotions, he saw behind him an Egyptian noble named Basilides, whom he knew to be lying ill several days' journey from Alexandria. He inquired of the priests whether Basilides had entered the temple that day; he inquired of everyone he met whether he had been seen in the city. Eventually he sent some horsemen, who discovered that at the time Basilides had been eighty miles away. Vespasian therefore took what he had seen for a divine apparition, and from the name 'Basilides' deduced the tenor of the oracle's response.*

The origins of the god Serapis have not yet been canvassed 83 in any Roman authorities.* The priests of Egypt give the following account: King Ptolemy,* the first of the Macedonians to put the power of Egypt on a firm footing, was engaged in building walls and temples, and instituting religious cults for the newly founded city of Alexandria, when there appeared to him in his sleep a young man of striking beauty and superhuman stature, who advised him to send his most faithful friends to Pontus to fetch his image: this would bring blessings to the kingdom, and its resting-place would grow great and famous. The youth then appeared to ascend into heaven in a sheet of flame.

Impressed by this miraculous omen, Ptolemy revealed his nocturnal vision to the priests of Egypt, who are used to interpreting such things. As they had but little knowledge of Pontus or of foreign matters, he consulted an Athenian named Timotheus, a member of the Eumolpid clan, whom he had brought over from Eleusis* to act as priest of the religious rites, and asked him what strange cult and what god was meant. Timotheus found some people who had travelled to Pontus and learnt from them that near a town called Sinope there was a temple, which had long been famous in the neighbourhood as the seat of Jupiter Dis: indeed, near it there also stood a female figure, which was commonly called Proserpina.*

Ptolemy was like most despots: easily terrified at first, but liable, when his panic was over, to think more of his pleasures than of his religious duties. The incident was gradually forgotten, and other thoughts occupied his mind until the vision was repeated in a more terrible and impressive form than before, and he was threatened with death and the destruction of his kingdom if he failed to fulfil his instructions. He at once gave orders that an embassy should be made ready with presents for King Scydrothemis, who was then reigning at Sinope; on the envoys' departure he instructed them to consult the oracle of Apollo at Delphi.* They made a successful voyage and received a clear answer from the oracle: they were to go and bring back the image of Apollo's father* but leave behind his sister's.

84   On their arrival at Sinope they laid their king's presents, petition, and instructions before Scydrothemis. He was in some perplexity. He was afraid of the god and yet alarmed by the threats of his subjects, who opposed the project: then, again, he often felt tempted by the envoys' presents and promises. Three years passed. Ptolemy's zeal never abated for a moment. He persisted in his petition, and kept sending more and more distinguished envoys, more ships, more gold. Then a threatening vision appeared to Scydrothemis, bidding him no longer thwart the god's design. When he still hesitated, he

was beset by every kind of disease and disaster: the gods were plainly angry, and every day the burden of their wrath grew greater. He summoned an assembly and laid before it the divine commands, his own and Ptolemy's visions, and the troubles with which they were visited. The king found the people unfavourable. They were jealous of Egypt and fearful of their own future; they surged round the temple.

The story now grows grander still. The god himself, it says, embarked unaided* on one of the ships that lay beached on the shore, and by a miracle accomplished the long sea-journey and landed at Alexandria within three days. A temple worthy of so important a city was then built in the quarter called Rhacotis, on the site of an ancient shrine of Serapis and Isis.* This is the most widely accepted account of the god's origin and arrival.

Some people, I am well aware, maintain that the god was brought from the Syrian town of Seleucia during the reign of Ptolemy, the third of that name. Others, again, say it was this same Ptolemy, but make the place of origin the famous town of Memphis,* once the bulwark of ancient Egypt. Many take the god for Aesculapius,* because he cures disease: others for Osiris, the oldest of the local gods; many, again, for Jupiter, as being the sovereign lord of the world. But the majority of people, either judging by what are clearly attributes of the god or by an ingenious process of conjecture, identify him with Father Dis.

Domitian and Mucianus were now on their way to the Alps. 85 Before reaching the mountains they received the good news of the victory over the Treviri, the truth of which was fully attested by the presence of the enemy general Valentinus. His courage was in no way crushed and his face still bore witness to the proud spirit he had shown. He was allowed a hearing, merely to see what he was made of, and condemned to death. At his execution someone cast it in his teeth that his country was conquered. He replied, 'I have death as my consolation.'

Mucianus now gave utterance to an idea which he had long cherished, though he pretended it was a sudden inspiration. Since by Heaven's grace, he said, the forces of the enemy had been broken, it would ill befit Domitian, now that the war was practically over, to stand in the way of those others to whom the credit belonged. Were the fortunes of the empire or the safety of Gaul at stake, it would be right that a Caesar should take the field; the Canninefates and Batavi should be consigned to minor generals. Domitian should stay at Lyons and there show the power and prosperity of the throne from close quarters. By abstaining from trifling risks he would be ready to cope with greater ones.

86   The ruse was detected, but Mucianus' deference meant that it could not be unmasked; they therefore proceeded to Lyons. From there Domitian is supposed to have sent secret messengers to Cerialis to test his loyalty, and to ask whether the general would transfer his army and his authority to him, should he present himself in person. Whether Domitian's idea was to plan war against his father or to acquire power and support against his brother was unclear; for with salutary restraint Cerialis parried his proposal and treated it as a boy's day-dream. Realizing that older men despised his youth, Domitian gave up even those limited functions of government which he had hitherto performed. He hid his thoughts from scrutiny beneath an ingenuous and unassuming appearance, feigning literary tastes and a passion for poetry. His aim was to conceal his real self and withdraw from all rivalry with his brother, whose gentler and altogether different nature he utterly misconstrued.

BOOK FIVE

Early in this same year Titus Caesar had been entrusted by his 1
father with the task of completing the reduction of Judaea.
While he and his father were both still ordinary citizens, Titus
had distinguished himself as a soldier. Now his efficiency and
reputation were steadily increasing, while the provinces and
armies vied with one another in their enthusiasm for him.
Wishing to seem independent of his good fortune, he always
showed dignity and energy in the field. His affable and
friendly conversation called forth devotion. He regularly
mingled with his soldiers at their duties or on the march
without compromising his dignity as general.

Three legions awaited him in Judaea, the Fifth, Tenth, and
Fifteenth, all veterans from his father's army. These were
reinforced by the Twelfth from Syria, and by detachments of
the Twenty-Second and the Third brought over from Alexandria. This force was accompanied by twenty auxiliary cohorts
and eight regiments of cavalry; also the Kings Agrippa and
Sohaemus and auxiliaries from King Antiochus, a strong force
of Arabs, who had the hatred for the Jews usual between
neighbours, and numerous individuals who had come from
Rome and the rest of Italy, each tempted by the hope of
securing the first place in the Emperor's still unoccupied affec-
tions. With this force Titus entered the enemy's country; his
column was drawn up in order, he sent out scouts everywhere,
and held himself ready to fight. He pitched his camp not far
from Jerusalem.

Since I am coming now to describe the last days of this 2
famous city, it may not seem out of place to recount here its
early history.

It is said that the Jews are refugees from Crete who settled
in the furthest part of Libya at the time when Saturn was
forcibly deposed by Jupiter.* Evidence for this is sought in the
name: Ida is a famous mountain in Crete inhabited by the
Idaei, whose name became lengthened into the foreign form
Judaei. Others say that in the reign of Isis* the superfluous

population of Egypt, under the leadership of Hierosolymus and Juda, discharged itself upon the neighbouring districts; while there are many who think the Jews of Ethiopian stock, driven by fear and hatred to emigrate in the reign of King Cepheus.* Another tradition makes them Assyrian refugees* who, lacking lands of their own, occupied a district of Egypt, and later took to building cities of their own and tilling Hebrew territory and the frontierland of Syria. Yet another version assigns to the Jews an illustrious origin as the descendants of the Solymi—a tribe praised in the poems of Homer*— who founded a city and called it Jerusalem* after their own name.

3   Most authorities, however, agree* that a foul and disfiguring disease once broke out in Egypt, and that King Bocchoris,* on approaching the oracle of Ammon* and inquiring for a remedy, was told to purge his kingdom and to transport all the victims into another country, for they had earned the disfavour of Heaven. A motley crowd was collected and abandoned in the desert. While all the other outcasts lay idly lamenting, one of them, named Moses, advised them not to look for help to gods or men, since both had deserted them, but to trust rather in themselves and accept as divine the guidance of the first being by whose aid they should get out of their present plight. They agreed, and set out blindly to march wherever chance might lead them. Their worst distress came from lack of water. When they were already at death's door and lying prostrate all over the plain, a drove of wild asses moved away from their pasture to a rock densely covered with trees. Guessing the truth from the grassy nature of the ground, Moses followed and disclosed some streams with an ample flow of water. This restored them. Continuing their march for six successive days, on the seventh they routed the natives and gained possession of the country. There they consecrated their city and their Temple.*

4   To ensure his future hold over the people, Moses introduced a new cult, which was the opposite of all other religions. All that we hold sacred they held profane, and they allowed practices which we abominate. They dedicated in the innermost part of the Temple an image of the animal whose

guidance had put an end to their wandering and thirst,* after first killing a ram, apparently as an insult to Ammon.* They also sacrifice bulls, because the Egyptians worship the bull Apis. Pigs are subject to leprosy, the foul plague with which they too were once infected; so they abstain from pork in memory of their misfortune. Their frequent fasts bear witness to the long famine they once endured, and, in token of their rushed meal, Jewish bread is made without leaven.* They are said to have devoted the seventh day to rest because that day brought an end to their toils.* Later, finding idleness alluring, they gave up the seventh year as well to sloth.* Others maintain that they do this in honour of Saturn, either because their religious principles are derived from the Idaei, who are supposed to have been driven out with Saturn and become the ancestors of the Jewish people; or else because, of the seven stars* which govern the lives of men, the star of Saturn moves in the topmost orbit and exercises the mightiest influence, and also because most of the heavenly bodies move round their courses in multiples of seven.

Whatever their origin, these rites are sanctioned by their 5 antiquity. Their other customs are perverted and abominable, and owe their prevalence to their depravity. All the most worthless rascals, renouncing their national cults, started showering them with offerings and tribute.* This is one cause of Jewish prosperity. Another is that they are obstinately loyal to each other and always ready to show compassion, whereas they feel nothing but hatred and enmity for the rest of the world. They separate themselves from others both in meals and in bed: though immoderate in sexual indulgence, they refrain from intercourse with foreign women: among themselves anything is allowed. They have introduced circumcision to distinguish themselves from other people.* Those who are converted to their customs adopt the same practice, and the first lessons they learn are to despise the gods, to renounce their country, and to regard parents, children, and brethren as worthless.

However, they take steps to increase their numbers. They count it a crime even to kill any of their later-born children,* and they believe that the souls of those who die in battle or under execution are immortal. Thus they think much of having children and nothing of facing death. They prefer to bury and not burn their dead. In this, as in their concern for and belief in an underworld, they conform to Egyptian custom. Their ideas of the divine are quite different. The Egyptians worship most of their gods as animals, or in shapes half animal and half human. The Jews acknowledge one god only, of whom they have a purely spiritual conception. They think it impious to make images of gods in human shape out of perishable materials. Their god is almighty and eternal, inimitable and without end. They therefore set up no statues in their temples, nor even in their cities, refusing this homage to their kings and this honour to the Roman emperors. However, the fact that their priests intoned to the flute and cymbals and wore wreaths of ivy,* and that a golden vine* was found in their Temple, has led some people to think that they worship Father Liber,* the conqueror of the East. But this is completely out of accord with their cult. Liber instituted joyous and cheerful rites, but the Jewish ritual is preposterous and sordid.

6   The country of the Jews is bounded by Arabia on the east, by Egypt on the south, and on the west by Phoenicia and the sea. On the Syrian frontier they have a distant view towards the north. Physically they are healthy and hardy. Rain is rare; the soil fertile; its products are of the same kind as ours with the addition of balsam and palms. Palm-groves have height and beauty, the balsam is a mere shrub. When its branches are swollen with sap one may open them with a sharp piece of stone or crockery, for the sap-vessels shrink up at the touch of iron. The sap is used in medicine. Lebanon, their chief mountain, stands shaded in eternal snow, a strange phenomenon in such a burning climate. Here, too, the River Jordan has its source and comes pouring down, but does not emerge in the Mediterranean. It flows undiminished through first one lake, then another, and loses itself in a third.

This last is a lake of immense size,* like a sea, though its water has a fouler taste and a most unhealthy smell, which poisons the local inhabitants. No wind can stir waves in it: no fish or water-fowl can live there. The sluggish water supports

whatever is thrown onto it, as if its surface were solid, while
those who cannot swim float on it as easily as those who can.

Every year at the same time the lake yields asphalt. As with
other arts, it is experience which shows how to collect it. In its
natural state it is a black liquid; when congealed with a
sprinkling of vinegar, it floats on the surface of the water. The
men who collect it then take it into their hands and haul it on
deck. Then without further aid it trickles in and loads the boat
until you cut off the stream. But this you cannot do with iron
or brass: it is repelled only by blood or a garment stained with
a woman's menstrual discharge. That is what the old authorities say, but those who know the district aver that floating
blocks of asphalt are pushed and dragged to shore by hand.
The steam out of the earth and the heat of the sun dries them,
and they are then split up with axes and wedges, like logs or
blocks of stone.

Not far from this lake are plains which they say were once 7
fertile and covered with large and populous cities; these plains
were destroyed by lightning.* Traces of the cities are said to
remain, and the ground, which looks scorched, has lost all
power of production. The plants, whether wild or artificially
cultivated, are black and sterile and wither into dust and
ashes, whether when in leaf or flower, or when they have
attained their full growth. Without denying that at some date
famous cities were there burnt up by fire from Heaven, I am
yet inclined to think that it is the exhalation from the lake
which infects the soil and poisons the surrounding atmosphere. Soil and climate being equally deleterious, the spring
and autumn crops all rot away. The River Belius* also flows
into the Jewish sea. Round its mouth is found a peculiar kind
of sand which is mixed with soda and smelted into glass.
Small though the beach is, its product is inexhaustible.

The greater part of Judaea is scattered with villages, but 8
they also have towns. Jerusalem is the Jewish capital, and
contained the Temple, which was enormously wealthy. A first
line of fortifications guarded the city, then came the palace,
and the inner defences enclosed the Temple.* None but a Jew
was allowed as far as the doors: none but the priests might
cross the threshold.*

When the East was in the hands of the Assyrians, Medes, and Persians, they regarded the Jews as the meanest of their slaves. During the Macedonian ascendancy King Antiochus* endeavoured to abolish their superstitions and to introduce Greek customs. But Arsaces at that moment rebelled,* and the Parthian war prevented him from effecting any improvement in the character of this grim people. Then, when Macedon waned, as the Parthian power was not yet ripe and Rome was still far away, they took kings of their own. The mob was fickle and drove them out.* However, they recovered their throne by force; banished their countrymen, sacked cities, slew brothers, wives, and parents, and committed all the usual royal crimes. But the kings fostered the Jewish superstition, since they strengthened their authority by assuming the priesthood.*

9   Gnaeus Pompey was the first Roman to subdue the Jews and set foot in the Temple by right of conquest.* That is the source of the information that the Temple contained no image of any god: their shrine was empty, the innermost sanctuary void. The walls of Jerusalem were destroyed,* but the Temple was left standing. Later, during the Roman civil wars, when the eastern provinces had come under the control of Mark Antony, the Parthian king Pacorus seized Judaea and was killed by Publius Ventidius.* The Parthians were driven back over the Euphrates, and Gaius Sosius* subdued the Jews. Antony gave the kingdom to Herod,* and Augustus, after his victory, enlarged it. After Herod's death, somebody called Simon,* without awaiting the Emperor's decision, forcibly assumed the title of king. He was punished by Quintilius Varus, who was governor of Syria;* the Jews were repressed and the kingdom divided between three of Herod's sons.* Under Tiberius all was quiet. Gaius Caesar ordered them to put up his statue in the Temple: they preferred war to that. But Gaius' death put an end to the rising. In Claudius' reign the kings had all either died or lost most of their territory. The Emperor therefore made Judaea a province* to be governed by Roman knights or freedmen. One of these, Antonius Felix,* indulged in every kind of cruelty and lust, wielding a king's authority with all the instincts of a slave. He had

married Drusilla, a granddaughter of Antony and Cleopatra, so that he was Antony's grandson-in-law, while Claudius was Antony's grandson.*

The Jews endured such oppression patiently until the gover- 10 norship of Gessius Florus,* under whom war broke out. Cestius Gallus, the governor of Syria, tried to crush it, but met with more reverses than victories. He died, either in the natural course or perhaps of disgust, and Nero sent out Vespasian, who, within two summers,* thanks to his reputation, good fortune, and able subordinates, had the whole of the flat country and all the towns except Jerusalem under the heel of his victorious army. The next year was taken up with civil war, and passed quietly enough as far as the Jews were concerned. But once peace was restored in Italy, foreign troubles began again; Roman wrath was increased by the thought that the Jews were the only people who had not given in. At the same time it seemed advantageous to leave Titus at the head of the army to meet all the eventualities of the new reign, whether good or bad.

Thus, as I have said, Titus pitched his camp before the walls 11 of Jerusalem and proceeded to display his legions in battle order. The Jews formed up at the foot of their own walls, ready, if successful, to venture further, but assured of their retreat in case of reverse. A body of cavalry and some light-armed cohorts were sent against them, and fought an indecisive engagement, from which the enemy eventually retired. During the next few days a series of skirmishes took place in front of the gates, and at last continual losses drove the Jews behind their walls.

The Romans then determined to take the city by storm. It seemed undignified to sit and wait for the enemy to starve,* and the men all clamoured for the risks, some through courage, but many others were wild and greedy for plunder. Titus himself had the vision of Rome* with all her wealth and pleasures before his eyes, and felt that their enjoyment was postponed unless Jerusalem fell at once.

The city, however, stood high and had been fortified with works vast enough to protect a city standing on the plain. Two enormous hills were surrounded by walls ingeniously

built so as to project or slope inwards and thus leave the flanks
of an attacking party exposed to fire. The rocks were jagged at
the top. The towers, where the rising ground helped, were 60
feet high, and in the hollows as much as 120. They were a
wonderful sight and seemed from a distance to be all of equal
height. Within this ran another line of fortification surrounding the palace, and on a conspicuous height stands the
Antonia, a castle named by Herod in honour of Mark Antony.

12 The Temple was built like a citadel with walls of its own, on
which more care and labour had been spent than on any of the
others. Even the cloisters surrounding the Temple formed a
splendid rampart. There was a never-failing spring of water,
catacombs hollowed out of the hills, and pools or cisterns for
holding rainwater. Its original builders had foreseen that the
peculiarities of Jewish life would lead to frequent wars, consequently everything was ready for the longest of sieges. Besides
this, when Pompey took the city, fear and experience taught
them several lessons, and they had taken advantage of the
avarice in the days of Claudius to buy rights of fortification,
and built walls in peacetime* as though war were imminent.
Their numbers were now swelled by floods of human refuse
and unfortunate refugees from other towns. All the most
desperate characters in the country had taken refuge there,
which only increased dissent.

They had three armies, each with its own general. The
outermost and largest line of wall was held by Simon; the
central city by John,* and the Temple by Eleazar. John and
Simon were stronger than Eleazar in numbers and equipment,
but he had the advantage of a strong position. Their behaviour towards each other mainly consisted of fighting,
treachery, and arson: a large quantity of corn was burnt.
Eventually, under pretext of offering a sacrifice, John sent a
party of men to massacre Eleazar and his troops, and by this
means gained possession of the Temple.* Thus Jerusalem was
divided into two hostile parties, but on the approach of the
Romans the necessities of foreign warfare reconciled their
differences.

13 Various portents had occurred at this time, but so sunk in
superstition are the Jews and so opposed to all religious prac-

tices that they think it wicked to expiate them by sacrifices or vows.* Embattled armies were seen to clash in the sky with flashing arms, and the Temple shone with sudden fire from heaven. The doors of the shrine suddenly opened, a superhuman voice was heard to proclaim that the gods were leaving, and at once there came a mighty movement of their departure. Few took alarm at all this. Most people held the belief that, according to the ancient priestly writings, this was the moment at which the East was fated to prevail: men would now start forth from Judaea and conquer the world. This enigmatic prophecy really applied to Vespasian and Titus; but men are blinded by their greed. The common people applied to themselves the promise of grand destiny, and even defeat could not convince them of the truth.

The number of the besieged, men and women of every age, is stated to have been 600,000.* There were arms for all who could carry them, and far more were ready to fight than would be expected from their total numbers. The women were as determined as the men: if they were forced to leave their homes they feared more in life than in death.

Such was the city and such the people with which Titus Caesar was faced. As the nature of the ground forbade a sudden assault, he determined to employ earthworks and mantlets. The work was accordingly divided among the legions, and there was a respite from fighting until they had got ready every means of storming a town that had ever been devised in ancient times or by modern ingenuity.

After the severe reverse at Trier Civilis reinforced his army 14 in Germany, and took his stand by the camp at Vetera. The position was a safe one, and he hoped to inspirit his native troops with the memory of their former victories there. Cerialis followed in his footsteps, with forces now doubled by the arrival of the Second, Sixth, and Fourteenth Legions, besides auxiliary infantry and cavalry, who had long received their summons and came hurrying on the news of victory. Neither general was dilatory, but a vast plain lay between them. It was by nature swampy, and Civilis had built a dam projecting into the Rhine, which stemmed the current and flooded the adjacent fields. The treacherous nature of the ground, with its precarious shallows, told against our men, who were heavily armed and afraid of swimming. The Germans, on the other hand, were used to rivers, lightly armed, and tall enough to keep their heads above water.

15   Provoked by the Batavi, the bravest of our troops opened the engagement at once, but soon fell into a panic when their arms and horses began to sink in the deep marshes. The Germans, who knew where to find the shallows, came leaping across them, often leaving our front alone and running round to the flanks or the rear. It was not like an infantry engagement at close quarters, but more like a naval battle. The men floundered about in the water or, finding firm foothold, tried to balance their whole body on it. Thus the wounded and the whole, those who could swim and those who could not, struggled with each other and perished all alike. However, considering the confusion, our loss was less than might have been expected, for the Germans, not daring to venture out of the marsh, withdrew to their camp.

The result of this engagement gave each of the generals a different motive for hastening on a decisive battle. Civilis wanted to follow up his success, Cerialis to wipe out his disgrace. The pride of the Germans thrilled with success; shame stimulated the Romans. The natives spent the night singing uproariously, while our men muttered angry threats.

16   At daybreak Cerialis formed up his cavalry and the auxiliary cohorts on his front, with the legions behind them, while he himself held a picked body in reserve for emergencies. Civilis did not extend his line, but halted them in wedge-formation, with the Batavi and Cugerni on his right, and the forces from across the Rhine near the river on the left.

Neither general followed the usual custom of haranguing the whole army. They rode along and addressed their various divisions in turn. Cerialis spoke of the ancient glory of the Roman name and of their victories old and new. He urged them to blot out for ever their treacherous, cowardly, and defeated enemy. They had to punish, not fight them. They had, he said, just fought against superior numbers and yet had routed the pick of the German troops; the remnant were fugitives in their hearts and wounded on their backs. He then gave special encouragement to each of the legions, calling the Fourteenth the conquerors of Britain,* reminding the Sixth that their authority had set Galba on the throne,* and telling the Second that in the coming fight they would for the first time dedicate their new colours and their new eagle to Rome's service. Then riding along to the army of Germany, he pointed with his hand and bade them recover their own river-bank and their own camp by the enemy's blood. They all cheered with increased eagerness. Some longed for battle after a long spell of quiet: others were weary of war and pined for peace. They hoped that the future would bring them recompense and rest.

Nor was there silence in Civilis' lines. As he formed them up 17 he appealed to the site to witness their valour. The Germans and Batavians were standing, he told them, on the field of their glory, trampling the charred bones of Roman soldiers under foot. Wherever the Romans turned their eyes they saw nothing but imprisonment, defeat, and catastrophe. The Germans must not be alarmed by that sudden change of fortune in the battle at Trier. It was their own victory which hampered them there: they had dropped their weapons and filled their hands with loot. Since then everything had gone in their favour and against the Romans. He had taken every possible precaution, as befitted a cunning general. They themselves were familiar with these soaking plains, but the swamps would be a deadly trap for the enemy. They had the Rhine and the gods of Germany before their eyes, and under the power of these they must go to battle, remembering wives, parents, and fatherland. This day would either gild the glory of their ancestors or earn the execration of posterity.

They applauded his words according to their custom by dancing and clashing their arms, and then opened the battle with showers of stones, slingshot, and other missiles, trying with taunts to lure on our men, who had not yet entered the marsh. The missiles exhausted, the fight began to warm up; 18 the enemy made an angry charge. Thanks to their great height and their very long spears they could thrust from some distance at our men, who were floundering and slipping about in the marsh. While this went on, a group of Bructeri swam across from the dam which, as I described above, had been built out into the Rhine. This started a panic and the line of our auxiliaries began to be driven back. Then the legions took up the fight and equalized matters by staying the enemy's wild charge.

Meanwhile, a Batavian deserter approached Cerialis, avowing that he could take the enemy in the rear if the cavalry were sent round the edge of the swamp: the ground was solid there, and the Cugerni, whose task it was to keep watch, were off their guard. Two squadrons of horse were sent with the deserter, and succeeded in outflanking the unsuspecting enemy. The legions in front, when the din told them what had happened, redoubled their efforts. The Germans were beaten and fled to the Rhine. This day might have brought the war to an end, had the Roman fleet hurried after them. As it was, even the cavalry were prevented from pursuit by a sudden downpour of rain and the onset of nightfall.

19   On the next day the Fourteenth Legion were sent to join Annius Gallus in Upper Germany, and their place in Cerialis' army was filled by the Tenth from Spain. Civilis was reinforced by the Chauci. Not daring to hold the Batavian capital,* he took whatever was portable with him, burnt everything else, and retired into the Island. He knew that the Romans had not enough ships to build a bridge, and that they had no other means of getting across. He also destroyed the mole built by Drusus Germanicus.* As the bed of the Rhine here falls towards the Gallic branch,* his removal of all obstacles gave it free course; the river was practically diverted, and the flow between the Germans and the island narrowed to the point that the dry land appeared to be continuous. Tutor and Classicus also crossed the Rhine, together with 113 senators from Trier, among whom was Alpinius Montanus, who, as I said above, had been sent by Antonius Primus into Gaul. He was accompanied by his brother Decimus Alpinius. By arousing sympathy and by offering presents, the others, too, were all busy raising reinforcements among these eagerly adventurous tribes.

20   The war was far from being over. Dividing his forces in four, Civilis in a single day attacked the strongholds of the

auxiliary horse and foot and the legions: the Tenth Legion at Arenacum,* the Second at Batavodurum, and the auxiliary horse and foot at Grinnes and Vada. Civilis himself, Verax his sister's son, Classicus, and Tutor each led one of the attacking parties. They could not hope all to be successful, but reckoned that, if they made several ventures, fortune would favour one or the other. Besides, Cerialis, they supposed, was off his guard; on receiving news from several places at once he would hurry from one garrison to another, and might be cut off on his way.

The party assigned to attack the camp of the Tenth considered it no light task to storm a legion, so they fell on the soldiers when they came outside and were occupied in cutting timber, and killed the camp prefect, five senior centurions, and a handful of the men. The rest defended themselves behind the fortifications. Meanwhile another party of Germans endeavoured to break the bridge which had been begun at Batavodurum, but nightfall put an end to the battle while the outcome was in the balance.

The attack on Grinnes and Vada proved more formidable. 21 Civilis led the assault on Vada, Classicus on Grinnes. Nothing could stop them. The bravest of the defenders had fallen, among them, commanding a cavalry squadron, Briganticus, who was, as I have said, a faithful ally of Rome and a bitter enemy of his uncle Civilis. However, when Cerialis came to the rescue with a picked troop of horse, the tables were turned, and the Germans were driven headlong into the river. While Civilis was trying to stop the rout he was recognized, and finding himself a target, he left his horse and swam across. Verax escaped in the same way, while some small boats put in to fetch Tutor and Classicus.

Even now the Roman fleet had not joined the fight. They had, indeed, received orders, but fear held them back, and the rowers were employed on various duties elsewhere. It must be admitted, also, that Cerialis did not give them time enough to carry out his orders. He was a man of sudden resolves and brilliant successes. Even when his strategy had failed, good luck always came to his rescue. Thus neither he nor his army cared much about discipline.

A few days later, moreover, Cerialis narrowly escaped being
22 taken prisoner and did not evade disgrace. He had gone to
Novaesium and Bonn to inspect the winter quarters that were
being built for his legions, and was returning with the fleet.
The Germans noticed that his escort straggled,* and that the
sentries were careless: so they planned a surprise. Choosing a
night black with clouds they slipped downstream and made
their way unmolested into the camp. For the initial massacre
they called cunning to their aid: they cut the tent-ropes and
slaughtered the soldiers as they struggled under their own
canvas. Another party fell on the ships, attached hawsers to
the sterns, and towed them off. Having surprised the camp in
dead silence, when once the carnage began they added to the
panic by making the whole place ring with shouts. Awakened
by their wounds the Romans hunted for weapons and rushed
along the passages, a few in uniform, most of them with their
clothes wrapped round their arms and swords drawn in their
hand. The general, who was half-asleep and almost naked,
was only saved by the enemy's mistake. His flagship being
easily distinguishable, they carried it off, thinking he was
there. But Cerialis had been spending the night elsewhere; as
most people believed, having an affair with a Ubian woman
named Claudia Sacrata. The sentries sheltered their guilt under the general's disgrace, pretending that they had orders to
keep quiet and not disturb his rest: so they had dispensed with
signals and calls, and had dropped off to sleep themselves.
In full daylight the enemy sailed off with their captive vessels
and towed the flagship up the River Lupia* as an offering to
Veleda.

23   Civilis was now seized with a desire to make a naval display. He manned all the available biremes* and all the ships
with single banks of oars, and added to this fleet an immense
number of small craft. These carry thirty or forty men apiece
and are rigged like Liburnian cruisers. The small craft he had
captured were worked with multi-coloured plaids, which
served as sails and made a fine show. He chose for review the
miniature sea of water where the Rhine comes pouring down
to the North Sea through the mouth of the Maas. His reason
for the demonstration—apart from typical Batavian vanity—

was to scare away the provision convoys that were already on their way from Gaul. Cerialis, who was less alarmed than astonished, at once formed up a fleet. Though inferior in numbers, he had the advantage of larger ships, experienced rowers, and clever pilots. The Romans had the stream with them, the Germans the wind. So they sailed past each other, and after trying a few shots with light missiles they parted.

Civilis retired across the Rhine without attempting anything further. Cerialis vigorously laid waste the Island of the Batavi, and employed the common device of leaving Civilis' houses and fields untouched.* They were now at the start of autumn. The heavy equinoctial rains had set the river in flood, covering the marshy, low-lying island until it looked like a lake. Neither fleet nor provision convoys had arrived, and their camp on the flat plain began to be washed away by the force of the current.

Civilis afterwards claimed that at this point the Germans 24 could have crushed the Roman legions and wanted to do so, but that he had cunningly dissuaded them. Nor is this far from the truth,* since his surrender followed in a few days' time. Cerialis had been sending secret messages, promising the Batavians peace and Civilis pardon, and urging Veleda and her relatives to change the fortune of a war that had only brought disaster after disaster, by doing a timely service to Rome. The Treviri, he reminded them, had been slaughtered; the allegiance of the Ubii recovered; the Batavians robbed of their homeland. By supporting Civilis they had gained nothing but wounds, defeat, and bereavement. He was a fugitive exile, a burden to those who harboured him. Besides, they had earned blame enough by crossing the Rhine so often: if they took any further steps, their side would take on itself the crime and the guilt, the Romans could count on vengeance and the wrath of Heaven.

Thus Cerialis mingled threats and promises. The loyalty of 25 the tribes across the Rhine was shaken, and murmurs began to make themselves heard among the Batavi. 'How much further must our ruin be prolonged?' they asked. 'One tribe cannot free the whole world from the yoke. What good have we done by slaughtering and burning Roman legions except to bring out others, larger and stronger? If it was to help Vespasian that we have fought so vigorously, Vespasian is master of the world. If we are challenging Rome in war—what an infinitesimal fraction of the human race we Batavians are! We must remember what burdens Raetia and Noricum and all Rome's other allies bear. From us they levy no tribute, only our manhood and our men. That is next door to freedom.* And, after all, if we have to choose our masters, it is less disgrace to put up with Roman emperors than with German women.'

Thus the common people: the chieftains used more violent language. It was Civilis' lunacy, they said, that had driven them to war. He wanted to remedy his private troubles by ruining his country. The Batavians had incurred the wrath of Heaven by blockading Roman legions, murdering Roman commanders, and plunging into a war which was useful for one man and deadly for the rest. Now they had reached the limit, unless they came to their senses and openly showed their repentance by punishing the culprit.

26   Civilis was well aware of their changed feelings and determined to forestall them. He was tired of hardship, and he felt, besides, the desire to live which so often weakens great souls. He demanded an interview. The bridge over the River Nabalia was broken down in the middle, and the two generals advanced onto the broken ends. Civilis began as follows:

'If I were defending myself before one of Vitellius' commanders, I could expect neither pardon for my conduct nor credence for my words. Between him and me there has been nothing but hatred. He began hostilities, I fostered them. Towards Vespasian I have from the beginning shown respect. When he was a private citizen, we were known as friends. Antonius Primus was aware of this when he wrote urging me to take up arms to prevent the legions from Germany and the Gallic levies from crossing the Alps. The instructions which Antonius gave in his letter Hordeonius Flaccus ratified by word of mouth.* I raised the standard in Germany, as did Mucianus in Syria, Aponius in Moesia, Flavianus in Pannonia . . .'

The rest of the work is lost. Civilis' own fate is unknown, though it seems that his people were not seriously punished for their rebellion. The Jewish War was crushed by Titus that summer, with the capture of Jerusalem and the destruction of the Temple, though pockets of resistance held out until 73, when Masada, the final stronghold, was taken.

Helvidius Priscus was exiled and put to death in about 74 for his opposition to Vespasian; and in 79 Caecina was accused of conspiring with Eprius Marcellus against the Emperor—the former was murdered at a dinner party on Titus' orders, the latter forced to suicide. Mucianus died in 76 or 77, writing several literary works in the final years of his life; his rival Antonius Primus, now out of favour with Vespasian, enjoyed a long and comfortable retirement in his home town of Toulouse. Verginius Rufus also retired under the Flavians, before emerging in his eighties to hold a final consulship in 97, the year of his death. Tacitus himself delivered the funeral eulogy.

Vespasian reigned as emperor for a further nine years, dying in 79. Titus succeeded him, but his rule was brief. He died of fever in 81 at the age of 40, and was succeeded by Domitian, who reigned for fifteen years, becoming a byword for cruelty and tyranny. He was assassinated by a palace conspiracy in 96, aged 44; and with him the Flavian dynasty came to an end.

EXPLANATORY NOTES

3 *consul for the second time*: his first consulship had been in 33.

the year when . . . Titus Vinius was his colleague: AD 69. The sentence imitates the opening of Sallust's *Histories* (1. 1). More generally, Tacitus places himself in the tradition of Roman annalistic historians like Livy by beginning with a new consular year rather than the death of Nero in June 68; but at the same time he defers narrating that opening until he has provided the background in 1. 4–10.

the foundation of Rome: the conventional date of foundation was *c.*753 BC, but other chronologies were also followed.

Battle of Actium: 31 BC: the battle where Octavian (the future Augustus) defeated Mark Antony and established himself as sole ruler of the empire.

the reigns of the deified Nerva and of the Emperor Trajan: Nerva, Domitian's successor, was officially deified after his death, as had been Julius Caesar, Augustus, Claudius, Vespasian, and Titus before him. Tacitus in fact never wrote the history of Nerva and Trajan: probably this passage is simply a way of obliquely praising their virtues by implicitly contrasting them with their predecessors.

5 *elsewhere than at Rome*: as governor of Tarraconensis, in Spain, Galba had risen against Nero; the Senate proclaimed him emperor after Nero's death.

greedy for news: other sources do not suggest such widespread regret for Nero. Tacitus introduces the theme of the corrupt mob, and prepares the way for Otho's accession with their support.

not to be paid to them: new emperors commonly gave a gift of money to each Praetorian Guardsman; but Nymphidius Sabinus (see below) had promised in Galba's name an amount so large as to be impossible to pay.

Nymphidius Sabinus: son of a freedman, he had commanded the Praetorian Guard since 65. He had helped to depose Nero in favour of Galba; but then was alleged to have sought to take power for himself, and was killed in the attempt.

6 *Petronius Turpilianus*: consul in 61, then governor of Britain.

thousands of unarmed soldiers: the numbers are probably exaggerated: the reference is to some of the marines enrolled by Nero (next paragraph), who met Galba with demands as he entered Rome.

A legion had been brought from Spain: VII Hispana (Tacitus calls it 'Galbiana'): it in fact seems to have left Rome for Pannonia before Galba's fall. Tacitus distorts the picture to emphasize the theme of an un-Roman Rome on the verge of revolution.

Vindex: Roman senator of Gallic origin. While governor in Gaul in 68 he revolted against Nero, precipitating the Emperor's downfall; he was however defeated in battle and committed suicide.

Clodius Macer . . . Fonteius Capito: Macer was commander of III Augusta in Africa. Capito, consul in 67, was governor of Lower Germany.

Fabius Valens: the first introduction of one of the leading figures in the work: he was then commander of the I Legion in Bonn. Other sources make Galba's responsibility more direct; Tacitus shows the Emperor's weakness, while Valens' willingness to act on his own account prefigures his domination of Vitellius' rebellion.

7 *looks and personal attraction*: Nero had died at the age of 31; Galba was 72, bald, and crippled by arthritis.

Cluvius Rufus: a favourite of Nero's. He wrote a history of his own times, which Tacitus later used for the *Annals*, and may have consulted here. It appears from this that Galba had placed him in command of all three Spanish provinces.

Verginius: Verginius Rufus (*c*.14–97); as governor of Upper Germany he had defeated Vindex. Other sources imply greater altruism in his refusal of the throne, and greater honesty on the part of Galba. Tacitus (typically) imputes sinister motives, the hints of jealous competition for the throne adding to the general sense of political instability.

Hordeonius Flaccus: Verginius' successor as governor.

8 *thrice consul*: in 34, 43, and 47. He was a favourite of Tiberius, Gaius, and (especially) Claudius, under whom he wielded considerable influence.

four legions: in fact there were currently only three legions there, III Gallica having been sent to Moesia (cf. 1. 79). Tacitus repeats the mistake at 2. 4, 2. 6, and 2. 76.

The Jewish War: the Jews had risen against Rome in 66.

9 *control of the Household*: senators were banned from visiting Egypt without the Emperor's permission; hence the governor was always a knight. He received the marks of honour previously enjoyed by Egyptian kings.

Tiberius Alexander: a Jew by birth, and nephew of the Jewish philosopher Philo: he had governed Judaea 46–8, then Egypt 66–70.

procurators: imperial agents of non-senatorial status, who governed minor provinces.

Titus Vinius his colleague: with this return to the opening words of the work, Tacitus signals the end of his preliminary survey, and the start of his narrative proper.

had broken their oath of allegiance: the rising was under Vitellius: Tacitus describes it in 1. 51.

10 *the rings of a knight*: rings were worn by knights as a mark of status. According to Plutarch, *Galba* 7, Icelus' promotion was for bringing Galba news of his elevation to the throne. Suetonius, *Galba* 21 claims that he was Galba's lover, but that would not suit Tacitus' picture of the Emperor's old-fashioned strictness.

Poppaea Sabina . . . Octavia: Octavia (*c.*40–62) was daughter of Claudius and first wife of Nero, who divorced and banished her, then had her killed. He then married Poppaea Sabina (*c.*31–65); but soon killed her in a temper. Poppaea's exact relationship with Otho is very doubtful: Tacitus later gave a completely different account in *Annals* 13. 45–6, and most sources clearly state that they were lovers. Tacitus mutes that here, throwing the blame more on Nero. Even as he explicitly links Otho to Nero, his narrative begins to enhance his moral character.

11 *imperial election*: a sarcastic oxymoron: the term 'election' was not used of selecting imperial heirs, but was the Republican word for when a magistrate was voted in by a citizens' assembly. Even under the Empire, such elections were largely in the hands of the Senate, not the emperor alone.

Marius Celsus: he is known to have written on military tactics, and may have been one of Tacitus' sources for these events.

City Prefect: senator in charge of the administration of the city of Rome and its garrison.

at the insistence of Laco: in other sources the adoption is entirely Galba's own idea, and there is no reference to this conference. Although Tacitus presents it as a possibility that Galba took the initiative, the overriding image is of the Emperor under the sway of evil subordinates.

Rubellius Plautus: a great-grandson of the Emperor Tiberius and a prominent Stoic, executed by Nero.

addressed him as follows: this speech, with its lengthy defence of an emperor adopting his heir, had strong contemporary resonances for Tacitus' audience: the current Emperor, Trajan, had been adopted by his predecessor Nerva.

curial statute: a law passed by a Roman assembly was required to adopt a man whose natural father was dead.

Gnaeus Pompey and of Marcus Crassus: Gnaeus Pompeius Magnus ('Pompey the Great', 106–48 BC), an ancestor of Piso on his mother's side, was partner of Julius Caesar (100–44 BC) in the unofficial 'First Triumvirate'; he then was Caesar's chief opponent in the civil war leading to the end of the Republic. Marcus Licinius Crassus (115–53 BC) was the third member of the 'First Triumvirate'; he was in fact not Piso's blood ancestor (his grandson had adopted Piso's grandfather).

Sulpician and Lutatian houses: two leading Republican families, with many distinguished members.

Marcellus . . . Agrippa . . . his grandsons . . . Tiberius Nero: Marcus Claudius Marcellus (42–23 BC), son of Augustus' sister, married Augustus' daughter Julia and was given honours apparently marking him for the succession. After his death, Marcus Vipsanius Agrippa (c.63–12 BC), Augustus' closest ally, married Julia and was similarly given exceptional honours. Then their sons Gaius Caesar (20 BC–AD 4) and Lucius Caesar (17 BC–AD 2) were both adopted by Augustus and designated his heirs. Finally, when they too died, Tiberius Claudius Nero (42 BC–AD 37), the son of Augustus' wife Livia by her first marriage, was adopted by Augustus and succeeded him on his death as the Emperor Tiberius.

12 *an elder brother*: Crassus Scribonianus.

only experienced misfortune: Piso's parents and eldest brother were put to death under Claudius; another brother was killed under Nero, and he himself had been exiled.

14 *each man chose another*: in early Italy, troops were raised by choosing one man, who chose another, who chose another, etc.

Fourth and Twenty-Second Legions: IV Macedonica and XXII Primigenia, both in Upper Germany.

15 *The next question was one of finance*: this had in fact happened earlier: Tacitus, by altering the sequence of events, gives the impression of discontent growing at Rome after Piso's adoption.

Antonius Naso ... Aemilius Pacensis ... Julius Fronto: Naso subsequently had a successful military and civilian career under Otho and Vespasian; Pacensis and Fronto appear later in the *Histories* as supporters of Otho.

16 *proscribing them and keeping them by us*: astrologers were widely consulted at Rome, but were also subject to repression, not least because of their potential for political subversion. It was illegal to consult them about the Emperor's future, and they were frequently expelled from the city.

17 *Tigellinus*: a close associate of Nero's: see 1. 72.

18 *Temple of Apollo*: a famous temple attached to the imperial palace on the Palatine Hill; the precise site is uncertain.

Umbricius: the most distinguished of the 'haruspices', one of the official societies of diviners at Rome: he wrote a book on divination.

19 *favourable to his plans*: Plutarch, *Galba* 24 says that Otho was terrified by this omen, thinking that the god was identifying him to Galba. Tacitus, by contrast, does not raise the possibility that Galba might have avoided his fate at this point.

Tiberius' House ... the Velabrum ... the Golden Milestone: Tiberius' House was a large imperial palace overlooking the Roman Forum; the Velabrum was a low-lying area near the Forum, the site of a market; the Golden Milestone was the monument marking the meeting-point of all the roads leading into the city.

20 *spared the sight of blood*: at best a half-truth. There had been a massacre just outside the city (1. 6).

21 *bounty for your loyalty*: at last the offer of bounty comes, but too late, and noticeably not proposed by Galba himself.

Vipsanian Arcade: a colonnade in the north or Rome, built under Augustus.

inclined to be passive: Suetonius, *Galba* 20 says that they dashed to help Galba, but lost their way: Tacitus increases the sense of the army's abandonment of the Emperor.

22 *Otho had been killed in the camp*: other sources make this the key in Galba's decision to leave the palace. In Tacitus, Galba has already decided to go—the main factor is the malign influence of Laco and Icelus.

24 *Polyclituses and Vatiniuses and Aegialuses*: Polyclitus, a freedman, was a favourite of Nero executed by Galba. Vatinius was another lower-class favourite of Nero; Aegialus is otherwise unknown.

25 *plain-clothes cohort*: the palace watch of the Praetorian Guard wore civilian clothes.

arsenal: within the Guards' barracks was the only permanent arsenal in Italy. Otho's actions here belie his words—he had just suggested that violence would be unnecessary.

Rostra: a platform by the Forum from which speakers addressed the crowd.

26 *Arsacids*: The royal family of Parthia. Vologaeses I was King of Parthia in 69; his son Pacorus II ruled in Tacitus' own day.

effigy of Galba: an image of the Emperor was attached to the pole of the standard.

Lacus Curtius: a monument in the Roman Forum, as were the temples of Julius and Vesta mentioned below.

27 *assigned by Galba to protect Piso*: Plutarch *Galba* 26 says that Densus protected Galba, not Piso. Tacitus' version shows Galba totally abandoned, and also explains Piso's brief escape.

28 *henceforward supreme*: in fact, Otho almost certainly controlled these appointments; but Tacitus is contrasting his licence with the old-fashioned strictness of Piso, whom he showed predicting exactly this at 1. 30.

29 *held that post*: from 62 to 68. Galba had deprived him of it.

into civil war: a close imitation of the famous description in Sallust, *Histories* 1. 12 of the corruption of Rome when her enemies were no more. The disasters of that earlier collapse into civil war are being replayed; but Tacitus focuses his analysis on the soldiers alone, on whose morals the whole state depends.

murder him: Plutarch, *Galba* 27 implies that Laco had been murdered earlier, with Galba, Piso, and Vinius.

30 *brothers had been executed*: Gnaeus Pompeius Magnus in 46; Marcus Licinius Crassus Frugi in 67.

fifty-seven years: Vinius was probably 47; either Tacitus or the transmitted text are in error.

mother's father was one of the proscribed: more probably his father's father: a Titus Vinius is known to have been proscribed (officially outlawed, and subject to summary execution) by the Second Triumvirate in 43 BC.

A scandal: in 39, when Calvisius was governor of Pannonia. He and his wife were recalled, and both committed suicide. Vinius was freed on Gaius' assassination in 41.

31 *distinction in Germany ... governed Africa ... Nearer Spain*: among other posts in his long career, Galba governed Upper Germany 39–41 (achieving a notable victory over the Chatti), Africa 45–7, and Nearer Spain 60–8.

32 *Pharsalia, Philippi, Perusia, and Mutina*: battles of the civil wars that had destroyed the Republic. Pharsalia and Philippi are both in north Greece; at the former, Julius Caesar defeated Pompey (48 BC); at the latter, Mark Antony and Octavian (the future Augustus) defeated Brutus and Cassius (42 BC). Octavian sacked the Etruscan town of Perusia (the modern Perugia) in 41 BC; and at Mutina (Modena) in north Italy Antony had been defeated in 43 BC by the combined forces of Octavian, Decimus Brutus, Hirtius, and Pansa.

intervention of Vespasian: Vespasian is in fact unlikely to have been a serious contender this early. As the scene shifts to Vitellius, Tacitus briefly reminds the reader of his ultimate conqueror.

provincial frontier: i.e. the frontier between Upper and Lower Germany.

33 *Sequani and Aedui*: two important tribes of central Gaul that had supported Vindex.

grants to their community: true: see 1. 8.

stubborn attachment to Nero: a major fire had devastated Lyons in 65; Nero had donated 4,000,000 sesterces to rebuild it.

34 *Treviri and Lingones*: Rhineland tribes that had supported the army against Vindex.

35 *leave the camp by night*: Tacitus here provides a foretaste of his depiction of Hordeonius in Book 4: a man who crassly adopts schemes which then backfire.

oath of allegiance: military oaths were taken on enlistment, or to a new commander; they were renewed at the start of each year.

Fifth ... Fifteenth: V Alaudae and XV Primigenia.

36 *quarters of the First Legion*: at Bonn.

37 *usually held by freedmen*: Vitellius may have done this merely because appropriate freedmen were not available in Germany; but it is also true that senior administrative posts that under earlier emperors were held by freedmen from 69 on were increasingly occupied by knights.

furlough fees: cf. Otho's similar action at 1. 46.

Pompeius Propinquus: see 1. 12—he had warned Galba of Vitellius' revolt.

a cheaper sacrifice: as often, Tacitus hints at real motives without explicitly citing them. He indicates his belief in Burdo's innocence, but leaves the reader to remember that the real guilty party who was to be protected was in fact Vitellius' chief lieutenant Valens (1. 7, 1. 52).

Batavi: a German tribe living at the mouth of the Rhine; Civilis was ultimately to lead them in a revolt against Rome (Books 4–5). Tacitus' account of Vitellius' motives is ironic: his actions have exactly the opposite of their intended effect.

38 *Italian Legion*: I Italica, founded by Nero in 66/7.

Trebellius Maximus: governor of Britain 63–9. Tacitus had given a slightly different version of these events in *Agricola* 16.

Twentieth Legion: XX Valeria Victrix, stationed in Britain.

Pennine Pass: the Great St Bernard.

39 *Twenty-First Legion*: XXI Rapax.

Germanicus: this title implied victory over Germany, where Vitellius had been governor (though in fact without military success); but it was also a family title of Gaius, Claudius, and Nero.

Divodorum: Metz.

40 *nearly 4,000 people had already been killed*: an emblematic episode. Tacitus shows the Vitellians out of control of their own forces: in his account, this is a major cause of their ultimate downfall.

Leuci: Gallic tribe living around Toul, between the Marne and the Moselle.

41 *part of the army*: Roman troops were levied from Lyons, and armies were garrisoned there. However, the citizens' argument is tendentious: Vienne was also a source of legionaries for Rome.

in supplication: the traditional dress and behaviour of suppliants in the ancient world.

Allobroges and Vocontii: the two major Gallic tribes of the western Alps.

42 *Lucus*: Luc-en-Diois.

Helvetii: they lived in Switzerland; they had fought against Caesar, who had praised their fighting qualities.

a *dispatch*: presumably an appeal for help. The Pannonian army subsequently supported Otho, then joined Vespasian.

43 *Mount Vocetius*: the Botzberg.

Aventicum: Avenches.

governor in Africa: probably in 60–1; he had also remained there for the following year serving under his brother.

44 *Novaria, Eporedia, and Vercellae*: Novara, Ivrea, and Vercelli.

fought against his party: see I. 45. In Plutarch, *Otho* 1, this looks like genuine clemency by Otho. Tacitus, as usual, gives it a sinister twist: his Otho is a hypocrite *trying* to appear merciful.

45 *received the news*: according to Plutarch, *Otho* 2, Otho summoned him to Rome. Tacitus suppresses Otho's part in an act that would have been to his credit.

incite Clodius Macer to civil war: cf. 1. 7 for these allegations.

46 *long before been conferred on Vitellius*: Vitellius had in fact claimed the throne only thirteen days before Otho.

47 *two months*: in fact only for one month: Caelius and Flavius took over in April.

48 *Caelius Sabinus and Flavius Sabinus ... Arrius Antoninus*: Caelius was a notable writer on law; Flavius Sabinus the son of Vespasian's brother (1. 46). Arrius Antoninus became consul again in 97; his grandson was the Emperor Antoninus Pius.

pontifical and augural colleges: two of the major societies of priests at Rome.

Cadius Rufus, Pedius Blaesus, and Saevinus Propinquus: Cadius had been condemned in 49, Blaesus in 59, after corruptly governing Bithynia and Cyrene respectively. Saevinus is otherwise unknown; the surname has been corrupted in the manuscript, and is conjectured here as Propinquus.

Hispalis and Emerita: Seville and Mérida.

granted Roman citizenship: presumably an attempt to win over Vitellius' supporters there.

ashamed to accept it: other sources imply Otho was more willing to accept the name. Tacitus, while linking Otho to Nero, slightly distances him, and so hints at his ultimate demonstration of his nobility.

49 *triumphal statue*: a statue of him in full triumphal garb; only someone in the imperial family could actually celebrate a triumph. Before this period, however, the statue was always accompanied by an award of triumphal ornaments (cf. 2. 77); unless Tacitus has simply omitted to mention them, this is the first known instance of a statue alone being granted.

Aurelius Fulvus, Tettius Julianus: Aurelius and Tettius both later had distinguished careers under the Flavians. Aurelius was paternal grandfather of the Emperor Antoninus Pius.

50 *an obscure refuge with the humblest of their clients*: this picture of the humiliation of the upper classes does not appear in other sources. Tacitus here, as in the rest of the episode, is reinforcing his standard themes: social order overturned by civil war, the differing responses to crisis, and the danger of mob rule.

prefect of the legion: an unusual title: he was probably the camp prefect, who superintended the camp. For Martialis cf. 1. 28.

51 *discipline of earlier days*: the same point had been made by Piso at 1. 30: Tacitus shows his gloomy predictions borne out in the event.

53 *all depend upon the safety of the Senate*: the idea that a city's essence is not in its buildings was an ancient commonplace. Otho's identification of Rome's essence with the Senate is more striking, especially in view of the senators' subsequent behaviour—part of Tacitus' ambiguous presentation of the institution.

54 *faced the east*: Plutarch, *Otho* 4 and Suetonius, *Vespasian* 5 treat this as a portent foretelling the rise of Vespasian in the East. Tacitus omits this natural interpretation, and instead concentrates everything on the Otho–Vitellius conflict. Vespasian comes to the fore only in Book 2; even there Tacitus resists showing his rule closely foreshadowed by divine omens (see 2. 78, and cf. 2. 1).

now we only hear of them in time of panic: traditional historians of the Republic like Livy listed portents for virtually every year. Tacitus places himself in their tradition by including such events; but the very irregularity of their appearance highlights the contrast between his work and theirs.

Pile Bridge: the oldest bridge in Rome, for religious reasons built entirely of wood. Its destruction by floods was frequent, but always treated as an evil omen.

Flaminian Way: the main route north from the city.

purification of the city: to propitiate the gods after the portents—a sacrificial victim was led round the religious boundary of the city.

55 *freedman Moschus*: freedmen had regularly commanded the fleet under Nero. For Aemilius Pacensis cf. 1. 20.

Suetonius Paulinus: a senior ex-consul, most famous for crushing the rebellion of Boudicca when governor of Britain in 58–61.

Aquinas: Aquino.

kinship to Galba: Dolabella was Galba's great-nephew, and according to Plutarch, *Galba* 23 had been named as a possible heir. Tacitus highlights the paradoxes of Otho's behaviour by juxtaposing this with his generosity towards Vitellius' younger brother: his current enemy is treated with greater magnanimity than his past one.

56 *Scribonianus' rising*: in Dalmatia in 42: he was defeated within five days.

sacred shields: these were kept in the Temple of Mars, but were removed every 1 March, taken round the shrines, and replaced on the 23rd.

57 *Galerius Trachalus*: a well-known orator. He was probably related to Vitellius' wife (cf. 2. 60), an additional reason for his moderation here. Tacitus does not mention this: he concentrates instead on the servility resulting from political instability.

59 *years now fitted him*: he was then 29.

if Vespasian himself assumed sovereignty: Tacitus has the Flavians planning their coup earlier than in any other writer; throughout this section Titus' own imperial ambitions are revealed. In Josephus they look more disinterested: he delays discussing their plans until after Vitellius becomes the sole (and immoral) ruler.

Queen Berenice: great-granddaughter of Herod the Great of Judaea; she ruled jointly with her brother Agrippa II over Galilee and the East Bank of the Jordan. She and Titus were lovers, and remained so for another ten years.

60 *origin of this worship*: Tacitus here gives two alternative versions of the cult's origins; others were also current in antiquity.

sea gave her birth: one version of the birth of Venus (later made famous by Botticelli) has her born in the sea from the castrated genitals of the sky-god Uranus. Cinyras was a famous mythical king of Cyprus, where she arrived.

Tamiras: in fact the name of a Semitic fertility goddess: possibly the original name of the goddess in this cult.

61 *Only the siege of Jerusalem remained*: not quite true: several fortresses, including Masada, were still uncaptured; but Tacitus is overstating the ease of the task, so as to stress Vespasian's opportunity to take the throne.

62 *seldom saw one*: the last visit by a member of the Emperor's family had been in 19.

63 *'Nero was at hand'*: these two chapters serve to move the action from the East to Rome and Otho. The theme of Nero, reintroduced here, is then continued further in 10, reminding the reader of Otho's ambiguous relationship to him.

Misenum: Miseno.

64 *Vibius Crispus*: a famous orator, prominent both before and after 69. He later was known as a close friend of Vespasian. His brother was Vibius Secundus, who had been exiled in 60 for corruption while governor of Mauretania.

65 *rebellion in Britain*: of Boudicca.

First Legion: I Adiutrix.

shameful support: it was thought dishonourable to use gladiators, who were slaves, as soldiers: legionaries were always free men.

Vestricius Spurinna: Tacitus probably knew Vestricius, as they shared a mutual friend in the Younger Pliny. He was now in his mid-forties.

an iron breastplate: usually worn only by ordinary soldiers.

66 *Albantimilium*: Ventimiglia.

Tungri: a tribe from Belgian Gaul.

Forum Julii: Fréjus.

67 *Antipolis*: Antibes.

Albingaunum: Albenga.

68 *Liburnian cruisers*: a form of swift warship.

utter servility: again the traditional Roman theme made famous by Sallust: the moral corruption of peace (cf. 1. 46). Tacitus, as

Sallust had before him, presents a stark and virtually inescapable
choice of evils: with the Roman conquest of the Mediterranean
the one remaining form of war that can arrest this moral decline
is civil war. Yet civil war is for him not a solution; it is itself, as
here, the appalling consequence of that decline.

Placentia and Ticinum: Piacenza and Pavia.

69 *the Po in sight*: Placentia is itself on the Po, but Tacitus here (a
little confusingly) refers to another point of the river, at the end
of Spurinna's march.

70 *parti-coloured plaid and trousers*: Gallic costume.

73 *Castores*: named for the twin gods Castor and Pollux, who had
a shrine there.

Prince Epiphanes: son of Antiochus IV of Commagene; see 2.
81.

74 *betray the army to his brother*: an ironic twist to the theme of
the fratricide of civil war that Tacitus elsewhere exploits. Both
sides distrust the potential brotherly loyalty, and assume that
their man will betray them; manifestly at least one of the accusations is false.

76 *mutiny nearly broke out afresh*: this contradicts 2. 27, where
Caecina's defeat is said to prevent the troops from mutiny.
Tacitus is now bringing to the fore the indiscipline of the civil
war, not least so as to link it with the destructive rivalry of the
commanders.

danger to the country: such character comparisons were common in ancient historical writing; but Tacitus here, as often,
filters his judgements through contemporary perceptions, and
indicates their limitations in the light of events. The ultimate
fates of the two emperors provide a partial corrective to the
criticisms expressed here; and it was, as he showed, Vitellius'
rebellion that had indirectly prompted Otho's coup.

78 *descended to flattery*: in Plutarch, *Otho* 8 Titianus and Proculus
give more serious reasons why Otho should fight at once, and
Paulinus' counter-arguments are less extensive. Tacitus weights
the argument strongly in favour of delay, and thus suggests the
irrationality of Otho's haste.

Brixellum: Brescello.

something for their idle troops to do: Caecina probably had
more serious reasons also: to strike (or at least look as if he
would strike) at the Othonians south of the Po. Tacitus plays

down its seriousness, again making the Othonians appear irrational by undermining the case for fighting immediately.

80 *Paulinus was much too wise*: Plutarch, *Otho* 9 says directly that it was indeed in hope of peace that some of the commanders argued for delay. Tacitus introduces this interpretation only to reject it with characteristically cynical reasoning. For him the moral corruption that pervaded both armies is more significant for understanding events.

free to covet wealth without fear: an idea closely derived from Sallust (e.g. *Catiline* 10–13, *Jugurtha* 41–2, *Histories* 1. 11–12)—central to his work is the sense that Rome's defeat of her enemies led to avarice and hence to moral and political ruin. Cf. also 2. 17.

strife first flared up: according to the legends of early Rome reported in historians like Livy, class conflict was present virtually from the beginning of the Republic. Tacitus is here imitating Sallust's polarized and over simplified picture of Roman history, reinforcing the sense of the degeneracy of his own day by contrasting it with the values of the past. In imitating Sallust, however, he caps him: for Marius, Sulla, and Pompey figured in Sallust's work as examples of late-Republican degeneracy—but Otho and Vitellius are implied to be worse still.

Gaius Marius . . . Lucius Sulla: Marius (157–86 BC) was the leading political and military figure of his day (consul seven times). In his last consulship (86), held after capturing Rome from his leading noble enemy Sulla (138–78 BC), he behaved with notorious (and illegal) cruelty. After his death, Sulla established himself as dictator (82–79), having numerous opponents killed in the process. Marius came from a provincial Italian town, but in fact, despite the widespread legend of his lower-class origins, his family was equestrian.

81 *the confluence of the Po and the Addua*: this is impossible: the Addua meets the Po much further away, and is an improbable objective for Otho's army. Either Tacitus is confused, or the text is corrupt.

83 *never been in battle before*: I Adiutrix had in fact fought at Castores (2. 24). XXI Rapax had been founded by Octavian (the future Augustus) a century earlier.

84 *no hesitation in granting terms*: Plutarch, *Otho* 13 provides much more detail on the negotiations; Tacitus moves swiftly to Otho's own response, on which he is to focus.

85 *firm resolve*: this is not fully consistent with the account of Otho's behaviour earlier. Tacitus now introduces the greater heroism associated with his imminent death.

possible to revive this cruel and pitiable war: Tacitus (unlike Plutarch, *Otho* 15) does not only present this point as the view of the characters, but endorses it with his own voice, and so implicitly enhances the nobility of Otho's actions.

he initiated our contest: a misleading statement: it is true only in that Vitellius revolted against Galba a few days before Otho independently assassinated him.

86 *distributed his money carefully*: to his tenants, according to other sources.

Servians: a loose identification of Galba, whose family name was in fact Sulpicius—Servius was his first name.

never remember it overmuch: there is tragic irony in this conclusion: Cocceianus was years later executed by Domitian for celebrating Otho's birthday.

87 *fell upon his dagger*: Plutarch, *Otho* 17 tells how the soldiers continued to oppose Otho's suicide, and to rebuke themselves for not preventing it. As before, Tacitus focuses all the picture on Otho's own actions.

Ferentium: Ferento.

Regium Lepidum: Reggio Emilia.

88 *Rubrius Gallus*: Nero's commander against Galba and Vindex.

'Conscript Fathers': the formal term of address to senators.

Eprius Marcellus: an informer under Nero, also a famous orator.

89 *Bononia*: Bologna.

safe-conducts: these would entitle him, among other things, to the use of post-horses for public business.

a few days later: if this is true, the order cannot have come from Vitellius himself, who was not yet in Italy.

reported in the theatre: on 18 April (the festival of Ceres was celebrated with shows and games on 12–19 April). The news, if this is true, reached Rome with unparalleled speed, given that Otho committed suicide on the 16th.

90 *not written at all*: official addresses of this sort were usually sent only by the emperor himself.

91 *rise by his vices*: Suetonius, *Vitellius* 12 has numerous details of Asiaticus' earlier relationship with Vitellius, including that they had been lovers. Tacitus shows Vitellius' weakness, but throws more blame on Asiaticus himself.

Albinus: previously a notoriously corrupt governor of Judaea.

Juba: the name of a famous past king of Mauretania. For procurators, cf. 1. 11 and p. xxvii.

Arar: the Saône.

eminent family: apparently a descendant of Mark Antony: see 3. 38.

92 *infant son*: he was 6 years old.

93 *pretending to be divine*: this brief episode highlights the un-Roman side to Gallic culture, prefiguring Books 4 and 5, where this theme is to the fore. However, the end of the paragraph unexpectedly elides the Gauls with the supporters of Otho: this also prefigures the later books, where the division between foreign and Roman continually breaks down. See in general the Introduction pp. xix–xxii.

the disgrace of appearing at the games in the arena: only gladiators, who were slaves, would normally fight in the arena. For astrologers cf. 1. 22; Suetonius, *Vitellius* 14 suggests Vitellius exiled them through fear of their criticisms of him—in Tacitus it looks more creditable. He makes Vitellius a paradoxical figure, juxtaposing his degenerate gluttony with his restoration of old values.

Plancius Varus: later governor of Bithynia under Vespasian.

94 *Interamna*: Terni.

95 *Lucius Arruntius*: Tiberius had appointed him governor of Spain, but then had kept him at Rome for at least ten years.

97 *extensive impunity*: contrast the favour previously shown to the Batavians (2. 66). The indiscipline of the troops, for Tacitus, is promoted by Vitellius' fickleness.

98 *very well pleased*: compare Tacitus' comment on the Cremonans' callousness in the previous paragraph. Their sycophancy is bound up with Vitellius' brutality, and both will meet with nemesis.

99 *Valerius Marinus . . . Pedanius Costa*: Marinus and Costa had been due to be consuls in October, Macer in November and December. Tacitus fails to mention that Marinus promptly went

over to Vespasian; it is more important to him to emphasize everybody's complaisance towards Vitellius.

Scribonianus Camerinus: nephew of Galba's heir Piso, executed in 67.

execution of a slave: crucifixion.

meditating war: with what follows we may contrast Josephus, *Jewish War* 4. 588–604, who makes Vespasian's decision to take the throne not the result of personal ambition, but of disinterested patriotism and pressure from others.

Third Legion: III Gallica. It had in fact already rioted against Vitellius, and this may well have been crucial in encouraging Vespasian to claim the throne. Tacitus, however, does not narrate the riot until 2. 85: he shows the Flavian rising fundamentally stemming from the Flavians themselves.

100 *youthful sons*: Titus was then 29, Domitian 17.

as follows: with Mucianus' speech here, compare Galba's adoption speech to Piso (1. 15–16) and Valens' arguments to Vitellius (1. 52), both concerned with the relationship between noble lineage and imperial ambition. In Josephus, *Jewish War* 4. 592–600 there is much less on this subject, and it is presented as general discussion, not Mucianus' own views.

101 *Corbulo's murder*: a famous general during the reigns of Claudius and Nero, murdered on the orders of the latter in 67. He was for Tacitus a particularly apposite example to have Mucianus introduce here: Domitian later married Corbulo's daughter.

insignia of a triumph: ornaments given to successful generals. Vespasian had won them while a commander during Claudius' conquest of Britain.

102 *promise of this omen*: this and other, much clearer omens are listed in various sources. Tacitus chooses to focus on the one whose meaning is vaguest: for him, Vespasian's power is not as clearly favoured by the gods, but is the result of his own ambitions. The interpretation specifically promising the throne is Vespasian's own.

Carmel: the site had been used for worship since Canaanite times, but the god's cult title at this period is doubtful.

103 *the third*: the 11th, according to Suetonius, *Vespasian* 6.

104 *Sohaemus . . . Antiochus . . . Agrippa*: Sohaemus was a notable pro-Roman, king of Emesa in Syria since 54. Antiochus IV

Epiphanes, king of Commagene on the upper Euphrates, 42–72; he was a descendant of the Seleucid dynasty that had once controlled much of the Near East. Agrippa II ruled with Berenice over a large part of eastern Palestine; he had gone to Rome with Titus (2. 1), but unlike Titus had not turned back *en route*.

old man's heart too: i.e. as well as Titus': see 2. 2.

105 *the keys of Egypt*: i.e. the coastal area, especially Alexandria.

more as the Emperor's partner than his subordinate: contrast his words at 77. Tacitus regularly presents Mucianus' relationship to Vespasian in such terms (compare 1. 10 and 2. 5): the theoretical subordinate who possesses a dangerously large share of imperial power—a typically Tacitean theme that becomes still more central in the *Annals*.

Dyrrachium: Durazzo.

106 *Brundisium*: Brindisi.

'*Funds . . . are the sinews of civil war*': a (near) quotation from Cicero, *Philippics* 5. 5: 'the sinews of war, funds without end.'

bold use of his lessons: cf. 2. 5 for Vespasian's avarice; Suetonius, too, treats this as his leading vice.

the Illyrian army espoused his cause: they were disaffected with Vitellius (2. 60).

107 *Antonius Primus*: a leading figure in Book 3. His crime under Nero was (in 61) to have witnessed a forged will.

Tampius Flavianus and Pompeius Silvanus . . . Cornelius Fuscus: the careers of Flavianus and Silvanus went in parallel: both had been governors of Africa; subsequently under Vespasian they were successively put in charge of Rome's aqueducts; and they finally were colleagues in a second consulship. Cornelius Fuscus was ultimately Prefect of the Guard under Domitian.

108 *more contemptible and indolent every day*: Vitellius' march was in fact not especially slow: he covered 1,100 (English) miles in at most 100 days. Tacitus distorts the picture to accentuate the contrast with the Flavians' vigour.

fattening up gladiators: soldiers would normally purchase and prepare their own food; gladiators (who were despised as slaves) were fed by their owners to ensure their health.

110 *the Cremera and the Allia*: two battles in early Roman history. At the Cremera in *c.*479 BC, virtually the entire Fabian clan was

destroyed; at the Allia in c.387 BC, the Gauls wiped out the Roman army and subsequently sacked the city. The events are couched in legend, but 18 July was traditionally seen as the anniversary of both, and was observed as a so-called 'black day', on which public business should not be transacted.

rescue of his slighted authority: tribunes under the Republic had the right to protect citizens from abuse of power. An appeal to them would imply that Vitellius was actually threatened by Helvidius; Tacitus ironically treats it as a mild measure. There is also irony in the word 'authority': that authority included Vitellius' own tribunician power as emperor, which should have made such an appeal unnecessary.

Thrasea: Thrasea Paetus, Helvidius' father-in-law, distinguished for his Stoic philosophy; this led him to resist Nero, who forced him to suicide. Vitellius had indeed opposed him—in order to be sycophantic to Nero.

111 *full rights over their freedmen*: these included the right to inherit from them, and to be supported by them in need: hence the freedmen's response. Earlier, especially under Claudius, freedmen in the imperial household had held senior administrative posts, but this practice was now dying out; for Tacitus, however, the existence of powerful freedmen is a consistent symbol of the evil reversal of the moral order.

Sixteen cohorts of Guards: an unprecedented number. Vitellius seems also to have allowed non-Italians into the Guards, contrary to normal practice.

112 *Vitellius' birthday*: Probably 7 September. This therefore in fact came after the events of the following paragraph: Tacitus completes the narrative of Vitellius' behaviour at Rome, then moves back in time to summarize the situation when the first news came of the Flavian revolt (2. 96).

King Tatius: the Sabine King Tatius had, in legend, ruled for a time jointly with Romulus, Rome's founder. The priestly college called the Titii was supposedly named after him.

not yet four months: i.e. it was August.

113 *war of his own*: Tacitus here again prefigures Book 4: Hordeonius' fears were in the event justified.

114 *distrusted and disliked*: Vespasian had governed Africa c.62. Tacitus is here emphasizing the contrast with Vitellius, and suppresses the idea, found in Suetonius, *Vespasian* 4, that Vespasian's administration was admired by many.

Valerius Festus: a relative of Vitellius, as we learn at 4. 49. He later had a meteoric rise under Vespasian.

Etesian winds: regular summer north-westerly winds in the Mediterranean.

capacity to endure toil was dulled: this picture of the German troops' loss of military virtue draws on standard Roman images of Romans corrupted by provincial luxury, but reverses them: the provincials here are corrupted by Vitellius' Rome.

115 *Hostilia*: Ostiglia.

Lucilius Bassus: Vespasian later made him governor of Judaea to finish crushing the Jewish revolt; but he died before completing the task.

attributed it to patriotism and the interests of peace: Josephus, *Jewish War* 4. 635, the one Flavian historian we possess, actually attributes it to Caecina's fear of the Flavian troops; but Tacitus has an interest in claiming that his predecessors were mere flatterers.

117 *Poetovio*: Pettau.

recently suffered defeat: the Thirteenth Legion had fought on Otho's side at Bedriacum.

enervate them: Antonius' key argument: Tacitus' words at 2. 99 have supported it.

118 *not defeated but deceived*: the Thirteenth Legion's own argument at 2. 44, but Tacitus showed it then as clearly false. Likewise, the claim that the cavalry shattered Vitellius' line is an exaggeration.

119 *Sarmatian Iazyges*: a Hungarian tribe east of the Danube.

Suebi: a group of German tribes north of the Danube; Sido and Italicus ruled the Suebian tribes Marcomanni and Quadi in Bohemia-Moravia.

120 *Opitergium and Altinum*: Oderzo and Altino.

news of its desertion: the fleet does not actually revolt until 3. 12, but Tacitus has described the preparations for its defection at 2. 100–1, and presents the desertion itself as inevitable.

Ateste: Este.

121 *Vicetia*: Vicenza.

the enemy's general had thus lost his native town: an ironic point, given that Tacitus has told the reader that Caecina himself is about to join the Flavians.

ambition: Tacitus questions Mucianus' motives, but also shows his warning in the event proved correct, given the actual brutality that results from Antonius' attack.

122 *a famous family*: Messala was probably descended from Valerius Messala Corvinus (64 BC–AD 8), himself of a distinguished ancient family, a writer, and a close political associate of Augustus. Messala wrote a history of this campaign, which Tacitus used as a source (3. 25, 3. 28); he is also one of the characters in Tacitus' *Dialogus*. Although only tribune, he was now in charge of the legion, since the legionary commander had fled to Vespasian (2. 85).

123 *excess of terror*: Flavianus' extravagant fear anticipates the notorious cowardice of Vitellius himself at the end of the book, and contrasts with Antonius' resoluteness.

gods of war: medallions depicting these gods were on the shafts of the standards.

124 *furnace of some baths*: sited beneath the floor of the bathhouse's heated room.

lictors: attendants who accompanied senior officials.

Atria: Adria.

125 *that very field*: i.e. Bedriacum. This is not strictly true, as they were then some miles from the field, but it prepares the way for the idea that another key battle is about to be fought on the same spot. Josephus, *Jewish War* 4. 640 treats this change of heart by the army as more the result of fear of Vitellius than pride; but to Tacitus the German army's loyalty to Vitellius is a central theme.

126 *occupy Cremona*: there was a lunar eclipse that night, which the Vitellians took as an evil omen, but to which Tacitus makes no reference; Heaven, for him, is not clearly on Antonius' side.

127 *a brave soldier*: this description of Antonius is closely modelled on Sallust's description of the rebel Catiline at his final battle (*Catiline* 60). The overtones are especially resonant: Catiline's combination of military heroism and moral perversity fits Antonius all too well.

128 *nor marched out to attack the enemy*: contrast the good generalship of Antonius in the same circumstances (3. 16–17): by the parallel Tacitus shows that the loss of Caecina has made all the difference to the Vitellians.

129 *victory by force*: Antonius does not, contrary to the soldiers'
fears, claim to be aiming for a surrender. The events that follow
the town's actual surrender (3. 31ff.) should be read in the light
of this speech.

130 *raised recently by Galba*: it had been formed in Spain in the
previous year.

131 *Fifteenth*: the manuscript actually reads 'Fourteenth'; but that
legion was not involved in the battle. 'Sixteenth' has also been
proposed as an emendation.

Mark Antony . . . Corbulo: Mark Antony (82–30 BC) had part-
nered Octavian (the future Augustus) in the Second Triumvirate;
then opposed him in the civil war. He had led III Gallica against
Parthia in 36 BC (unsuccessfully, despite Antonius' words here).
Corbulo had led it against the Armenians in AD 62–3.

132 *the Syrian custom*: III Gallica had served in Syria since 40 BC.

133 *inclined to this view*: to the decision to attack, or to the men's
eagerness for plunder? Tacitus leaves it, and hence also
Antonius' responsibility for the sequel, unclear.

'tortoise' formation: the shields were interlocked to form a
continuous cover.

134 *Gaius Pliny*: Pliny the Elder, the author of the surviving *Natural
History*. Among his many other scholarly works was a history of
this period, now lost.

135 *olive-branches and ritual bands*: symbols of surrender: cf. 1. 66.

136 *assistance to the Vitellian cause*: Tacitus' account does not entirely support this charge; but cf. 2. 70.

Forty thousand soldiers: Dio 64. 15 has the plundering largely
carried out by the Vitellians themselves; for Tacitus the Flavians
are entirely responsible.

137 *Mefitis*: goddess who protected against malaria.

the consulship of Tiberius Sempronius and Publius Cornelius:
218 BC. In that same year Hannibal, the great Carthaginian
general, crossed the Alps and invaded Italy; he was forced out
only in 203 BC. The Gauls had also invaded Italy just a few years
previously, in 225–222 BC.

138 *When Caecina had left Rome*: the story moves a month back,
picking up events in Rome from the end of Book 2. This accen-
tuates the irony of Vitellius' complacent apathy: Tacitus has just
shown us the collapse of his cause.

Aricia: Ariccia.

139 *no bill had been passed rescinding the magistracy*: such a bill would have to be passed by a popular assembly. Under the Principate these were a mere formality; but formalities still mattered.

Caninius Rebilus: lieutenant of Caesar, who was made consul for the last day of 45 BC, after his predecessor had died in office.

Servilian Park: an imperial mansion at Rome.

Caecina Tuscus: son of Nero's wet-nurse. Nero had made him governor of Egypt, then banished him.

caught up Vitellius' young son: a standard oratorical technique to attract sympathy. Vitellius is taken in, but has also, of course, ulterior reasons for being 'persuaded'.

140 *Junii and Antonii are his ancestors*: distinguished Republican families. Blaesus was probably a descendant of Mark Antony, and possibly Nero's cousin.

a leisurely advance: compare Vitellius' own march to Rome (2. 71); Valens' behaviour is shown as essentially 'Vitellian'. In fact his tardiness may have been the result of his earlier illness (2. 99), which Tacitus now ignores.

141 *Ariminum*: Rimini.

Hercules Monoecus: Monaco.

142 *Stoechades*: the Îles d'Hyères.

sent there by Claudius: in 43.

143 *doubt about the change*: the Twentieth was especially slow to change its loyalties.

Brigantes: a powerful tribe of northern England.

King Caratacus: king of the Catuvellauni, in southern England; he led a revolt against the Romans under Claudius, but was defeated in 51.

144 *Sixth Legion*: VI Ferrata; the legion that went over to Vespasian in 3. 44 was VI Victrix.

Fonteius Agrippa: according to Josephus, *Jewish War* 7. 91, he was killed here in battle soon after. Tacitus ignores this aftermath of the story: his main interest is in the responsibility for the turbulent empire being transferred into Flavian hands.

Pontus: in northern Turkey. It had been a 'client kingdom'—nominally independent, but under Roman control. In 64 it had been incorporated into the Roman province of Galatia. Polemo II had been its king from 38 to 64.

Trapezus: Trabzon.

145 *Chobus*: the Khobi.

146 *despising Vespasian*: Antonius' troops' fatal insubordination is, for Tacitus, thus mirrored in his own attitude towards his superiors; compare 3. 53, and Bassus and Silvanus at 3. 50.

Eleventh: XI Claudia, stationed in Dalmatia.

Annius Bassus: he had previously served under Vespasian in the Jewish War.

Fanum Fortunae: Fano.

147 *Pompeius Strabo fought against Cinna at the Janiculum*: Pompeius Strabo was father of Pompey the Great; he defended Rome when in 87 BC, during the civil war, it came under attack from Cinna. The Janiculum is the hill across the River Tiber from the main area of ancient Rome.

Sisenna: a politician of the first half of the 1st century BC, about which he wrote an influential history.

148 *my labours will prove useless*: a revealing comment. Desire for personal glory was thought a perfectly acceptable and indeed admirable trait among the Romans, but such an exclusive concentration on it would still be uncomfortable. Antonius does not appear to rate his side's success as valuable in itself.

149 *committing suicide*: other sources tell a similar story involving Otho; but, given Tacitus' portrayal of their respective characters, it suits his Vitellius much better.

150 *Latin rights*: these gave all citizens of such towns certain legal rights, but without full Roman citizenship; full citizenship was given only to their magistrates.

Mevania: Bevagna.

151 *Tarracina*: Terracina.

Narnia: Narni.

152 *Petillius Cerialis*: a major figure in Book 4. His career advanced under Vespasian: twice consul, and governor of Britain 71–4.

154 *Urbinum*: Urbino.

the end of the war: the close identification of Valens and Vitellius culminates here: his death is linked to the end of Vitellius' cause.

Anagnia: Anagni.

Juvenalian Games: games instituted by Nero in 59 to celebrate his coming of age.

155 *Age had enfeebled Sabinus*: he was about 61.

156 *Silius Italicus*: politician and poet: his *Punica*, a long epic poem on the Hannibalic War, still survives.

without bloodshed: with Vitellius, as with Sabinus, Tacitus shows imperfectly realized good intentions as a key factor in the disaster that follows.

an old man: he was 57 (3. 86).

Pompey . . . Antony: misleading examples: Pompey was murdered without Caesar's knowledge, while Antony committed suicide.

Claudius' colleague: Lucius Vitellius had Claudius as his colleague in his last two consulships and his censorship (cf. 1. 9). However, to call Vespasian his 'dependant' is probably an exaggeration: Vespasian rose to prominence at the time of Vitellius' father's greatest influence, but we know of no further connection between them.

157 *opportunely dying*: Suetonius, *Vitellius* 14 records a rumour that Vitellius killed her. Tacitus omits this: he has consistently, as here, shown Vitellius' love for his family (e.g. 1. 75, 2. 59, 2. 89).

Caesar . . . Gaius . . . Nero's: Caesar was assassinated by a group of other senators at a meeting of the Senate. Gaius was killed in 41 by a small group of conspirators in a corridor of the palace. Nero fled Rome on the news of Galba's revolt, and went to a villa a bit under four (English) miles away, where he killed himself.

158 *Sacred Way*: the oldest street in Rome. It ran from the Roman Forum (where the Temple of Concord was also sited) towards the palace.

house of Flavius Sabinus: on the Quirinal Hill in the north-east of the city.

Capitol: fortified hill in the centre of Rome, containing the famous temple to Jupiter Optimus Maximus.

Verulana Gratilla: wife of Arulenus Rusticus (3. 80); she was exiled after his execution in 93. Tacitus' words hint at an unfeminine lack of modesty on her part, of which Romans traditionally disapproved.

159 *Aventine*: hill in the southern quarter of the city.

160 *merely an excuse for war*: other sources have Vitellius actively arranging the attack on Sabinus; Tacitus shows him as increasingly passive and ineffectual.

'Grove of Refuge': the saddle between the two peaks of the Capitol. In legend Romulus, the first king of Rome, had established a right of asylum there.

Tarpeian Rock: a cliff, probably on the south-east side of the Capitol; condemned criminals were traditionally executed by being flung from it.

the most common account: in fact, other surviving sources (probably deriving from Flavian propaganda) make the Vitellians clearly responsible. Tacitus here weights the evidence in the other direction, but allows no side to escape blame.

the temple: of Jupiter Optimus Maximus.

161 *could have defiled*: Tacitus here refers to various legends connected with the Capitol. Omens at its foundation were said to have promised it as the 'Capital of an Empire' ['caput imperii'], a significant play on the name 'Capitol'. Then the Etruscan king Lars Porsenna supposedly attacked Rome in c.507 BC seeking to restore the monarchy; the ultimate negotiated settlement left Rome a republic. Tacitus here says that Rome surrendered to Porsenna; the normal patriotic account had the Romans successfully withstanding him, but Tacitus chooses the version which most closely parallels the current situation. Finally, the Gauls sacked Rome in c.387 BC; patriotic legend had the Romans on the Capitol holding out against them.

burnt before in civil war: in 83 BC, during the civil war that brought Sulla to power. The perpetrator was never identified.

Tarquinius Priscus ... Servius Tullius ... Tarquinius Superbus: in legend Tarquinius Priscus, Servius Tullius, and Tarquinius Superbus (= 'The Proud') were, respectively, the fifth, sixth, and seventh (and last) kings of Rome.

Suessa Pometia: a town of the Volscians, a neighbouring Italian tribe.

his second consulship: about 507 BC.

consulship of Lucius Scipio and Gaius Norbanus: i.e. 83 BC: the gap was in fact about 425 years.

his famous 'Fortune': Sulla was nicknamed 'Felix'—'The Fortunate'.

Lutatius Catulus: major politician of the early 1st century BC, who dedicated the rebuilt temple in 69.

162 *commanding what he had banned*: cf. the similar behaviour of Vitellius: both sides, for Tacitus, are now controlled from below.

a linen mantle: dress of a worshipper of the Egyptian goddess Isis.

163 *Gemonian Steps*: flight of steps leading up to the Capitol, on which the bodies of executed criminals were exposed.

from bloodshed: Tacitus presents these as alternatives, but his own account has supported both interpretations.

Temple of Feronia: just under three (English) miles outside Tarracina.

164 *Vergilius Capito's*: he had been governor of Egypt 47–52.

165 *Saturnalian holiday*: festival celebrated in a carnival atmosphere, starting on 17 December.

Ocriculum: Otricoli.

deflecting popular resentment: i.e. by placing responsibility for the disaster on Mucianus' shoulders.

Salarian Way: road leading into Rome from the north-east.

'*The Red Rocks*': a prominent cliff-face a few miles north of the city.

166 *Fidenae*: Castel Giubileo.

Arulenus Rusticus: husband of Verulana Gratilla (3. 69). He was a Stoic associate of Thrasea Paetus and Helvidius Priscus (see 2. 91), and was eventually executed by Domitian after publishing eulogies of them.

a knight named Musonius Rufus: an influential teacher (his pupils included Epictetus), some of whose discourses still survive. He was banished by Nero in 65 and recalled by Galba; later he was banished again by Vespasian and recalled by Titus. However, at 4. 10 he is not a knight, but a senator. Tacitus may be wording this passage loosely, and mean only that he was of equestrian family; but he also hints at the derogatory implication that he joined the embassy illegitimately.

167 *Vestal Virgins*: the important cult of Vesta at Rome was served by six aristocratic women, vowed to virginity for thirty years.

Colline Gate: in the north-east corner of the city.

Sallust's Gardens: a park lying outside the city walls to the west of the Colline Gate.

168 *twice when Sulla mastered Rome, once under Cinna*: Sulla's armies had conquered Rome in 88 and 82 BC, Cinna's in 87 BC.

their holiday: the Saturnalia (3. 78).

Guards' camp: it lay just outside the Colline Gate.

169 *shameful hiding-place*: other sources give more detail of Vitellius' humiliating attempts to escape: Tacitus now treats him more sympathetically, drawing a veil over his degradation.

soldier of the German army: i.e. one of his own troops.

the site of Galba's murder: the people had celebrated Vitellius' accession in similar fashion (2. 55): the parallel reinforces Tacitus' portrait of the mob's fickleness.

Vitellius' father: the text is unclear here: probably some words are missing in which Vitellius' father was described.

Luceria: Nocera.

170 *deserted Galba for Vitellius*: Caecina in particular.

all fear of violence was at an end: Tacitus' ironic hint at Domitian's cowardice is noteworthy: so too is the reminder of the last and worst of the Flavians directly after the death of their unworthy predecessor.

171 *plundering Cremona*: unlike in Josephus, *Jewish War* 4. 654 Antonius is not here restrained by Mucianus. The reminder of the atrocity against Cremona (3. 32–4) emphasizes once again Antonius' brutality against his own people, now turned against the very city of Rome; we may contrast his noble sentiments at 3. 60. Through the whole of the opening of this book Tacitus casts over the Flavian victory the shadow of future tyranny.

173 *praetorship with the powers of a consul*: this position is unparalleled. It was presumably connected with the fact that Vespasian and Titus were both still absent, as well as with a desire to honour the three Flavians equally.

a pretext: a triumph could only be obtained for a victory over a foreign enemy. The Sarmatian expedition may be connected with the Dacian attack at 3. 46; Tacitus does not make the connection, and so denies the triumph even a shred of validity.

restore the Capitol: a significant move: the temples on the Capitol were believed central to the prosperity of Rome. However, under standard senatorial procedure religious matters ought to have been transacted *before* secular ones.

Valerius Asiaticus: son-in-law of Vitellius; he apparently died within a few weeks of this episode.

honour to a new emperor: the text is missing some words here, although the general sense is clear.

fortune in life: this famous digression is significantly placed: as the Flavian rule begins, Helvidius is established as the paradigmatic opponent of tyranny. It also establishes Eprius Marcellus as his enemy, and so gives him too a paradigmatic role, preparing the way for the debate that follows.

174 *that school of philosophy*: i.e. Stoicism.

Eprius Marcellus: he ultimately committed suicide after being accused of conspiracy against Vespasian; hence there is an irony in his complaisant stance towards the Emperor in the following scene.

175 *Soranus and Sentius*: like Thrasea, Barea Soranus had been forced to commit suicide under Nero. Sentius may be Cn. Sentius Saturninus, who must have known Vespasian, as they both held commands under Claudius during his conquest of Britain; but details of his fate are unknown.

176 *any Brutus or Cato*: two Brutuses were famous opponents of tyranny: Lucius Junius Brutus in legend expelled Tarquinius Superbus, the last king of Rome, and became the first consul of the new Republic; Marcus Junius Brutus (85–43 BC) led the assassins of Julius Caesar. Marcus Porcius Cato (234–149 BC) was famed for his unbending rectitude, as was his great-grandson of the same name (95–46 BC), who fought against Julius Caesar.

Vespasian's age: he was now 60.

in those days administered the Treasury: in Tacitus' own day, two ex-praetors were selected by the Emperor to be the chief treasury officials; this had also been the practice under Nero.

interposed his veto: under the Republic, tribunes had the right to veto senatorial motions. This is the last known case when the veto was used—and it is striking that it is on behalf of the autocrat, not an assertion of liberty. Of course, the Emperor himself also had tribunician power: this formed the legal basis of his authority to override the Senate.

took care to remember it: i.e. to pass on to Vespasian that Helvidius had allotted him only a subordinate role.

Publius Celer: a Stoic who had been bribed to give evidence against Barea Soranus in 66.

177 *adopted the power of an emperor*: Tacitus consistently shows
    Mucianus taking over imperial prerogatives: see 2. 83, and cf. 2.
    5, 4. 44–7, and 4. 68.

    Gaius Piso: this Piso had led a conspiracy against Nero, but was
    betrayed and forced to commit suicide.

178 *Chatti*: a powerful people of western Germany.

    the neighbouring island: i.e. the part of the Netherlands between
    the diverging mouths of the Rhine.

    Julius Paulus: the text has been corrupted around this point—
    'Claudius Paulus' has also been conjectured as the name.

    Sertorius: Quintus Sertorius (c.123–72 BC), a Roman governor
    of Spain who for some years led the Spaniards in a war against
    Rome, claiming to be the legitimate Roman authority. His am-
    biguous position between Roman and foreign is mirrored in
    Tacitus' portrait of Civilis; and Tacitus' phrasing here directly
    imitates Sallust's description of Sertorius (*Histories* 1. 88).
    Sertorius, like Hannibal, had only one eye.

179 *prefects*: subordinate officials with this title were in charge of
    local military districts.

180 *the Island*: see 4. 12.

    Mogontiacum: Mainz.

    Gaius' farcical expeditions: Gaius had visited Germany in 39–
    40, and sought to stage-manage a military victory for himself.

    Frisii: they inhabited modern Friesland, in the north-east
    Netherlands.

    Nervian: the Nervii were a tribe inhabiting land near Brussels.

182 *Aedui and Arverni*: the Arverni were a powerful tribe inhabiting
    the Auvergne. For the Aedui see 1. 51. Both had supported
    Vindex.

    the East is used to tyrants: a standard Roman stereotype of the
    submissive Easterner. However, Tacitus undermines Civilis' case
    by putting this argument in his mouth. On the one hand, the
    Jews were currently in revolt; on the other, he has shown Civilis
    himself aiming at kingship (4. 18).

    born before the days of tribute: an exaggeration—tribute began
    to be levied in 27 BC, nearly a hundred years earlier.

    Quintilius Varus was killed: when governor on the Rhine in 9,
    Varus had been surprised by a German attack: his three legions
    were wiped out and he committed suicide.

    Ubii: German tribe inhabiting the area round Cologne.

183 *stationed in the rear*: a regular German custom, according to Roman writers.

Vetera: Xanten.

increase in the number of their cavalry: cavalry were better paid than infantry.

184 *First Legion*: I Adiutrix.

Gallus hesitated: Tacitus leaves it unclear whether Gallus had received Hordeonius' messages in 4. 19: he shows the troops taking the actual responsibility for fighting, and the commanders' motivation as doubtful. We can compare the hints of treachery in the same paragraph; all this reinforces the sense that Civilis may indeed have Roman support, as alleged, and thus that the war with him is a civil war.

185 *Bructeri and Tencteri*: tribes on the east bank of the Rhine, the Tencteri opposite Cologne, the Bructeri to their north.

186 *to hold two legions*: at full strength each legion would have about 5,000 men.

188 *the legions from Mogontiacum were in pursuit*: cf. 4. 19: however, Hordeonius had countermanded the order. Again Tacitus leaves unclear how much was known and the troops' precise motivation.

189 *'the anger of heaven'*: such sceptical rationalism towards omens is typical of ancient historians: but the inclusion of the omen in the narrative at all would carry for a Roman hints at disaster to follow.

Novaesium: Neuss.

they encamped . . .: some words are missing from the text here.

Gelduba: Gellep bei Krefeld.

190 *Menapii and Morini*: Gallic tribes on the west bank of the Maas.

Agrippinenses: their chief town, the modern Cologne, took the name 'Colonia Agrippinensis' after a colony was placed there in 50 by Agrippina (the wife of Claudius and mother of Nero), whose birthplace it was. The tribe took its new name from the town.

Marcodurum: Düren.

191 *Caecina's edict*: Caecina was entitled to issue edicts as consul. This was presumably a manifesto in favour of joining the Flavians.

193 *Asciburgium*: Asberg.

196 *Chatti, Usipi, and Mattiaci*: the Usipi were a tribe of the east bank of the Rhine south of Cologne; the Mattiaci were a branch of the Chatti, inhabiting the area round Wiesbaden.

supposed to be plotting revolution: Tacitus pointedly highlights the panic of the Roman populace at the supposed rebellion in Africa, juxtaposing it with the real threat in Germany, towards which they show no response. The real story behind the African 'rebellion' is told in 4. 48–50.

197 *Julius Frontinus*: he later had an outstanding career: thrice consul, governor of Britain, and supervisor of the city's aqueducts. He wrote treatises, which still survive, on military strategy and Rome's aqueduct system.

Crassus Scribonianus: brother of Galba's heir Piso: see 1. 48.

Seventh Legion: VII Galbian; VII Claudia had in fact also fought for the Flavians at Cremona, and was sent to Pannonia.

198 *repeated blushes were taken for signs of modesty*: Tacitus here ironically alludes to Domitian's notoriously florid complexion.

nothing was done about Piso: as Galba's 'rightful heir', Piso was still potentially controversial. By juxtaposing this episode with the reference to a potential coup by his brother Tacitus reinforces the point.

disgracefully tampered with: Nero had not only added various festivals, but had altered the names of the months.

taken refuge with Vespasian: at 4. 39, however, Tettius' supposed anti-Flavianism was only an excuse for his demotion; the real motive was to honour Grypus. By showing that his actual flight to Vespasian achieved his restoration of rank, Tacitus hints at conflict and embarrassment among the Flavians.

Demetrius, a professor of Cynic philosophy: a famous philosopher, often referred to by Seneca; he was eventually banished by Vespasian on the advice of Mucianus. The hostility that he aroused here may have been because of his own well-known friendship with Stoics like Soranus, whom Publius had betrayed. His allegiance was to Cynicism, an influential school of Greek philosophy advocating the adoption of a primitive life according to nature. Despite what Tacitus implies here, Demetrius' defence of Publius may well have been consistent with Cynic doctrine, which stressed the importance of reconciliation and justice, and combined harangues against vice with understanding for those who strayed from the moral line.

Junius Mauricus: brother of Arulenus Rusticus (3. 80). He was exiled by Domitian after his brother's execution, then recalled by Nerva in 97; he became an adviser to Trajan.

199 *Paccius Africanus . . . suggested to Nero the murder of the two brothers Scribonius*: Paccius Africanus had been consul in 67; this episode does not seem to have seriously hindered his career, since he later became governor of Africa. His alleged victims were Publius Sulpicius Scribonius Proculus and Scribonius Rufus; they had been summoned by Nero to Greece in 67, then were forced to commit suicide.

Vibius Crispus: cf. 2. 10 for Vibius' own ambiguous behaviour under Nero.

the senatorial age: the minimum age for a senator was 25.

Aquilius Regulus: Messala's half-brother, and a notorious informer under Nero. In 67 he had accused Marcus Licinius Crassus Frugi (brother of Galba's heir Piso), and Crassus' father-in-law (Quintus Sulpicius Camerinus Pythicus) and brother-in-law; all three were executed. Orfitus was the consul of 51, executed in 66 by Nero as a result of Regulus' accusation.

200 *divided amongst his creditors*: so there was no money to tempt Nero.

stuffed yourself with seven million sesterces: an informer obtained a quarter of his victim's estate after his conviction.

201 *under Caesar's nose*: i.e. Domitian, who was presiding.

Antistius Sosianus: he had actually been exiled for his treason against Nero, but he had subsequently obtained his recall by informing against his fellow exiles. However, there is an irony in the senators 'reaffirming the original penalty', since the original exile was under the very laws they are now opposing.

202 *Sena*: Siena.

a mutiny almost broke out among the soldiers: with what follows compare the mutiny of the Batavians at 4. 19: Mucianus' control of the situation here contrasts with Flaccus' vacillation.

203 *the regular term of service*: Guards served for a term of sixteen years; regular legionaries for twenty.

204 *the then governor, Marcus Silanus*: in 39. However, Tacitus is apparently mistaken about the governor at the time: it was not Silanus (whose tenure there had been some years earlier), but another Lucius Piso, the father of the current governor.

the safest course is war: Mucianus himself had used similar arguments to Vespasian at 2. 76–7. Tacitus now hints that the risk of revolution in Africa is real, contrary to what he had suggested at 4. 38: however, the implication of what he says here is that it was at least partly those groundless suspicions at Rome that encouraged Piso to consider rebellion now. Certainly Mucianus' assassin seems, in Tacitus' account, to have been sent on the basis of rumour alone.

205 *His name will recur again and again in this narrative*: he became infamous as an informer under Domitian; but he was eventually himself convicted of corruption and exiled.

Adrumetum: Sousse.

206 *Oea*: Tripoli.

Garamantes: they inhabited the desert interior of modern Libya.

207 *at once launched his fastest corn-ships*: this had probably happened before Titus' departure for Judaea. Tacitus uses the movement of the ships to effect the transition back to Rome; he also closes the narrative of events in Rome and Africa with Vespasian's solution to the grain crisis that had triggered them at 4. 38.

Lucius Vestinus: a friend of Claudius; he had been governor of Egypt in 59–62.

Plautius Aelianus: he had had a long political career, and was now the senior of the pontiffs, one of the four major colleges of priests at Rome, to which only a limited number of senior aristocrats might be appointed.

a pig, a sheep, and an ox: this triple sacrifice to Mars was a standard part of the purification ceremony.

Jupiter, Juno, and Minerva: Juno and Minerva, as well as Jupiter, were worshipped in the Capitoline temple.

208 *the empire was coming to an end*: Tacitus' irony is apparent, given that he has just described the temple's restoration.

Druids: priests of the Celtic tribes: they had been subjected to major Roman prohibitions and persecutions.

209 *committed adultery*: Caesar had a notorious reputation as a womanizer, not least during his campaign in Gaul.

210 *Baetasii . . . Marsaci*: the Baetasii were a Belgic tribe; the Marsaci inhabited the Netherlands.

210 *Sacrovir*: Gallic chieftain who had led a revolt in 21; it was
swiftly crushed and he committed suicide.

Galba's reduction of the tribute: in fact Galba had only reduced
the tribute for certain tribes: the Treviri and the Lingones had
been penalized (1. 53). Tacitus' own narrative has undermined
Vocula's arguments.

211 *given themselves and their wives and children to the flames*:
notably at Saguntum in Spain, when captured by Hannibal in
219 BC. Tacitus' phrasing here closely recalls Livy's famous
description of the Saguntines' mass suicide (Livy 21. 14. 4)—
indeed, the style of the whole speech is modelled on Livy.

212 *Quirinus*: name given to the deified Romulus, legendary founder
of Rome.

213 *if any quarrel arose with the Gauls*: the implication is a striking
one: the new 'Gallic Empire' may itself be riven by Roman-like
civil war.

Veleda: for some years an important figure for German nation-
alist sentiment: however, she was eventually captured in 77 and
taken to Rome. Female leadership was, for the Romans, a standard indication of foreign degeneracy: compare 3. 69.

214 *Vindonissa*: Windisch.

leave their camp: the whole of the following section is modelled
on Livy's celebrated description of the humiliating Roman
surrender to the Samnites at the Caudine Forks in 321 BC (Livy
9. 5ff.). The imitation emphasizes the defeat here as a low point
for Roman power: but it also hints at the ultimate Roman
success—Livy showed them eventually turning the tables on the
Samnites.

215 *Mars, supreme among gods*: the Teutonic god Tiu was identified
with the Roman war-god Mars; however, normally Wodan
(identified with Mercury) was regarded as the supreme god. This
may have changed in wartime, or Tacitus may simply be at error
here.

closed to us the rivers: the Romans were strongly predisposed
to regard rivers like the Rhine as natural boundaries of their
empire. The Tencteri's demands here would thus appear to a
Roman reader to challenge the integrity of their power.

216 *those luxurious habits which enslave Rome's subjects*: again
the Sallustian theme: that civilized luxury leads to moral corruption (cf. 1. 46, 2. 37, 2. 99). Hence the Tencteri, for a

Roman reader, accurately identify a problem, but their solution, the destruction of the Roman Empire, would be seen as disastrous.

217 *Sunuci*: German tribe west of Cologne.

the Germans swam across: cf. 4. 12 for the Batavi's skill at swimming.

the devices by which he lay in hiding: the story was told in the lost part of the *Histories*. Sabinus and his wife lived for nine years in a hidden vault beneath a monument, where two sons were born to them. The parents were eventually discovered and executed; the sons appear to have survived.

218 *Remi*: tribe of north Gaul, around modern Reims.

Domitian's indomitable passions: Mucianus again appears to be virtually usurping the Emperor's role; however he is, for Tacitus, more perceptive than others about Domitian's true character (cf. 4. 40).

Arrecinus Clemens: his sister was Titus' first wife. His appointment here set him on a notable career: twice consul, governor of Nearer Spain, and in charge of the city's water supply. But Tacitus' reference to Domitian's favour that won him the post is highly ironic: Domitian ultimately had Clemens executed.

great distinction under Gaius: another sinister irony: the elder Clemens had in fact been one of Gaius' assassins.

able to fill both positions: the commander of the Guards would normally have been a knight, not a senator.

Second: II Adiutrix.

220 *Vangiones, Triboci, and Caeracates*: German tribes from the west bank of the Rhine.

Bingium: Bingen.

Nava: the Nahe.

221 *Rigodulum*: Riol.

222 *country of the Mediomatrici*: this paragraph again (cf. 4. 62) is closely modelled on Livy's account of the Caudine Forks.

223 *as the war is practically over*: this is hardly borne out by the narrative. Cerialis, as often in Tacitus' portrayal, is overconfident.

allies and enemies alike: Ariovistus, the king of the Suebi (cf. 3. 5), was summoned to Gaul to aid one tribe against the other, but took over part of the country himself. In the end, Julius Caesar defeated him in battle, and proceeded to conquer the rest of Gaul in 58–51 BC, claiming always to be there at the invitation of the Gauls themselves.

223 *the Cimbri and the Teutons*: German tribes from what is now Denmark. In the late 2nd century BC they had migrated and attacked southern Gaul and Italy, only to be defeated by the Romans in a series of battles.

you govern this and other provinces yourselves: this was in fact very rare at that time. Vindex had been the one prominent example.

224 *depravity and greed*: Cerialis repeats Tacitus' phrase from 4. 14: this was indeed the Roman behaviour that had provoked the revolt.

227 *Tolbiacum*: Zülpich.

228 *the regular season of the summer winds*: late August or early September.

229 *deduced the tenor of the oracle's response*: the name 'Basilides' is Greek for 'son of a king': Tacitus has Vespasian taking it as a divine confirmation of sovereignty. However, this story seems to belong more naturally to a time before Vespasian was aware of his victory, and it appears as such in Suetonius, *Vespasian* 7. Tacitus' transferring it here focuses attention instead on the future rule of Vespasian's own sons, and especially Domitian, to whom the book will shortly turn.

not yet been canvassed in any Roman authorities: the following story, found also in Plutarch, *On Isis and Osiris* 28, is in fact not the correct origin of the Serapis cult. Ptolemy took an existing cult at the previous capital of Memphis, where the dead Apis, the Egyptian sacred bull, was identified with the god Osiris under the name Oserapis; he then transformed this into the central royal cult of Alexandria. Tacitus alludes to the true story among the alternatives he offers at the end of his main version: see 4. 84.

King Ptolemy: Ptolemy I Soter (*c.*367–283 BC), general of Alexander the Great, made himself king of Egypt when Alexander's empire broke apart after his death. He made Alexandria his capital; it had been founded by Alexander after his conquest of Egypt in 332 BC.

230 *Eleusis*: A town near Athens, the site of the Eleusinian Myster-
ies, a famous initiation cult worshipping the goddess Demeter
(identified with the Roman Ceres). The Eumolpids were the clan
supplying the cult's hereditary priests.

Jupiter Dis . . . Proserpina: Jupiter Dis was Pluto, god of the
underworld; Proserpina was goddess of the underworld, daughter of Ceres and Jupiter.

the oracle of Apollo at Delphi: Apollo was god of prophecy; his
oracle at Delphi was the most famous in the Greco-Roman
world.

image of Apollo's father: Apollo was the son of Jupiter and Leto;
hence his 'father and sister' are Jupiter and Proserpina respectively. This, of course, depends on identifying the image of
Jupiter Dis which Ptolemy is to bring back with Jupiter himself.

231 *embarked unaided*: a standard element in ancient stories of the
introduction of new cults.

an ancient shrine of Serapis and Isis: this temple in Rhacotis (in
the west of the city) was in fact built under Ptolemy III Euergetes
(reigned 246–221 BC). Tacitus' confusion is shown by the fact
that he now seems to admit that the cult of Serapis already
existed in Egypt.

Memphis: the correct version: see 4. 83.

Aesculapius: Roman god of healing.

233 *Saturn was forcibly deposed by Jupiter*: in mythology, Saturn
was Jupiter's father: Jupiter overthrew him and became ruler of
the gods. The connection of Saturn with the Jews may be an
attempt to explain the institution of the Sabbath—see 5. 4.

the reign of Isis: in Egyptian myth, the wife of the god Osiris.
Some Greek writers believed them to be a historical king and
queen of Egypt.

234 *King Cepheus*: mythical Greek king; his supposed homeland
varies.

Assyrian refugees: perhaps a version of the story in Genesis 12:
Abraham went to Canaan from Haran in Syria.

poems of Homer: in *Iliad* 6. 184, 204: they appear to be a tribe
of south-west Turkey.

Jerusalem: in Greek and Latin 'Hierosolyma'.

Most authorities, however, agree: the idea that the Jews were
descended from lepers expelled from Egypt was common
among Greek writers. The particular version here, which is only

very loosely related to the biblical account, originated with an Alexandrian Greek called Lysimachus. Tacitus omits Lysimachus' account of Jewish sacrilege during the Exodus: he reserves the moral paradoxes of Judaism for later.

234 *King Bocchoris*: king of Egypt *c*.720–715 BC. This is impossibly late: the Bible places the Exodus several centuries earlier.

the oracle of Ammon: a famous oracle at Siwa; the Egyptian god Ammon was identified by the Romans with Jupiter.

their city and their Temple: in Jewish sources Jerusalem was only captured by King David centuries later, and the Temple was built by his son Solomon.

235 *wandering and thirst*: i.e. an ass. The myth that there was an image of an ass in the Holy of Holies was widespread among Greek and Roman authors; however Tacitus contradicts it himself at 5. 5 and 5. 9 below.

insult to Ammon: among the Egyptians, rams were sacred to both Ammon and Osiris. This is unlikely to be the true explanation of the Jewish use of rams (and bulls) in sacrifice; but it was one found among Jews themselves to explain the use of a lamb for the Passover offering (Philo, *Questions and Answers on Exodus* 1. 8; also *Midrash Exodus Rabbah* 16: 3). Tacitus' introduction of it here suits his picture of paradoxical Jewish reversal of existing practices.

without leaven: unleavened bread was certainly distinctively Jewish. However, it was prescribed only for Passover (e.g. Exodus 12: 15–20, 12: 34) and for certain sacrificial rituals (e.g. Leviticus 2: 4–11; also Mishnah *Menachot* 5: 1–2); at all other times leaven was eaten. Tacitus' failure to mention this again reinforces his polarized opposition between Jews and non-Jews.

end to their toils: according to Tacitus, crossing the wilderness took seven days, as opposed to the forty years in the Bible. The biblical explanations for the Sabbath are, of course, very different: e.g. Genesis 2: 3, Deuteronomy 5: 15.

the seventh year as well to sloth: a reference to the Sabbatical year, when the land was to lie fallow and debts were remitted: see e.g. Leviticus 25: 2–7, Deuteronomy 15: 1–18.

the seven stars: the seven zodiacal 'planets': Sun, Moon, Mercury, Venus, Mars, Jupiter, and Saturn.

offerings and tribute: before the destruction of the Temple, all Jews, including converts, sent it annual tribute; other offerings were also common. After the destruction of the Temple, the Romans compelled all Jews to send the offerings as tribute to Rome.

distinguish themselves from other people: in fact other Eastern nations, including the Egyptians, also practised circumcision. Once again, the Bible explains the custom differently (Genesis 17: 11–14).

later-born children: i.e. extra children born once the father claimed to have reached the desired family size, or after he had made a will (under Roman law, a new living child would automatically invalidate the old will). The Romans regularly exposed unwanted infants, abandoning them to die or be picked up by others; this was prohibited under Jewish law.

236 *wreaths of ivy*: this is untrue. The error may arise from a misinterpretation of the feast of Tabernacles, where branches of palm, myrtle, and willow were used in the ceremony; but it is also likely that Tacitus is adapting his account of Judaism to reinforce the apparent similarity with the cult of Bacchus, a similarity which he can then expose as merely superficial.

a golden vine: it hung above the gate of the sanctuary.

Father Liber: Bacchus, the god of wine; his worshippers wore ivy wreaths and danced to music.

a lake of immense size: i.e. the Dead Sea.

237 *destroyed by lightning*: a reference to the story of the destruction of Sodom and Gomorrah (Genesis 18–19).

the River Belius flows into the Jewish sea: the Nahal Naaman: it in fact flows into the Mediterranean near Acre.

enclosed the Temple: both here and at 5. 11 Tacitus seems to have misinterpreted his source. Jerusalem had three sets of walls, but they were not concentric, as he implies; nevertheless, an enemy attacking from the north-west (the easiest approach) would have to carry all three before reaching the Temple, which stood on Mount Moriah at the eastern extremity of the city. The Temple, however, had its own fortifications, which were in addition to these three walls.

cross the threshold: an oversimplification. The Temple had four courts, and foreigners could enter the first, but only priests the fourth.

238 *King Antiochus*: Antiochus IV Epiphanes of Syria (reigned 175–164 BC). He banned Jewish religious practices in 167, but was

faced with a revolt led by the priestly family of the Hasmoneans; after his death, his anti-Jewish decrees were rescinded. The Hasmoneans ultimately took the kingship, obtaining substantial autonomy for the Jews in 142 BC, though true independence did not come until after the death of Antiochus VII in 129 BC.

238 *Arsaces at that moment rebelled*: an anachronism. Antiochus IV campaigned against Parthia in 165; but the revolt of Arsaces I, the founder of the Parthian Empire, had in fact occurred in 247, under Antiochus II.

The mob was fickle and drove them out: entirely false. Tacitus is constructing a picture without regard to the actual events, simply relying on the standard Roman stereotype of tyrannical rule.

assuming the priesthood: from 152 BC the Hasmonean rulers took the title of High Priest. Earlier Jewish kings, unlike the Hasmoneans, claimed direct descent from David, and so were not even of priestly family.

right of conquest: in 63 BC.

The walls of Jerusalem were destroyed: they were, however, rebuilt shortly afterwards.

Publius Ventidius: Antony controlled the East 42–31 BC. Pacorus (not in fact king, but the son of King Orodes) captured Jerusalem in 40 BC and placed the Hasmonean Antigonus on the throne, but in 38 BC was defeated by Publius Ventidius Bassus, Antony's chief lieutenant.

Gaius Sosius: governor of Syria, who helped Herod capture Jerusalem in 37 BC.

gave the kingdom to Herod: Herod the Great (*c*.73–4 BC). Antony had in fact already made him king in 40.

Simon: a slave of Herod's: he was in fact only one of several aspirants to the throne in the anarchy after Herod's death.

governor of Syria: for Varus see 4. 17; he governed Syria 6–4 BC.

three of Herod's sons: Archelaus, Antipas, and Philip. But Tacitus does not mention that Archelaus was deposed in 6, and his domain turned into a Roman province.

made Judaea a province: the part of Judaea formerly ruled by Archelaus had in fact been put under governors by Augustus in 6. In 41 Claudius gave it to Agrippa I, grandson of Herod the Great, but on Agrippa's death in 44 it reverted to direct Roman rule.

Antonius Felix: governor of Judaea 52–60; he was a freed slave of Claudius' mother.

239 *Antony's grandson*: Claudius' mother was Antony's daughter. Felix's wife Drusilla was the daughter of the Jewish king Agrippa I, and no relation to Antony. An earlier wife, the daughter of Juba II of Numidia, *was* the granddaughter of Antony and Cleopatra. Her name is unknown; conceivably she too was called Drusilla, but it is more likely that Tacitus has conflated the two women.

Gessius Florus: governor 64–6.

two summers: i.e. 67–8.

wait for the enemy to starve: however, according to Josephus famine did ultimately play a major role in the Jewish defeat.

vision of Rome: an ambiguous motivation: the soldiers wish for the wealth of Jerusalem; for Titus, the main 'conquest' will be of Rome. Tacitus sets the war with the 'foreign' Jews against a reminder of the moral problems arising from the Flavians' conquest of their compatriots: see Introduction pp. xvii–xxii.

240 *built walls in peacetime*: the northernmost wall was built by Agrippa I before his death in 44.

the central city by John: John of Gischala had headed the recent resistance in Galilee; he then had fled to Jerusalem and taken it over. However, most of the city was captured from him by the powerful revolutionary leader Simon bar Giora. Tacitus is again confused over Jerusalem's topography: Simon in fact now controlled virtually all the city except the area of the Temple, John held only the outer area around the Temple.

gained possession of the Temple: according to Josephus, *Jewish War* 5. 98–105, this in fact happened after Titus had begun his siege of the city. Tacitus has the Romans facing more united opposition after Eleazar's fall, and less exploiting enemy divisions.

241 *expiate them by sacrifices or vows*: i.e. as the Romans traditionally did.

600,000: this seems exaggerated; it may derive from Titus' own attempts to play up the magnitude of his victory.

243 *the conquerors of Britain*: XIV Gemina had served in Britain since its conquest in 43.

set Galba on the throne: VI Victrix in Spain had been the first legion to hail Galba as Emperor.

244 *the Batavian capital*: Batavodorum. It lay in the north-eastern suburbs of the modern Nijmegen.

Drusus Germanicus: Nero Claudius Drusus Germanicus (38–9 BC); brother of Tiberius and father of Claudius.

the Gallic branch: i.e. the Waal.

245 *Arenacum*: Rindern.

246 *his escort straggled*: i.e. while marching along the bank.

Lupia: the Lippe.

biremes: ships with two banks of oars.

247 *houses and fields untouched*: so as to make Civilis' supporters suspect that he was secretly in league with the Romans. The same tactic had been employed by various characters in earlier historians, including Coriolanus and Hannibal in Livy.

Nor is this far from the truth: however, Tacitus' subsequent narrative implies that the Germans wished to hand Civilis over, and that his voluntary surrender forestalled them. He subtly corrects Civilis' argument, even as he apparently endorses it.

248 *next door to freedom*: contrast 4. 14: Tacitus' own narrative has shown the actual extent of Roman repression.

ratified by word of mouth: Civilis had used the same half-true pretexts at 4. 13: Tacitus closes the narrative of the revolt by referring back to its opening.

GLOSSARY OF PLACE-NAMES

Adrumetum Sousse
Albingaunum Albenga
Albantimilium Ventimiglia
Altinum Altino
Anagnia Anagni
Antipolis Antibes
Aquinas Aquino
Arar Saône
Arenacum Rindern
Aricia Ariccia
Ariminum Rimini
Asciburgium Asberg
Ateste Este
Atria Adria
Aventicum Avenches
Batavodorum in north-east
 Nijmegen
Belius Nahal Naaman
Bingium Bingen
Bononia Bologna
Brixellum Brescello
Brundisium Brindisi
Byzantium Istanbul
Chobus Khobi
Divodurum Metz
Dyrrachium Durazzo
Emerita Merida
Eporedia Ivrea
Fanum Fortunae Fano
Ferentium Ferento
Fidenae Castel Giubileo
Forum Julii Fréjus
Gelduba Gellep bei Krefeld
Hercules Monoecus Monaco
Hispalis Seville
Hostilia Ostiglia

Interamna Terni
Luceria Nocera
Lucus Luc-en-Diois
Lupia Lippe
Marcodurum Düren
Mevania Bevagna
Misenum Miseno
Mogontiacum Mainz
Mutina Modena
Narnia Narni
Nava Nahe
Novaesium Neuss
Novaria Novara
Ocriculum Otricoli
Oea Tripoli
Opitergium Oderzo
Pennine Pass Great St Bernard
Perusia Perugia
Placentia Piacenza
Poetovio Pettau
Regium Lepidum Reggio Emilia
Rigodulum Riol
Sena Siena
Stoechades Îles d'Hyères
Tarentum Tarento
Tarracina Terracina
Ticinum Pavia
Tolbiacum Zülpich
Trapezus Trabzon
Urbinum Urbino
Vercellae Vercelli
Vetera Xanten
Vicetia Vicenza
Vindonissa Windisch
Vocetius Botzberg

The following places have not been definitively identified, or else have no modern equivalent: Actium, Aquileia, Bedriacum, Bovillae, Castores, Forum Alieni, Grinnes, Minturnae, Pharsalia, Philippi, Sinuessa Spa, Vada.

INDEX

Except in the case of foreign monarchs with Roman citizenship (who are normally referred to, in Tacitus and elsewhere, by their local name, not their full Roman names), and of well-known Roman authors like Livy, Sallust, and Cicero, the index gives the full names of people, as far as these are known. Where Tacitus employs only some of these names in referring to a character, the names that we know from other sources (apart from the abbreviated personal names listed below) are italicized.

Standard Roman abbreviations are used for the following personal names: Appius (abbreviated as Ap.), Aulus (A.), Decimus (D.), Gaius (C.), Gnaeus (Cn.), Lucius (L.), Marcus (M.), Publius (P.), Quintus (Q.), Servius (Ser.), Sextus (Sex.), Tiberius (Ti.), Titus (T.). These names are ignored in alphabetization: the exception is the Emperors Gaius, Tiberius, and Titus, who are invariably referred to by their personal names. For a full explanation of Roman names, see Introduction pp. xxix–xxx.

American Literature

British and Irish Literature

Children's Literature

Classics and Ancient Literature

Colonial Literature

Eastern Literature

European Literature

Gothic Literature

History

Medieval Literature

Oxford English Drama

Poetry

Philosophy

Politics

Religion

The Oxford Shakespeare

A complete list of Oxford World's Classics, including Authors in Context, Oxford English Drama, and the Oxford Shakespeare, is available in the UK from the Marketing Services Department, Oxford University Press, Great Clarendon Street, Oxford OX2 6DP, or visit the website at www.oup.com/uk/worldsclassics.

In the USA, visit www.oup.com/us/owc for a complete title list.

Oxford World's Classics are available from all good bookshops. In case of difficulty, customers in the UK should contact Oxford University Press Bookshop, 116 High Street, Oxford OX1 4BR.